Contents

A Note on the Translation

Most of the essays in this volume had not previously been translated into English and I translated them from Polish. Witold Kula's "Our Part (A Pessimist's Voice)" was originally published in English translation in *Gal-Ed*, the journal of the Institute for the History of Polish Jewry and Israel-Poland Relations in Tel-Aviv; with the editors' permission, I prepared a new translation for this volume. Three other essays were previously available in English, and they are reprinted here: Aleksander Smolar's "Jews as a Polish Problem"; Jan Błoński's "The Poor Poles Look at the Ghetto," translated by Anna Zaranko; and Julian Tuwim's "We, Polish Jews," translated by Madeline Levine.

Agnieszka Marczyk

Introduction: Poland and Anti-Semitism

ADAM MICHNIK WITH AGNIESZKA MARCZYK

Léon Poliakov, author of *The History of Anti-Semitism*, one of the greatest books ever written on the subject, was once asked why he wrote that book. "I wanted to know why they were out to kill me," he replied. "It was almost personal."

Our reason for compiling this anthology was also personal: to prove that anti-Semitism is not something Poles drink in with their mother's milk, as is generally perceived. This sentiment is expressed time and again, and it is always troubling. Polish culture has long recognized the poison of anti-Semitism and tried to counteract it.

After the disgrace of the virulent anti-Semitic campaign conducted by the Polish communist regime against the students who demanded the extension of civil liberties in 1968, the writer and film director Tadeusz Konwicki wrote in *Kalendarz i klepsydra* (*The Calendar and the Hourglass*):

> Polish Jews are no more but their problem lives on. A problem which none-theless remains unresolved. Unresolved in its most essential aspect—in the realm of our conscience. And even if the tombstones of Jewish graveyards turn to dust, if new generations transform the last remaining synagogues into con-cert halls or art galleries, and the last European forgets that a numerous Jewish people once lived on the banks of the Vistula—ghosts of murdered Jews will haunt our homes at night. And if one day, or one night, they stop haunting us, they will always come to us on Judgment Day or the Night of the Dead, they will come in a great procession of our grandfathers and our grandsons, a procession of saints and sinners—our kith and kin.
>
> The coexistence of Poles and Jews was complicated in this mistreated land. There were good years, even beautiful ones, but there were also ugly, trouble-some times, sometimes downright tragic. It is perhaps better to forget this everyday rhythm of shared fate, both good and bad; but it is difficult to forget that Providence has allowed us to survive, to remain in this vague universe of the living. And this accident of biological deliverance, this gift from hypotheti-cal heaven—though we still do not know its ultimate meaning—obligates us

to celebrate a Great Feast of All Souls to honor these brothers who perished forever, brothers who were closest to us and yet completely foreign, brothers who were both liked and hated, stepbrothers in this shared, unlucky fate.[1]

With sadness and indignation, Konwicki goes on to say that despite this complex and tragic coexistence, time and again, "ghastly shrieks of anti-Semitism can be heard throughout Poland." They help "strip Poland of honor and esteem" and "make Poles objects of revulsion to the world." And he leaves no doubt as to his own position: "Anti-Semitism is a strike at Poland's heart. Racism is a way of ripping Poland out from the map of Europe. Fascism is self-annihilation."[2]

His words accompanied our work on this anthology. "Polish Jews are no more but their problem lives on." There are still anti-Semites, and they appear whenever a political conflict breaks out. "They come in all shapes and sizes," the philosopher Leszek Kołakowski wrote in 1956, "like annoying insects: some study leaflets on ritual murder and demand that Jews be slaughtered, some talk of lower races, others of 'cultural otherness,' and others still are content with an animosity that is often difficult to capture and readily manifests in everyday life without any help from theories."[3]

In 2002, the scholar Ireneusz Krzemiński carried out extensive research on the persistence of anti-Semitic stereotypes in Poland, and his findings were alarming. He found that one in nine Poles (11.6 percent) believed that the Jewish people are collectively responsible for the crucifixion of Christ. And that one in four (27 percent) claimed that Jews are secretly plotting to rule the world. Were similar findings obtained in any West European country, there would have been an uproar in the media and the public sphere. In Poland, there was practically no response.

In the fall of 1997, Prelate Henryk Jankowski publicly claimed, "The Jewish minority in the Polish government cannot be tolerated because the nation is afraid of it."[4] In the 1980s, Jankowski had been the priest of the Solidarity shipyard workers in Gdańsk, and he had worked closely with Lech Wałęsa. The Western press was outraged by his anti-Semitic proclamation. In Poland, there was a troubling silence among government officials, church authorities, and intellectuals. Rev. Stanisław Musiał, a Jesuit priest who often worked with the Catholic weekly *Tygodnik Powszechny*, could not bear this silence. He published a scathing article in which he argued that Jankowski's statement was not simply a political remark, but rather an anti-Semitic statement of Nazi provenance, and the Church should call it a sin. The silence and the weak, ambivalent responses to Jankowski's anti-Semitism, Musiał argued, were a disgrace and trivialization of evil. To move the hearts and minds of fellow Poles, Musiał wrote:

> "Not tolerating" another person solely on account of his biological descent is an intellectual dark alley: here we enter a terrain where all rationality ends, where all lights of reason go out; indeed, we enter the realm of absurdity and death. To hold a grudge against Napoleon, for example, for having been born in Corsica and having his own and not any other parents is completely absurd—he could not do anything about it. We can judge him for his words and deeds, but not for his heritage.[5]

To drive the point home, Musiał then asked his readers to do a brief thought experiment: suppose that in 2050 there is a conclave to elect a new pope, and among the electors (all of whom are potential candidates for the papacy), there are eight Polish cardinals, eminently qualified for the position. And imagine how shocked and outraged Poles would be, Musiał continued, if the presiding cardinal announced, "for the good of the Church no one is allowed to vote for any of the 'Polish minority' candidates" because "they are 'biologically' Polish."[6]

Like Musiał, the writers reproduced in this anthology condemn both anti-Semitism and silent acquiescence to it. In various ways and from widely different perspectives, they appeal to reason, ethics, emotions, and imagination, and they seek to inscribe Jewish experiences into a Polish and a human horizon. Individually, their voices were sometimes as isolated as Musiał's was in 1997. But collectively they constitute an important component of Polish history—one that is little known beyond Poland's borders. The goal of this anthology is to bring their voices together and show that resisting anti-Semitism is as deeply rooted in Polish culture as anti-Semitism itself.

In its original version, published by the Scientific Papers Authors and Publishers Society UNIVERSITAS in Poland, this anthology consists of three volumes of approximately 900 pages each. It contains over 300 newspaper articles, editorials, literary and satirical pieces, poems, essays, and scholarly studies. Despite this, it is far from exhaustive, and it only hints at many recent scholarly and public debates. For example, just the essays on the pogrom perpetrated by Poles on the Jewish inhabitants of Jedwabne in 1941 would fill a large volume. Authors represented in the original version of the anthology include journalists, poets, sociologists, historians, political commentators, writers, Communists, dissidents, Catholics, Polish Jews, and Jewish Poles who forged their own complex identities, refusing to let anyone define their identities for them. Anti-Semites, whether in the government or in the general population, were quick to arrogate the right to decide who was Jewish, and this was most poignantly expressed by an Israeli friend, a 1968 émigré, who once said with a sad smile: "Poland is the only country in the world where I was not allowed to be Polish."

This English-language version of the anthology is necessarily much shorter than its Polish counterpart, but it seeks to represent the diversity of the authors, arguments, and identities represented there. It is an experiment in cultural transposition—an attempt to bring a long-standing internal Polish debate to audiences beyond Poland. To someone unfamiliar with the Polish cultural and historical context, these debates can seem puzzling because of their language, tacit assumptions, symbols, and contextual references. To anchor this selection of essays and make them more intelligible, it is therefore essential to start with a brief excursus into Polish history and the history of Polish-Jewish relations.[7]

Poles and Jews in the Nineteenth Century

Throughout the nineteenth century—when Western Europe experienced modernization and nation-building—Poland was partitioned between the continent's most conservative monarchies: Russia, Prussia, and Austria. Between 1772 and 1795, the vast Polish-Lithuanian Commonwealth, a union of the Kingdom of Poland and the Grand Duchy of Lithuania, was divided between its three stronger neighbors and subjected to harsh colonial rule. On the eve of the partitions, the Commonwealth, headed by an elected king, was home to a diverse multiethnic society. Poles were the majority, while the largest minorities included Lithuanians, Ukrainians, Belarussians, and Jews, who had lived in these lands since the eleventh century. Their numbers had grown steadily over time, largely because of migration from other parts of Europe, and by the 1790s there were around 800,000 Jews in the Commonwealth, accounting for 9 percent of the population. This was the largest Jewish community anywhere at the time, and it represented one-third of the world's Jewry.[8]

Until the sixteenth century, Jews in the Commonwealth were under direct royal authority, which gave them the status of free subjects, and made it possible for many families to establish themselves as bankers, merchants, and royal administrators. They participated in dense networks of trade and international exchange, providing goods and services to the rich and powerful across Europe and beyond. With time, the king's power in the Commonwealth weakened, and in 1539 noble families were granted jurisdiction over Jews and all commoners living in their domains. This transfer of authority eventually led to restrictions on Jewish rights and to closing off many areas of employment previously open to Jews. On the eve of the partitions in 1772, the vast majority of Polish and Lithuanian Jews lived in small towns and shtetls. They spoke Yiddish and prayed in Hebrew. They typically worked as local traders, artisans, or lease-holders for mills, breweries, and other businesses. Over the centuries, this Jewish community created a complex, thriving civilization—it was in the Commonwealth cities, towns, and villages that Jewish scholarship blossomed; spiritual luminaries, writers, and poets created their masterpieces; and Vilnius (Vilna) gained the reputation of the "Jerusalem of Lithuania."

Once the Commonwealth was partitioned, most of its Jewish inhabitants found themselves under Russian rule. In 1791, in an attempt to segregate Jews within the Russian Empire, Catherine the Great created the so-called Pale of Settlement—a region in western Russia where Jews could legally obtain permanent residence. The Pale became much larger when swaths of the Commonwealth were added to it in 1795. Polish and Lithuanian Jews living there were granted some rights, but they were also subjected to military conscription and stripped of the relative autonomy of local self-government, which they had enjoyed under the Commonwealth. The first half of the nineteenth century was a time when Jewish communities in the German states and in Western Europe grappled with everything that goes under the name of *Haskala*—which means "wisdom" and "erudition," and refers to the Jewish Enlightenment, which involved modernization, religious reform, and the economic and cultural assimilation which accompanied these. By the early 1900s, assimilation was quite extensive among German and West European Jews, but it was still very limited among their East European counterparts.

For Poles, the partitions were a time of foreign rule, and of continued attempts to regain their national independence and preserve their national identity. The first half of the nineteenth century was dominated by a call to arms, and Polish fighters organized several insurrections in all three partition zones. By the 1830s, Adam Mickiewicz, the foremost of the Polish Romantic poets, created an enduring image of Poland as the "Christ of

Nations"—martyred on the three-armed cross of Russian, Prussian, and Austrian rule, and destined to rise again. During this time, Polish military uprisings were also animated by a sense of solidarity with all the oppressed peoples throughout Europe, expressed in the revolutionary call "For Your Freedom and Ours." During this time, a number of Polish Jews sided with the fighting Poles. Colonel Berek Joselewicz, for example, led a Jewish regiment in the 1794 Kościuszko Uprising—named for its leader, the brigadier general who had fought in the American War of Independence; another Jewish regiment fought alongside Poles in Warsaw during the November Uprising of 1830–1831; and the Jewish banker Leopold Kroneberg supplied arms to Polish fighters during the January Uprising of 1863–1864.

The insurrectionaries had limited resources and their power was no match for the Russian Army. When the January Uprising was crushed by the tsar's troops, Poles began to believe that the partitions were permanent. The next generation of activists denounced armed struggle and focused on education, language, and culture, making efforts to build national consciousness at the grassroots level—among the peasants and small-town dwellers. Oppression resulting from attempts to forcibly integrate Poles into the partitioning empires worsened in the final decades of the nineteenth century, in the aftermath of the emergence of Austria-Hungary (1867) and German Unification (1871), when Bismarck launched campaigns against Catholics and ethnic minorities in the newly established Reich. Throughout the century, in the absence of statehood, a disproportionately large responsibility for preserving Polish identity fell to the intellectual elites, literature, and the Catholic Church. With time, Catholicism emerged as a defining aspect of Polish national identity.

Throughout the nineteenth century, Polish anti-Semitic stereotypes were very similar to those in the rest of Europe, and their roots reached to the Middle Ages and earlier periods. Religious anti-Semitism, for example, which presented Jews as "Christ's murderers," survived not only into the partitions era but also into the twentieth century. And, in the face of industrialization and rapid social change that took place in Russia and Eastern Europe toward the end of the nineteenth century, various social groups—such as peasants, workers, and some members of the urban intelligentsia—began subscribing to the image of "Jew the financier, exploiter of poor Christians." Beliefs about an alleged Jewish conspiracy to rule the world were also voiced with increasing frequency. Though nineteenth-century Polish elites decried the absurdity of the centuries-old blood libel, many in the countryside still believed that there was a kernel of truth to accusations that Jews kidnapped Christian children and murdered them for ritual purposes.[9] Finally, the emergence of workers' movements and mass political parties throughout Europe in the 1890s was coupled with the creation of new stereotypes, which equated Jews with subversive Marxists and anarchists, and prefigured the later anti-Semitic canard of *Żydokomuna* (Judeo-Bolshevism.)

In the face of growing anti-Semitism among Poles, many Jews expressed loyalty toward the Russian government and sought its protection. This was especially necessary after 1881, when pogroms became more frequent, and Jews depended on government authorities and police to protect them. Yet the Russian government's role was ambiguous, since pogroms were also alarmingly common in Russia, and tsarist security forces seem to have provoked a number of pogroms in the Pale of Settlement.[10]

The Interwar Years: Polish Independence and the Crisis of Democracy

In 1918, Poland regained independence after more than a century of colonial rule, and the Second Polish Republic was founded. The end of the First World War was not clear-cut anywhere, but it was especially long and complicated in Eastern and Central Europe. The November 11 armistice brought an end to fighting on the Western Front in 1918, but hostilities in eastern parts of the continent did not cease until 1921. In Poland, this period witnessed several armed conflicts about the new republic's borders and borderlands: the Battle of Lviv, the Greater Poland Uprising, three uprisings in Silesia, Polish-Czech border clashes, the Polish-Ukrainian War, the Polish-Lithuanian War, and the Polish-Soviet War of 1920. The last of these was a major war caused by the expansionist ambitions of both the emerging Soviet Russia and Poland, and it lasted from February 1919 until October 1920. Soviet campaigns were successful in the early months of the war, and when the Treaty of Versailles was being negotiated in the spring of 1919, many feared a Bolshevik advance into Europe's heartland. It was not until the summer and fall of 1920 that Marshal Józef Piłsudski led the Polish Army to victory, and the border between the two states was ultimately settled by the 1921 Treaty of Riga.

During these years, powerful shock waves shaped the economic life of the region. Like Weimar Germany and other neighboring new republics,

Poland experienced runaway hyperinflation between 1918 and 1923, after which relative stabilization ensued. The economic crisis was made more difficult by the fragmentation of Polish life in the aftermath of the partitions. Russia, Germany, and the Austro-Hungarian Empire each left behind its own administrative and legal infrastructure, hospitals, banks, schools, currencies, markets, and trade networks. All these now had to be integrated into a single system. As in the Polish-Lithuanian Commonwealth, society in the Second Republic was multiethnic and multilingual. Poles accounted for roughly two-thirds of the population, while the remaining one-third included Ukrainians, Lithuanians, Jews, Russians, Belarussians, Czechs, and Germans.

In the midst of the postwar military and economic upheavals, parties, statesmen, and politicians competed to shape Poland in accordance with their divergent visions and ideals. The 1918 political scene had its roots in the 1890s, when the Polish Socialist Party (PPS) and the precursor of the National-Democratic Party (SND) were founded in exile in Paris. The PPS emerged during the 1892 conference of the Second International, and its program emphasized both workers' rights and Polish national independence. Józef Piłsudski, who became the head of the Polish state in 1918, was active in the PPS from its inception until 1914. He was inspired by the traditions of the multiethnic Polish-Lithuanian Commonwealth and by the early nineteenth-century Polish insurrectionaries. After the defeat of the 1905 workers' revolution in Russia and Poland, Piłsudski began calling for the formation of a Polish military force that would eventually challenge the partitioning powers. He started training military units (the Polish Legions) in 1909 in Galicia, and when the First World War broke out in 1914, he led them in campaigns against Russia. In November 1918, when Germans were leaving Warsaw, Piłsudski (just released from the Magdeburg prison where he had been held since 1917) claimed control of the city, and shortly thereafter he became the head of the emerging Polish state. In the early 1920s, he and the PPS advocated a tolerant, multiethnic Poland, where all minorities would enjoy equal rights and protections.

Their most important rivals, the National Democrats, evolved from the Polish League, which had been founded in Paris in 1887. Throughout the 1890s, under the leadership of Roman Dmowski, Zygmunt Balicki, and others, National Democrats embraced the principle of Polish national interest. Instead of planning uprisings that were doomed to fail, Dmowski argued, Poles should send deputies to the Duma and pressure Russia into gradual extensions of Polish autonomy. At first, Dmowski demanded that Jews show loyalty to Polish national interests (as he understood them), especially by limiting trade with the partitioning powers. After 1912, he turned to aggressively anti-Semitic rhetoric, and, over the course of the interwar years, became fanatically xenophobic and hostile toward Jews, eventually advocating their expulsion from Poland. Throughout the interwar decades, the National Democrats advocated the idea of an ethnic Polish state (Poland for the Poles), often evoking various conspiracy theories (such as an alleged Jewish-Masonic plot) to explain Poland's problems and difficulties.

Other major parties active in 1918 included the Polish Peasants' Party (PSL), the Christian Democrats (PSChD), the Polish Communist Party (KPP), and the Jewish Bund (founded in Vilnius in 1897). During the early 1920s, ruling coalitions included the National and Christian Democrats, the PSL, and minor right-wing parties. But coalitions proved difficult to sustain, and, much as in neighboring Weimar Germany, governments fell with alarming frequency. To make matters worse, the Second Republic's first elected president, Gabriel Narutowicz, was assassinated shortly after the election of 1922. The president was elected by members of the Parliament, and Narutowicz, who received the votes of Jewish and other minority deputies, won a narrow victory over the National Democratic candidate. An extremist zealot decided to kill him and rid Poland of a president who enjoyed Jewish and minority support. Four years later, in May 1926, Piłsudski seized power in a coup d'état, with the aim of restoring a modicum of stability to Polish political life. His government, which became known as Sanacja (from the Polish "healing," "cleansing"), gradually marginalized parliamentary elections and proceedings, and turned into a dictatorship, though one which nonetheless tolerated some political and cultural pluralism. Piłsudski ruled until his death in 1935, and was succeeded by several colonels who governed until 1939, when Germany invaded Poland.

The Great Depression ruined economic life throughout Europe, and in Poland its effects were felt acutely between 1929 and 1935. Agricultural prices plummeted, industrial production was devastated, and, during the worst period of the crisis, unemployment soared to over 40 percent. Until 1935, the Parliament was dominated by the Nonpartisan Bloc for Cooperation with the Government (BBWR), and in 1937 the Camp of National Unity (OZN) became the main progovernment organization. The BBWR included Jews while the OZN excluded them but both used authoritarian measures that often targeted the political opposition. In 1930, for example, with orders from Piłsudski himself, more than a dozen opposition politicians were arrested and imprisoned in the Brest fortress (among them Wincenty Witos who had served as prime minister in the early 1920s). Without having committed a crime, they were tried and given prison sentences; they were then forced to choose between prison and exile. In 1934, a group of young nationalist activists founded the violent and anti-Semitic National Radical Camp (ONR). Though the government outlawed them just three months later, the group, with its fascist ideology and violence, remained active and highly visible until the Second World War. In this context, anti-Semitism, which punctuated public life in Poland throughout the interwar years, reached a new level of intensity.

In 1921, the Second Republic was home to over 2.8 million Jews, accounting for 10.9 percent of the population. This was the largest Jewish community in Europe, and it was second only to the Jewish diaspora in the United States. During the interwar years, as in the second half of the nineteenth century, Jewish assimilation in Poland was not as extensive as in Germany and Western Europe. The vast majority of Polish Jews, 77 percent, were urban dwellers, and almost a quarter lived in just five cities: Warsaw, Łódź, Vilnius, Krakow, and Lviv. Throughout Poland's eastern borderlands there were hundreds of shtetls, many of which were 80 to 90 percent Jewish. By 1939, the size of the Jewish community grew to over 3.3 million.[11] While a majority of ethnic Poles worked in agriculture, Jews were employed primarily in manufacturing and commerce—some were industrial entrepreneurs but most were artisans, traders, lease-holders, and small shopkeepers. The 1931 census, moreover, showed that many thrived in the so-called liberal professions: they accounted for 56 percent of the Second Republic's doctors, 45 percent of teachers, 33 percent of lawyers, and 22 percent of journalists.[12]

Jewish cultural and political life in interwar Poland was diverse and dynamic. In addition to several Zionist parties, there were non-Zionist socialists, and activists committed to the traditional religious worldview. The Zionist movement had been initiated by Theodor Herzl in 1897, and by the interwar years it developed several competing branches. In addition to religious Zionists (the Mizrachi), there were liberal Zionists; radical Marxist Zionists who came together in the Poale Zion Party; and Revisionist Zionists, gathered around Vladimir Jabotinsky. Zionists had a determined opponent in the Bund, the largest Jewish socialist party, which advocated the autonomy of Jews in the diaspora. Religious Jews were represented by Agudas Yisroel, a party led by rabbis who called for both Jewish autonomy in Poland and respect for Jewish religious customs and traditions.

Over 80 percent of Jews in interwar Poland spoke Yiddish, but some were also beginning to use Hebrew on a daily basis, and for many intellectuals and professionals, Polish was becoming the primary language. Ideological differences often overlapped with linguistic preferences. Zionists promoted Hebrew; the choice of Polish typically went hand-in-hand with support for assimilation; while Bund Socialists saw Yiddish as the natural language of the East European diaspora. Each of the main cultural-political groups organized its own education system, and Jewish children attended Zionist, Bundist, and Orthodox schools throughout Poland.

In the decade before 1914, Yiddish literature had gone through a period of dynamic development, but cultural projects were temporarily suppressed by the violence and dislocations of the First World War. The interwar years, in turn, and especially the early 1920s, proved to be a time of intense aesthetic experimentation and new achievements in both Polish and Jewish culture. Polish and Yiddish newspapers and journals quickly proliferated and reached wide circles of readers; a Hebrew press also attempted to gain a foothold in the new landscape of art, politics, and culture. While Polish writers and painters in cities like Warsaw, Krakow, and Poznań experimented with expressionism, futurism, and various avant-garde projects, Jewish modernist writers and artists came together in groups like Di Khalyastre in Warsaw, the Jung Idysz in Łódź, and the Jung Vilne in Vilnius. In Warsaw, the most influential Polish literary group, the Skamander poets, brought together vitalism, urban themes, and focus on everyday life to launch an assault on the pieties of partitions-era literature. Among the Skamanders there were Jewish Poles, or Polish Jews, especially Julian Tuwim and Antoni Słonimski,[13] who set out to construct their own complex identities while actively participating in Poland's conflict-ridden public life.

Throughout the interwar years, Polish anti-Semitism took on a variety of forms, which ranged from exclusionary, racist rhetoric to violent outbreaks and pogroms. During the First World War, and in the turbulent years between 1918 and 1921, anti-Jewish violence was widespread in military conflict zones, and at least eight large pogroms took place between November 1918 and August 1919. By this time, the pejorative stereotype of *Żydokomuna* (Judeo-Bolshevism) was gaining ground among Poles and fueling fears that Jews supported the enemies of the newly established Polish state. In its most basic form, *Żydokomuna* refers to the accusation that Jewish Communists imported a hostile ideological system to Poland from Soviet Russia and sought to aid the Soviet state in its attempts to subjugate Poland.

Those who clung to this stereotype pointed to Jewish members of the Polish Communist Party (KPP), disregarding the fact that even if Jews were overrepresented in the KPP leadership, the total number of Jews in the KPP was a miniscule fraction of the entire Jewish population in Poland. Not to mention the fact that the KPP was a multinational party, and its ranks also included Poles, Ukrainians, Belarussians, and Germans. Anti-Semitic hysteria peaked during the Polish-Soviet War, when Warsaw was surrounded by Bolshevik forces in the summer of 1920. Among other things, a decree was issued to incarcerate thousands of Polish-Jewish soldiers and officers in a military detention camp in the nearby town of Jabłonna. Anti-Jewish frenzy was so intense that it did not matter that these soldiers had volunteered to fight in the Polish Army against the Bolsheviks.

Pressured by the Allies, Poland signed the Minorities Treaty at Versailles, and the 1921 Polish Constitution granted civil, religious, and political rights to Jews and other communities. But even with the extension of rights, and with no official quotas limiting the number of Jews in various professions, many realms of employment were closed to them in the 1920s—not by law, but by social norms and habits. Most Polish Jews could not, for example, find employment in state or local administrations, the courts, the police force, or the military. And when the state took over factories, Jews were often removed from nearly all levels of management.[14] Throughout the 1920s, anti-Semitic rhetoric persisted in Polish politics and culture, with the National Democrats usually taking the lead.

In the 1930s, in the wake of the Great Depression, anti-Jewish violence, boycotts, and discrimination became a powerful force in Polish public life. The year 1934 proved an important turning point. During this year, the Polish Parliament worked on a new constitution, which was finally adopted in April 1935, shortly before Piłsudski's death; it increased presidential powers and renounced some of the protections granted to Jews and other minorities back in 1921. Also in 1934, the Polish government signed a nonaggression declaration with Nazi Germany, and the ultranationalist National Radical Camp (ONR) activists, who were especially active on university campuses, started advocating the principle of *numerus clausus*. At first, they demanded all universities reduce the number of Jewish students to 8 percent; by 1937, however, they wanted a complete ban on admitting Jewish students to post-secondary education   al institutions. During this campaign, ONR groups carried out brutal physical attacks on Jewish students and disrupted lectures of professors who condemned these attacks. Violence was particularly frequent in Vilnius, but it happened throughout the country. At the Lviv Polytechnic University, for example, three Jewish students were murdered during the 1938–1939 school year. Although no countrywide legislation setting quotas on Jewish students was enacted, in 1937 the minister of education allowed universities to create the so-called ghetto benches—racially segregated seating areas for Jewish students in lecture auditoriums. And many universities passed *numerus clausus* statutes on their own initiative. In the 1920s, 20 percent of university students in Poland had been Jewish—during the 1937–1938 school year, this figure dropped to 10 percent.[15]

By attacking Jewish students, ONR activists wanted to limit the number of Jews in the labor market. They went even further by organizing boycotts against Jewish stores, and in this they were joined by National Democratic activists throughout Poland. The government did not oppose the boycotts and other forms of economic discrimination against Jews, and both boycotts and violence escalated after 1935. Several pogroms took place in various towns and villages between 1935 and 1938,[16] and both National Democratic ideologues and some government politicians began advocating the expulsion of Jews from Poland.

Anti-Jewish violence, discrimination, and prejudice inflicted immense suffering among Polish Jews and poisoned public life in interwar Poland. In September 1939, Nazi Germany invaded Poland, and the Nazi invasion was followed by the Soviet one. Poland's western regions were annexed by Germany, its eastern borderlands were annexed by the USSR, and the Nazi General Government was established in the middle. It soon became the main site of the Shoah.

Poles and Jews during the Holocaust

In September 1939, there were more than 3 million Jews in Poland. In May 1945, there were between 40,000 and 60,000. Over the course of a few years, up to 6 million European Jews perished in the Nazi Holocaust; most had lived in Poland and the Soviet Union.[17] The principle underlying the murders was racial extermination: Jews were singled out for annihilation solely because they were Jews.

Between 1939 and 1941, Jews were forcibly confined in ghettos, where overwhelming numbers were killed by starvation and disease. Then came mass extermination. In the General Government, this was code-named

Operation Reinhardt and lasted from October 1941 until November 1943. Starting in March 1942, Nazi authorities opened killing centers in Bełżec, Sobibór, and Treblinka. Later that year, Majdanek, Chełmno, and Auschwitz served as additional extermination sites. Parallel to this, after the Nazi invasion of the USSR in June 1941, SS units and Einsatzgruppen began massive execution actions in the former Soviet territories. These actions aimed at killing entire Jewish communities, often by shooting them in forests in the vicinity of their homes. Meanwhile, in the General Government, Operation Reinhardt was followed by a period which the Germans often called the *Judenjagd* (Jew hunts), and during which surviving Jews who had escaped from ghettos and extermination camps were captured and executed.

The Shoah took place largely in Polish lands, in the context of a brutal war between two totalitarian regimes. As Timothy Snyder has recently shown, between 1933 and 1945, the Nazi and Soviet regimes deliberately murdered around fourteen million civilians in the "bloodlands," the region that "extends from central Poland to western Russia, through Ukraine, Belarus, and the Baltic States."[18] In addition to Jews murdered in the Holocaust, victims included Ukrainians Poles, Russians, Balts, and others. Snyder emphasizes that his total of fourteen million deaths, overwhelming as it is, is a conservative estimate. It does not include the millions of soldiers who perished on the battlefields in this region; civilian casualties of war; or those who died from exhaustion or illness in concentration camps, as a result of forced labor, or during deportations or evacuations.[19] The exact number of Polish civilian victims of the war is not known, but Snyder offers the best available estimate when he writes that around one million were killed by the Germans, another million died as a result of mistreatment or as civilian casualties of war, and approximately 100,000 were killed by the Soviets—including the 21,892 military personnel, police, and intellectuals executed by the NKVD in the Katyń Forest in the spring of 1940.[20]

In different ways, the Second World War was the most traumatic chapter in both Jewish and Polish history. Both communities were victims, but their suffering was not symmetrical, and it was not a shared suffering. As Antony Polonsky writes: "Far from healing the divisions between Poles and Jews, the Nazi Holocaust, carried out as it was largely on Polish soil, considerably strengthened those barriers of suspicion, fear, and even hatred between the two communities which had already begun to grow alarmingly in the last years before the outbreak of the war."[21] After the war, the behavior of Poles toward Jews during the Holocaust became the dominant subject of painful Polish-Jewish debates.

The evolution of these debates is intertwined with postwar Polish history, and we will return to it later, but we should first signal what historians have been able to establish. Source materials in this realm include survivor testimonies, letters, diaries, and memoirs; eye-witness accounts (often collected during trials or other formal depositions); photographs; and Polish, German, and Soviet documents created by various levels of wartime administration. Rigorous studies have been carried out by Jewish, Polish, and other historians, especially in the years after 1989, and the work of historians at the Polish Center for Holocaust Research has been particularly important. Yet despite the availability of painstakingly careful studies, we do not have—nor are we ever likely to have—comprehensive summary statistics that show how Poles behaved toward their Jewish neighbors. But we do know that the range of these behaviors and attitudes spanned the full spectrum from self-sacrificial solidarity to murderous pogroms.

Throughout the war, the most common attitude among Poles was passivity or indifference. In survivor memoirs and testimonies, this theme resounds with painful frequency. Survivors often recount that when they were being confined in ghettos, rounded up for deportations, or forced to march through towns or villages, most Poles looked on or looked away. When they escaped ghettos or death camps and asked for help, whether in the cities or in the countryside, Poles often stood by or walked away.[22] An important reason for this indifference was the pervasive fear of the Germans, as well as the numbing that occurs when brutal violence is ubiquitous in the context of war. And in late 1941, the Nazis instituted the death penalty for anyone who aided Jews. While Poles were not always executed for sheltering or aiding their Jewish compatriots, reprisal executions—carried out on both individuals and entire communities—were common throughout the war. Yet even as historians acknowledge the role of fear, other questions remain: How did anti-Semitism contribute to the passivity of so many Poles? And how did this passivity affect the course of the Nazi Holocaust?

In addition to the large silent majority of bystanders, there was a small minority of Poles who sheltered or assisted Jews during the Shoah, risking their lives in the process. Many acted individually, extending help to either acquaintances or strangers, providing food or a hiding place, which could mean the difference between life and death for Jews trying to survive on the "Aryan" side of various towns and cities. In Warsaw, an underground organization called the Council to Aid Jews (Rada Pomocy Żydom, or Żegota) functioned between 1942 and 1944. It brought together people with various political orientations, both Poles and Jews, and it was the only organization of this kind in all of occupied Europe. It provided food, medical supplies and care, forged identity documents, and money to Jews hiding on the "Aryan" side of Warsaw. The Council also helped place Jewish children from the Warsaw Ghetto with individual families and in Catholic orphanages and convents. We do not have reliable estimates of how many Poles offered assistance to Jews during the war or how many Jews survived because of such help. As of January 1, 2016, there were 6,620 Poles honored as Righteous among the Nations at the Yad Vashem memorial in Israel, constituting a quarter of all those honored there.[23]

At the opposite end of the spectrum were Poles who participated in the persecution of Jews, whether by profiting from their expropriation and extermination, perpetrating violence against them, or, more rarely, by murdering them. Shoah survivors provide repeated testimonies about Polish looters who came to take Jewish property and valuables in the wake of deportations from ghettos or after Jewish businesses were destroyed by the Germans. There are also frequent reports about Polish blackmailers (*shmalt-zovniks*) and various forms of extortion. Sometimes, when Jews escaped from ghettos or death camps, and Poles discovered their hiding places, they demanded money or valuables in exchange for not turning them in to the Nazis. And some Poles offered to shelter and provide food for Jews but demanded payments in return, threatening to denounce Jews to the Germans if payments were not made.[24]

The countryside was also the site of looting, blackmail, denunciations, and anti-Jewish violence. Jan Gross and others have analyzed instances when Polish peasants who lived in the vicinity of the Bełżec and Treblinka killing centers searched for gold and valuables among Jewish corpses and in the ashes of the dead.[25] Barbara Engelking's research suggests that it was exceedingly difficult for Jewish victims to find refuge in Polish villages throughout the country in the final phase of the Holocaust in the General Government, between 1942 and 1945. After analyzing several hundred sources, Engelking has identified 792 cases of Polish peasants either murdering Jews or turning them over to the Germans, which meant certain death.[26] Murders were committed by individuals or families and by groups of peasants. Jan Grabowski offers additional evidence for murders perpetrated by Polish peasants—the scale of the phenomenon is currently under investigation.

Historians from the Polish Center for Holocaust Research expect that the final count may be in the tens of thousands.[27]

The worst wave of group anti-Jewish violence took place in the Podlasie region, in the wake of the German invasion of the Soviet Union in June 1941. In the power vacuum created when the Soviet occupying forces withdrew and German administration was not yet established, Poles carried out anti-Jewish pogroms in a dozen villages.[28] The largest of these was in the town of Jedwabne on July 10, 1941. Poles from the town and surrounding villages taunted Jews and carried out lynchings for several days, finally forcing a few hundred Jews into a barn and setting fire to it.[29]

Two other issues must be signaled in this brief overview: the stance toward Jews taken by the Polish Catholic Church and by various Polish underground military organizations. As Dariusz Libionka points out, Nazi policy toward the Polish Catholic Church varied depending on location. In territories annexed by the Third Reich in 1939, German authorities sought to fully dismantle all Church institutions, whereas in the General Government Church leaders and clergy were persecuted but Church institutions remained largely intact. Despite this broader context of persecution, throughout the war there were many situations in which Polish nuns, priests, parishes, convents, or orphanages offered shelter to Jews, often issuing baptism certificates to protect them in case they encountered the Nazis. Yet, as with the general population, those who offered assistance seem to have been the exception and not the rule. In addition, Libionka has examined official Church documents in the period between 1939 and 1945 and found that the Polish episcopate remained largely silent about the Shoah. Condemnations of the Holocaust did not appear in documents from any of the three Church Councils held by the Polish bishops during the war, and they were also absent in the episcopate's correspondence with the Vatican.[30] Libionka argues that both fear and negative attitudes toward Jews among the Polish bishops contributed to this silence.

Several Polish underground military organizations were active throughout the war, and they took different stances toward Jews and the Holocaust. The largest and most important of these was the Home Army, a nonpartisan umbrella group that answered to the Polish government-in-exile in London. The other major military formations were the Peasant Battalions, the communist People's Guard, and the right-wing National Armed Forces (NSZ). Individual instances of anti-Semitism took place at various times in the ranks of all these organizations, but there were important differences in their overall stance toward Jews. The most consistently supportive group was the communist People's Guard, while the leadership and members of the NSZ were the most hostile. They had inherited the ultranationalist ideology of the interwar National Democrats, with its chauvinist anti-Semitism. Source materials about the behavior of the members of the NSZ toward Jews are extremely limited—we know that some of them murdered Polish Jews, but we do not know how many.[31] On the other hand, there were instances of sworn nationalists and anti-Semites who aided and sheltered Jews during the war because they felt that this was dictated by Christian ethics.

By and large, the leadership of the Home Army opposed anti-Semitism and anti-Jewish violence. For example, the Home Army's weekly newspaper, *Biuletyn Informacyjny,* never published anti-Semitic articles and called on its readers to offer assistance to Jews; its editor, Aleksander Kamiński, was later honored at Yad Vashem. The Home Army also publicly condemned, and in some cases executed, Polish blackmailers who extorted money from hiding Jews and threatened them with denunciations. The Polish government-in-exile in London condemned the Holocaust, called on Polish society to provide aid to Jews, and made repeated attempts to convince the Allies to intervene militarily to stop the mass exterminations. Finally, and most controversially, the Home Army supplied a small number of arms and explosives to the Jewish fighters during the 1943 Uprising in the Warsaw Ghetto but did not join in the fighting. From the point of view of the Home Army commanders, political and military circumstances in April 1943 ruled out direct participation of Polish underground military units in the Ghetto Uprising. The Jewish fighters in the Ghetto thus fought alone and felt abandoned by the outside world. In this case, and in most ongoing historical debates about the Home Army's relationship with Polish Jews, the question is whether it could have done more to help.[32]

Without access—or even potential access—to enough sources to warrant definitive statistical conclusions about the relative frequency of various behaviors of Poles toward Jews during the Shoah, we are left with trends revealed by the ongoing analyses of available sources. And the emerging picture suggests that there were three general types of behavior. There was a silent and passive majority. There was a small minority of those who took advantage of the Holocaust or perpetrated violence; these were often ordinary people who lived in extraordinarily violent times, not simply criminals or the socially marginal. And, finally, there was also a small minority of Poles who overcame fear and the surrounding abyss of violence and offered help.

Anti-Semitism in the Polish People's Republic

When the Second World War ended in Europe in May 1945, Poland was under the control of Stalin's Red Army. The Allies and Soviet leaders negotiated a new European order at the Yalta and Potsdam Conferences, and the Poland established after these negotiations was radically different from the interwar Second Republic. As a result of the Yalta Conference, Stalin received Churchill's and Roosevelt's consent to pull Poland entirely into the Soviet sphere of influence. Poland lost political sovereignty, the government passed into the hands of Communists chosen by Stalin, and Poles lost the ability to decide their own fate. Borders were moved westward as the Soviet Union annexed interwar Poland's vast eastern borderlands, and in the west Poland received a smaller amount of territory that had belonged to Germany before the war. This shift was followed by massive population transfers: Poles from the annexed borderlands were repatriated, Germans from the western territories were expelled, and the relatively few Ukrainians who remained in the southeast corner of the new Polish state were forcibly resettled to other areas of the country. These shifts, together with the Holocaust, made postwar Poland a state without significant ethnic or religious minorities.

Between late 1944 and 1947, conditions akin to civil war prevailed throughout the country, as the Communists, who were closely aligned with and dominated by the Soviet Union, sought to consolidate power. They gradually limited the rights of noncommunist parties and activists, and sought to eliminate the remaining Home Army and other underground military units. By 1948, a Stalinist Polish government was consolidated, and eight years of brutally repressive rule followed.

Between 1945 and 1948, tens of thousands of Polish Jews who had spent the war years in the USSR returned to Poland but most soon immigrated to the United States, Western Europe, or Palestine, where the State of Israel was founded in 1948. During this time, acts of anti-Jewish violence were sometimes perpetrated by members of the anticommunist underground and by Polish civilians. Violence broke out in Rzeszów, and pogroms took place in Krakow and Kielce between June 1945 and July 1946. In Kielce, the

Pogrom started with a rumor that Jews kidnapped a Polish child and at least forty Jews were killed. In addition to reactivating the centuries-old blood libel that accused Jews of kidnapping Gentiles for ritual murder purposes, pogrom perpetrators often fused the fear of imminent Soviet domination with the prewar myth of Judeo-Bolshevism; and they feared that returning Polish Jews might demand the return of their property and homes confiscated by the Nazis and later taken over by Poles.

Among other things, the Stalinist regime established in 1948 made it possible for Jews to find employment in realms that had previously been closed to them. This included positions in various branches of state administration, like courts, censorship offices, the military, and the secret service. The resulting presence of Polish Jews in the state apparatus gave renewed momentum to Judeo-Bolshevik stereotypes and accusations, as did the presence of high-profile Polish-Jewish officials like Hilary Minc (who served as deputy prime minister for economic affairs) or Jakub Berman (who headed the Stalinist secret service and was in charge of regime propaganda), both of whom belonged to the ruling triumvirate headed by Poland's president and Communist Party General Secretary Bolesław Bierut.

Stalin died in 1953, and in February 1956 Nikita Khrushchev delivered his famous "Secret Speech" at the Twentieth Congress of the Communist Party of the Soviet Union; he condemned Stalinist excesses and the "cult of personality" that had ostensibly led the Communist Party astray. This marked the beginning of "the thaw"—a promise of greater pluralism and democratization within communism—in the USSR and throughout the Eastern Bloc. This proved very short-lived in Hungary, where a revolt against the Soviet-dominated government was put down by Soviet troops in early November 1956. In Poland, there was a general workers' strike in Poznań in June 1956, and it was brutally suppressed by the government. A political breakthrough came just a few months later, however, when in October the leadership of the ruling Polish United Workers Party (PZPR) (hereafter referred to as simply the Communist Party) changed, Stalinist practices were condemned and political prisoners were released. Władysław Gomułka came to power and served as the head of the government and the first secretary of the Communist Party until 1970.

In the months leading up to the October breakthrough, two factions vied for dominance within the party. The so-called Pulavians advocated liberalization within the party-state and eventually supported Gomułka in his bid for power. Most of them were intellectuals and many had Jewish roots.

The opposing Natolin faction wanted to maintain a rigid authoritarian system of power; many of its members were ethnic Poles and they used both nationalist and anti-Semitic rhetoric in their attempts to gain dominance. The Natolin faction carried out their campaign not just in Warsaw but also in small towns and villages throughout Poland, and their party-approved brand of anti-Semitism reached large parts of the Polish population. Many Jews lost their jobs in state and party administration, education, and small local businesses. The accompanying climate of anti-Semitism provoked a new wave of Jewish emigration (which was now possible because of the liberalization of the regime), and historians estimate that around 50,000 Jews left Poland between 1957 and 1958.[33]

The next countrywide episode of anti-Semitism came a decade later, when factional intrigues within Poland's ruling party coincided with the Israeli victory in the Six Day War in June 1967. During the Six Day War, the United States supported Israel while the Soviet Union supported the surrounding Arab states, and when the Israeli Army won a decisive victory over Egypt, Jordan, and Syria, the Soviet Union broke off diplomatic relations with Israel, ordering its satellite states to do the same. In Poland, Mieczysław Moczar, the minister of the interior who was planning to advance in the party-state hierarchy and hoped to eventually succeed Gomułka, used this context as occasion to initiate an anti-Semitic purge in the party and attack his opponents for their alleged "Zionism." The term had little to do with the actual historical Zionist movement; it was a code word for scapegoating supposedly "Zionist" supporters of "Israeli capitalism"—which is to say, Poles with Jewish backgrounds.

In the early months of 1968, waves of antigovernment protests swept throughout Europe, the United States, and other regions of the world. In the States, these protests took place in the context of the civil rights movement, and they were galvanized by opposition to the Vietnam War. In Western Europe, protesting students condemned capitalist exploitation and often expressed socialist convictions, and in Eastern Europe, students and intellectuals protested against the prolonged communist dictatorship. In Poland's neighboring Czechoslovakia, protests of the Prague Spring challenged Soviet dominance, and the newly elected first secretary of the Communist Party, Alexander Dubček, began introducing liberalizing reforms.

The Prague Spring was eventually terminated by the invasion of the Warsaw Pact army in August 1968, but when it started in January 1968, it inspired hope for potential transformation in Poland. The direct trigger for the Warsaw protests, however, came from the realm of Polish culture. Since November 1967, Adam Mickiewicz's play *Dziady* (*Forefathers' Eve*) was playing at the National Theater in Warsaw. Mickiewicz had written the play during the early partitions era, when much of Poland was under Russian rule and Poles organized uprisings against the tsar. In 1967, the director, Kazimierz Dejmek, accentuated the play's revolutionary elements, and audiences applauded enthusiastically during all patriotic and anti-Russian lines. By mid-January, Gomułka's government decided to temporarily suspend further performances of Mickiewicz's play, arguing that its message was anti-Soviet. A censor's ban on Mickiewicz was for Poles what a ban on Shakespeare would have been for the English. Outraged students and intellectuals organized protests at Warsaw University, criticizing the government's heavy censorship, its unabashed betrayal of communist ideals, and its restriction of the few civil rights and liberties that had been granted in 1956. Protests gained momentum throughout February, and on March 4, party authorities announced that two of the protest leaders would be expelled from the university. The Communist Party did not have the right to expel students from school, as this decision belonged to university administrators. On March 8, students and intellectuals organized a massive rally to protest the party's illegal move, as they continued to voice grievances against the government. The rally was violently suppressed by riot police, but the protest spread to universities throughout the country and continued for another month. In the end, a few dozen students were brought to trial; some were expelled from school, while others received prison sentences of up to three-and-a-half years.

A number of the Warsaw student leaders had Jewish roots, and Gomułka's government used this as an excuse to create a vulgar anti-Semitic narrative that blamed Jews for provoking the March protests, claiming that the protests did not reflect the general mood among Poles. The government's smear campaign was replete with offensive pamphlets and anti-Jewish caricatures, at times reminiscent of the Nazi press in the 1930s. A number of liberally minded professors, who had either Jewish roots or Jewish family members, were expelled from universities throughout Poland; among them were luminaries of Polish twentieth-century thought such as Zygmunt Bauman and Leszek Kołakowski. Throughout this time, Moczar took advantage of the widespread anti-Semitic hysteria and intensified the "anti-Zionist" purges in the party, the military, and among reporters and other professionals. All this led to yet another wave of Jewish emigration from Poland, and an estimated 15,000 Polish Jews and Poles with Jewish backgrounds left Poland during 1968 to 1970.[34]

The absurdity and crude brutality of the 1968 anti-Semitic campaign discredited Poland in the international arena, and both governments and intellectuals expressed disbelief and dismay. Gomułka lost power in December 1970, after ordering a bloody suppression of workers' strikes and protests in northern Poland. Moczar was removed from party leadership, and Edward Gierek's new government sought to distance itself from the events of 1968. Throughout the next decade, communist propaganda avoided anti-Semitic rhetoric, but discussion of Polish-Jewish relations remained taboo.

The political climate changed in 1980, when the Solidarity movement launched its sustained challenge against the government. After a wave of shipyard worker strikes led by Lech Wałęsa and others in Gdańsk and other cities, the government agreed to negotiate. In the summer, government representatives and strike committees signed the 1980 August Accords, which outlined basic workers' rights and established Solidarity as an independent trade union—not subject to Communist Party control. Edward Gierek was forced to resign, and Solidarity began pressuring the new government to ensure fair wages and respect both workers' rights and broader civil rights and liberties. In December 1981, however, General Jaruzelski's government decided to clamp down on Solidarity by instituting martial law. Over the course of the next two years, thousands of activists were imprisoned, including many Solidarity leaders and prodemocratic intellectuals. By the mid-1980s, Solidarity was significantly weakened, but by then Mikhail Gorbachev was initiating unprecedented reforms within the Soviet Union (*glasnost* and *perestroika*), and this soon led to greater autonomy of communist parties throughout the Soviet bloc. In 1988, General Jaruzelski's government decided to seek a compromise with Solidarity, and the Round Table talks took place in the spring of 1989. The resulting Round Table Agreement legalized independent trade unions and separated state structures from the ruling Communist Party by introducing the office of the president and a new lower house into the Polish Parliament. Candidates endorsed by Solidarity won a landslide victory in elections held on June 4, initiating the collapse of communism.

The 1980 August Accords created an atmosphere of greater political and intellectual openness, and for the first time in postwar Poland, public reflections about anti-Semitic abuses and Polish-Jewish relations began to emerge. In March 1981, Warsaw University organized a conference focusing on the events of 1968, and commemorations took place in Krakow and Wrocław. In response, anti-Semitic ideologues took to the streets once again, and the Warsaw conference was picketed by a newly formed extremist group that called itself the Grunwald Patriotic Association. They embraced radically nationalist slogans, praised the 1968 anti-Semitic purges, and criticized Solidarity for spreading "anarchy" and "counterrevolution." Despite this episode, a few months later another important sign of reckoning with Poland's anti-Semitic past came when the Kielce Solidarity activist Jerzy Stępień and Bishop Mieczysław Jaworski honored the victims of the Kielce Pogrom. And in December 1981, shortly before the imposition of martial law, Krystyna Kersten published the first extensive Polish analysis of the Pogrom and the events that led up to it.

General Jaruzelski carefully avoided anti-Semitic propaganda, and in 1983 he sought to improve Poland's reputation by organizing an official international ceremony to commemorate the fortieth anniversary of the Uprising in the Warsaw Ghetto. Marek Edelman, the only surviving Ghetto Uprising leader, however, refused to participate and wrote: "Celebrating our anniversary here—where our entire social life is weighed down by humiliation and bondage, where words and gestures have been stripped of truth—is a betrayal of our struggle; it is participation in something that is the very opposite of our struggle, an act of cynicism and contempt. I will not be a part of this."[35]

Throughout the 1980s, reflections about Polish-Jewish and Christian-Jewish relations began to appear in various Polish Catholic, émigré, and underground periodicals. This was inspired in part by Pope John Paul II's condemnation of anti-Semitism as a negation of Christian ideals and his 1986 visit to the Great Synagogue in Rome. The most important breakthrough, however, came in 1987 when the literary critic Jan Błoński raised the issue of Polish moral responsibility during the Shoah in his essay, "The Poor Poles Look at the Ghetto," published in the Catholic weekly *Tygodnik Powszechny*.

Until the publication of Błoński's essay, Polish and Jewish perspectives on the Holocaust differed so much that genuine dialogue was nearly impossible. Jewish views were informed by the experiences of Shoah survivors:

> In their eyes, the Poles had stood aside while the Nazis had implemented their murderous plans. The small amount of assistance provided was, in their eyes, outweighed by the activities of the denouncers and blackmailers, while the attitude of the majority was, at best, indifferent. This feeling of alienation was

strengthened by the postwar insecurity and the anti-Jewish outbreaks which culminated in the Kielce Pogrom of July 1946 in which at least forty Jews were murdered.[36]

Polish collective memory, on the other hand, was dominated by images of Poles who helped and sheltered Jews, and this was believed to have been the behavior of the majority. The losses inflicted on Poles by the brutal German occupation had various psychological consequences, and two of these were particularly important in the Polish-Jewish context: Poles did not investigate their potential guilt or responsibility during the Holocaust, and they did not acknowledge the specificity of the Shoah. Instead, they sought to represent Polish and Jewish wartime suffering as equal. Against these collective images, Błoński called on Poles to reexamine their role during the Holocaust and to start this collective reflection with an admission of guilt. This guilt, he argued, stemmed from Poles' indifference: "participation and shared responsibility are not the same thing. One can share the responsibility for the crime without taking part in it. Our responsibility is for holding back, for insufficient effort to resist."[37] Błoński's claims caused a stormy debate in Poland, and while many attacked him for going too far, his essay initiated a new period of deeper, more honest, and more painful reflection about Polish attitudes and behaviors during the Holocaust. A number of Jewish historians saw Błoński's essay as a sign that genuine Polish-Jewish dialogue about the Shoah could perhaps begin.[38]

Working through the Past

When Poland became a democratic republic after the collapse of communism, and censorship and communist propaganda disappeared from public life, a new landscape of debates, cultural projects, and historical initiatives emerged. And during this last quarter-century the small community of Polish Jews revived Jewish religious and secular life throughout the country. Although there are only an estimated 8,000 to 15,000 Jews living in Poland today, there are active synagogues, Jewish elementary schools, Hebrew schools, Jewish community centers, and other institutions in cities like Warsaw, Krakow, Wrocław, Łódź, and others. The Union of Jewish Religious Communities in Poland has been active since 1993, while the Rabbinical Association of Poland was established in 2008, becoming the first representative body of Polish rabbis in the postwar era. In larger cities,

Jewish religious life is diverse and includes both Orthodox and Progressive communities. Secular Jews organize various cultural and literary meetings and conferences, and Jewish periodicals like *Midrasz* and *Słowo Żydowskie* have become important forums of discussion and dialogue.

In November 1990, the Polish Bishops' Conference issued a pastoral letter that condemned anti-Semitism and expressed contrition for all its historical manifestations in Poland. In the years since 1990, Poland and Israel have established and maintained a strong diplomatic relationship, and many Poles have grown aware of the haunting absence of the great Jewish civilization that once existed in this region. Successive Polish governments and various Polish and Jewish cultural foundations have worked together to bring contemporary Jewish culture to Poland and to recover at least some aspects of the historical legacy of the Polish Jewry. Annual Jewish cultural festivals have been taking place in Krakow since 1988 and Warsaw since 2004; and Warsaw has been home to an annual Jewish Book Fair since 1998. In small towns and villages, youth groups and various local organizations have been working to restore abandoned Jewish cemeteries and recover other traces of Jewish history.

While some of these initiatives have not been free from a certain dose of nostalgia, which idealizes the past and falls far short of authentic wrestling with history, they have made Jewish culture newly visible in Polish public life. And the POLIN Museum of the History of Polish Jews, which opened its doors in the fall of 2014, offers rigorously researched and imaginatively curated exhibits on the many centuries of Jewish life in Poland.

In both historical scholarship and public debates about Poles and Jews during the Shoah, the most important turning point came with the publication of Jan Gross's *Neighbors* in 2000. Using survivor testimonies, court depositions, and other sources, Gross analyzed how Poles perpetrated the Jedwabne Pogrom in July 1941. When Błoński had written his seminal essay on Polish moral responsibility during the Holocaust, he focused on indifference and stopped short of arguing that, at times, Poles were co-perpetrators. He argued that despite the virulence of Polish anti-Semitism in the 1930s, Poles did not participate in genocide, but "when one reads what was written about Jews before the war, when one discovers how much hatred there was in Polish society, one can only be surprised that words were not followed by deeds. But they were not (or very rarely). God held back our hand."[39]

Gross shocked public opinion by showing that there were instances when Poles murdered Jews during the Holocaust—without either German or

Soviet coercion. He was immediately accused of falsifying history and deni-grating Poland, and fierce debates around his book soon gave rise to dozens of publications.[40] Gross's detractors questioned his use of historical sources, his understanding of the wider historical context, and even his motivations in writing the book. Some proposed alternative histories of the Jedwabne massacre, arguing that the Nazis were the main perpetrators who "forced" a group of Poles to participate, others claimed that Poles had acted out of a justified anger at Jews who had allegedly been collaborating with the Soviet occupier (Jedwabne is located in the territory annexed by the Soviet Union between September 1939 and June 1941).[41] Despite these voices, both the leadership of the Catholic Church and the Polish president expressed con-trition on behalf of the Polish nation. In May 2001, Polish bishops came together in the Warsaw Cathedral to beg God's forgiveness for the Jedwabne crime, and in July, during an official anniversary ceremony in Jedwabne, President Aleksander Kwaśniewski said: "Our conscience will be clear if the recollection of those days creates terror and moral indignation in our hearts. We are here to carry out a collective examination of conscience. We pay homage to the victims and we say: never again."[42]

Gross's book also became a catalyst for new investigations of Poles' behaviors during the Holocaust. Much of this work has been carried out by historians affiliated with the Polish Center for Holocaust Research, which was founded in 2003. Over the last decade, books and articles by historians like Barbara Engelking, Jan Grabowski, Dariusz Libionka, Jacek Leociak, Dariusz Stola, Krzysztof Persak, and many others, have helped Poles con-front and work through some of the darkest aspects of Polish culpability during the Shoah. The collective process of wrestling with history has also found reflection in theater and cinema. Tadeusz Słobodzianek's 2008 drama *Nasza Klasa* (*Our Class*) examined the Jedwabne Pogrom, and Władysław Pasikowski's 2012 film *Pokłosie* (*Aftermath*) explored both the Jedwabne mas-sacre and the lingering present-day refusals to accept responsibility for it. In 2013, Paweł Pawlikowski's film *Ida* portrayed the history of a young Jewish woman whose parents were murdered during the Holocaust by a Pole; it received the Academy Award for Best Foreign Language Film. These films, together with historical scholarship that analyzes painful truths, have caused waves of controversy and apologetic rhetoric. But most importantly, they have helped advance the collective process of working through the past, and today this process is more extensive in Poland than in any other country in East Central Europe.

This is not to say that Poland is free of anti-Semitism, which continues to persist among segments of the Polish population and becomes manifest primarily in two ways. First, it is openly embraced by far-right groups, and especially by the National Radical Camp (ONR), which was revived in 1993. As in the rest of Europe, radical extremists remain on the margins of public life in Poland, but they are becoming more visible and are making overt attempts to enter the political mainstream. Over the last several years, for example, they have organized massive annual marches on Polish Independence Day, and in the 2015 elections, several far-right candidates won parliamentary mandates. A second major way in which anti-Semitism enters Polish public life is when populist politicians or parties resort to anti-Semitic rhetoric during election campaigns. In this case, anti-Semitic slogans or insinuations are used instrumentally to gain votes, and then put aside once elections are over. These, and various instances of anti-Semitic prejudice, however, do not have a monopoly on defining Polish-Jewish relations today. They exist in the context of a democratic public sphere; they are open to scrutiny, criticism, and condemnation.

Finally, a few words about the selection and language of the essays reproduced in this volume. In Polish journalism and public debates during the interwar period, one often comes across the phrase *kwestia żydowska*, which can be rendered as "the Jewish problem," or "the Jewish question." The immediate, inescapable association this phrase evokes today is the *Judenfrage*—the racist, artificial, inhuman "question" posed by the Nazi regime, and "solved" at the Wannsee Conference and in the death camps of the Shoah. The Polish interwar *kwestia żydowska* was different from the Nazi *Judenfrage* but it, too, had its roots in intolerance, fears, and racism. It was a cliché used by anti-Semites who wanted to indicate that Jews in Poland were a "problem"—a supposedly "objective problem" that contributed to interwar Poland's misfortunes. *Kwestia żydowska* amalgamated various stereotypes that equated Jews with the harmful effects of modernity (as allegedly exploitative financiers, liberals, Marxists, and so on—the contradictions did not matter), and in the late 1930s it was often used by anti-Semites who advocated mandatory Jewish emigration from Poland.[43] This phrase, however, was at times also used by opponents of anti-Semitism, sometimes with purposeful distance ("the so-called Jewish question") but often without. No critic of anti-Semitism today would use the phrase "the Jewish problem" when discussing interwar Poland—we would say that Polish-Jewish relations were problematic and

that Polish anti-Semitism was a problem. When some of the authors reproduced in this anthology used *kwestia żydowska* in their texts, they meant "the
problem of anti-Semitism," but they remained immersed in the conceptual
and linguistic vocabulary of their time. We chose to retain that vocabulary both to preserve the historicity of the texts and to invite readers to
re-imagine the challenges faced by those seeking to articulate critiques of
anti-Semitism in interwar Poland.[44]

In those days, anyone who saw the boycott of Jewish businesses as a
moral duty of the Catholic Pole *and yet* argued that violence against Jewish
shops and merchants was never justifiable was seen as a dangerous philo-
Semite. Anyone who claimed that Jewish students should accept *numerus
clausus* policies for the sake of their honor *and yet* argued that assailing these
students with brass knuckles and razors was not allowed could be attacked
as a "Jew sympathizer." And a politician who argued that Jews should be
expelled from Poland *and yet* wanted to make exceptions for those who
served in the Polish Army was accused of sentimentality unfit for public
office. These were years when even the most open-minded journalists advocated assimilation, heedless of the fact that for Jews this implied the renun-
ciation of their religion, language, cultural traditions, and customs.

The essays reproduced in this volume have played an important role in the
Polish public sphere over the course of the twentieth century. Together, they
tell a story about a crucial element of Polish political and cultural life. This
story starts with Czesław Miłosz, who was not only a great poet and a Nobel
Prize laureate but also one of the keenest critics of the ailments of Polish
mentality, a critic who avoided distortions and hypocrisy. Ksawery Pruszyński
represented the liberal wing of the Polish conservative intellectual tradition,
while Maria Dąbrowska was the voice of liberal, leftist circles and a great
moral authority in Polish literature. Kazimierz Wyka, Jerzy Andrzejewski,
Mieczysław Jastrun, Witold Kula, and Stanisław Ossowski were leftist writers and humanists, who became "fellow travelers" of Poland's communist
government between 1944 and 1948. One of their reasons for accepting the
antidemocratic regime was the Communist Party's radical rejection of anti-
Semitism. Several essays come from the period known as "the thaw" when
anti-Semitism became a subject of public debate when Poland was turning
away from Stalinism in 1956 and 1957. Leszek Kołakowski was the leader of
the rebellious young generation of idealistic Communists, Konstanty Jeleński
was an eminent émigré writer, and Jerzy Turowicz was the editor of the
liberal Catholic weekly *Tydognik Powszechny*, which was closed down in

1953 after it refused to publish an official obituary for Stalin, which glorified his criminal deeds. In 1958, Tadeusz Mazowiecki became the editor of the Catholic monthly *Więź*, which brought together young Catholics who rejected Stalinism and Stalinist anti-Semitism; in 1989, he became Poland's first noncommunist prime minister.

The remaining essays were written by prominent writers who represent various political orientations—leftists, Catholics, émigrés, and members of the anticommunist opposition. Their essays often refer to one another and document the many ways in which Polish intellectuals wrestled with anti-Semitism.[45] This volume, like any publication of this type, is open to criticism, and certain texts, some might argue critical ones, are missing. Perhaps most important is the absence of Jan Gross's writings. Since the publication of his book *Neighbors* in Poland in 2000, he has played a pivotal role in galvanizing Polish debates about anti-Semitism; we therefore use the year 2000 as a turning point in the periodization of this anthology, but we do not include his work since it is already well known to international audiences.

Anti-Semitism has always gained vitality in Poland during times of political crisis, and it has always been an element of antidemocratic discourses. The authors reproduced here represent diverse currents within Polish democratic culture, and their essays ultimately remind us that silence in the face of hate and discrimination is tantamount to acquiescence and conformity. Breaking through this conformity requires courage. And the courage to speak out against all forms of discrimination—whether it is advanced by individuals or governments—is still very much in demand today.

Notes

1. Tadeusz Konwicki, *Kalendardz i klepsydra* (*The Calendar and the Hourglass*), (Czytelnik, 2005), 269.
2. Ibid., 270.
3. This is a quote from Leszek Kołakowski's essay "Anti-Semites: Five Familiar Theses and a Warning" which is reproduced in this volume. The quote appears on page 143.
4. As cited by Rev. Stanisław Musiał in "Czarne jest czarne" (Black Is Black), originally published in the weekly *Tygodnik Powszechny*, Nov. 16, 1997; reprinted in the Polish version of this anthology Adam Michnik, ed., *Przeciw antysemityzmowi 1936–2009* (*Against Anti-Semitism, 1936–2009*) (Scientific Papers Authors and Publishers Society UNIVERSITAS, 2010), 3:734. Rev. Musiał SJ (1938–2004) was a Jesuit, philosopher, theologian, and member of the editorial

board of *Tygodnik Powszechny* from 1981 onward. He became a member of the Polish Episcopate's Commission for Dialogue with Judaism in 1986, and was the Commission's secretary until 1995. His essay "Black Is Black" received the 1998 Grand Press Award in Poland.

5. Michnik, *Przeciw antysemityzmowi 1936–2009*, 3:741.

6. Ibid., 3:741.

7. A necessarily brief overview of the relevant historical context is provided in this Introduction. For a more detailed analysis of various themes and turning points in the history of Polish-Jewish relations see, for example, Robert Blobaum, ed., *Antisemitism and Its Opponents in Modern Poland* (Cornell University Press, 2005).

8. For statistical estimates of the size of the Jewish community in the Polish-Lithuanian Commonwealth see, for example, "Poland before 1795," *YIVO Encyclopedia of Jews in Eastern Europe*, n.d., http://www.yivoencyclopedia.org/article.aspx/Poland/Poland_before_1795.

9. For more on this subject, see, for example, Joanna Tokarska-Bakir, *Legendy o krwi. Antropologia przesądu* (*Legends about Blood: The Anthropology of Prejudice*), (Wydawnictwo W.A.B., 2008).

10. See, for example, Paweł Śpiewak, *Żydokomuna: interpretacje historyczne* (*Judeo-Bolshevism: Historical Interpretations*), (Czerwone i Czarne, 2012); and Jerzy Zdrada, *Historia Polski, 1795–1914* (*The History of Poland, 1795–1914*), (Wydawnictwo Naukowe PWN, 2007).

11. *Mały Rocznik Statystyczny* (*Abridged Statistical Almanac*), (Główny Urząd Statystyczny, 1939). See also Anglo-American Committee of Inquiry, Appendix III: Estimated Jewish Population of Europe, http://avalon.law.yale.edu/20th_century/angap03.asp.

12. Iwo Pogonowski, *Jews in Poland: A Documentary History. The Rise of Jews as a Nation from Congressus Judaicus in Poland to the Knesset in Israel* (Hippocrene Books, 1993), 28.

13. See Julian Tuwim's essay "We, Polish Jews" in this volume on pages 63–68.

14. See, for example, Ludwik Honigwill, "Tragedia żydowskiej inteligencji" (The Tragedy of the Jewish Intelligentsia), *Myśl Socjalistyczna* 61, no. 3 (1936).

15. *Mały Rocznik Statystyczny* (*Abridged Statistical Almanac*) (Główny Urząd Statystyczny, 1939.)

16. See, for example, Jolanta Żyndul, *Zajścia antyżydowskie w Polsce w latach 1935–1937* (*Anti-Jewish Incidents in Poland between 1935 and 1937*), (Fundacja im. Kelles-Krauza, 1994).

17. See data provided by the United States Holocaust Museum: https://www.ushmm.org/wlc/en/article.php?ModuleId=10008193.

18. Timothy Snyder, *Bloodlands: Europe between Hitler and Stalin* (Basic Books, 2010), vii.

19. Ibid., 411–412.

20. Ibid., 140.

21. Antony Polonsky, *My Brother's Keeper? Recent Polish Debates on the Holocaust* (Routledge, 1990), 2.

22. For examples of memoirs in which this indifference is documented see Erna
    F. Rubinstein, *The Survivor in Us All: A Memoir of the Holocasut* (Archon Books,
    1983); Krystyna Żywulska, *I Survived Auschwitz* (Tchu Publishing House,
    2009); and Fred E. Katz, *Ordinary People and Extraordinary Evil: A Report on
    the Beguilings of Evil* (State University of New York Press, 1993). See also
    Emmanuel Ringelblum, *Polish-Jewish Relations during the Second World War*, ed.
    Joseph Kermish and Shmuel Krakowski (Howard Fertig, 1976).
23. For the most recent count of those honored at Yad Vashem, please see http://
    www.yadvashem.org/righteous/statistics. For examples of the kind of assistance
    provided, see, for example, Timothy Snyder, "The Righteous Few," in *Black
    Earth: The Holocaust as History and Warning* (Tim Duggan Books, 2015), 298–318.
24. For examples of documentation of these attitudes, see, for example, Ringelblum,
    Polish Jewish Relations during the Second World War; and Raul Hilberg, *Perpetrators,
    Victims, Bystanders: The Jewish Catastrophe, 1933–1945* (HarperCollins, 1992).
25. Hilberg, *Perpetrators, Victims, Bystanders*, 214; and Jan Gross, *Golden Harvest: Events
    at the Periphery of the Holocaust* (Oxford University Press, 2012).
26. Barbara Engelking, *Jest taki piękny słoneczny dzień . . . Losy Żydów szukających
    ratunku na wsi Polskiej 1942–1945* (Stowarzyszenie Centrum Badań nad Zagładą
    Żydów, 2011), 15–16. Available in English: *Such a Beautiful Sunny Day . . . Jews
    Seeking Refuge in the Polish Countryside, 1942–1945* (Yad Vashem, 2016).
27. Jan Grabowski, *Hunt for the Jews* (Indiana University Press, 2013). For estimates of
    the numbers of Jews murdered by Poles, see the following interviews: Barbara
    Engelking in the weekly *Wprost*, January 2, 2011, https://www.wprost.pl/
    tygodnik/224996/Spojrzmy-prawdzie-w-oczy.html; and Alina Skibińska, in
    the daily *Rzeczpospolita*, January 12, 2011, http://www.rp.pl/artykul/592972-
    Chlopi-mordowali-Zydow---rozmowa-o-ksiazce-Grossa.html#ap-1.
28. See, for example, Andrzej Żbikowski, "Pogromy i mordy ludności żydowskiej w
    Łomżyńskim i na Białostocczyźnie latem 1941 roku w świetle relacji ocalałych
    Żydów i dokumentów sądowych" (Pogroms and Murders of Jews in the
    Łomża and Białystok Regions in the Summer 1941, as Related by Survivors
    and Recorded in Court Documents), *Wokół Jedwabnego* (*Around Jedwabne*), vol.
    1 (Wydawnictwo Instytutu Pamięci Narodowej, 2002), 159–272.
29. The most influential analysis of this Pogrom is Jan Gross's *Neighbors* (Princeton
    University Press, 2001) (originally published in Polish by Fundacja Pogranicze
    in 2000).
30. Dariusz Libionka, "The Catholic Church in Poland and the Holocaust, 1939–
    1945," in *The Holocaust and the Christian World*, ed. Carol Rittner, Stephen D.
    Smith, and Irena Steinfeldt (Continuum International, 2000), 74–78.
31. Instances of murders are discussed, for example, by Joseph Kermish, "The
    Actions of the Council for Aid to Jews (Zegota) in Occupied Poland," in *The
    Nazi Holocaust: Part 5: Public Opinion and Relations to the Jews in Nazi Europe*, ed.
    Michael Robert Marrus, 2 vols. (Walter DeGruyter Press, 1989), 2:506–507.
32. For balanced overviews of the behaviors and attitudes toward Jews in the
    Home Army, as well as other underground Polish military organizations, see,

for example, Joshua Zimmerman, *The Polish Underground and the Jews, 1939–1945* (Cambridge University Press, 2015); and Antony Polonsky, *Jews in Poland and Russia, vol. 3, 1914–2008*, (University of Illinois Press, 2012).

33. Historians provide various estimates. Marcos Silber, for example, provides the most accurate available estimate of Polish Jews who immigrated to Israel between 1957 and 1960 (44,389 people) in "Foreigners or Co-nationals? Israel, Poland, and Polish Jewry (1948-1967)," *Journal of Israeli History* 29, no. 2 (Sept. 2010), 213–232. During this time, Polish Jews immigrated not only to Israel but also to other countries, so the final figure is certainly higher.

34. See, for example, Jerzy Eisler, *"Polskie miesiące"—czyli kryzys(y) w PRL ("Polish Months" —Crises in the Polish People's Republic)* (Wydawnictwo Instytutu Pamięci Narodowej, 2008).

35. As cited by Joanna Szczęsna in "Ostatni Mohikanie i nowy naród" (The Last of the Mohicans and a New Nation), *Gazeta Wyborcza*, June 28, 2003.

36. Polonsky, *My Brother's Keeper?*, 2.

37. Jan Błoński, "The Poor Poles Look at the Ghetto," reproduced in this volume, on pages 273–285.

38. For an analysis and documentary presentation of this debate, see Polonsky, *My Brothers' Keeper?*

39. Jan Błoński, "The Poor Poles Look at the Ghetto," quoted in this volume, on page 285.

40. For an overview of these debates, see, for example, Antony Polonsky and Joanna B. Michlic, eds., *The Neighbors Respond: The Controversy over the Jedwabne Massacre in Poland* (Princeton University Press, 2003).

41. This is analyzed in various studies, see, especially, Marci Shore's "Conversing with Ghosts: Jedwabne, Żydokomuna, and Totalitarianism," in *The Holocaust in the East: Local Perpetrators and Soviet Responses*, ed. Michael David-Fox, Peter Holquist, and Alexander M. Martin (University of Pittsburgh Press, 2014), 5–28.

42. Aleksander Kwaśniewski, "Sąsiedzi sąsiadom zgotowali ten los" (Neighbors Did This to Neighbors), *Gazeta Wyborcza*, July 11, 2001.

43. For a nuanced analysis of how this phrase functioned on the pages of an interwar nationalist youth periodical *Odrodzenie* in the 1930s, which was typical of right-wing mentality at the time, see Dariusz Libionka, "Kwestia żydowska—myślenie za pomocą clichés. Przypadek 'Odrodzenia' 1935–1939," (The Jewish Question: Thinking in Clichés, the Case of "Odrodzenie"), *Dzieje Najnowsze* 3 (1995): 31–46.

44. Throughout the volume, the phrases *kwestia żydowska* or *problem żydowski* are translated as "the Jewish question" or "the Jewish problem." When authors use the less charged *sprawa żydowska*, we render it as either "the Jewish issue" or "the Jewish cause," depending on context.

45. Throughout the anthology, authors' notes and citations appear as footnotes. We provide additional clarification in editors' notes, which appear at the end of each chapter.

PART I

Prologue

I

Jews—the 1920s

CZESŁAW MIŁOSZ

Editors' Introduction

Czesław Miłosz (1911–2004) was a poet, essayist, and prose writer; he received the Nobel Prize in Literature in 1980.[1] Born in the small Lithuanian town of Szetejnie (Šeteniai), he studied law in Vilnius during the interwar period, when Vilnius and much of Lithuania were part of the Second Republic of Poland. While in Vilnius, Miłosz spoke out against the anti-Semitic abuses of Polish nationalist radicals. He spent the Second World War in Warsaw, where he was active in underground literary circles, and where he provided assistance to Jews hiding on the "Aryan" side of the city. He is honored at Yad Vashem as one of the "Righteous among the Nations." After the war, Miłosz briefly served as the cultural attaché of the People's Republic of Poland in Washington, DC and later in Paris. In 1951, when Andrei Zhdanov, Stalin's deputy for cultural policy, ordered Polish writers to produce social realist literature, Miłosz defected and sought political asylum in France. He immigrated to the United States in 1960 and taught Slavic literature at the University of California, Berkeley. In 1993, he moved to Krakow, where he spent the rest of his life.

Miłosz's poetry is often about simple everyday objects and situations, but just as often he explored philosophical questions and the realms of history and metaphysics. He was also deeply interested in the dialogue between science and religion, and in the effects of modernity on the human psyche.

In 1943 he wrote two poems about the Uprising in the Warsaw Ghetto. "Campo di Fiori" offers a heart-rending contrast between a carefree merry-go-round on the Polish side of the wall and the burning Ghetto on the other. "Biedny chrześcijanin patrzy na getto" (The Poor Christian Looks at the Ghetto) was later echoed in Jan Błoński's 1987 essay "Biedni Polacy patrzą na getto" (The Poor Poles Look at the Ghetto), which galvanized discussions about Polish moral responsibility during the Holocaust.[2] Miłosz's most famous essay collections include *Zniewolony umysł* (*The Captive Mind*, 1953), an analysis of how Polish intellectuals succumbed to the allure of communism, and *Rodzinna Europa* (*The Native Realm*, 1959), a contemplative memoir exploring what it means to come from multiethnic and multilingual Eastern Europe.

The text reproduced here is not a typical Miłosz piece. It is a chapter from his anthology *Wyprawa w dwudziestolecie* (*A Voyage into the Interwar Years*, 1999), in which he brought together historical sources, newspaper editorials, records of parliamentary proceedings, pamphlets, letters, diary entries, and other documents to create a portrait of Poland between 1918 and 1939. In this collage of voices and debates, Miłosz attempted to come to terms with both the achievements and the wretchedness of this time in Polish history. He did not aim to create an exhaustive historical account but rather wanted to make the interwar decades come alive for contemporary Poles.

Historical context is essential for reading Miłosz's collage of texts, and in the Introduction we have provided a discussion of the most important social, political, and economic challenges that faced the multiethnic Poland when it regained independence in 1918. Here, we should only reiterate that throughout the 1920s various political parties with radically different visions of Poland competed for power, and while the Polish Socialist Party (PPS) advocated tolerance and respect for minorities, the National Democrats wanted Poland to be an ethnic state and often resorted to virulently anti-Semitic rhetoric.

Most of the texts Miłosz compiled in this chapter come from the Vilnius-based weekly *Przegląd Wileński* (*The Vilnius Review*); they provide overviews of issues discussed in various Jewish newspapers throughout the 1920s. There are also three longer articles on the attitudes of Polish socialists, Jewish assimilation, and the dilemmas confronting the Zionist movement. Miłosz wanted these texts to speak for themselves and limited his own interventions to a minimum, providing a brief introduction and very short commentary in each chapter. This chapter begins with his narrative about what he considered to be the most significant phenomena in Jewish life and Polish-Jewish relations in the 1920s and 1930s. His prose will surprise anyone familiar with his great essays—in this book, instead of writing, Miłosz dictated his commentaries to an assistant, often choosing to speak in telegraphic, staccato sentences.

The interwar years are now receding into the distant past, and the texts reproduced here will inevitably present readers—both in Poland and outside—with some puzzles and ambiguities. Their rhetorical style is also quite different from contemporary debates about racism and tolerance. Yet this mosaic of texts opens our collection of essays because it puts readers face to face with people who had high stakes in Polish-Jewish relations in interwar Poland. The voices Miłosz brought together in this collage belong to a world that would be decimated by the Second World War and the Holocaust. Without the backdrop of these voices, all postwar Polish debates about anti-Semitism would remain incomplete and overly abstract.

At that time, Poland was a "land of civil servants." Aleksander Wat used this phrase in *Mój wiek* (*My Century*), and I draw upon it because it captures those realities well.[3] This was an extension, as it were, of the old division into peasantry and gentry—though clerks no longer necessarily had to come from the gentry, and one should, after all, include among them all those who held permanent posts—policemen, railway men, and provincial civil servants. A post, even a low-ranking one, meant a lot, given the impoverishment of the largest part of the population—that is, the peasantry. There were still a great number of large landed estates in the countryside, as the agrarian reform—passed by the Sejm (Parliament) in 1920—made only feeble progress over the course of the entire interwar period. This was in contrast to the neighboring Baltic States, where land reform had taken on the character of national struggle: in Lithuania against Polish landowners and in Latvia against German ones. In Lithuania, landowners were typically left with just 80 hectares [200 acres] each, and in Latvia with only 40.

Jews remained entirely outside the realm of civil servants and peasants, and this very segregation helps understand the resulting tensions. The historic Polish-Lithuanian Commonwealth had been home to the largest number of Jews in the world; it was the center of their flourishing spiritual life, religious movements, and modern Yiddish literature, which was just beginning to emerge. As a result of the partitions, an enormous number of Jews who had settled in the eastern expanses of the country found themselves under Russian rule; they were forbidden to enter Russia's heartland, and the Russian border was retained in the form of the so-called Pale of Settlement.[4] Those referred to as Russian Jews, who played such an important role in the Russian Revolution, and also contributed much to Russian culture, were simply Polish Jews seized by the Russian state.

The Poland that emerged in 1918 was still a country where Jews comprised a large percentage of the population. They numbered over three million, and they could be considered a separate nation, differing from fellow citizens in religion, customs, and occupation—primarily in trade and tavern-keeping, and partly also in skilled labor and labor for hire. The vast majority spoke Yiddish; schools taught in Yiddish, and books and newspapers were published in Yiddish. One should bear in mind that for several centuries Yiddish was restricted to closed-off Jewish communities, and its forays beyond their confines date to the nineteenth and twentieth centuries. Yiddish books and newspapers published in Poland were read throughout Europe; outside of Europe, the literary blossoming of the Yiddish language had an equivalent only in the large East European Jewish community in New York City. Vilnius was the main Yiddish cultural center, while New York's Yiddish literature and theater thrived in the first decade of the twentieth century. Jewish theater in New York celebrated its greatest successes during the First World War.

The Jewish population in Poland was astonishingly diverse—both economically and culturally. Alongside an affluent plutocracy there were the poor masses, making their living from cottage industries and petty trade. Likewise, in the realm of culture, the religious Orthodox, who were the majority, had little in common with those who embraced emancipation, only some of whom remained faithful to the Yiddish language.

As early as the partitions period, some Jews started breaking free of the religious community's control, sending their children to state schools that taught in Russian in the east, and in German in the Austrian and Prussian zones. This—especially under Russian rule—gave rise to the phenomenon of the "Litvaks," Jews who were culturally Russian. Jews started to learn Polish at the end of the nineteenth century and the beginning of the twentieth. Greatest progress was made in Galicia. The need for texts in Polish, including religious ones, can be gleaned from the lifework of Isaac Cylkow, a Warsaw synagogue preacher who translated the Old Testament from Hebrew into Polish.[5]

An important phenomenon in the interwar period was the fast intellectual emancipation of young Jews, who read modern writers and philosophers, abandoned religion, and participated in—mainly socialist—political movements. Some chose the PPS, but—before the war—they also opted for either the Social-Democratic Party of the Kingdom of Poland and Lithuania or the Bund, a party founded in Vilnius during the tsarist period, which was, as it were, a parallel of Polish socialism. Another type of emancipation gave rise to the Zionist movement, which, in turn, diversified into a right and a left wing, no less radical than the socialists and the Communists.

To explain what took place in Polish-Jewish relations, one can evoke a certain exotic analogy. In Poland, Jews were urban dwellers; statistics treating the population as a whole would be misleading because in towns and cities Jews were a very large part of the population, and in some places they were the majority. They were also, especially in small towns, nearly synonymous with trade. Something similar happened in Indonesia, where the Chinese were in the Jews' position. The Indonesian peasant earned his living solely from farming and he did not look kindly upon the Chinese shopkeeper. The shopkeeper's children, in turn, breaking free from family influence, joined the ranks of the Indonesian Communist Party. As a result, anti-Chinese sentiment acquired both ideological and nationalist hues, and this eventually led to mass slaughters of the Chinese.

Centuries of Jewish presence in Poland made it the place where thriving Jewish cultural traditions were preserved up until the days of the Holocaust—traditions little known or appreciated by fellow Poles. Historians tend to associate the emergence of Jewish messianic movements with the misfortunes that befell Jews in the seventeenth century. These were, above all, the massacres in Ukraine during the Khmelnytsky Uprising.[6] It was then that the self-proclaimed messiah Sabbatai Zevi from Smyrna gained many followers in Poland. In the next century, however, a new false messiah—Jacob Frank—appeared; like Zevi, who reached the heights of immorality by converting to Islam, Frank, who was excommunicated by Jewish communities, received baptism. His followers, who were granted noble titles after being baptized, as was customary in Poland, started the family lines of the so-called Frankists.

Messianism was related to Hassidism, which evolved mainly in the towns of eastern Galicia, and led to the veneration of the Tzadikim—figures renowned for their piety and miracles. Jews who embraced emancipation, and wished to count themselves among progressive Europeans, were reserved toward the Jewish religious literature produced in Poland. For example, it took Martin Buber to translate the *Tales of the Hasidim* (into German).[7] In Poland, the writings of famous Hassidic figures—like Rabbi Nachman of Breslov—were not available in Polish.

Few Jews wrote in Polish before the First World War, but among those who did were Julian Klaczko; the poet and translator Antoni Lange; the literary critic and historian Wilhelm Feldman; the poet Bolesław Leśmian; and the critic Ostap Ortwin, among others. By the interwar years, there were already many like them, and Warsaw's literary circles were largely Jewish—both writers and audiences. This, by the way, was associated with yet another division, since those who wished to remain Jewish while writing in Polish accused colleagues who completely turned away from Jewishness of being traitors. Roman Brandstaetter was one of the leading Zionist writers, and his life was to take a rather unusual course—after a long stay in Palestine, where he spent the Second World War, he became a Christian and died a Roman Catholic. But Poland was a country that produced eminent Yiddish and Hebrew writers. Before the First World War, these were Isaac Leib

Peretz, a great poet and novelist who wrote in Yiddish, and Sholem Asch. After 1918, two members of the Association of Jewish Writers, the Singer brothers—Israel Joshua and Isaac Bashevis—gained international renown. Vilnius was perhaps the liveliest intellectual center. It is worth noting, by the way, that Jews in America attach great significance to their place of origin. Hailing from Vilnius was the greatest honor; it was somewhat less prestigious to be from Warsaw; and being from Galicia conferred the least prestige. The Young Vilne group of Yiddish writers gained fame in Vilnius in the 1930s, and among its members who survived the war there were Chaim Grade, the poet Szmerke Kaczergiński, and Abraham Sutzkever.

Many points of friction existed between Jews and Poles, starting with the main one between the Catholic peasant—with his mores—and the small-town Jew, who observed different customs. The notion that Jews were Christ's murderers, promulgated by the clergy for centuries, became fused with a superstitious fear of secretive Jewish machinations in commerce. Some peasants were already aspiring to become shopkeepers, and the extensive anti-Semitic propaganda campaign advanced by the National-Democratic Party and a significant portion of the clergy was addressed, above all, to this peasant and petty-bourgeois mentality. A different image—that of a Jewish factory owner with ties to international capital—helped advance propaganda among workers. At the time, anti-Semitic brawls were staged primarily at the universities, mostly by law and medical students, and this was tied to propaganda that targeted Jews practicing the liberal professions.

Focus on the so-called Jewish question was a characteristic quality of political life during the 1920s and 1930s, and it constituted a significant part of Roman Dmowski's program and writings.[8] In 1919, Poland signed an agreement dealing with minorities, and, in accordance with it, Article 109 of the 1921 Constitution stated: "Every citizen has the right to keep his nationality and cultivate his language and national qualities. Other state laws will guarantee that minorities in the Polish state will be able to enjoy the full and free exercise of their national identities with the help of autonomous minority associations, which shall have legal public status within the framework of a general association of self-governing bodies. The state shall have the right to control their activity and supplement their financial resources as needed."

Taking advantage of this, Polish Jews exhibited an astounding amount of energy in organizing mutual-aid societies and educational institutions at various levels. There were schools that taught in Yiddish, but there were also some that taught in Hebrew, as well as in Polish—the famous Epsztajn High School in Vilnius, for example. Conflicts with city councils concerning subsidies for these schools were often discussed in the Jewish press. These schools provided general education, but there were also purely religious ones—the cheders and the yeshivas, with the latter functioning as a kind of religious university.[9]

Polish-Jewish relations did not take the same course in the 1920s as they did in the 1930s. Their true deterioration came during the latter, due in part to what was happening in the neighboring states, that is, in Germany and in the countries of East Central Europe, where fascist movements were afoot. It is worth pointing to some of the Polish government's attempts "to solve the Jewish problem" by securing loans from America to support small-scale manufacturing and handicraft in centers of Jewish destitution such as Warsaw and Łódź. These attempts were unsuccessful, and, as Jerzy Giedroyc writes in his *Autobiography*, in return for underwriting the loans, American Jews demanded that the Polish government promise it would not support the emigration of poor Jews to America, since the influx of these impoverished countrymen was contributing to anti-Semitism.[10] In any case, in the 1930s there was a proliferation of various ideas—advanced by demagogues—about Jewish emigration from Poland, which, incidentally, was not contrary to the Zionist notion of creating a Jewish state in Palestine. Generally, one has to say that while the so-called assimilationists among Jews, those who proposed gradual merging with Polish society, were heeded in the first interwar decade, they lost nearly all influence in the second. The Bund decisively supported the idea that Jews should stay in Poland, though it emphasized the traditional culture of Yiddish-speaking Jews. In the Bund's view, socialism would automatically solve conflicts among national groups.

The presence of Jews in Poland created configurations that are difficult to convey today. On the one hand, there was appreciation of their intellectual liveliness and inventiveness in culture and everyday life, expressed in the saying, "*z nimi trudno, bez nich nudno*" (it's difficult with them but boring without them). This coexisted, on the other hand, with anti-Semitic obsessions that bordered on psychosis, and, in the late 1930s, on outright madness, making it impossible to clearly perceive the threat of war.

Poles harbored many stereotypes of the figure of the Jew, and these did not necessarily have referents in reality. Jews as a separate group, or even a nation of Polish Jews, found themselves in a territory seized by great powers, which is to say outside the realm of Polish statehood. No wonder they looked after their own group interests, interests that were not identical with those of the Poles. They were not particularly happy about getting conscripted into the Russian, Austrian, or German armies, and this may have contributed to the emergence of the image of the Jew as a reluctant soldier, even an outright coward. Jews who fought in the Polish uprisings proved how wrong this image was.

A new stereotype emerged as a result of Jewish youth's marked attraction to revolutionary ideas and to various stripes of socialism—including those of the Bolshevik variety—an attraction that can also be seen as an outcome of the Russification of the Jewish social strata educated under tsarist rule. This was expressed in Polish military men's mistrust of educated Jews, despite the fact that they joined Piłsudski's Legions and fought in the 1920 war, while having to overcome significant obstacles in the process. Instead of being sent to the front, Jewish intellectuals were interned in a camp in Jabłonna, and their futile attempts to take part in the war were preserved in a song:

Jabłonna, ach Jabłonna
nadzieja nasza płonna

Jabłonna, oh Jabłonna
Our hope is in vain

I cite this song as it was sung to me by Alfred Tarski, a Jabłonna detainee, and a famous mathematical logician, known in America as the "Einstein of the West Coast."

The right-wing National Democratic movement openly proclaimed a program hostile to Jews, though this was just one part of their idiosyncratic interpretation of Polish history. In their worldview, most emphatically articulated by Jędrzej Giertych, an international conspiracy had threatened Poland for centuries.[11] Accordingly, Catholic Poland became an object of special hatred among Protestants in the seventeenth century, and their international plot generated the Swedish invasion.[12] The Freemasons then picked up the mantle of Protestant hostility against Poland, and they, in turn, tried to undermine it in cahoots with similarly scheming Jews. Although Poland had liberated itself from the three partitioning powers, it was still ensnared in the tentacles of a Jewish international, which was collaborating with the Communist International. The National Democratic propaganda targeted Poles engaged in petty trade, who viewed every Jew as a competitor.

Socialists saw these issues entirely differently, and Tadeusz Hołówko—
Piłsudski's man, who, nota bene, was to die at the hands of a Ukrainian
nationalist in 1931—is worth citing:

A Polish shopkeeper supposes, and believes devoutly, that all Poles have a
patriotic duty to let him fleece them. But, he thinks, Poles must never let
Jewish shopkeepers do the same, even if buying from them might be somewhat cheaper. And since we socialists say that all middlemen-shopkeepers,
whether Jews or Poles, should be done away with, and that every worker and
intellectual should go to his own cooperative—there is an easily understandable bourgeois and reactionary anger at us, and we are accused of being Jewish
lackeys.

But is the Jewish wheat merchant not a brother to the Polish landowner,
who sells him the still-standing crops, well aware that the merchant will specu-
late and raise wheat prices, and that this will directly affect Polish workers and
intellectuals in the cities? Are Jewish money changers not kinsmen to our own
native rentiers, who buy dollars and franks from them and invest their savings
in these currencies? These rentiers lambast Piłsudski for his alleged role in the
rising price of the dollar, all the while secretly rejoicing that their savings are
"growing" without work and effort.

Given that this is how things are, it is rather amusing that we socialists get
accused of harboring some special sympathy toward Jews.

Our sympathies simply reveal our culture and our respect for mankind.

We shall never agree to, and we shall never stop protesting against the degradation of Jewish dignity. Cutting off Jewish beards, throwing Jews out of
train cars, mistreating them in the military, and harassing them in the state
administration—all this brings shame and disgrace to Poland. A Jew is a citizen
of the Polish Republic. It is not his fault that 600 years ago King Casimir the
Great allowed his ancestors to settle in Poland. He has the same rights as every
other citizen because he has the same responsibilities.

Unfortunately, brutality toward Jews has engulfed all social strata—and here,
again, the greatest harm we inflict is upon ourselves.

First of all, it is absurd to push away Jews who identify as Poles. They are the
intelligentsia—and often the best and brightest, both intellectually and culturally.

Absurd things are taking place: Jews with great knowledge and European
renown, often professors at prestigious foreign universities, Jews who identify
as Poles and who are Poles in both culture and spirit, are being refused positions in mathematics, medicine, and biology departments, not to mention law,
history, and philology. Solely because of their backgrounds.

And how often do professors refuse to accept young and promising Jewish
scholars as their assistants, again, solely because of their backgrounds?

Is it really possible to bring "elements foreign to the Polish spirit" into mid-
wifery, chemistry, botany, and similar disciplines? Do we really have so many

true scholars that we can push cherished and esteemed people away from Polish scholarship?

Are the things happening here not unthinkable anywhere else in Europe?

We have an eminent historian who has educated a whole generation of young historians, whose works have expanded the spiritual horizon of Poland's entire contemporary intelligentsia, and who is now skillfully and passionately defending Polish causes abroad. And in *Gazeta Warszawska* (*The Warsaw Gazette*)—a newspaper that aspires to the status of a cultured periodical—we read the proclamations of various Peasant-National circles in Warsaw, circles of butchers, sausage-makers, and shopkeepers who have never heard the name Łukasiński before, but who do not want this historian to represent Poland abroad because he is Jewish.[a]

It does not matter that this man taught Polish society to truly love Poniatowski, Łukasiński, and Dąbrowski.[13] His right to Polishness can be denied by any butcher, illiterate, or profiteer, solely because their Polish mothers had the misfortune of giving birth to them.

And isn't Poland's best theater company —with its invaluable cultural contributions to the Polish stage—maligned by "eminent" Polish "critics," only because its talented director has Jewish ancestors?

It is like this everywhere: among lawyers, doctors, engineers—wherever the expansion of the ranks of Polish intelligentsia is at stake.

Unfortunately, things are different when it comes to making money, even when this proves ruinous to the state. I am referring to the tender solidarity between the Polish and Jewish bourgeoisie.

Descendants of Poland's most renowned noble families head the Supervisory Boards of banks owned by the Jewish plutocracy. In the tobacco business, Reverend Adamski and Professor Głąbiński come to the rescue of Jewish factory owners. And in the oil and coal industries, Polish and Jewish bourgeoisie engages in brotherly cooperation.

It is really not that difficult to discern who is more needed in Poland. Is it the intellectuals who have Jewish roots but who are Polish in their culture and spirit, who are passionately expanding the cultural heritage of the Polish nation, and whom we socialists defend? Or the likes of the Polakiewicz brothers, or the Szereszewski family from Grodno, so enthusiastically defended by "true patriots" and National Democratic anti-Semites? And this is Polish

---

[a] Szymon Askenazy—C. Miłosz. [Editors' note: Szymon Askenazy (1865–1935) was a distinguished historian who wrote primarily about Polish insurrectionary activity in the early nineteenth century. In the early 1920s he was Poland's first representative to the League of Nations. Among other things, he wrote a detailed study of Walerian Łukasiński (1786–1868), who was an officer in the Polish Army during the Napoleonic era, and a political conspirator against Russia in the 1820s. He was imprisoned by tsarist authorities in 1830 and spent nearly four decades in prison, becoming a symbolic figure in the Polish struggle for independence during the partitions era.]

society's second mistake: it is not afraid of capitalist sharks but it fears an
assimilated, or assimilating, intelligentsia with Jewish roots.

—Tadeusz Hołówko, *Kwestia narodowościowa w Polsce*
(*The National Question in Poland*), Warsaw, 1922

The anti-Jewish mood at the universities reached greatest intensity in the
1930s, but the question of the so-called *numerus clausus* emerged already in
the early 1920s.

Following the example of other universities, youth in Vilnius organized an
academic assembly which resolved (or, as our newspapers say, "carried up a
resolution"!) to demand limits on the percentage of Jewish students. There
is not much one can say about the *numerus clausus* principle itself. It is not a
new idea, and it was systematically used by the tsarist government in Russia.
It is not currently feasible because it contradicts the Constitution, which is
binding in the Polish state, and which guarantees equal rights to all citizens,
regardless of national or religious differences. The *numerus clausus* principle
also clearly undermines the state, since no state can voluntarily allow a large
part of its youth to mature into citizenship in a foreign milieu, outside the
state's influence and control. Not to mention the ethical issues involved.

If the idea of nationalizing universities might make some sense in Krakow
or Warsaw, analogous striving at the university in Vilnius is completely
absurd, and it can only be explained by a herd-like instinct to imitate. Vilnius
University, meant to serve the so-called Eastern Lands, or parts of Lithuania
and Belarus annexed by the Polish state, cannot, by its very nature, be predominantly Polish. Its character can be—and indeed is—Polonizing. But that
is an altogether different matter.

In our region, as the Sejm elections have demonstrated, Poles comprise
an insignificant percentage of the population, and, as the educational system
develops, university students will become more and more nationally diverse.
There will come a time when Belarusians and Lithuanians will be in the
majority. Striving to "nationalize" Vilnius University is therefore not a feasible
project. Unless, after putting limits on Jews, quotas on other "non-nationals"
will be introduced. This, in turn, will soon lead to the establishment of national
universities—Belarusian, Ukrainian, Lithuanian, Jewish, and so on. Is this what
the National Democrats truly desire?

—"Z mego notatnika" (From My Notebook),
Przegląd Wileński (*The Vilnius Review*),
no. 47-48, December 17, 1922[14]

A few reviews of the Vilnius Jewish press offer a sense of the issues that
were most frequently discussed. As one can easily notice, ceaseless arguments

about language were underway. On the one side were the traditionalists and the Bund, in favor of education in Yiddish; on the other were the Zionists, who insisted on introducing schools that would teach in Hebrew. In any case, all kinds of events are described here, such as a hooligan attack on a May Day march, which was attended primarily by Bund members and the Zionist left, and in which the police seemed to side more with the hooligans than the march participants.[15]

In the Warsaw periodical *Der Moment* (*The Moment*) we find Deputy Pryłucki's enthusiastic article about the Vilnius "Pomoc Pracy" (Worker Assistance Society), founded by a humble but tireless activist, Doctor Beniamin Fin.

From Jewish periodicals, we learn that the Anski Historical and Ethnographic Society has decided to publish a journal *Archiwum Żydowskie* (*The Jewish Archive*) in collaboration with some of the most distinguished Jewish scholars and writers. It will also publish an artistic album of the city of Vilnius and cantor Bernsztajn's book collection of synagogue and folk songs.

—Miecz(ysław) Gold(sztajn), "Przegląd wileńskiej prasy żydowskiej"
(Vilnius Jewish Press Review), *Przegląd Wileński*
(*The Vilnius Review*), no. 20, November 26, 1923

Tog (*The Day*) features an interview with Mr. Ludwik Chomiński, vice-president of the agrarian "Liberation" (PSL-Wyzwolenie) parliamentary club.[16] According to Deputy Chomiński, Poland's worst malady is the dissonance between the Constitution and the administration's treatment of national minorities, especially in the Kresy (Eastern borderlands) region.

"We are striving"—Deputy Chomiński said—"to introduce autonomous local governing bodies in all districts with mixed populations. Only this way, will it be possible to remedy the administration's mistakes in the so-called Kresy."

He identified the most important tasks of the current parliamentary session as follows:

"The defense of the social classes represented by PSL-Wyzwolenie, the enforcement of the Constitution and agrarian reform, and decisive parliamentary struggle against the current government."

When asked about the significance of the merger between PSL-Wyzwolenie and Mr. Dąbski's rather large group, Mr. Chomiński said:

"First of all, this means consolidation and tightening of opposition ranks against the current government. And second, this merger simultaneously completely eliminates Witos and his role in the former Russian partition."

Deputy Chomiński describes the leftward turn in the political mood of the peasant masses, perceptible especially in the parliamentary clubs of the agrarian "Piast" Party (PSL-Piast) and the National Workers' Party (NPR), as the greatest service rendered by the Chjeno-Piast government, which keeps discrediting itself every day because:

"National Democracy is a sore on the body of the Polish state organism; it was able to develop only because of the murky residues of recent history. National Democracy is a system on the verge of exhausting itself. It has no future. The country demands the construction and reform of all kinds of state instruments—and this by no means belongs to the National Democrats' vocation. The influence of PSL-Wyzwolenie thus grows every day, not only in the former Congress Kingdom, but even in Witos's stronghold in Western Galicia. Recently, we have even made some headway into the Poznan district." (. . .)

The press also cites Deputy Wygodzki's characteristic speech at a meeting of the Parliamentary Education Committee.[17]

Sternly denying accusations that the Jewish educational system is anti-state, Dr. Wygodzki describes the *credo* of the Vilnius Jewry this way:

"We, the national minorities, were not—and we are not—Poles. We wish to remain loyal citizens, but on the condition that our culture, and especially our schools, get total freedom. The closing of these schools would make me, personally, an enemy of the Polish state."

—(Miecz(ysław) Gold(sztajn), "Przegląd wileńskiej prasy żydowskiej"
(Vilnius Jewish Press Review), *Przegląd Wileński*
(*The Vilnius Review*), no. 18, October 28, 1923

Tog (*The Day*) notes with satisfaction that the entire parliamentary left wing, including the national minorities, conducted joint deliberations. Meanwhile, in *Der Moment* (*The Moment*), Deputy Pryłucki attempts to demonstrate that this joint session is best viewed as no more than a polite gesture, since the participants neither proposed a program (even a minimal one) nor signed a binding protocol.[18]

According to Mr. Pryłucki, the problem of the Polish left lies in the fact that it does not have an honest, democratic program for national minorities.

Unzer Frajnd (*Our Friend*) considers this issue from a different point of view, and says, among other things:

"The Polish left has to understand that it will be able to stand up to the reactionaries only by joining hands with the national minorities. It is essential to recognize the prudence of a united front of all opposition forces in the country. Sooner or later, this unification will find realistic expression in daily life, unless the Polish opposition allows itself to get crushed under the wheels of the frenzied reactionaries. The country is going through one of its most difficult moments. And this was brought about solely by the instability of the Polish leftist parties.

(. . .) We are fighting for national schools because we are convinced that only such schools can serve the needs of the Jewish masses."

We should also point out the voice of Mr. Szyfman, an education activist from the Hebrew camp who, on the pages of *Unzer Frajnd*, proposes taking joint action on behalf of the entire Jewish educational system.

If we are able to confirm the information provided by some Jewish dailies, which say that the Jewish National Assembly in Kaunas has found a *modus vivendi* for the Jewish educational system (Yiddish and literature would be obligatory in Hebrew schools, and Hebrew would have to be taught in Yiddish schools), Jewish education activists from these mutually inimical camps will have to seriously consider both internal and external coordination of their efforts in this immensely difficult moment for Jewish education.

—Miecz(ysław) Goldsztajn, "Przegląd wileńskiej prasy żydowskiej"
(Vilnius Jewish Press Review), *Przegląd Wileński*
(*The Vilnius Review*), no. 21, December 16, 1923

Because of last week's Warsaw conference for teachers from schools teaching in Yiddish, we devote today's edition of our press review to questions concerning Jewish education.

Here is what Mr. N. S., a leading contributor to *Nasz Przegląd* (*Our Review*) says about this problem in an article entitled "Spór o szkołę żydowską" (A Dispute about Jewish Schools):

"The struggle for national rights, which Jews are waging in trying political circumstances, is made especially difficult by internal disputes arising from the fact that Jewish culture is bilingual. While other national minorities base their educational and autonomy-related goals on a uniform model of public schools, Jews engage in fierce struggles among themselves about both the language of instruction and the character of schooling.

The Orthodox are trying to inject new life into the old cheder by introducing "secular subjects" and new teaching methods; Zionists are establishing public schools, which are partly religious and partly secular, and which teach in Hebrew; and the workers' democratic movement announced the idea of secular, non-religious schools that teach in Yiddish —and managed to create a network of its own public schools in recent years."

The proliferation of Jewish schools is, indeed, astounding. The Vilnius region—where Jewish culture tends to be highly developed, and where Jewish intelligentsia is most organized and active—is becoming the natural source of vital energies for the Jewish education system.

The vast majority of education organizers are labor activists. Thus, the system, which is in its early stages, bears clear markers of class affiliation, expressed, among other things, in the elimination of religion and Hebrew as "reactionary" subjects. Slowly, however, schools that teach in Yiddish are becoming available to ever wider social strata.

Hebrew is being introduced in response to parents' demands. And class-oriented Jewish schools are systematically striving to become national schools, which gives Mr. N. S. reason to claim:

"We should be happy about the healthy developments in the left-wing political camp because as soon as Hebrew was introduced in 'radical' schools, it became possible to build bridges to secular Zionist schools, with the goal of combining efforts to eliminate the ossified cheders. The struggle for national rights will start following a normal course only when it is based upon a uniform Jewish public school model—even if there are some differences across individual schools. This will disarm our most dangerous adversaries who refuse to grant us rights by claiming that we have not yet reached agreement among ourselves."

—Miecz(ysław) Gold(sztajn), "Przegląd wileńskiej prasy żydowskiej"

(Vilnius Jewish Press Review), *Przegląd Wileński*

(*The Vilnius Review*), no. 1, January 13, 1924

Who knows whether the greatest obstacle to achieving national autonomy, both within the Polish Republic and in other states, is not the disharmony within the Jewish community itself?

This applies, above all, to the question of the language used in schools. While democratic and worker circles view Yiddish as the national language, the large and influential Zionist party recognizes only Hebrew. In addition, the Orthodox want to preserve the old-fashioned cheder, while introducing the study of the state language into its curriculum.

Moreover, while the Jewish bourgeoisie wants autonomy to extend to social welfare issues, radical members of the Jewish community demand only cultural autonomy.

Attainment of cultural autonomy for the Jewish minority depends largely on whether individual factions within the Jewish community can come to agree about their demands.

—Miecz(ysław) Goldsztajn, "Przegląd wileńskiej prasy żydowskiej"

(Vilnius Jewish Press Review), in *Przegląd Wileński*

(*The Vilnius Review*), no. 5, March 9, 1924

Deputy Wygodzki addressed the question of whether Jews are Poland's enemies by publishing an interesting article in the Jewish dailies. He said, among other things:

"Abandoning all good manners, state dignitaries and church officials have spoken out against Jews so brutally in recent times that one can no longer remain silent. . . . What do you want, gentlemen? 'Jews'—you say—'are Poland's enemies.' But where is your proof? 'We are the noblest nation in the world'— you convinced yourselves of this when Poland was still enslaved. Incidentally, as with other enslaved nations, a particular psychology based solely on emotion emerged among you during your time of bondage. According to this ideology, the East is barbaric, and you have to bring Western culture there. Germans are a morally rotten nation, and you have to make them better. And Jews—the very same Jews who, having left you, thrived so magnificently in America, and created such an astonishing culture in Palestine—these Jews are, in your opinion, a nation whose spiritual and economic culture is inferior. They bring nothing but harm to Poland. Polish towns therefore have to be 'Polonized,' and a policy of eradication, boycott, and other such things should be directed at Polish Jews. Isn't it time to re-examine all these notions and this stale psychology?"

And Deputy Wygodzki claims decisively:

"If you look at this whole issue with your eyes wide open, and make use of your common sense, you will immediately understand what filth you've stepped into. . . . You will also easily grasp that whenever people say that Jews (which ones?) are Poland's enemies, they are simply lying. All Jews living within the borders of the Polish state have close economic and cultural ties to Poland. If the Polish state were to be destroyed, or experience a misfortune, Jews would certainly suffer as well. Despite your hostile anti-Semitic policies, we are not your enemies. We impatiently await for the moment when you realize that nothing good comes of the current policies—either for us or for you."

—Miecz(ysław) Gold(sztajn), "Przegląd wileńskiej prasy żydowskiej"
(Vilnius Jewish Press Review), *Przegląd Wileński*
(*The Vilnius Review*), no. 16, September 28, 1924

(. . .) It is, nonetheless, high time for Jewish activists and journalists to stop seeing anti-Semitism everywhere.

An excellent journalist, Mr. S. Stupnicki, rightly points to this phenomenon in the *Lubliner Tugblat* (*The Lublin Daily*). While discussing a minor local issue, he writes, among other things:

"Jews are so used to being maligned and having special laws issued for them, that anything that anyone does, any change in the existing order of things, or any economic undertaking—even if no one means to bring them any harm, or if the change makes things better for them—is discussed as a restriction of rights.

Ill intentions toward Jews are immediately sensed and an alarm is sounded. Though understandable, this is very sad. It is a result of whole millennia of experience. For centuries, Jews have suffered because of human anger or stupidity, and it has become hard to believe that anyone could do anything, or introduce reforms, without targeting Jews.

This psychology, common among the Jewish masses, must be fought. Civic awareness should be instilled in Jews. A Jew should clearly perceive what is going on around him. He should stop seeing the world as consisting only of enemies and bad people who hunt him down and wish him harm. He should, finally, understand that one cannot keep living according to old forms forever, that changes must take place in life, farming, forms of trade, and trade relations."

This topic is also indirectly tied to a matter broached by Dr. H. Gliksman in the most recent issue of *Literarisze Bleter* (*Literary Journal*).

It is lamentable that the Jewish ghetto disappeared only in the physical sense. The spiritual ghetto has remained, and it has been modernized and adapted to new circumstances, which makes it even harder to fight against this relic of the Middle Ages. Every year, one can see the expansion of the Chinese wall that separates the Jewish and Christian communities.

—Miecz(ysław) Gold(sztajn): "Przegląd wileńskiej prasy żydowskiej"
(Vilnius Jewish Press Review), *Przegląd Wileński*
(*The Vilnius Review*), no. 15, September 27, 1925

In the *Literarisze Bleter* (*Literary Journal*) a talented, young writer, I. J. Zyngier draws an interesting parallel between Jewish communities in Vilnius and Warsaw—cities that always found themselves in analogous political circumstances. Mr. Zyngier says the following about the time of the Russian partition:

"Jewish Vilnius has borrowed from Russia everything that is good and beautiful, everything that makes Russia different from other European states. This was expressed in simplicity, authenticity, relation to man, struggle, principles, and social activism. Meanwhile, Warsaw has borrowed nihilism, indolence, and tardiness. After the Russians departed, Vilnius threw off the imposed Russian language. The 50,000 Vilnius Jews have more children in their own public schools than Warsaw Jews do, and there are over 300,000 Jews in Warsaw. Vilnius, moreover, has three Jewish schools with eight grades (not Warsaw 'Jewish' with 'Mosaic' religion, but truly Jewish), a Jewish trade high school, vocational schools, and evening courses; yet good Russian qualities—perseverance, a fighting spirit, and working for the common good—have remained.

Vilnius is, after all, the only city that has won the fight to have its rightful demands met in the municipal council (36% of general monies are allocated to Jews). Vilnius has also succeeded in winning rights for the seminary, and having students take their exams in Yiddish before a ministry representative.

Warsaw, meanwhile, is managed by loyalists, Galician tramps, and its own nihilists."[19]

Regarding the German partition, the author of "Vilnius and Warsaw" claims:

"Vilnius has taken over European punctuality and diligence. People work in Vilnius. And so, Vilnius has wonderful and superbly managed cultural and philanthropic institutions. If Warsaw has taken anything over from Europe it is European egotism, European 'loyalty' toward everything, and Europe's wretched tolerance (?), together with the shimmy, gaiety, lightheartedness, and vanity."

And Mr. Zyngier reaches the following conclusion:

"The warm attitude of Vilnius teachers toward Jewish schools, language, and culture remains unmatched.

(. . .) Vilnius has been, and shall remain, our cultural center."

—Miecz(ysław) Gold(sztajn), "Przegląd wileńskiej prasy żydowskiej"
(Vilnius Jewish Press Review), *Przegląd Wileński*
(*The Vilnius Review*), no. 6, March 22, 1926

Local Jewish press offers extensive commentary on the May Day events in Vilnius.

Mr. Sz. Fraj published the following remarks in the *Wilner Tog* (*Vilnius Day*):

"Was it not May Day that gave you—'patriots'—an independent Poland?

Do you know that the call for Polish independence was first made with pride and courage under May-Day banners?

Do you know that the great masses, which you attacked so barbarically yesterday, fought for your country's freedom when it suffered under Cossack and
gendarme whips—while you were licking the occupiers' boots?"

The *Wilner Tog* also poses the following questions to government authorities:

"Why did fascists feel that they could disregard the authorities' pledge to
maintain order at all costs, and found it most convenient to attack the demon-
strators right outside the Voivodship Office?

Do things really have to be this way? Will the authorities continue to force
Jewish companies to fund *Dziennik Wileński* (*The Vilnius Daily*) by their adver-
tisements (in the trade registry), thus enabling the daily to pay for articles
which call for pogroms, and which have been especially abundant on its pages
this past week?"

—Miecz(ysław) Gold(sztajn): "Przegląd wileńskiej prasy żydowskiej"

(Vilnius Jewish Press Review), *Przegląd Wileński*

(*The Vilnius Review*), no. 9, May 9, 16, 1926

The Jewish community's internal problems were discussed in many Yiddish
newspapers. There was, however, no lack of Jewish papers in Polish. *Nasz
Przegląd* (*Our Review*), edited by Jakub Appenszlak, came out in Warsaw.[20] It
represented the Zionist ideology, which was gaining more and more adherents in Poland because of the impoverishment of the Jewish masses and growing anti-Semitism. Polish-Jewish writers who wished to maintain a Jewish
national identity while choosing the Polish language—rather than Yiddish or
Hebrew—as their means of expression, published in *Nasz Przegląd*.

Is assimilation really triumphant?

In our press review, we included an article by Sz. I. Stupnicki, who complains
about the triumph of assimilation. Similar complaints have resounded rather
frequently in recent times, mostly in Yiddishist circles. The authors of these
laments often follow more or less the following train of thought:

"We congratulate ourselves on having a flourishing Jewish national
movement but the young generation is already starting to speak Polish.
And that is not all. Even older people give in to the youth and strain their
tongues, wishing to communicate with the youth in the vernacular. We
have not seen anything like this before, not even in the era of burgeoning assimilation. The need to assimilate used to be debated in Hebrew and
Yiddish; now the need to develop national consciousness is written about
and discussed in Polish."

Our national cause would, indeed, be in serious trouble, if not for the fact
that those who grumble about the downfall of Jewishness make a cardinal mistake when they view language as the sole manifestation of Jewish nationality.

This very notion is, in fact, the most assimilationist thesis, since it draws no distinction between the Jewish people, who are dispersed throughout various countries, and other nations, which are clustered in individual territories. And it is a great paradox that Yiddishists are the ones who succumb to this illusion, since this way of thinking annihilates their own theory of the nation.

For how did contemporary Yiddish come into being? After leaving Palestine and settling in various lands, Jews initially spoke Hebrew among themselves. As time passed, despite the existence of ghettos, and despite the reign of socio-religious separatism, which far outstripped the dreams of even the most extremist of today's nationalists, Jews have taken over the language of their surroundings—mostly German. They spoke their local provincial dialects, as the philologist, specialist, and lawyer N. Pryłucki explained in a recent Town Hall lecture. And it was only thanks to Jewish mobility that this blend of dialects, along with an admixture of elements of Hebrew, coalesced to create a separate Yiddish language—especially given the fact that, over time, most Jews migrated to Slavic lands, where "Yiddish-Teitsch" was enriched by new elements, and grew increasingly independent from its Old-German roots.

Jewish nationality is now developing under different circumstances. We can see that in German countries Yiddish has disappeared, unable to compete with the related *hochdeutsch*. Things are taking a similar turn in America and England, despite the influx of new immigrants. According to recent claims made by observers as talented and diligent as Mr. Sz. J. Jackan and Mr. Pejsach Kapłan, the young generation speaks only English, without relinquishing their Jewish nationality. And an analogous process is taking place here in Poland as well, though it is much slower because there are cohesive Jewish masses here, and not only their language but also their ideas, culture and customs set them apart from indigenous nationals. This is taking place despite the efforts of anti-Semitic government authorities, who make it very difficult for Jews to learn Polish. It is a process that no human force can hold back. It has been this way throughout the long years of Jewish history, and it is this way now.

Is this assimilation? Not in the least. Mr. Stupnicki's own reasoning testifies to this when he complains that even a Chassidic rebbe talks to his children in Polish and adds:

"Speaking Polish is the first and most important step toward true assimilation. Polish cannot be compared to German or French. Unfortunately, there is practically no Jewish literature in Polish. It is not just that Polish literature and press are strictly nationalist, not just that they offer only weak reflections of the universal human spirit—they are also strictly Catholic. And so, whoever switches to Polish is not simply switching to a European language; this switch has to be characterized as a move toward Polish nationalism, a step on the way toward Catholicism. And this process is taking place at a tremendously fast pace."

What can we do about it? Since the process of linguistic "Polonization" cannot be halted, the Polish language needs to become one of the realms in which we can keep developing our Jewish nationality. What was possible with German, French, English, and Russian can also happen with Polish. And this is precisely the spirit that permeates the work of authors who write Jewish books and articles in Polish. Let us leave the struggle against Polish nationalism and clericalism mostly to the Poles themselves. This struggle is underway, by the way, and though it is perhaps not as swift as in other nations, it is not quite as hopeless as Mr. Stupnicki surmises.

The comparison between Vilnius and Krakow is unfortunate. Mr. Stupnicki makes Vilnius—with its burgeoning Yiddish newspapers, schools, and institutions—a model for Krakow, where "assimilation" has allegedly progressed so far as to make the survival of Jewish newspapers impossible. Vilnius has belonged to Poland for merely a few years; it is a borderland city, surrounded by Belarusian nationals. Until recently, the Jewish intelligentsia in Vilnius was as (linguistically) "Russified" as the Jewish intelligentsia in Krakow or Warsaw is "Polonized" today. It will be possible to compare the two cities only in thirty years. We shall see who ends up looking better.

There is no reason to despair. Jewish nationality is developing differently from other nationalisms. We have, above all, Zionism with its Hebrew culture, which is moving from Palestine to the diaspora. We have the Yiddish culture, which is developing its depth and breadth, though not its height, in the sense that its penetration among the intelligentsia is less extensive than among the masses. We have, finally, our common Jewish culture, which keeps evolving regardless of the vernacular spoken by any given individual or group. When we realize this, we can fight against assimilation more effectively than when we recognize its alleged triumphs. For if the Hebrew and Yiddish camps view each other as symptoms of assimilation, if fanatics on both sides perceive assimilation in Polish-language Judaica, and if we keep hampering instead of cooperatively supporting and complementing one another—then we shall truly pave the way for assimilation.

—S. H., "Czy istotnie asymilacja triumfuje?"
(Is Assimilation Really Triumphant?), in
Nasz Przegląd (*Our Review*), no. 1, January 4, 1930

Zionism at the brink of a new era

Deliberations of the Eighth Congress of Poland's Zionist Organization begin in Warsaw today. The agenda includes matters of extreme importance for deepening the Zionist ideology and the future development of the movement. The only party which is based on the idea of a Jewish state, and which plays a vital role in the national life of the golus,[21] is entering a new phase of existence in the context of changing realities. The Congress must take stock of the past, understand the essence of the present, and map out a path for the future.

Today's changing conditions are expressed in the fact that the economically ruined masses of Polish Jews, brought to despair by hopeless destitution, *are moving from passive waiting for the improvement of their lot to a feverish struggle for the possibility of existence.*

This struggle resembles the efforts of the proverbial drowning man who grasps at straws. The pauperized masses thrash about as they look for a way out, but paths to a better life are closed off to them, as are the gates of emigration.

At this dramatic moment, it is hardly surprising that the organization situated at the very heart of Jewish life is painfully aware of the shockwaves of the cataclysm that engulfs the Polish Jewry. For many long years, Zionism has fought for the moral victory of the Zionist principle. It won this victory after the First World War—the political horizon was brightened by the recognition of the Balfour Declaration, the San Remo Resolution, and the League of Nations' endorsement of the creation of Eretz Israel, a Jewish national home. After this moral victory, large numbers of pioneers left for Palestine. Armed with perseverance and ready for greatest sacrifices, they started building the foundations of this home; they dried out swamps, made fallow and sandy lands fertile, established agricultural colonies, and erected modern Jewish cities. But the hungry, homeless, and persecuted masses in East European countries did not have time to wait for the completion of the pioneers' work. The great ports were closed off to them, only Jaffa and Haifa remained open. And the moral victory was now proclaimed to be material—thanks to its moral victory, the Zionist organization obtained the keys to the gates of Palestine. Without waiting for the preparation of Eretz Israel to receive the immigrant masses, East European Jews demanded these keys: the gates were opened and waves of mass emigration started flowing, the waves of the so-called Fourth Aliyah.[22]

This Aliyah included creative people who were capable of productive, hard, and exhausting work—pioneers' work. The first modern Jewish city, Tel Aviv, was erected by the sea. New settlements, plantations, gardens, and groves came into being. But the majority of the Fourth Aliyah was made up of penurious petty merchants and middlemen, poor artisans, and déclassé petty bourgeoisie. They could not yet be fed by the Palestinian land, which was just barely invigorated by the first phase of farming, most of it still not liberated from the burden of sand and boulders that had weighed it down for centuries. Thus, after the influx of immigrants there came an outflow. A crisis started in Palestine, but it basically extended only to densely populated cities—Tel Aviv, Haifa, Jerusalem —weak centers of small-scale industry and trade. The crisis did not affect Jewish agriculture and halted at the borders of rural settlements. This Palestinian crisis is essentially a continuation of the economic crisis of Jewish petty bourgeoisie in Eastern Europe. The middleman who first went bankrupt on Nalewki Street, went bankrupt again on Allenby Street in Tel Aviv. Different geographical coordinates did not alter his situation. And his situation would be the same, by the way, in economically developed countries like the United States or Australia, where there is currently also no place for déclassé petty bourgeoisie.

One of the two bourgeois Zionist factions, Al Hamishmar, calls for selective immigration procedures, admission for no one but pioneers, and elimination of "unproductive" social strata. The second faction, Et Livnot, which has a majority in the Zionist organization, has thrown the doors of immigration wide open. It was, in fact, impossible to act otherwise, to stop the powerful surge of immigration, and refuse to open the gates for all who were knocking. From the point of view of Zionist theory, the position of Al Hamishmar was entirely legitimate. But if only a select few were actually admitted to Palestine, Zionism would have to sidestep the demands of Jewish realities and the need to resettle the masses, which became central and urgent. The organization would thus refuse to take up the challenge posed by reality, and it would have to admit its weakness. It would retreat to a sideline position, becoming an ideological camp unable to take up existing challenges. By slowly preparing people capable of settling Eretz Israel, and waiting for a more opportune moment, the organization would diminish the role of Zionism in Jewish life, and it would have to give up "intangibles" like fervor, enthusiasm, and mass mobilization, which are vitally important for every movement. It would, perhaps, avoid many mistakes. But to act is to make mistakes. Adherents of Et Livnot took up reality's challenge, they took up a task that was too great for them, counting, among other things, on the possibility that great momentum might create unexpected, opportune circumstances. Like every undertaking, this had some aspects of a game. And there was faith in the ability of the "unproductive" to adapt, faith in the energy of "Nalewki and Dzika Streets," in private initiative, and in the power of the initiative of the Jewish "*luftmensch*."[23]

This faith is not without some basis in reality. In our nation, the homeless, the "unprofessional," and the unfortunate have shown an often stunning ability to adapt to the worst of circumstances. They have displayed vitality, resilience, and ingenuity. They could brilliantly exploit every opportunity, make deals, and create business networks as well as new branches and fields of production. If the Jewish traveling salesman could facilitate economic contacts between Kamchatka and Central European industry before the war—why should the same salesman prove helpless in Palestine? The so-called unproductivity of the Jewish masses is a little fairytale used by doctrinaires in their demagogic propaganda. In economic life, the middleman's role is no less important than the producer's. The middleman reaches the market and the consumer, and a producer who does not reach the market through the middleman goes out of business. In Russia, the prosperity of the Jewish population, along with trade and industry, was destroyed in the name of "productivization."[24]

Trade and industry, the economic organs that allow for the exchange of material goods and enable the functioning of intermediaries, encountered unfavorable circumstances in Palestine. Unrest in Syria, an uncertain political situation in Mesopotamia, torpor in Transjordan, and indeterminate relations throughout the entire Middle East, deprived Palestine of an economic "hinterland," and diminished its significance as a liaison between East and West. England, which has mandate authority in Palestine, did not make investments necessary for the development of economic life there. It did not allot land for Jewish settlement purposes, and it limited itself to taking responsibility for maintaining peace and order. The mistake of Et Livnot was that it counted on favorable political circumstances and influx of investment capital from Jewish sources and mandate authorities. So far, these hopes have been in vain. The generosity of world Jewry proved too limited in relation to Palestine's needs; Jews are incapable of carrying out this massive settlement undertaking by themselves, without outside help.

Had the gates not been opened for the Fourth Aliyah, there would have been no great wave of immigration; without immigration, there would have been no crisis . . .

In other words: if nothing were done, no mistakes would have been made along the way. . . . If this is all that is at stake, then the opponents of the majority in the Zionist party are right. But how significant is this correctness in the face of the great demands placed on Zionism by Jewish realities?

The crisis of this most recent wave of emigration has intensified internal struggles within the Zionist Organization, especially in Poland. Even if one brackets these struggles, and the sometimes scathing criticism that the fighting factions direct at each other, the regional fragmentation of the party prevents the Zionist Organization in Poland from focusing its efforts and acting efficiently. Besides the federation and the fractions, there are four central committees: in the former Congress Kingdom, in the Vilnius region, and in eastern and western Małopolska (Lesser Poland). In these circumstances, coordinated activity is difficult to imagine.

The Congress that starts today thus faces the task of consolidating the movement in the framework of a single organization in the lands of the Polish Republic. Regional differences in the "mentality" of Polish Jews, and animosities among the movement's individual leaders, make this difficult. Yet both the changing realities and the need to reinforce the Zionist position among the various worldviews that compete for the allegiance of Jews today make the consolidation and unification of regional groups a pressing imperative.

Only after unification will it be possible to solve problems concerning Zionism's domestic and foreign policy, the reform of its organizational structures, and effective dissemination of its fundamental principle.

The Zionist Organization's "domestic policy" must face the fact that a powerful assimilation process is underway among Polish Jews, and that this process is reinforced by factors that incite class struggle and drive fragmentation, which undermines the idea of national unity.

The so-called golus-work thus becomes a crucially important responsibility.

When it was possible to think that Palestine's actual present capacity was more or less equivalent to the emigration potential of the Jewry, concentration of all activities on Palestine was tantamount to performing real and most important work.

But right now, Palestine cannot take in all the Jews who want to emigrate. The situation in Palestine has stabilized: those who were weaker and unprepared for struggle went under, and those who were stronger remained afloat. A gradual configuration of social strata is emerging. Before the emergence of new economic and political phenomena that will open the country's gates, the Zionist Organization must undertake the painstaking, daily work of raising awareness among the masses, the intelligentsia, and the youth. It must deepen national culture, and participate in the maintenance and development of Jewish educational institutions.

Last year, when I wrote in this newspaper about Zionism's arrival at a turning point, I wondered: who would give us a Fifth Aliyah capable of sacrifices? Where would this "army of workers" come from? Would it not be from the nation's body? From national schools? What milieu would create it if not Jews who are educated and live immersed in their own culture and national aspirations?

And what is taking place all around us? What kind of "national institutions and schools" do we have? What does our "unity" look like? A year ago, we could talk about a satiated and half-assimilated Western European and American Jewry. Today we can talk about a financially ruined Polish Jewry, undergoing assimilation at an accelerated pace. There is no need to point to the abnormality of this phenomenon and its unavoidable consequences.

All our powers must concentrate on organizing our national life. Will the Eighth Congress of Polish Zionists realize the importance of this task?

When it comes to "foreign policy," reality is forcing Zionists to carry out a political offensive.

At present, the postulate of an "offensive" is the only notion in Jabotinsky's entire program of "revision," which has not only maintained vitality but gained in significance. Whoever observes the behavior of the mandate government, and the indifference or hostility of the English press, which conveys how British public opinion views the creation of a national home for the Jewish people, cannot doubt the futility of the approach of patient waiting embraced by the Zionist headquarters in London. English policy in the East is increasingly tilting toward the Arab side: when writing about Transjordan, for example, the authoritative *Times* emphasized the exclusively Arab character of this country, without even mentioning the possibility of extending Jewish settlements beyond the Jordan River. And the prospect of making Transjordan an independent state, and fully separating it from the Palestinian Mandate, is becoming realistic.

Under these circumstances, Zionism must demand its rights before the world, and it must invoke the promises that were made.

We should hope that the Congress of Polish Zionists, which represents the masses who have sacrificed the most for Palestine by performing the difficult settlers' work, will decisively demand the fulfillment of promises—and call on the London headquarters to begin Zionism's "political offensive."

—Jakub Appenszlak: "Syjonizm u progu nowej ery"
(Zionism at the Brink of a New Era), *Nasz Przegląd*
(*Our Review*), no. 181, July 3, 1927

Editors' Notes

1. "Żydzi—lata dwudzieste" from *Wyprawa w dwudziestolecie* by Czesław Miłosz © 1999 Czesław Miłosz, used by permission of the Wylie Agency (UK) Limited.

2. Błoński's essay is reproduced in this volume on pages 273–285; it is reprinted from Antony Polonsky's edited volume devoted to the discussions this essay generated in Poland after its publication in 1987: Polonsky, ed., *"My Brother's Keeper?" Recent Polish Debates on the Holocaust* (Routledge in association with the Institute for Polish-Jewish Studies, Oxford, 1990).

3. Aleksander Wat (1900–1967) was a poet and writer best known for his spoken memoir *Mój wiek* (*My Century*), which was recorded as a conversation with Czesław Miłosz in Berkeley in 1964–1965, and first published in Polish in 1977. It chronicles Wat's life, and both his engagement and later disillusionment with communism. The exact phrase Wat uses is *kraj urzędniczej inteligencji*, which Richard Lourie rendered as "a land of white-collar intelligentsia" in Aleksander Wat, *My Century* (NYRB Classics, 2003).

4. The following historical referents mentioned in this essay are discussed in the Introduction to this volume: the partitions of Poland, nineteenth-century Polish uprisings and Jewish support for the insurgents, the Pale of Settlement, pre-1914 and interwar Polish and Jewish political parties (including the Polish Socialist Party, the National Democrats, Polish agrarian parties, and the Bund), Roman Dmowski, Vladimir Jabotinsky, Józef Piłsudski, the Polish Legions, the Polish-Soviet War of 1920, and the military internment camp in Jabłonna. Please see "Poles and Jews in the Nineteenth Century and "The Interwar Years: Polish Independence and the Crisis of Democracy" in the Introduction for any needed clarification.

5. Miłosz uses the words *kaznodzieja* (preacher) and *Stary Testament* (Old Testament) in this sentence.

6. The Khmelnytsky Uprising (1648–1657) was a Cossack revolt in the Polish-Lithuanian Commonwealth. The insurgents committed atrocities against the civilian population and carried out dozens of anti-Jewish pogroms; historians estimate that tens of thousands of Jews were killed.

7. Martin Buber (1878–1965) was a philosopher and scholar of religion. Born in Austria, he lived in Germany after the First World War and immigrated to

Palestine in 1938. He is best known for his existentialist philosophy of dialogue articulated in his book *Ich und Du* (*I and Thou*, 1923) and for his translations and analyses of Hassidic tales and teachings.

8. For a discussion about how the cliché *kwestia żydowska* (which can be rendered as "Jewish question," "Jewish problem," or "Jewish issue") functioned in interwar Poland, please see the final section of the Introduction.

9. Cheders were religious schools for young boys; after their Bar Mitzvah at the age of thirteen, boys could continue their education in yeshivas.

10. Jerzy Giedroyc (1906–2000) was the editor of the Paris-based Polish émigré monthly *Kultura*, which provided a sustained critique of the Polish communist government, and offered a forum for literary and political discussions for several decades.

11. Jędrzej Giertych (1903–1992) was a nationalist activist in interwar Poland and an émigré editor in Great Britain after the Second World War. He was expelled from the émigré nationalist group Stronnictwo Narodowe for his extreme nationalist views.

12. The Swedish invasion of the Polish-Lithuanian Commonwealth (1655–1660) came in the aftermath of the Thirty Years' War, which had engulfed Central Europe between 1618 and 1648. Although the Swedes were unable to establish permanent control over the Commonwealth, they inflicted enormous losses and casualties, and decisively weakened the Polish-Lithuanian state.

13. Prince Józef Poniatowski (1763–1813) was a military leader when Poland was partitioned in the 1790s, and the Polish minister of war during the Napoleonic period. Jan Henryk Dąbrowski was a general active in the 1790s and early 1800s. He is among Poland's national heroes, and the Polish national anthem evokes the military formation called the Polish Legions, which he organized in Italy in 1797.

14. The author of this piece is not provided in the Polish original.

15. Since the 1880s, May Day (May 1) has been celebrated as International Workers' Day in various countries. On May Day in 1926, Zionist parties and Bund organized a peaceful march in Vilnius, and they were attacked by Polish nationalist street squads, who brutally beat both male and female participants; around fifteen participants were wounded.

16. Ludwik Chomiński (1890–1958) was a leader of the left-leaning Polish Peasants' Party "Wyzwolenie" (PSL-Wyzwolenie). In October 1923, when this press review was written, Poland was ruled by a coalition known as Chjeno-Piast. It was a united front of Christian and right-leaning parties (ChZJN) and the center-right Polish Peasants' Party "Piast" (PSL-Piast), whose leader, Wincenty Witos (1874–1945), served as Poland's prime minister.

17. Jakub Wygodzki (1856–1941) was a doctor, medical researcher, and political activist in Vilnius. He was a deputy in the Polish Parliament throughout the 1920s.

18. Noach Pryłucki (1882–1941) was a journalist and lawyer from Vilnius. He served in the Polish Parliament throughout the 1920s.

19. The Polish word *ugodowiec* (loyalist) refers to the second half of the nineteenth century, when many lost hope that Poland could become sovereign again and advocated various forms of accommodation with the partitioning powers.

20. Jakub Appenszlak (1894–1950) was a publisher, journalist, and liberal Zionist activist. He was the editor of the Warsaw daily *Nasz Przegląd* (1923–1939).

21. The Yiddish word *golus* means exile from the Land of Israel; it refers to the Jewish diaspora.

22. Historians identify six Aliahs, or waves of mass Jewish emigration to the Land of Israel, between 1881 and 1947. The Fourth Aliah (1924–1931) included mostly East European Jews, many of whom left as a result of both poverty and growing anti-Semitism.

23. The Yiddish word *luftmensch* refers to someone who is impractical and dreamy, who does not have a definite occupation or job skills.

24. The "productivization" of Jews in Imperial Russia refers the tsarist administration's attempts to change how Jews functioned in the economy. Most often, this meant moving Jews from petty trade into agriculture.

PART II

1936–1939: The Mustard Gas of Racism

2

The Przytyk Market Stands

KSAWERY PRUSZYŃSKI

Editors' Introduction

Franciszek Ksawery Pruszyński (1907–1950) was a journalist, writer, and diplomat, best known for his keen newspaper reports about Poland and Europe. He was born in Wolica Kierkieszyna in Volhynia (today's Ukraine) and studied law at the Jagiellonian University in Krakow, where he joined the conservative youth organization Myśl Mocarstwowa (Imperial Thought). Starting in 1930, he published in the Krakow conservative daily *Czas* (*Time*) and various leading Polish papers and periodicals. He was a nonconformist and combined elements of both conservative and democratic-liberal traditions. Like many Polish conservatives at the time, he opposed radical agrarian land reform (which would parcel out all landholdings to individual peasant families), and he emphasized his loyalty to Catholicism while supporting the separation of church and state. Throughout the 1930s he openly criticized both fascism and communism as totalitarian ideologies, and he opposed the ethnic nationalism embraced by the National Democrats. In 1936 he was a correspondent in Madrid, where he supported the democratic and left-leaning Republicans who fought against General Franco in the Spanish Civil War. Throughout the 1930s, Pruszyński traveled widely and published several books, including *Podróż po Polsce* (*A Voyage through Poland*, 1937), and *W czerwonej Hiszpanii* (*In Red Spain*, 1939). His books available in English include *Unfinished Journey: A Film Script* (1944), *Adam Mickiewicz: The Life Story of the Greatest Polish Poet* (1956), and *The Polish Invasion* (2010). During the Second World War, he joined the Polish Army and fought for the Allies in the Battles of Narvik (1940) and Falaise Pocket (1944). He also spent a year as a press attaché in the Polish Embassy in the

USSR (1941–1942). He returned to Poland after the war and later served as the Polish People's Republic ambassador to the Netherlands.

The essay reproduced here was originally published in the Warsaw weekly *Wiadomości Literackie* (*Literary News*) on July 12, 1936. *Wiadomości Literackie* was the most influential periodical of liberal Warsaw intellectuals, and it was viciously attacked by the National Democrats throughout the interwar period. Pruszyński's piece was published a few months after the Przytyk Pogrom, which took place on March 9, 1936. Within a few weeks after this Pogrom, there were violent anti-Semitic outbreaks in Odrzywół and Mińsk Mazowiecki, and another pogrom took place in Brest-on-the-Bug (formerly Brest-Litovsk) in May 1937.

Przytyk is a small town near Radom, which is about sixty miles south of Warsaw. In the middle of 1935, National Democratic activists called for a general boycott of Jewish trade there. During the boycott, National Democratic street squads repeatedly demolished Jewish market stands and beat their owners. In response, a group of about twenty young Jewish men formed a *zelbszuc*, a self-defense unit. After one of the National Democratic squad attacks on Jewish market stands, members of the *zelbszuc* fought back. According to eyewitnesses, the police joined in, fighting on the side of the National Democrats. After about an hour of fighting, *zelbszuc* member Szulim Chil Leska shot and killed a Polish assailant, and a crowd of furious Poles retaliated by attacking Jewish homes, workshops, and shops. Homes and shops were demolished and looted, and Jews were brutally beaten; at least twenty-four suffered severe injuries. The shoemaker Josek Minkowski was killed and his wife, Chaja, was beaten and died from her injuries after being transported to a hospital. On March 12 the independent Senator Moses Schorr condemned the massacre in the Polish Sejm (Parliament), and shortly thereafter the Bund and the Polish Socialist Party (PPS) called for a one-day, countrywide general strike.

Pogrom participants and Jewish fighters were put on trial, and Pruszyński describes the proceedings and the atmosphere in the courtroom. Eleven of the fourteen Jewish defendants received guilty verdicts and prison sentences. Leska was sentenced to eight years in prison, and two other Jews accused of using firearms were sentenced to six and five years each. Twenty-two out of the forty-three Polish defendants received sentences of six months to a year in prison. The four Poles accused of killing the Minkowski couple were acquitted because of "insufficient evidence." It did not matter that the couple's children recognized the killers, who were their neighbors.

One by one, fifty-seven people, referred to as "defendants," file into the center of the room, a rectangle bordered on one side by the judges' table, by defense stands on two sides, and a policeman on the fourth side. Some five hundred people, described as "witnesses" in court papers, follow them in. But the proceedings hardly seem like a trial, and the setting doesn't look like a typical court of justice. It's as if several hundred different filmed versions of the same event were brought into a great film lab, and, once developed, the rolls were unfurled, their content examined, discussed, and dissected.

The camera lenses, however, were not wide-angled enough. For three weeks, we are taken around a very small setting—a town's marketplace; its main street and pavement; the surrounding suburbs; the bridge on the Radomka River; the vicinity of Herberg's mill; market stands and pubs. For three weeks, men wearing the robes of judges, prosecutors, and defense attorneys will put fragments of the film up to the light, examine the details, and compare them with one another. But all this will not result in any grand, evenly flowing, or rhythmically unfolding great film. Cuts from various cameramen and film examined from different angles, under different lighting, cannot be spliced into a single whole. At the end of all this work, it will appear as if one camera was used to film the same things two, three, or even four times. Black shadows will appear on whole reams of film. Specific moments will be captured only through sudden, sharp contours. We will see a farm boy urging a boycott and being freed from police custody by the crowd; right after, we will see the same farmers-market crowd blockading a police station that looks like the interior of a small house. We'll see a man reaching out from a garret, pointing a gun out the window; we'll hear shots; a peasant will fall down in the street. A phantom car spraying gunshots will suddenly appear—a car not found in any other footage. Then, for a moment, the scene will come into dreadfully clear focus: we'll be in the rooms of a Jewish home; its window frames will seem to be sagging from the weight of stones, and three small, frightened children will be pulled out from under a cot by their legs, hair, and heads—thick-set peasants swinging wagon crossbars over them. It will be dark in the cramped hallway, and again we won't see the faces of people using clubs to crush the base of the skull, the parietal bone, and the bluish, veiny convexity of the temples of a poor Jewish shoemaker.

For a moment, the images will break off entirely, and then we'll float on streams of film shot by experienced cameramen: there will be police reports, the court physician's depositions, the inspection of the body, and

reports from Radom administrative workers. Then, through a torn peas-
ant shirt, we'll probe a deep, even wound in the desiccated body of the old
peasant, made by the bullet that came from above. Again, they will lift up
Josek Minkowski's crushed skull for us, pounded with clubs even after he
died; they will tell us to take a good long look at what was left of Chaja
Minkowska's head, smashed with wagon crossbars or the blade of a scythe.
But no one will show all that transpired before, as it actually happened.
After three weeks, it won't even be possible to determine how to splice the
individual fragments of the horrifying film together, to see how successive
events followed one another—the boycotting Strzałkowski and his arrest
by the police; the fight and rout in the Przytyk townsquare; and finally, the
events by the river. Time and again, as the judge justifies the sentence, he
will have to repeat the words "impossible to determine." Despite fifty-seven
defendants, twenty defense attorneys, several hundred witnesses, and three
weeks of work. The court will refuse the witnesses' testimonies, and, one
by one, the prosecutor will condemn the falsity of these statements. Yet
despite entreaties, appeals to the sanctity of the court oath, and reminders
about legal punishments and justice, a vast number of the witnesses will give
contradictory, meandering, and fanciful testimonies. The crowd won't sympathize with laws that govern oath-taking, truthful testimony, and punishments for perjury. It will sympathize with the row—or rather two rows—of
defendants.

   The defense attorneys in this trial—concerning events in a small town
whose location was hardly known before March 9, 1936—include stars of
the Polish bar, known for highly publicized, sensational, dramatic, and spectacular cases. They include Leon Berenson, the great defense attorney from
the 1905 and Brest trials. But the proceedings are reminiscent of a staged
play. And one would be hard pressed to recall a trial so ordinary in its tragic
horror. Every defendant is vulnerable to the lawyers' leading and probing
questions. Perhaps that man over here is the protagonist of these events; perhaps the one next to him is their evil spirit, the Szela of the new peasantry,
the Shylock and Apostate of Przytyk.[1] The interrogation lights move from
young Wójcik's determined, crude, peasant, Kalmyk face to Leska's pale
and reserved one, with eyes half-closed; they slide along the shoulders of a
stout peasant who looks like Zagłoba, and along Haberberg's black beard.[2]
After a few days, the exhausted lights shut down. In this trial—involving
these fifty-seven people and several hundred witnesses, only a few of whom
are articulate before the magistrate—there are no tragic, great, heroic, or

criminal figures. There are no powerful people—no hidden figures pull-ing the strings. Anti-Semitic campaigns had more and better agitators in many other regions in contemporary Poland—regions exposed to National Democratic activity much earlier and much more fully than those in the vicinity of Przytyk. The famous "Przytyk voivode," Korczak, is a common, typical peasant. He speaks like a peasant, he argues like a peasant, he has a peasant's vocabulary, and lives like an impoverished peasant, a man whose soil is poor, who makes a living by subleasing land from others, hoping to sell his horse someplace or another, harboring distant dreams about having his own lime fertilizer business someday. One other thing we can say about this man—the man shown in the Jewish press as the *spiritus movens* of the Przytyk events, chieftain of the Przytyk hordes, a Radomian Hitler, and a threat to the government in Warsaw, the man who mindlessly rehashes the canon of Polish anti-Semitism when he talks—is that he grew closer to the town than the other peasants. They went to town once a week; he went every day. Perhaps he listened to the radio from time to time, perhaps he talked to people from other places more often, and he might have read the newspaper more frequently. He became a spark in the Radom events by coincidence. The gunpowder that was lying here could have been set off by a candle stub.

For there is one more perspective, one more implicit film image that the reporter must take in, since he has no stake in the trial's legal and procedural outcomes, and he views all this purely as a cross-section of the situation of Jews in Poland. He must notice that the vast majority of the accused, both on the Polish and the Jewish side, are young. They say that the young are the best at registering the invisible currents floating in the ether of their time—that age, maturity, family, and work have not yet blunted their politi-cal sensitivity. And these young Poles are peasants, but there is more to it. They are subsistence farmers and landless sons from large families, inheri-tors of farmland divided into tiny strips. If they ever chose to write, they could add shocking new pages to *Pamiętniki chłopów* (*Peasant Memoires*).[3] They represent the classic rural proletariat in Poland, a country which has no equal in Europe when it comes to the size of its agrarian population and the scale of its rural destitution. And this agrarian proletariat is not from the Baranowicze and Równe region but from well beyond the Vistula; it is a proletariat from the better-off half of Poland—from Minister Kwiatkowski's "Poland A." Socialist Radom is nineteen kilometers from here, and the Poznań district—the Polish Denmark, an economic oasis—is not much more than a hundred kilometers away. The defendants can read and write; they went to school. They belong to political parties, and they boycotted not only Jewish market stands but also an ordinance that limited electoral rights. These are the defendants responsible for Przytyk.

It is hardly trivial, unimportant, or coincidental that the largest of all our trials involving anti-Semitic disturbances is a peasant trial. And the people on trial are not "kulaks"—wealthy countryside farmers—but young subsistence farmers and landless peasants, who turn twenty-something and realize that there will not be enough of their father's land for them. The agricultural laborers who are the protagonists of Wanda Wasilewska's novel *Ojczyzna (Fatherland)* ask what Poland gave them in exchange for the years of the war for independence, and they demand payment in the form of socialism.[4] Here, in front of a blockaded police station in Przytyk, a different group of peasants—soldiers from a 1920 volunteer regiment—also asks what Poland gave them, though their demand for compensation is different from the outcry in the famous novel.

The court was unable to determine exactly who was responsible for the horrible death of the poor Jewish couple from Przytyk. But it was peasant hands that put wagon crossbars, stones, clubs, and knives into motion. Perhaps the peasant wasn't killed by Leska; perhaps he was felled by Jewish fire. The defendants Leska, Haberberg, Banda, Wójcik, and Kubiak are not the ones marching directly toward us in the metaphorical newsreel projected onto newspaper screens throughout Poland; and witness Snopek is not the only one to say gleefully that the pogrom "was something to look at." In this newsreel, we are confronted by a large peasant crowd stampeding toward us. A crowd just like the one in Przytyk when peasants, alarmed by news from town at 3 PM, hastily turned their horses around to go "defend their own." This crowd is the hero, the culprit, the defendant, and the prosecutor in the trial. And to find out who was in this crowd, one has to walk among Przytyk's Jewish houses, one has to go to Potworów and to the countryside.

"Did Jews sell a lot before this boycott?," Esquire Kowalski, the National Democratic defense attorney asks every Jew.

"They did," a Jew answers.

"Well, and how many Jewish stands were there on a typical market day?"

"Seventy or eighty."

"*Eighty*," the attorney emphasizes every time.

"Well, and during the boycott, before March ninth and in the morning of March ninth, before the riot, how many Jewish stands were there?"

"Jewish ones . . . ," the Jew says, "maybe eight or ten."

"Eight, ten," Kowalski repeats, "and how many peasant stands?"

"Sixty," says the Jew.

"Sixty," Kowalski confirms, "and were there peasant stands in the market before that?"

"No, there were not," the Jew replies.

"There were not. So, there were no peasant stands before," the attorney repeats to himself, "and now, after the boycott, there are."

This kind of questioning, having nothing to do with the substance of the trial, is the *leitmotif* used by the defense lawyers with every witness. Their strategy is based on two things: on the one hand, to defend each of the accused against charges of violence and terror; on the other, to draw attention to the economic success of the boycott, which, in a matter of a few weeks, raised the specter of starvation and dire poverty for the Jewish masses. We don't know whether the boycott relieved the misery of the Polish villages, whether it had permanent consequences, or whether its function was to establish a peasant stronghold in town and actually move peasants from the plow to the market stand. What is obvious and certain is that the boycott was bringing economic ruin to a few thousand Jews living in Przytyk. Everyone should see it for himself. Przytyk is 90 percent Jewish and perhaps one of the poorest towns I could find during my long journey through the pauperized borderlands. Two national groups took part in the "Przytyk war," in the pogrom, the "upheaval" that took place there. A visitor will wonder what they could have been looking for in Jewish Przytyk, why they envied these people living in their crooked huts. And that's not the only thing that will surprise anyone who is not intimately familiar with local issues.

What happened here on March 9 began as a boycott organized by peasants against a Jewish town. What ended with the death of the peasant and the corpses of the Minkowski couple started as a fight for the market stand. That's right, not a shop but a market stand. The Jewish population makes its living from trade. The Jewish aristocracy hold positions in great banks; the middle class own shops; the proletariat runs the market stand. The Przytyk town-square market stand was attacked by the peasantry—by a human mass lifting itself out of the countryside. And it was overwhelmed in a very short time.

Here, again, there are things that are difficult to understand. We all got used to the fact that peasants strive for parceled land from large estates, wishing to take it without compensation—we see this as natural, understandable, and

legitimate. All of us city dwellers are convinced that waves of peasant loath-
ing are eroding the foundations of manor-house columns, and that, even
more important, large-scale and radical land redistribution will draw peasants away from communism, or Witos, and win them over for Składkowski
or Grażyński.[5] And yet the trials we have witnessed in recent years, focusing
on peasant riots in towns like Łapanów, Lisko, or Tarnów, showed peasants
fighting against taxes and the corvée, against the starost, the bailiff, and the
policeman.[6] But the trials currently underway show peasants attacking the
impoverished shoemaker Minkowski, or Icek Banda and the Jewish stand
with eggs, calico, or hats. Peasants are expropriating Jewish stands without
compensation. Why?

To understand why, we need to carry out three successive experiments.
We could first read *Pamiętniki chłopów* (*Peasant Memoires*). If we read them
perceptively, we'll see that the space occupied by the so-called manor
in the contemporary Polish countryside—in its dreams and its destitution—is incredibly small; we won't encounter the word "manor" until
after reading over a hundred pages. For thousands of villages and hundreds of thousands of peasants, the manor is something bordering on the
exotic. Second, we would need to take a plane ride over Poland, to get a
bird's-eye view of lands stretching from Czerniowce to Gdańsk, and from
Vilnius to Katowice. Our search for the immense estates, vast territories,
and landlords' endless fields would be in vain. From the bird's-eye perspective, Poland is a fragmented chessboard of thin patches of land. To understand the Przytyk tragedy, we need, finally, to open Józef Poniatowski's
and Theodora Oberlander's books dealing with Poland's agrarian overpopulation. They would first tell us that even with the recovery of the
entire reserve of the wastelands, the total area of land to be parceled out
will amount to 3 million hectares [approx. 12,000 square miles], at best.
According to Poniatowski, if even more radical measures were taken, an
additional 600,000 hectares [approx. 2,300 square miles] might be parceled out. This maximum land reserve would make it possible to establish 600,000 six-hectare [fourteen-acre] farms. The yearly—and mostly
rural—population growth in Poland is 400,000 people. According to
Oberlander, the available reserve of land would be used up almost entirely
by land additions for smallholder peasants. And the landless? The fast-
multiplying, rabbit-like generations of our countryside? Seasonal migrations and permanent emigration have ceased almost entirely. There is no
industrialization. Przytyks are starting to occur.

The fight for the market stand does not break out because market stands could provide jobs for all the unemployed in the countryside. The fight breaks out because there is nowhere else to go. Because roads are blocked; there is not enough land; starting a new farm is costly, even if land were available; and the market stand is closest at hand. It is what's most easily available, most immediately profitable. The market stand won't help things, however; it won't take in people without work. It will provide relief, but not complete relief. Yet today's countryside views the merchant as a rich man— he is the owner of a treasure trove with sugar, petroleum, matches, and iron. Only if we look on from above do we see that this petty Jewish merchant is actually a pauper. For the peasant, he is the man we hear about in the courthouse lament—the man who rakes in several dozen zlotys a day. One dozen would make the peasant happy. The man in a yarmulke eats herring and potatoes, while the peasant in the sheepskin coat eats only potatoes. Simply put, a group whose standard of living is even lower than that of the Jewish Ghetto is now challenging this Ghetto.

Once again, this might seem quite natural. Poland would simply be undergoing a process that took place everywhere in the West a hundred— or a few dozen—years earlier. In conservative England and republican France, in Germany, Austria, Denmark, and Czechoslovakia, agrarian regulation always pushed rural masses into cities and small towns. This was how Karlsbad and Prague became more Czech, and Lublana became more Slovenian; this, finally, was how the cities and small towns around Poznań became more Polish. But all this happened earlier in other places, and it happened without Przytyk-like violence. That's because elsewhere, excessive countryside procreation and the overpopulation of villages was accompanied by economic booms that favored industrial development. It was not just about farms getting smaller—factories were also opening their doors in the cities. The small-town and merchant population was moving from the market stand to the shop, from the shop to capital, and from capital to industry. This movement not only emptied out trading posts in towns but also created new workplaces by opening factories. In Poland, industrial development is stalled, stuck in place. During the boom years, yearly employment growth was minimal relative to the massive, bottom-up increase in the number of potential workers. The pauperized masses of Minkowskis, Leskas, and Bandas will not move to shops in Radom. Haberberg, the mill owner, won't build a great factory, and he won't employ thousands of Strzałkowskis, Wójciks, and Kubiaks. He won't become a Kroneberg or a Bloch in two generations.[7] The peasant, whom the Jew would employ in that scenario, will now become his competitor. He will paw the Jew's bread rolls with dirty, sweaty hands, pretending he wants to buy them. He will knock the hats from his counter into the mud. He will chase buyers away. He will keep him hungry. He will kill him.

It's not just that the Przytyk Jew is unable to replace his small-scale operation by a modern shop in Radom—he cannot replace the workshop by a plant, or the mill by a factory. He is not simply unable to move up—he has nowhere to go. Before the war there was industrial development; now the new chimneys billowing smoke in Radom and in the "security triangle" belong to state-run factories.[8] Before the war, there was emigration; now there is none. Zionist organizations have opened Palestine to Jews from Germany, but they keep it nearly closed to Jews from Poland. Those who think that Jews will leave after Przytyk should know that only one person moved to Palestine after everything that happened here. And those who bring up the example of the Poznań district should remember that around Poznań there were no Przytyks, Mińsk Mazowieckis, and Grodnos—places where locals removed Jews by the specter of pogroms. Around Poznań, the mirage of Berlin floated over the Ghetto—the great, magnificent Berlin, the Berlin of assimilation and wealth. Before and after the war, thousands of Jews from the Poznań district immigrated to Germany. The mirage was more potent than the specter. But in today's circumstances, the only place Jews from Przytyk can go is the cemetery.

All this is meant to sketch out a certain problem that goes beyond the Przytyk case, though its cross-section is revealed by Przytyk. We need to dispassionately ascertain the opportunities in the countryside today—opportunities that have eluded the countryside and those that beguile it. Mierosławski is said to have predicted that Poland will have a future only once the last bishop is hanged on a noose made from the guts of the last nobleman. Perhaps there was a rural Mierosławski at Korczak's meetings, claiming that there wouldn't be happiness in Poland until the last debt collector is hanged by the last Jew's intestines. Demagogy is always the same—only rarely does it leave its dry riverbeds to seek new ones.

There was—we should finally note—no opposition against the disturbances that swept the Opoczno and Radom provinces. There was only the policeman. The intellectual wasn't there. The village teacher wasn't there. Yet there are teachers and schools in villages around Przytyk. There are teachers in Przytyk itself. We saw one of them standing before the judges, playing a rather sad role in all that transpired. In today's Przytyk, the school is a place where children fight and hate. Little Korczaks and little Minkowskis are battling away. Hatred from the street is spilling into the classroom. It is spilling far and wide throughout the whole country and not encountering any dams. It is also not encountering anything that would redirect the flood— born of impoverishment and not of agitation—into more useful, creative, and constructive channels. And various groups wish to see it only as leaven for a future revolution, a bloody wave that will carry their banners.

Editors' Notes

1. In addition to Shakespeare's Shylock, Pruszyński evokes figures from Polish history and literature here. The Apostate was a figure in Zygmunt Krasiński's *Nie-boska komedia* (*The Undivine Comedy*, 1833); he was the leader of a revolutionary Jewish group whose ideology mixed elements of Jacobinism and Saint-Simonianism. Jakub Szela (1787–1860) was a Galician peasant who led the serfs' uprising against the Polish gentry in 1846; he symbolizes brutality and peasant rage at landowners.

2. The Kalmyks are the inhabitants of present-day Russian Federation's province of Kalmykia, which lies in the Caucasus region, by the Caspian Sea. In colloquial Polish, the adjective "Kalmyk" is a racist slur meant to indicate stupidity. Onufry Zagłoba is the fictional protagonist of Henryk Sienkiewicz's *Trylogia* (*Trilogy*), which was published in parts throughout the 1880s, and which focused on the Polish-Lithuanian Commonwealth in the second half of the seventeenth century. Wójcik, Leska, and Haberberg were involved in the Przytyk trial.

3. *Pamiętniki chłopów* (*Peasant Memoires*, 1935–1936) was a book that resulted from a writing contest organized by the Polish Institute for Social Economy in 1933. Peasants from throughout the country sent in 498 essays, which describe their destitution and hunger, and testify to the state's inability to improve their lot.

4. Wanda Wasilewska (1905–1965) was a writer and social activist affiliated with the Polish Socialist Party (PPS) and the communist movement in interwar Poland. After the Second World War, she lived in the USSR. Her 1935 novel *Ojczyzna* (*Fatherland*) belongs to the genre of propaganda literature and portrays the emergence of class consciousness among peasants who work as hired rural laborers.

5. Wincenty Witos (1874–1945) was the leader of the Polish Peasants' Party "Piast" (PSL-Piast) in Galicia; in the early 1920s, he held the office of the prime minister of Poland three times; in 1930, the authoritarian Sanacja government imprisoned him and other opposition politicians in the Brest fortress. Felicjan Sławoj-Składkowski (1885–1962) was a member of Piłsudski's

authoritarian government after his 1926 coup d'état, serving as the minister of the interior for much of the decade between 1926 and 1936; he openly supported economic discrimination against Jews. Michał Grażyński (1890–1965) became the voivode of Polish Silesia after Piłsudski's coup. He instituted a controversial policy of limiting cultural and economic rights and freedoms of the German minority in his province.

6. In interwar Poland, the starost was a government representative in the provincial administrative unit the size of a county. The word *szarwark* refers to the Polish version of the corvée—peasants were required to perform unpaid work in projects benefiting their local community; this included road and bridge repairs, and the construction of flood barriers.

7. Leopold Stanisław Kronenberg (1812–1878) was a member of the wealthy Kroneberg family; in 1870, he founded the Warsaw-based Bank Handlowy, one of the oldest banks in Europe. He also invested in railroads, tobacco and sugar factories, steel and coal, and insurance companies. Jan Gotlib Bloch (1836–1902) was a financier and industrialist known as the "king of the railroads."

8. The "security triangle" was an ambitious economic project in the triangular region contained between the San and Vistula Rivers; it was led by Deputy Prime Minister and Minister of the Treasury Eugeniusz Kwiatkowski in the 1930s. The goal was to lower unemployment, build up a Polish military defense industry, and lift up the impoverished eastern rural region of Poland, which Kwiatkowski referred to as "Poland B."

3

Annual Shame

MARIA DĄBROWSKA

Editors' Introduction

Maria Dąbrowska (1889–1965) was a novelist, journalist, and playwright. Born in Russów, in central Poland, which was under Russian rule until 1918, she studied natural sciences, sociology, and economics in Lousanne and Brussels, and settled in Warsaw after the First World War. Throughout the interwar period, Dąbrowska expressed concern about the fate of the peasants and the poor; she supported agrarian reform and advocated tolerance toward national and religious minorities. She was affiliated with democratic socialist circles, and with Edward Abramowski's cooperative movement, which championed the ideal of cooperation against the notion of class war, and preferred gradual reform to revolution. She gained fame and a permanent place in the pantheon of Polish writers when she published her novel *Noce i dnie* (*Nights and Days*, 1932–1934). This family saga, a parallel of Thomas Mann's *Buddenbrooks* or Marcel Proust's *Remembrance of Things Past*, tells the story of several generations of a Polish family and paints a portrait of Polish society at the turn of the twentieth century. It made Dąbrowska a great moral authority in Polish intellectual circles for the rest of her life. After the Second World War, she maintained an independent voice and repeatedly criticized Poland's communist government, speaking out against censorship and limitations of civil rights and liberties, and advocating amnesty for political prisoners in 1956. In 1964 she was among the thirty-four signatories of a famous protest letter against censorship addressed to Prime Minister Józef Cyrankiewicz by Polish writers and intellectuals. Dąbrowska's diaries, spanning the years 1914 to 1965 and published posthumously in 1988, provide a wealth of insights into the history of

Polish intellectuals and the moral dilemmas faced by the Poles. Her books available in English include *A Village Wedding and Other Stories* (1957) and *A Polish Christmas* (2001).

The article reproduced below was originally published in the daily *Dziennik Popularny* on November 24, 1936. *Dziennik Popularny* was a joint publication of the left-wing of the Polish Socialist Party (PPS) and the Polish Communist Party (KPP), and it represented one of their many efforts to create a united front against fascism and extremist nationalism. The daily came out in 1936 and 1937, at which point it was closed down by the government. Dąbrowska wrote this article in response to the intensifying anti-Semitic rhetoric and violence perpetrated by both the National Democrats and the ultranationalist National Radical Camp (ONR) activists, who campaigned for quotas on the number of Jewish students admitted to universities and carried out brutal attacks on Jewish students.

In nearly all university towns in Poland, the beginning of every academic year brings an outbreak of anti-Jewish excesses, which insult both civilization and the most basic human and civic feelings. The writer's hand no doubt repeatedly reaches for the pen to condemn the barbarity of the enraged youth and the negligence of the instigators. And it retreats with desperate awareness that such efforts are futile. Those who today make clubs, knives, brass knuckles, and iron crowbars hidden in a schoolbag into symbols of the Polish student—are they capable of at least registering, if not understanding, words dictated by honesty and profound civic concern? How low would one have to stoop to have at least an illusion of being able to move primitive hearts and tiny brains? Yet the dismal message borne by the facts makes it impossible to remain silent, even if one is sadly certain that one speaks to the deaf, the savage, to people without conscience. Those who wish to blame Jews for all the bad things taking place in Poland (Poles have always displaced their guilt and defeats onto others) need spontaneous manifestations of anti-Semitism. They need them as proof that the Jewish issue is a pressing one, that it requires immediate and radical solutions.[1]

The regularity and perfect coordination of the brawls, which always take place in the same pre-established order, deprives them of any semblance of spontaneity. These outbreaks are planned, carried out methodically, and executed in cold blood, in circumstances that rule out any possible justification. Because coming to lectures with hidden weapons, with the evil intention to beat defenseless colleagues, or even just to pick on them and degrade their human dignity, is not a spontaneous reflex; it sounds more like savored cultivation of moral degeneration. Whoever calls it anything else does what has unfortunately been quite popular in Poland—he attempts to make hideousness appear beautiful. At the same time, masked or open defenders of this savagery forget one thing, or rather do not wish to know it. Namely, that even if a spontaneous reflex was at play here, any "spontaneity" that consists in persecuting, beating, and injuring helpless people, and destroying public and private property, could—at most—be explained regretfully by the debased cultural level and ignorance of the activists.

But such things do not deserve any special treatment and cannot be explained away by any mitigating circumstances when perpetrated by students—the young generation's intellectual, and thus perhaps also cultural, elite. Sadly, hundreds of thousands of unemployed paupers who have nothing to lose, and whose despair could push them to incalculable acts, suffer injustice and unhappiness with inexhaustible dignity; they are shining examples of culture and prudence.

Meanwhile, the avant-garde of brawls and social disorder includes the "elite" of those in whose unworthy hands the nation has entrusted its highest good: knowledge, the fountain of life.

This year, the student pogrom epidemic has spilled out from universities into the streets. Students are smashing windows, breaking into shops, and using metal weapons to hit people who are calmly going about their business; then they run away like cowards, incapable of taking responsibility for their transgressions. In Vilnius, the students' depressingly fanatical madness has already caused street riots, and, without pausing, this madness has demagogically provoked events reminiscent of the dark seventeenth century, which preceded the downfall of our fatherland.[2]

In addition, on the same university campuses, these denigrators of academic and national dignity are already moving beyond thoughtless racial hatred, and crude, undiscriminating competition by disparaging the very knowledge that society seeks to offer them with such trust. Two years ago, in a university courtyard, Professor Handelsman was treacherously attacked from behind and hit on the head with brass knuckles, with obviously murderous intention. This year, eggs were thrown at Professor Bartel in the street. Finally—and this is without precedent—students threw eggs at the world-famous scholar, Professor Wolfke, during his lecture, which is to say, while he was carrying out the noblest act of sharing priceless knowledge.[3]

They offended the majesty of the greatest value by means of which the nation inscribes itself into world civilization—the majesty of great, inventive scholarship. Such deeds, duly initiated in December 1922, were used to drag Poland to the level of backward tribes that meet luminous, light-bearing spirits with animalistic hatred in their primitive souls and with stones up their sleeves.[4] If things continue this way, Polish scholars, the nation's pride, will start emigrating from this country where knowledge is disparaged—just as they emigrated in the past, during the era of fiercest foreign oppression.

And scholars from other countries will start bypassing Poland, where Curie-Skłodowska[5]—if she came back to life—would probably also be attacked with eggs. For neither she nor any of the great intellectuals could have anything but condemnation and disgust for what is going on at Polish universities.

Here, great thuggery is coming to Poland not from below but from above; and if it encounters no resistance, it will soon turn against all that is lawful, enlightened, noble, and judicious. To return to the question of anti-Semitism, which today is turning into a mere political part of a pro-gram that brings reaction, fanaticism, and ignorance to Poland—this is not the place to teach enraged people that the Jewish issue has been intertwined with Polish life too organically and for too long to be settled or eliminated in any ad-hoc way.

This is not the place to explain to club-wielding youth the tragedy and complexity of the Jewish issue, and we ourselves—through the class egotism of our gentry, our great historic social sins—have cultivated and created its abnormal hypertrophy over the centuries.

This is not the place to point out how to respond to the underdevel-opment of the national economy. This, finally, is not the place to explain to politicians blinded by hatred and to misled children that curtailing the rights of any national minority whatsoever would be a moral and politi-cal defeat of the Polish state. We will have to leave the consideration of these significant and painful problems for another time. For there is one more thing I have to discuss—the saddest thing of all. I have said some bitter and caustic words about the youth, even though my heart bleeds when I say them. But what is one to say to those responsible for the youth's misdeeds?

And there are so many of them! We writers are guilty—we who are incapable of finding timely words, words powerful enough to move blunted consciences. Our nationalist party is guilty because it incites riots without considering the irreparable harm this does to young, depraved minds. Because participation in the deliberate beating and persecution of the defense-less leaves an indelible mark of moral inferiority on one's entire life. The priests are guilty because they are passionately concerned about . . . Spain.[6] Yet they have never used their authority to condemn the brawls and vio-lence perpetrated in the name of Catholicism and the cross. Taking vows at Częstochowa,[7] hearing confessions, giving Communion and blessings to young terrorists, hanging crosses, emblems of love and peace, in auditoriums so that—after these vows and confessions, and under these crosses—people would beat and denigrate their neighbors, whoever they might be, humili-ate irreproachable scholars, and incite street brawls—all this, for God's sake, cannot help bolster the Church's dignity!

At least not among authentically Christian souls with even the faint-est sense of moral purity. The education system is guilty because it leaves youths morally and intellectually unprepared for university, unable to match the academic performance of Jewish students, ignorant of our social and economic history and the sources of processes currently taking place in our social life; it leaves the youth dull and crude.

Some in the press are guilty—those who perfidiously pretend to bemoan the most savage abuses, while actually praising them, and who report on student events unfairly, and sometimes, unfortunately, also deceptively. Parents, caretakers, and family members are guilty because they do not simply fail to oppose the youth's savagery, but, on the contrary, support it, or, in the best-case scenario, offer silent, friendly approval. The guilty include those who loudly condemned the "paedocracy" before war—when the youth heroically opposed the military power of the invaders—but who are silent now.[8] And what can one say about professors throughout Poland? At a moment like this, they should have stood by Professor Wolfke with a single voice, expressing their attitude toward denigrating knowledge. They are not just scholars confined to their offices and laboratories—they are also mentors of the young generation. As of this writing, only Professor Michałowicz has made a noble and honorable statement.[9] Others either remain silent or make pilgrimages to the centers of student terror.

Ultimately, one can take pity on the wretched youth, since they know not what they do; and sometimes, in their spiritual aberration, they even believe that they are serving some—sadly pitiful—Ideal. But we—old sinners, corruptors, and passive enablers—we should know that we are responsible for others' mortal sins, sins that bring nothing but harm, ill repute, and shame to Poland.

Editors' Notes

1. Throughout the essay, Dąbrowska uses the phrases *sprawa żydowska* and *zagadnienie żydowskie*, which are best rendered as "the Jewish issue," and which are related to but distinct from *kwestia żydowska* (which is translated as "the Jewish question" or "the Jewish problem" throughout the volume), an anti-Semitic cliché used in interwar Poland. For more about the historical context of this language, please see the final section of the Introduction.
2. Dąbrowska is referring to the political discord among Polish nobility, which contributed to the weakness of the Polish-Lithuanian Commonwealth, and its inability to resist the partitions, or joint conquest by Prussia, Russia, and Austria, which removed the Commonwealth from the map of Europe in 1795.
3. Professor Marceli Handelsman (1882–1944) was a historian who taught at the University of Warsaw after 1915. He initially supported Piłsudski but grew

critical when the latter turned toward authoritarianism in the late 1920s and 1930s. Handelsman openly criticized the government's acquiescence to the introduction of "ghetto benches" at the universities. Professor Mieczysław Wolfke (1883–1947) was a physicist affiliated with the Warsaw Polytechnic. Professor Kazimierz Bartel (1882–1941) was a mathematician and politician, who served three terms as Poland's prime minister under Piłsudski between 1926 and 1930.

4. December 1922 refers to the assassination of independent Poland's first elected president, Gabriel Narutowicz, by an ultranationalist zealot.

5. Curie-Skłodowska is the full name of the physicist and Nobel Prize laureate Marie Curie (1867–1934).

6. This is a reference to the Spanish Civil War (1936–1939), in which a nationalist coalition led by General Franco was opposed by the democratic and left-leaning Republicans.

7. The Black Madonna of Częstochowa is Poland's most important Catholic shrine.

8. In the Polish context *paedocracy* (government by children) refers to the partitions era when realist politicians condemned young activists who organized insurrectionary actions and plotted against the partitioning powers. They argued that these youths, often students, indulged in futile actions that end in inevitable defeat and cause retaliatory repressions against the entire nation.

9. Professor Mieczysław Michałowicz (1876–1965) was a pediatrician and politician. He taught at the University of Warsaw starting in 1920, and between 1935 and 1938 he served as a senator of the Polish Republic; in 1939, he became the leader of the newly founded centrist Alliance of Democrats.

PART III

1939–1945: On Both Sides of the Wall

4

Jews and Polish Commerce

KAZIMIERZ WYKA

Editors' Introduction

Kazimierz Wyka (1910–1975) was a literary historian and critic. Born in the small town of Krzeszowice, near Krakow, he studied Polish literature at the Jagiellonian University. He had left-leaning liberal views and was close to writers like Jerzy Andrzejewski and Czesław Miłosz. After the Second World War, he taught at the Jagiellonian University and later served as its vice rector; he was also a cofounder of the Institute of Literary Research at the Polish Academy of Sciences, and the Institute's director between 1953 and 1970. Wyka published dozens of studies and influenced a generation of Polish literary historians and critics (Jan Błoński was one of his students). Wyka's most important books include a study of Polish modernism, *Modernizm polski* (1959), and a study of one of Poland's best-known Second World War poets, *Krzysztof Baczyński, 1921–1944*.

The text reproduced here comes from Wyka's book *Życie na niby* (which can be rendered *Living as If* or *Pretending to Live*), a compilation of sketches and reflections about life under the Nazi occupation and its effects on Polish society. Wyka wrote these during the war and in its immediate aftermath and published some of them in various periodicals after the war. The book was first published by the Książka i Wiedza press in Warsaw in 1957, when the turn away from Stalinism in Polish politics allowed for greater pluralism in public and intellectual life.

The disappearance of the million-strong mass of Jews from trade and finance will doubtless remain the central psycho-economic fact of the occupation years. This disappearance—even if we count the survivors—is final and definitive, a permanent fact of life in Poland today. Less permanent, though equally important, is the Poles' reliance on inertia as they attempted to automatically take the place vacated by Jews. I call this takeover inertial and automatic because, from the point of view of those jumping into the void left by the Jews, this entire process, to put it succinctly and bluntly, boiled down to this: replace the *unbaptized* with the *baptized*, but keep the entire hideous psychology of the con artist, the petty merchant, and the exploiter—a psychology tied to social function, not to national identity. The elation on the part of the Polish "third estate" can basically be reduced to one hope: now that there are no Jews, let us take their place without changing anything, let us take over all the habits, which the national moralists had identified with typical Jewish mentality—but now these habits will be national, noble, and sacrosanct.

This issue is central to understanding the psychology of the occupation economy; it must be analyzed with utmost care if it is not to overwhelm the nation's moral health.

Let us say it clearly: the woes of Polish economic life were not that Jews were prominent everywhere—from the market stand to the largest bank. The problem was that the financial world was excluded from the moral fabric of the nation's life. The economic and moral realms came into contact only through taxation, and even there they were pushed apart by bribery and lies. The petty bourgeoisie and Judeophobes invoked the old familiar tune: they opined that Jews were to blame for this, implied that nationally conscious merchants would have done better, and so on and so forth. The occupation showed the opposite to be true. Jews were excluded and the "national" merchant finally made his appearance. Did anything change? It turned out that the decisive factor here was not group or national psychology but rather the *nature of the economic base within the political system*. As soon as German policy had separated trade and social responsibility, as soon as trade was relegated to the side—as a private feeding ground for the conqueror and a sanctuary for individual spoils-taking—the psychology of those who benefited came to resemble those who had been removed by the occupier. Because before the war, other factors—namely, belated forms of economic liberalism—were also changing our economic life into a feeding ground. And everyone knows that hyenas always flock to the carcass but lions never do.

The more significant question is whether the *forms of the elimination of the Jews and the ways Polish society exploited this elimination* were morally acceptable. Speaking only for myself, uncaring of whether anyone else concurs, I will repeat: no, a hundred times no. These forms and hopes were ignominious, demoralizing, and base. In short, the attitude of the average Pole toward the tragedy of the Jews can be described as follows. Germans committed a crime by murdering Jews. We Poles would not do that. Germans shall be punished for this crime, they have sullied their conscience. But we are left with nothing but the benefits, now and in the future, without sullying our conscience, without staining our hands with blood. One would be hard-pressed to find a more hideous type of moral justification in our society. The fools who cling to it should remember that the destruction of Jews was merely the first stage in the purification of the *Weichselraum*—we were next in line.[1]

And thus a situation that had occurred in recent Polish history once before was repeated—this time on a much larger if purely psychological, scale. No one captured the moral anguish caused by regaining Zaolzie better than Churchill who said that Poland pulled Zalozie out of the backpack of the German soldier who was occupying the Sudetenland.[2] This time, the Polish shopkeeper—believing his actions to be perfectly moral—pulled the keys to the cash box of his Jewish competitor out from under the sword of the German executioner, while this executioner perpetrated an unprecedented crime. Germans get the blame for the crime; we get the keys to the cash box. The shopkeeper forgot that the "lawful" destruction of an entire nation is a fragment of an unparalleled process, unseen in history, which certainly could not have been orchestrated merely so that the sign over somebody's shop would change names.

The means by which Germans exterminated Jews burdens their conscience. But the *Polish reaction to this burdens our conscience*. A golden tooth pulled from a corpse will always bleed, even if everyone forgets from whose mouth it came. This is why we cannot allow this reaction to be forgotten or to persist—it carries a whiff of petty necrophilia. To put it more simply, since it came to pass that Jews are no longer involved in Poland's economic life, the benefits should not simply accrue to the baptized shopkeepers. *The entire nation and the state have the right to benefit.* Jewish business that has been eliminated cannot simply be replaced by structurally and psychologically similar Polish business because the entire process would not then make the least bit of sense. Yet precisely this kind of commerce made itself at home during the provisional circumstances of the occupation, and now many think that it will remain here for all time. After this brief experience, and the replacement of the unbaptized with the baptized, we should not allow anyone to pull the wool over our eyes by claiming that "national trade" is different.

But let us return to the occupation itself. Did Polish businesses take advantage of that unusual situation? Did a truly enterprising merchant class—one with wide horizons—appear? I say no, it did not, and I will show why this could never have happened under these specific wartime conditions. During these years, two contradictory phenomena became linked in the merchant class's attitude: *the necessity of risk-taking* and *the sufficiency of inertia.*

To bypass official regulations, Polish businessmen no doubt had to take constant risks. And, most often, the success of their risk-taking was dependent on the whim of the authorities. People got away with the greatest scams, or they were caught for the most trivial things if, unluckily, the authorities suddenly decided to crack down. Risk was lessened by the truth—tried and tested since the first year of the occupation—that a supply of cash would always offer a way out. Economic risk was inversely proportional to the capital at one's disposal: an unlucky novice entrepreneur caught with tobacco or pork fat was typically sent to a camp, while a wholesaler selling entire train cars, which were allowed to "slip away" from military deliveries, was protected from danger by the very scale of his scam, and by the number of interested and silent parties.

Thus, in practical terms, risk, seemingly so great that many today wonder how any trade at all was even possible in the General Government, was significantly diluted.[3] More importantly, however, this risk was psychologically undemanding because it was not a creative type of risk; it was not a struggle against real dangers, such as those that spurred the development of the great capitalist societies of the West. During the occupation, entrepreneurship and initiative-taking did not stride proudly and openly—they frequented the recesses of bribery, with deals accompanied by toasts among the parties to scamming and theft. It was, in a word, a posthumous renaissance of petty and middle bourgeoisie in an era in which we know that liberal forms of trade are a thing of the past, that they will be replaced by other economic forms, such as cooperative movements and state regulation. The occupation is not the only example in our history of a sudden blossoming of a specific economic form at a time when, in the general dialectic of economic phenomena, it already belongs to the past. Another is the existence of large landed estates.

The *sufficiency of inertia* canceled out the potentially positive consequences of increased risk-taking during the occupation years. For various reasons, the merchant could rely on inertia, and thus act in ways that
impeded the proper spirit of salesmanship. First of all, experience quickly
showed that it was better to sit on the sidelines than to show initiative
because one paid smaller tributes to the various offices and supervisory
agencies. Merchants' prudence pushed trading under the table, to the back
room, or outside the shop. Inertia became even greater when Jewish competition automatically fell away. Easy gains do not inspire anyone to exert
effort. The final reason for the inertia was the most demoralizing of all,
and its effects increased as liberation approached. It lay in the difference
between the price a merchant paid for his wares and what he charged for
them—a difference that grew over the years. If he bought his goods—
like vodka or cigarettes—at official prices, this passive profit became outright stunning. Vodka obtained in rations for a dozen zlotys brought 500 to
600 zlotys when served "in shot glasses." A cubic meter of wooden planks
obtained for a few dozen zlotys brought in well over a thousand, and so on.
Naturally, this inertia-based profit, deriving from the very fact of *possessing
the merchandise*, could be maximized when a large quantity of goods was
obtained at official prices. This, in turn, depended on good relations with
the Germans. Business with them was both the most risky and most inert.
Merchandise sold at the right time made it possible to retreat to a peaceful
nest behind one's shop and wait there patiently for new spoils. One could
outfit this nest with new furniture and mediocre paintings, one could fill
the pantry. . . . This was not commerce but spoils-hunting, interspersed by
periods of satiated purring.

To conclude, none of the factors that gave Polish merchants their special position during the occupation were progressive or permanent. These
businessmen owed their prominence to the ad hoc and cruel whims of the
occupier. If German victory came, these whims would have immediately
evaporated, and only a desire to pretend otherwise prevented merchants from
putting up signs like those hanging in Gdynia, Poznań, or Łódź: "*Reserved
for Frontline Soldiers.*"[4] There was astounding shortsightedness in the trust
with which Polish merchants repaid the occupier—testifying to the fact
that most local merchants lacked any understanding of society or the nation
at large. Social relations in the German Reich were no secret—the Polish
third estate had been completely eliminated there—and this awareness
should have opened bourgeois eyes the way it opened peasants' eyes. Local

merchants were simply happy because they were still *doing business*, while a mere dozen kilometers away other Polish merchants could not do the same.

The combination of risk and inertia did not provide any worthwhile permanent economic stimuli because it *brought together speculative attitudes* that have nothing to do with real commerce, which is based on high volume and small profit. And this amalgam of speculation gave birth to the psycho-economic dispositions that we are still witnessing today. The merchant got used to not being subject to any controls—and he will have to lose this habit. He got used to expecting his goods to bring immediate profit, without much effort to attract customers—and this he will have to let go. In a word, if those merchants who appeared during the occupation want to remain in the new Polish society, alongside other, more cooperative forms of trade, they must forget the easy pickings of those years.

Editors' Notes

1. When used by the Nazis, the German word *Weichselraum* referred to the basin of the Vistula River and denoted territories inhabited by Poles.
2. In the hopes of preserving peace in Europe, Great Britain and France agreed to the Nazi occupation of the Sudetenland, a region in Czechoslovakia, at the Munich Conference on September 29, 1938. Zaolzie was a borderland region disputed between Poland and Czechoslovakia after the First World War; it became part of Czechoslovakia in 1920. In 1938 the Polish government took advantage of the Nazi occupation of the Sudetenland and Czechoslovakia's weakness, and demanded Zaolzie; Polish troops entered Zaolzie on October 2, 1938, and Poland annexed Zaolzie. It was returned to Czechoslovakia in 1945.
3. The General Government was established by the Nazis after they invaded Poland in 1939; it is discussed in "Poles and Jews during the Holocaust" in the Introduction.
4. The cities of Gdynia, Poznań, and Łódź did not get included in the General Government; they were annexed by the Third Reich. The Polish population of these cities was deported into the General Government and their belongings were seized by the Germans. Stores that had belonged to Poles prior to 1939 were to be given out to German veterans after Germany would win the war; German authorities therefore put up signs "reserved for frontline soldiers" in these stores.

5

We, Polish Jews

JULIAN TUWIM

Editors' Introduction

Julian Tuwim (1894–1953) was a poet, satirist, and translator. Born into a
Jewish family in Łódź, he moved to Warsaw in 1916 to study law and philosophy. There he participated in various literary initiatives and published
his poems in literary periodicals. In 1920, he cofounded the Skamander
literary group together with Antoni Słonimski, Jan Lechoń, and others, and
they quickly gained great popularity. Later, Tuwim belonged to the liberal
intellectual circle gathered around the weekly *Wiadomości Literackie* (*Literary
News*, first published in 1924), which was viciously attacked by National
Democratic propaganda throughout the interwar years. He spent the war
years in exile, going from Romania to France, then to Portugal and Brazil,
eventually settling in New York City in 1942. He returned to Poland in
1946, where he expressed support for both the new Polish communist government and the Soviet Union, which he saw as a counterweight to fascism.

His most important interwar poetry collections include *Sokrates tańczacy*
(*Dancing Socrates*, 1920), *Rzecz czarnoleska* (*The Czarnolas Affair*, 1929), and
Treść gorejąca (*Blazing Meaning*, 1936). His poem "Bal w operze" (The Ball at
the Opera, 1936), an apocalyptic vision of a fascist dictatorship, is among the
masterpieces of twentieth-century Polish poetry.

Tuwim wrote the essay reproduced here in April 1944 in New York. It
was originally published in September 1944 in the London-based, liberal-
democratic monthly *Nowa Polska* (*New Poland*), which was edited by Antoni
Słonimski, and represented the voice of those Polish émigrés who sought
dialogue with the emerging communist Poland. One important thing to

note in this outcry in the face of the Shoah is that Tuwim decided not to condemn Stalinist crimes during the war; he grouped all antifascism into a single category, making no distinction between democratic antifascism and Stalinist antifascism, which was becoming the most important, and most brutally repressive, force on the European continent.

Tuwim's essay was translated by Madeline G. Levine, and her translation originally appeared, in a slightly different version, in *The Polish Review* 17, no. 4 (Autumn 1972): 82–89. It was revised and updated by Madeline G. Levine for this volume in 2014.

To my Mother in Poland
or to her most beloved shade

I.

. . . Immediately I hear the question, "Where does that *we* come from?" The question is justified to a certain extent. Jews, whom I have always assured that I am a Pole, ask it of me; and now Poles, for the majority of whom I am and will remain a Jew, will ask it of me. Here is my answer for all of them.

I am a Pole because I like it that way. This is a completely private affair to me, one which I have no intention of explaining, clarifying, demonstrating, or justifying to anyone. I do not divide Poles into "pure" or "not pure." I leave that to the pure racists, to native and non-native Hitlerites. I divide Poles, just as I do Jews and other peoples, into wise and stupid, polite and nasty, intelligent and dull, interesting and boring, abusive and abused, refined and coarse, and so forth. I also divide Poles into fascists and antifascists. Obviously, these two camps are not monolithic; each displays shades of varying intensity. But a clear dividing line between them exists and it will shortly become very easy to draw it. Shades will remain shades, but the line itself will most decidedly become brighter and deeper.

I might say that on the political level I divide Poles into anti-Semites and anti-fascists. Because fascism is always anti-Semitism. Anti-Semitism is the international language of fascists.

2.

If, however, it actually comes down to the justification of my nationality or, rather, my national identity, then I am a Pole for the simplest, most primitive reasons—mainly rational, partly irrational, but without any "mystic" coloring. To be a Pole . . . this is neither an honor, nor a glory, nor a privilege. The same is true of breathing. I have not yet met a man who is proud that he breathes.

A Pole—because I was born, grew up, and was educated in Poland; because in Poland I was happy and unhappy; because without a doubt I would return to Poland from exile even were heavenly delights to be guaranteed me somewhere else.

A Pole—because from a sentimental superstition that I cannot explain by any reasoning or logic, I yearn to have the Polish earth (no other) absorb me after my death.

A Pole—because that is what I was told I was, in Polish, in my parents' home; because from infancy I was nourished on the Polish language; because my mother taught me Polish poems and songs; because when the first shock of poetry arrived it was discharged in Polish words; because that which became most important in my life—poetic creation—is unthinkable in any other language, no matter how fluently I might speak it.

A Pole—because it was in Polish that I confessed the turmoil of first love, and in Polish that I stammered about its happiness and storms.

A Pole, too, because the birch and the willow are nearer to me than the palm and the citrus; because Mickiewicz and Chopin are dearer to me than Shakespeare and Beethoven. Dearer for reasons which, again, I cannot justify by any logic.

A Pole—because I have adopted from the Poles a certain number of their national vices.

A Pole—because my hatred for *Polish* fascists is greater than for fascists of any other nationality. And I consider this a very important feature of my Polishness.

But above all else: a Pole because I like it that way.

3.

I hear voices responding to this: "Fine. But if you are a Pole, in that case why 'We, JEWS'?" I humbly reply: BECAUSE OF THE BLOOD.—"So it's racism?"—No. Not racism at all. Precisely the opposite.

There are two kinds of blood: blood in the veins and blood from the veins. The first is a body fluid; therefore its study is properly the domain of physiologists. Whoever ascribes to this blood any special attributes and mysterious powers other than its organic ones turns cities into ruins, butchers millions of people, and ultimately, as we shall see, brings down slaughter upon his own tribe.

The second is the blood that the ringleader of international fascism is extracting from humanity in order to document the triumph of his gore over my gore; it is the blood of millions of innocent murdered people, not blood concealed in the arteries but blood revealed. Since the beginning of the world there has not been such a flood of martyrs' blood, and the blood of the Jews (not "Jewish blood") is flowing in the broadest and deepest streams. Its blackened torrents are already flowing together into a turbulent, foaming river . . . AND IN THIS NEW JORDAN I ACCEPT THE BAPTISM OF ALL BAPTISMS: A BLOODY, FERVENT, MARTYRS' BROTHERHOOD WITH THE JEWS.

Accept me, Brothers, into the honorable fellowship of the Innocently Spilled Blood. I wish to belong to this community, to this church, from this day forward.

May this ORDER—the Order of the Jew Doloris Causa—be awarded to the Polish poet by the people which gave him life. Not for any merits, for I have none before you. I shall regard it as an advance and as the highest award for those few Polish verses which will, perhaps, outlive me and whose memory will be linked with my name, the name of a Polish Jew.

4.

On the armbands that you wore in the Ghetto the Star of David was painted. I believe in a Poland in which that star, the one on the armbands, will be one of the highest decorations awarded to the most valiant Polish soldiers and officers. They will wear it on their breast with pride next to the ancient Virtuti Militari. There will also be a Cross of the Ghetto, a deeply symbolic name. There will be an Order of the Yellow Patch, conferring more honor than any other decoration until now. And in Warsaw (as in every other Polish city) some fragment of the Ghetto will be left standing, preserved, and maintained in unaltered condition, just as we find it, in all the horror of its charred remains and devastation. We will surround this monument to the ignominy of our enemies and the glory of our martyred heroes with chains forged from Hitler's captured guns, and every day we will entwine fresh live flowers in the iron links so that it may remain forever a fresh and living memory for future generations and a sign that our anguish for them is always alive and fresh.

One more thing will be added to this church of national relics.

We will bring children there and tell them about the most monstrous martyrdom of people in the history of the world. In the center of the monument, its tragic aspect heightened by the contemporary Glass Houses of the rebuilt city that (God willing) shall surround it, there will burn an eternal flame. Passersby will remove their hats before it.

And whoever is a Christian will make the sign of the cross. . . .

Therefore, with pride, with mournful pride, we who remained alive by a miracle and by chance will wear the order that eclipses all others—the order of the Polish Jew. With pride? Let us say, rather, with contrition and burning shame. Because we received it for your torment, for your glory, Redeemers!

. . . So perhaps not "We, the Polish Jews," but "We, Specters, we, Shades of our murdered brothers, the Polish Jews" . . .

5.

We, the Polish Jews. . . . We, eternally alive—which is to say, those who perished in the ghettoes and the camps, and we, the specters—that is, those who will return to our country from beyond the seas and the oceans and, amidst the ruins, will horrify with our bodies preserved intact and the spectral-ness of our apparently preserved souls.

We, the truth of the graves, and we, the illusion of existence; we, the millions of corpses and the several thousands, perhaps several tens of thousands, of seeming non-corpses; we, an infinitely immense fraternal grave; we, a Jewish cemetery such as history has never seen and never will see again.

We, asphyxiated in gas chambers and melted into soap that will never wash off the traces of our blood or the stain of the world's sins against us.

We, whose brains spattered on the walls in our miserable dwellings and against the walls where we were shot in masses . . . only because we were Jews.

We, a Golgotha on which an impenetrable forest of crosses might stand. We, who two thousand years ago gave to humanity the one Son of Man, innocently murdered by the Imperium Romanum—and that single death sufficed for him to become God. . . . What religion will arise from the millions of deaths, tortures, humiliations and crucified arms in their final despair?

We, the Shloimes, Srules, Moshkes, sheenies, kikes, yids. We, whose names and epithets vie in worthiness with the names of all the Achilles, Bolesławs the Brave, and Richards the Lion-Hearted.

We, once more in the catacombs, in the "bunkers" beneath the Warsaw pavement, slogging through the stench of the sewers to the astonishment of our companions the rats.

We, with carbines on the barricades, in the ruins of our bombed-out houses; we, soldiers of freedom and honor. . . .

"*Jojne, idź na wojnę!*" "Jewboy, go into battle!" He did, my dear sirs, and he died for Poland.

We, for whom "each threshold was a fortress" in each house crashing down upon us.

We, the Polish Jews, hiding in the forests, feeding our terrified children on roots and grass; we, crawling, creeping, on the alert, with an antique double-barreled shotgun acquired by a miracle or begged for with filthy money. . . .

"And have you heard the joke about the gamekeeper Jew? It's a riot! The yid, you see, fired his gun and shat his pants from terror! Ha ha!"

We Jobs, we Niobes, we, doing penance for the hundreds of thousands of our Jewish Ursulas. . . .[1]

We, deep pits of shattered, smashed bones and twisted corpses covered with welts.

We are a shriek of pain! A shriek so prolonged that the most distant ages will hear it. We are a Lament, we are a Howl, we are a Chorus chanting the funeral *el mole rachamim*,[2] the echo of which will be passed down from century to century.

We, the most magnificent heap of bloody manure in history, with which we have fertilized Poland so that the bread of freedom will taste better for those who survive us.

We, a macabre reservation; we, the last of the Mohicans, the survivors of a massacre, whom so new Barnum can take around the world proclaiming on colorful posters: "An unheard of sight! The biggest sensation in the world! The Polish Jews—alive and real!" We, a Chamber of Horrors, Schreckenskammer, Chambre des tortures! "Nervous persons are asked to leave the hall!"

We, sitting and weeping by the rivers of lands beyond the seas, as those others wept by the rivers of Babylon. Throughout the entire sweep of the world Rachel mourns her children, but they are no more! By the Hudson River, the Thames, the Euphrates, the Nile, the Ganges, and the Jordan, we wander in our diaspora, crying, "Vistula! Vistula! Vistula! Our own mother! Gray Vistula, rosy not from the dawn but from blood!"

We, who will not find even the graves of our children and our mothers, in so many layers will they lie, so dispersed will they be throughout the entire breadth of the land in a single burial! And there will not be one spot singled out for you to lay flowers, but like a sower of grain you will scatter them with broad sweeps of your arms. Perhaps by chance you will hit the right place.

We, the Polish Jews. . . . We, a legend dripping tears and blood. Who knows if it will not be necessary to describe it in Biblical verse, "That with an iron pen and lead / They were graven in the rock forever!"

(Job 19:24). We, the apocalyptic stage of history. We, the Lamentations of Jeremiah:

> In the dust of the streets
> lie the young and the old;
> my maidens and my young men
> have fallen by the sword;
> in the day of thy anger thou hast slain them,
> slaughtering without mercy.
>
> . . . . . .
>
> they flung me alive into the pit
> and cast stones on me;
> water closed over my head;
> I said, "I am lost."
> I called upon thy name, O Lord,
> from the depths of the pit . . . .
>
> . . . . . .
>
> Thou hast seen the wrong done to me, O Lord;
> judge thou my cause.
>
> . . . . . .
>
> Thou wilt requite them, O Lord,
> according to the work of their hands.
> Thou wilt give them dullness of heart;
> thy curse will be on them.
> Thou wilt pursue them in anger and destroy them
> from under thy heavens, O Lord.

(Lamentations II, III)[3]

A gigantic and ever-growing spectral Skeleton is hovering over Europe. In his empty eye sockets shines the fire of perilous rage, and his fingers are clenched in a bony fist. He, our Leader and Dictator, will dictate to us our rights and our demands.

New York, April 1944

Notes on Translation

1. A reference to the great Renaissance poet Jan Kochanowski's daughter, whose death is movingly lamented in his elegiac cycle *Treny* (*Laments*, 1580).
2. The opening words of the Jewish prayer for the repose of the dead.
3. English version of these excerpts from *Lamentations* II and III, as from Job (cited earlier), based on Revised Standard Version of the Hebrew Bible.

6

The Orchestration of Rage

MICHAŁ BORWICZ

Editors' Introduction

Maksymilian Boruchowicz, pseudonym Michał Borwicz, (1911–1987) was a writer, historian, and literary sociologist. Born into a Jewish family in Krakow, he studied Polish literature at the Jagiellonian University. In the interwar period, he published in left-leaning literary journals, and he joined the Polish Socialist Party (PPS) in 1936. He was captured by the Nazis in 1942 and sent to the Janowska labor and extermination camp on the outskirts of Lviv. He escaped in 1943 and joined the PPS underground military formation to fight against the Nazis. Between 1945 and 1947, he served as the director of the Krakow branch of the Jewish History Commission (run by the Central Committee of Polish Jews), which worked on documenting the Holocaust. He emigrated from Poland in 1947 and spent the rest of his life in Paris, where he received a doctorate in sociology at the Sorbonne. His research focused on the history of Polish Jews and the Shoah; he published widely in leading French historical journals.

The text reproduced here consists of selections from his book *Organizowanie wściekłości* (*The Orchestration of Rage*), which was originally published in Warsaw by Ogólnopolska Liga do Walki z Rasizmem (The Polish League for Fighting Racism) in 1947. It analyzes Polish attitudes and behaviors toward Jews during the Holocaust.

Myth and Living People

The ways in which the non-Jewish Polish population reacted to Jews during the occupation would remain a mystery if we do not take its psychological dimension into account. Separated from the rest of the population by
ghetto walls and stigmatizing signs, Jews became distant and foreign. Only
yesterday—despite antagonisms, quotidian jealousies, and anti-Semitic propaganda—they were people. Flesh-and-blood people. Neighbors with strengths
and weaknesses that anyone could get to know through personal contact.
Now their actual qualities—physical and spiritual, good and bad—began to
get blurred by being separated from the world; they were slowly changing
into an abstraction. Attitudes toward Jews were ceasing to be attitudes of people toward people; they were slowly changing into attitudes of people toward
a concept. Adolf Rudnicki (*Dzienniki* [*Diary*] in *Kuźnica* [*The Forge*], no. 1)
aptly emphasized this in his description of the atmosphere surrounding the
reactions of certain circles to the Uprising in the Warsaw Ghetto:

> The glow of the fire was visible in every corner of the city, at all hours of
> the day. When talking about all this, about children who were getting burned
> alive, people said, "It's in the ghetto"—and it sounded like it was happening
> somewhere far away. People said, "It's in the ghetto"—and peace of mind
> returned. But it was in Nowolipie, on Muranowska and Świętojerska Streets, a
> dozen meters away. A hundred meters away in space and fifteen months away
> in time—and that sufficed.

Incomprehensible? On the contrary, we will understand once we realize
one thing: this was not a way of looking at people fighting heroically in the
Ghetto; it was a way of looking at a generalized concept: the Jews.

Before the war people used to say: "Every anti-Semite has his Jew." It
is time to understand the implications of this universally familiar saying
(which is, of course, true): the Jew whom the anti-Semite "had" (i.e., the
one he acknowledged, valued, or found likable, with all the reservations, by
the way, that one person might feel toward another)—was a Jew he knew
personally. Whereas the Jewry (which, as an anti-Semite, he hated) was typically the collectivity of Jews whom he did not know personally and who
were strangers to him—Jews about whom he had formed opinions mainly
on the basis of anti-Semitic propaganda and concepts floating in the air.
Because a relationship with an individual whom one knows—or whom
one has just merely encountered—is a relationship with a human being.
A relationship with a generalized concept is shaped by propaganda.

During the German occupation, the Jewish population became foreign and unknown, distant and—despite all the bloody events—almost abstract. After that, the voice of intrusive propaganda claimed a monopoly. (. . .).

Let's take a vile brochure that circulated in occupied Poland—similar to many others, signed with the name, or pseudonym, of one Zbigniew Kowalewski, and entitled "Christianity's Mortal Enemy." In business-like manner, the author set about the task commissioned to him by German propaganda. For example, in this pamphlet Emperor Nero—inventor of "living torches" and one of the main persecutors of Christians—becomes a nearly idealized figure. According to the brochure, he ordered the persecution of Christians "in good faith," and merely from misguided motives. What explains such passionate love for Nero? The hireling author expounds: "Emperor Nero . . . was not a supporter of the Jews, and his top minister Burrus was an anti-Semite." This sentence contains almost the entire program Germans forced onto the nations they occupied: the most important thing is to be an anti-Semite; the rest doesn't matter. Let's honor Nero because

> Emperor Nero realized the great danger threatening Rome and sent an army led by Caius Cassius Gallus against Judea. But the storming of the city of Jerusalem was unsuccessful. Gallus suffered a defeat, and had to retreat as a result of heavy losses. Emperor Nero therefore ordered Flavius Vespasian, his most eminent strategist, to lead the war. Heading a powerful army, Vespasian set out against Jerusalem. And then something unexpected happened. Nero was murdered, and civil war broke out in Rome.

And so, one more crime—presented as one of the greatest of crimes—is added to all the Jewish crimes against Christianity: the killing of Nero, the proverbial and bloodiest murderer of Christians.

The brochure contains even more puzzling things. We know, for example, that early Christians spoke out against nationalism and overturned the boundaries of nationality. That they heeded the poor and the paupers while speaking out against the high and the mighty. But all this doesn't square with the racism and social "hierarchism" (in the German sense of the word) proclaimed by the Nazis. And so, the Jews are shown as treacherous promulgators of those dangerous ideas, while Christians appear as those who "everywhere opposed" this "world revolution" allegedly planned by the Jews. This is a clever way of making the uncritical reader simultaneously feel contempt for both Jews and the idea of the reconciliation of nations, which Nazism hated so much.

Besides illustrations (the kind we've already discussed), the brochure features quotes against Jews excerpted from the work of various authors. The quotes come, for example, from such alleged champions of Christianity as Mirza Hassan Chan, Chiamhig Big,[1] and . . . Voltaire. Needless to say, Christianity hardly benefits when such figures are portrayed as its defenders.

But it would be a mistake to think that all this nonsense was invented by the author of this brochure. No, the brochure was a summary of a book of a few hundred pages that was in turn a Polish adaptation of a number of German books. This is the sequence: The "defense" was written in accordance with official sources and official instructions. Its rubbish was repeated in many similar brochures, all relying on the same source. It thus gives some sense of the methods involved: not only lies and distortions, but also, and above all, the use of anti-Semitism to undermine the reader's moral and intellectual discipline.

This kind of undermining had a specific aim. As with everything German, it was planned and scrupulously thought-out, down to the last detail—which is why it is worth returning to later. (. . .).

The Functions of Things Left Behind
by the Victims

Germans were practical. Mass executions of Jews were preceded and punctuated by (enormous) levies imposed on them. Independent of this, from the very beginning Germans took Jewish apartments and furniture, valuables, and supplies. This ranged from "legal requisitions," and the effectively equally legal practice of having soldiers of various ranks and civilians—big fish and small fry—occupy Jewish apartments, all the way to fully official decrees or "order slips" submitted to the Judenrats. All these were merely preparatory activities. It was general plunder. What's more, the so-called "expulsions" (meaning simply murder) were preceded by the so-called "resettlement"—from villages to small towns, from small towns to larger towns, and vice versa, and from one part of town to another. The goal of these decrees was not only to uproot the persecuted from their home environment, to disorient them, and to make them completely defenseless, but also to successively strip them of their belongings. Resettling was accompanied by prohibitions that disallowed bringing goods exceeding certain quotas, which varied wildly according to place and circumstances. German authorities sealed and confiscated the remaining property. A similar procedure was also methodically applied after the "expulsions." And that's not all: Nazi "practicality" meant everything was planned out down to the very last step, and accompanied victims to their deaths, even after death. Clothes were stripped from those led to gas chambers, and golden teeth were pulled from corpses.

It is completely understandable that the total plunder of the material possessions of several million murdered people could not take place without leaving scraps along the way. Even a pillager as methodical and immeasurably greedy as the Nazi occupier could not prevent scraps of these scraps from getting into the hands of the local population.

Besides things victims gave to their acquaintances for safekeeping, there were the so-called "post-Jewish" apartments and "post-Jewish" shops. Let's repeat so that we can understand this clearly: these were crumbs of crumbs and scraps of scraps. Germans, by the way, did everything to force the population to make use of them. In many cities, even before Jews were locked up in ghettos, Poles' apartments were taken over by Germans and the expelled were sent to "post-Jewish" homes.

As always and in all places, there was no shortage of people waiting greedily for spoils left behind by the victims.

To a greater or lesser extent, all those who derived financial gain from the "de-Jewification" of Poland became adherents of racism. Was it because being dishonest or inhumane was in their nature? Not in the least. Rather, preoccupied with "seizing" property in the climate of the occupation (i.e., at a time when, due to circumstances created by the occupier's largesse, one had to disregard moral principles proclaimed in peacetime and violently snatch nearly everything), they learned "first-hand" the correctness of slogans jammed into their heads with the help of utter simplifications. Because regardless of the line of argument employed, these slogans ended with the claim that things will be better when there were no Jews.

And an artificial situation emerged to testify to the alleged correctness of such claims. With one caveat: that things were better for those who lined their pockets or who took over the place vacated by the Jews. And the "better" referred strictly to their financial situation. These people did not think (or rather they thought—since it was, after all, difficult not to think—but they didn't make the connection) that meanwhile things were getting worse for millions of Poles. They preferred not to understand that the "improvement" they were told about was not a result of reforms that could bring further economic development, but was rather simply an outcome of spoils left behind by a specific number of brutally murdered people. Nor did they grasp that together with these crumbs of post-German plunder they had swallowed the poison of depravity, which would disgrace them in various ways for many long years.[a]

The Will to Believe

The number of these kinds of people was, however, relatively small. And they shouldn't even be the focus. What's worse is that once they became consciously or unconsciously ready to ingest the German poison, they became its carriers—they might have perhaps even experienced the dissemination of this poison as a commitment to so-called "convictions." They influenced others who derived no benefits from the further spreading of these toxic notions. There thus emerged a psychological climate that facilitated uncritical reception of suggestions propagated by the occupier. A climate in which German insinuations were not just left without scrutiny—but in which people wanted to believe them.

[a] In this context, it is worth recalling Jerzy Putrament's remarks: "The slaughter (of Jews) created a gap in society. . . . Poles did not replace Jewish doctors, dentists, and lawyers. The same thing happened with artisans; after the elimination of Jewish craft, there were not enough Polish craftsmen. Yet one Jewish stratum was replaced with a surplus: merchants, shopkeepers, wholesalers, black market dealers. Profiteers.

For half a century, homegrown anti-Semitism was hatching in Poland, explaining all our national and social misfortunes by the presence of a few million Jews. Today, the anti-Semites' dreams have come true. Jews are no longer there as a few-million-strong social class. And here is what is most significant: we are missing the productive Jewish groups—professionals and artisans, while the parasitic Jewish group was immediately replaced with an even worse, more swindling, more ruthless cast of Polish petty merchants.

. . . A petty merchant as hideous as this "new" petty merchant bred by the Germans doesn't exist anywhere else. He doesn't exist and he has never existed anywhere else in the world.

. . . A bribe given to one of the Germans at the right time—and now this merchant has an apartment, and he has things left behind by Jews. Cleverly conducted swindles, ten-fold rip-offs, boorish ruthlessness, profiteering, blackmail—this is how he got to where he is today.

. . . Look inside this merchant's brain. The only functioning levers in there are those attached to quick, immediate gain. No other motivations can hatch there. No scruples besides physical fear. No drives besides physiology.

Does he need books? Perhaps only as kindling. Does he need Poland? No, because one has to work to build Poland, and, under the Germans, he had it good without working." ("Odbudowa psychiczna" [Psychological Reconstruction] in the weekly Odrodzenie [Rebirth], nos. 4-5).

Zofia Nałkowska describes the musings of a simple woman who, living near the Ghetto walls, witnessed the atrocities committed behind them.[2] This woman told Nałkowska about one event after another, each more shocking than the one before it; she expressed empathy, she could not control her emotions, she wept. And she kept repeating, "It's unbearable, unbearable." But Nałkowska observed that the empathy was mixed with peculiar asides: "But Ma'am," the woman said, "it'll be better for us if the Germans destroy them. They hate us even more than they hate the Germans." With her usual restraint, Nałkowska writes: "She seemed offended by my words of naïve persuasion and retorted: 'Who said it? No one had to say it. I know it myself, and everyone who knows them will tell you the same thing, Ma'am. If Germans lost this war by some chance, Jews would just murder us all. You don't believe it? Even the Germans themselves say it. They said it on the radio. . . .'" And Nałkowska comments: "She knew better, she needed that faith for some reason. (. . .) The woman who works at the cemetery saw and heard it herself. But for her, too, things became so intertwined with commentary that she lost her sense of reality." Elsewhere, Mieczysław Jastrun notes: "When the uprising [in the Warsaw Ghetto] was dying out, one of the students asked me if I knew that Jews who escaped from the Ghetto were murdering Poles. In vain I tried telling her that she fell for false rumors spread by the Germans. Always agreeable and very intelligent, this time she dug her heels in. She did not believe my words. It was only then that I understood: she wanted it to be so; that is why she believed even this story, intended for the lowest rabble."[3]

This "desire to believe" was also indirectly propped up by the deposit of tradition—or, to be more precise, by the deposit left on the margins of tradition—that was layered in people's minds. This factor, and its influence on attitudes toward Jews, was described by Jerzy Andrzejewski in his astute article on "The Problem of Polish Anti-Semitism."[4] Namely, for a long time Jews were a notorious subject of jokes and anecdotes. There was a tradition of having a puppet Jew in Polish nativity scenes, and everything could give occasion for humor: Orthodox Jews, the accent of Jews who spoke Polish, conservatism and progressivism, assimilation and lack of assimilation, military service and avoidance of military service, wealth and poverty, and all other possible qualities. A joke does not yet testify to hatred. On the contrary, it can often express tolerance or even mocking sympathy. Except that "[l]aughter is certainly healthy—so long as it is humor. But true humor comes from human solidarity. Scornful jokes and ridicule have no need for this strong and stable basis. They typically glide around on life's surface, indifferent to any hierarchy of values. Humor is rare. It accompanies people who know what they want and who value moral judgments. The weaker and the meaner people are, the more easily they succumb to ridicule, jokes, and laughing at someone else's expense. Snickering is the revenge of the weak, or the weapon of people who artificially elevate themselves."[5] "Are Jews really that funny? But what nation or what person doesn't have amusing features? Jews certainly have their share of oddities. But (. . .) [w]hen one jokes and derides the Jewish accent, the name Rappaport, and the red-haired wig, one doesn't have to think about the dire poverty of the Jewish proletariat, and all the humiliations and suffering that Jews have to bear upon their shoulders. Ridicule tends to be a good sleeping pill for conscience. During the German occupation, jokes and macabre laughter sometimes also surrounded the train cars that carried Jews to Majdanek and Treblinka."[6] While this laughter did not have to translate into approval for crime—on the contrary, many of those who were laughing might have condemned the German madness—it often played the role of something more than a "sleeping pill for the conscience." It is well-known, by the way, that left behind in the margins of tradition were not only jokes and anecdotes about Jews, but also a large number of slogans, prejudices, and negative concepts. These also played a significant role in creating the psychological conditions for easier acceptance of prearranged German judgments about Jews—an acceptance that precluded the subjection of these judgments to the rigorous control of criticism. More and more frequently, even those not used to analyzing social problems began to see a "problem" instead of human beings. As Stanisław Stomma[7] rightly observes, "when one attempts to solve a problem without noticing the person, the path to all kinds of atrocities is wide open." It is—to use Stomma's words—"one of the most successful mirages invented by the devil to ensnare mankind."[b]

Blackmailers

Scraps of property left behind by murdered Jews were not the only source of income. There were others. Saving themselves from inevitable death, many

---

[b] Stanisław Stomma, "Oskarżenie ze wszystkich najstraszniejsze" (The Most Terrible Accusation of All), *Tygodnik Powszechny*, no. 49, 1946.

Jews secretly left the Ghetto and lived on so-called "Aryan papers." And a whole multitude of people took to tracking them down and exposing them. Here we are not talking about official spies and agents, but blackmailers. These individuals were not concerned with "race." When they identified Jews, they did not turn them in to the Gestapo, but rather forced them to pay for silence. They were tireless leeches, with elaborate means at their disposal. They had their own organizations, their own observation shifts positioned in the streets, their own relay teams, their own messengers and contacts. Otwinowski talks about it:[8] "I know the terror of Warsaw streets during the occupation. . . . I know the double terror of these streets because I walked them with the stride of a regular Pole that I am, and also with the stride of a Jew the fervent 'Polish' patriots saw in me when they looked at my profile and my black hair. I know those glances—all too frequent, unfortunately— not just the glances cast by the fans of fast and easy money, but also by seemingly cultured people. . . . I know how much it costs, and how difficult it is to forget when it's not a German, but a seemingly decent-looking civilian who uses regular, just barely roguish language to propose: 'Give me all your valuables or . . . see that watchman on the corner?'"

Sometimes, even though the person accosted wasn't Jewish—as in the above example—he still had to pay because he preferred to avoid an encounter with the Gestapo for reasons other than race: "I also know the worst fear," Otwinowski adds in another passage from the same article, "the fear of a man trapped by this kind of proposition, who not only happens to have no money, but also lacks the right documents, or obviously falsified documents. Sometimes, thanks to the blackmailers, people who proved their 'Aryan' descent were 'caught' because in the course of a search the Gestapo found that they were carrying underground publications or other 'compromising little things.'" There were also cases when avowed anti-Semites fell into the clutches of German thugs this way. In any case, the distance between a blackmailer and an officially registered informer was exceedingly small. After a bit of time, whoever established contact with the German police through his anti-Jewish activity often became a fully paid informer under the police's command.

These remarks describe Nazi methods of orchestrating rage; they touch upon current manifestations of this phenomenon only occasionally, and only in relation to the legacy of the occupation years.

And this legacy, unfortunately, is as rich as it is dismal. It derives its identity from a long chain of murders and plunderings—crimes that have a Nazi character in a double sense: Nazism cultivated the atmosphere of hatred that gave rise to them, and Nazism taught this way of murdering. If the murderers donned the swastika, it was simply to show the loyalty of astute students to their master, or the loyalty of epigones to the inventor. One of the best known examples of anti-Jewish violence in the postwar period was the Pogrom in Kielce on July 4, 1946.[9] Its course was sufficiently covered in both Polish and foreign press. We know that it started with a crude and consciously concocted provocation, i.e., with blood libel fabrications about "ritual murder" allegedly committed by Jews. We also know that though this slander was completely contrived a few dozen people fell victim to the Pogrom (which was accompanied by pulling Jews off trains and murdering them).

A few months earlier, similar things happened in the town of Rzeszow. There was also a pogrom there—also under the pretext of revenge for "ritual murder." They even actually found a murdered child. When people heard this news, many mothers in town raised a lament and went running down city streets, wailing that their little sons or daughters were being killed. The number of children allegedly murdered by Jews grew as people spread the news by word of mouth. And only after the Pogrom did it turn out that none of the Catholic mothers were actually missing their children. But there was a missing mother. The mother of that murdered child. And not only the mother—there were no family members or acquaintances who could identify the body of the murder victim. . . . Was it perhaps the body of a Jewish girl who, having miraculously survived the occupation, was killed precisely so that her body could be found?

The organizers of these pogroms standardized and staged them wholesale.

One day—during the Kielce Pogrom—the police in Częstochowa were notified that in the suburbs (at 2 Zacisze Street) a crowd was trying to lynch a man believed to be a Jew and accused of murdering a young girl. When they arrived at the scene, the police determined that the person apprehended by the crowd was an "indigenous" Pole who had nothing to do with the Jewry—he was Eugeniusz Witkiewicz, a worker at the "Metal" factory. And among those killed by the murderous crowd in Kielce there were also two non-Jews. There is no way to avoid "collateral damage" . . .

There were other similar undertakings in Częstochowa at the time, but the decisive stance of local authorities prevented violence. A proclamation signed by Father Teodor Kubina (the Częstochowa Diocese bishop), and by representatives of the district and city administrative authorities, con-demned the Kielce crime and stated, among other things: "Despite this, we had occasion to confirm that here in Częstochowa, there are also people—fortunately few in number—who, as in Kielce, are trying to do everything to push the ignorant rabble to the kind of crime Kielce witnessed with horror. Because of this . . . we proclaim and make an appeal: *All claims about the reality of ritual murder are lies.* No one in Kielce, in Częstochowa, or any-where else in Poland was harmed by Jews for religious and ritual purposes. We are not aware of even a single case of a Christian child being kidnapped by Jews. All the currently circulating information and versions of this claim are either an intentional fabrication of criminals, or an unintentional fabri-cation of misled people trying to provoke a crime."

I am looking at a thick book about "Jewish ritual murder," published by Nazi propaganda. Independent of its criminal intentions, this book has frightening significance for the critical reader, though for reasons altogether different than those envisioned by Nazi propagandists. With typical German pedantry, the book lists anti-Jewish violence where the pretext was outrage at alleged "ritual murder." In other words: for the critical reader, this book serves as a history of anti-Jewish provocations (connected with the blood libel). "Ritual murder" is a fabrication. But crimes against Jews in which it served as a pretext are not a fabrication. They are a fact. Will the long chain of these crimes not arouse the consciences and outrage those who bring up the word "conscience" so easily and so frequently, but only with murderous aims?

Adam Polewka[10] rightfully wrote:[c] "During the liquidation of the Jews, people learned to plunder their belongings, and even tear clothes off of their bloody corpses. Whoever reaches through blood to grab someone else's belongings will never have any scruples. The road to looting and ban-ditry is wide open."[d]

The post-Nazi orchestration of rage brings severe harm to both sides. For Jews—who, after a terrible cataclysm, find themselves in a unique

---

[c] "To boli. . . ." [It hurts. . . .], in "W trzecią rocznicę zagłady getta w Krakowie" (On the Third Anniversary of the Liquidation of the Krakow Ghetto), 1946.
[d] As if to confirm Polewka's words, here is a press report (from a whole series of simi-lar ones): "Unknown perpetrators recently desecrated a Catholic cemetery in Dębica, in the Rzeszów district. Taking advantage of the cover of darkness, they opened twenty-five tombs. Looking for gold and valuables, they threw the caskets on the ground, broke them, and tampered with the bodies. An investigation is underway." (September 1946).

situation—it deepens the sense of injustice. It interferes with the process of returning to a productive life and cultivating a healthy sense of criticism toward both oneself and one's surroundings. For those infected by the venom of anti-Semitism, on the other hand, it fundamentally distorts the categories of thinking and acting. These words should not be taken metaphorically. On the contrary: to assess the scale of destruction brought by anti-Jewish prejudice one need only look at the homegrown "theories" it inspires. In fields like the philosophy of history, politics, economics, art, and all others, diagnoses that take reality into account are replaced by fanciful concepts about the alleged role of Jews, concealing everything that is real. Those under the sway of the aversion we've been discussing need to be told how these notorious delusions falsify scholarship and social thought, how they replace thought with magic formulae. There are people, finally, who understand the full nonsense of this psychosis, but who for whatever reason maintain distance toward it. They do not speak out against it, convinced that it has penetrated too deeply into the body of other concepts, and that attacking the anti-Jewish psychosis would wreak havoc on an entire configuration of outdated platitudes, mistakes, and superstitions. They don't appreciate the fact that this configuration is precisely what is most dangerously destructive.

Truths repeated too often become trivial. The wear and tear lessens their power to evoke a response, but it hardly lessens their significance. When we discuss this problem today, it is necessary and beneficial to keep some basic things in mind.

The bloodiest of all wars, which is now behind us, was—in a certain sense—a Jewish war. Not because Hitler advertised it as a war against Jews, but because it brought out the ultimate consequences of all the methods that were used over the centuries to victimize the Jewish people, above all others. Revival and re-activation of stale prejudices to make them into battle cries, pseudoscientific justification of witch-hunts, construction of theories from half-truths and appearances of truth, evocations of "collective responsibility," criminality dressed up to look like an idea, the use of brute physical force as the strongest argument, inciting religious and national antagonisms for one's own egotistical benefit, playing to the crowd's basest instincts—these were attributes of anti-Jewish violence and witch-hunts over the centuries. In this last war, all nations and all countries where the Nazi invader set foot had a dismally distinct experience of all these methods. Examine, if you will, the bloody machinery that worked with textbook precision during those years, and marvel at the indivisibility and universalism of these methods.

This war was also "Jewish" for another reason. Nazi degeneration affected Jews to the greatest degree, and the incredible potential to dehumanize executioners was realized most fully and with greatest precision in actions against Jews. There was also the torturers' full and complete complicity—a complicity which made it possible to carry out the Nazi program down to the very last detail in the Jews' unparalleled martyrdom. The initial parts of this program (whose ultimate direction was revealed in actions against Jews and therefore hardly ambiguous) were also carried out on other nations. The war years thus brought "achievements," which not only outstripped all ability to make sane predictions, but also crossed the very boundaries of the imaginable. . . . They revealed the capacity of the poisons we discussed, and their tendency to spread. They proved that once these poisons have physical force they cannot be controlled. They are like the plague. Individual bacilli contain the beginnings of an epidemic, and once the epidemic breaks out there is no way to "regulate" it or limit its effects. An epidemic can only be fought. Decisively. Right from the outset.

Editors' Notes

1. The brochure Borwicz discusses drew, among other things, on Theodor Fritsch's rabidly anti-Semitic *Antisemiten-Katechismus* (1887), later reprinted as *Handbuch zur Judenfrage*. In this book, Fritsch lied, falsified history, and made up allegedly historical figures; Mirza Hassan Chan seems to be one of these fabrications.

2. Zofia Nałkowska (1884–1954) was a writer and publicist. In the interwar period she wrote several novels, and after the war she published a nonfiction collection of stories *Medaliony* (*Medalions*, 1946), in which she used detached, dispassionate prose to narrate the horrific realities of the occupation years. Borwicz is citing one of the stories from this collection.

3. This is a quote from Mieczysław Jastrun's essay "The Power of Ignorance" in this volume on page 87.

4. Jerzy Andrzejewski's essay "The Problem of Polish Anti-Semitism" is reproduced in this volume on pages 95–112.

5. This is a quote from Andrzejewski's essay "The Problem of Polish Anti-Semitism"; it appears in this volume on page 103.

6. This is a continuation of the quote from Andrzejewski's essay in this volume on page 104.

7. Stanisław Stomma (1908–2005) was a politician and publicist. Between 1946 and 1953 he was the editor of the Catholic monthly *Znak* and a member of the editorial board of the Catholic weekly *Tygodnik Powszechny*. Between 1957 and 1976, he served as a Znak club deputy in the Polish Parliament.

8. Stefan Otwinowski (1910–1976) was a prose writer, playwright, and publicist. He described the war years in the novel *Czas nieludzki* (*Inhuman Time*,
   1961) and in the drama *Wielkanoc* (*Easter*, 1946).
9. The Kielce Pogrom is discussed in "Anti-Semitism in the Polish People's
   Republic" in the Introduction, and in the editors' introduction to Stanisław
   Ossowski's essay "With Kielce in the Background" on pages 116–115.
10. Adam Polewka (1903–1956) was a writer and publicist. In the interwar period,
    he was the director of Teatr Robotniczy (Workers' Theater) in the town of
    Sosnowiec; he joined the Polish Communist Party in 1932. After the war, he
    was a deputy in the Polish Parliament between 1945 and 1956, an editor of the
    daily *Echo* in Krakow, and the literary director of the Juliusz Słowacki Theater
    in Krakow.

PART IV

1945–1947: The Power of Ignorance

7

The Power of Ignorance

MIECZYSŁAW JASTRUN

Editors' Introduction

Mieczysław Jastrun (1903–1983) was a poet. Born into a Jewish family in the village of Korolówka in eastern Galicia, he studied philosophy and Polish and German literature at the Jagiellonian University. During the interwar period he published in the monthly *Skamander*, the weekly *Wiadomości Literackie (Literary News)*, and other leading periodicals. Between 1939 and 1941 he lived in Soviet-occupied Lviv, and after the Nazi invasion of the Soviet Union moved to Warsaw, where he survived on the "Aryan" side of the city. After the war, he joined the Polish Communist Party (PZPR) and served as deputy editor of the leftist cultural weekly *Kuźnica (The Forge)*, where he published many of his works. He left the Communist Party in 1957 to protest the government's turn away from the liberal ideals that animated the reforms in October 1956. He then publicly defended free speech and joined other leading Polish writers and intellectuals in signing a letter protesting censorship in 1964, which became known as the "Letter of the Thirty-Four" and became a symbol of the emerging anticommunist opposition.

In addition to beautiful lyrics, Jastrun wrote a number of essays in which he wrestled with the experience of the Shoah, analyzed Stalinism, and defended a universal humanist reading of Polish and European culture. His most important essay collections include *Mit śródziemnomorski (The Mediterranean Myth*, 1962) and *Wolność wyboru (Freedom of Choice*, 1969); a number of his poems are available in English translations in *Memorials, A Selection* (Diálogos, 2014). The essay reproduced here was initially published in the cultural weekly *Odrodzenie (Rebirth)* on June 17, 1945, in Krakow. It expresses Jastrun's reaction to anti-Semitism in Polish society in the immediate aftermath of the war.

Anti-Semitism, which was already deeply rooted in Poland before this war, has not weakened—despite the murder of over three million Jews and people designated as Jews by the Nazi inquisition. In the realm of morality, this fact is no less horrible than that of the mass-scale Nazi crime. It would seem that this slaughter, unparalleled in history and carried out by a despised enemy who persecuted the Polish population so ruthlessly and brutally, would inspire the tormented and tortured Polish society to some collective reaction of compassion, a sense of brotherhood in suffering. After all, *dum vulnirati fratres. . . . [sic].*[1]

Meanwhile, Jewish blood, spilled so profusely by the barbarian enemy of the nation and free humanity, inflamed the crowd's dormant instincts. This crowd is, above all, the petty bourgeoisie; it includes some of the intellectuals. When Jews were being deported from the Warsaw Ghetto in the summer of 1942, when they were burned alive there during Easter 1943, voices like these resounded most frequently: "At least we are not the ones doing it," "Too bad about the apartment buildings, but new and more beautiful ones will be built," "Germans have preempted Jewish attacks on us," and so on. During the 1943 Soviet raid on Warsaw, when the Jewish district set on fire by the Germans was still burning, one of the tenants shared with me his suspicion that Jewish insurrectionaries were throwing flares to guide the pilots to the most vulnerable locations in the city.

Since I am relating these minor but characteristic facts, I cannot refrain—though not without a sense of sorrow and shame—from quoting words that have long ago disappeared in the second fire and second smoke of martyred Warsaw.[2] Young office girls ran out onto the terrace of one of the tallest Żoliborz buildings to look at the fire in the Ghetto—it was during the first days of the Jewish Uprising—and they called out joyfully into the spring air, which was being shaken by explosions and saturated with smoke: "Come, look at how they're frying Jew-chops!" Anyone who thinks that some new stunning thirst for blood spoke through them would be mistaken. They were merely victims of the power of ignorance that accrued over the centuries.

If not for the universality of anti-Semitic prejudice, its deep-rootedness, and its allegedly obvious claims, it would have been impossible for whole hordes of blackmailers to sell—with impunity and in plain sight—the blood of Jews, most often Poles with Jewish backgrounds, who were hiding in Warsaw. Germans often relied on the Shakespearean *Merchant of Venice*: as if some satanic Shylock ever actually demanded a pound of a Christian's flesh when a contract was breached, centuries later, these "Christians" from the General Government repaid him with hundreds of pounds of "Jewish" flesh.

During the Warsaw Ghetto Uprising, I carefully observed the reactions of students enrolled in underground courses in Żoliborz and Praga.[3] Most of the students from Żoliborz High School, a place with democratic traditions, viewed the final act of the tragedy of the Polish Jews humanely, with compassion and understanding. Meanwhile, high school youth from Praga simply amused themselves with jokes about the events taking place on the other side of the wall. When the Uprising was dying out, one of the students asked me if I knew that Jews who escaped from the Ghetto were murdering Poles. In vain I tried telling her that she fell for false rumors spread by the Germans. Always agreeable and very intelligent, this time she dug her heels in. She did not believe my words. It was only then that I understood: she wanted it to be so; that is why she believed even this story, intended for the lowest rabble. To be capable of gazing upon the greatest martyrdom in the history of the world with indifference one undoubtedly had to have strong faith not only in the perniciousness of the "Jewish element" but in something more—in terrible danger, in the Jews' demonic powers.

For many, this faith was only theoretical; it could not withstand the test of daily life. And this explains why avowed anti-Semites often helped their alleged enemies. There were also instances when helping Jews required perseverance, and there was noble simplicity in the astonishing acts of devotion of a portion of society that ensured the survival of a handful of intellectuals with Jewish backgrounds. There were also left-leaning and democratic activists, who saved our society's dignity in our relationship with Jews and in other matters, as they have always done throughout our history.

Right now, however, I do not wish to speak about these phenomena but about representatives of the bourgeoisie and the intelligentsia, people who constitute the largest and most typical part of the nation. In their everyday life, these people do not lack strengths and virtues—they love their families, Warsaw, and their fatherland. But at times when even a stone would have shed tears, they stubbornly retreated into somber hatred, into blind superstition. Whole tomes could be written about the power of this superstition, but this is neither the time nor the place for a historical analysis of this phenomenon. We can only point out that—despite everything—today's society is not inclined to make hasty generalizations, even under particularly favorable circumstances. Despite their rightful and justified hatred for Germans for the crimes of the Nazi regime, most Poles do not wish to annihilate the

German nation; they do not want women and children to burn or to suffo-
cate in gas chambers. Yet this, after all, would be only revenge—horrifying,
but only revenge. Meanwhile the "Jewish issue" continues to move minds
to hatred—toward whom? Toward a shadow, a phantom, a handful of people
who survived a ghastly pogrom.

Press reports of instances when Poles murdered surviving Jewish families emphatically testify to the fact that Poland has organizations that have
taken up the dismal effort of continuing the bloody work of the Nazis. It
is utterly natural that the instinct for self-preservation forces Polish citizens
of Jewish descent—those who managed to survive the occupation period
amidst unfathomable difficulties—not to reveal their background in free,
democratic Poland.

Despite the unequivocal stance of the most democratic of all of Poland's
governments, most survivors of slaughter do not trust their "Aryan" compatriots, to use that idiotic Nazi term. Presumably, this lack of trust in the
Polish masses is not yet another manifestation of Jewish "cunning" and
"wickedness." We only need to keep our eyes and ears open to understand
the fears of the survivors.

Things did not go the way Julian Tuwim had predicted in his article
about Jews and the Jewish issue that he had sent from America, and which
(as far as I know) has not yet been published anywhere.[4] Tuwim predicted
that the word "Jew" would become honorable, and Jews still surviving in
Europe after the slaughter of millions would walk with the halo of martyrdom over them. Tuwim—one of those Polish poets who reacted most
directly—was mistaken; he was mistaken in his messianic, anti-rationalist
evaluation of the situation. But his mistake belongs to a rather respectable
tradition that reaches all the way back to Mickiewicz's messianic illusions.[5]

Decimated by villainous assassins, regularly tortured in concentration
camps and death camps, the Polish nation did not extend a brotherly hand
to "Israel"—despite the fact that the government of the Polish Republic
gave it "rights equal in all respects," to use a phrase from the "Principles"
of Mickiewicz's Legion.[6] Or, to be more precise, this applies not to the
entire Polish "nation" but to the reactionary part of the nation. This time, as
before, Polish literature, an essential expression of the Polish people, did not
abandon those dying a martyr's death. Władysław Broniewski's well-known
poem "To Polish Jews," Czesław Miłosz's "Giordano Bruno," several of Jerzy
Zagórski's stanzas, and plays by Stefan Otwinowski and Flora Bieńkowska
testify to this.[7]

During this last war, Jewish history was too shocking not to find reflections in literature—even one that follows history as lazily as ours. Some of the works that evoke this theme, however, are still burdened by an idealistic understanding of history. Hence the presence of messianic notions like "guilt" or "mission"—both equally backward and equally harmful. A dystopia of hatred cannot be surmounted by a utopia of humanitarian preaching. Non-rationalist, anti-materialist ways of approaching the question leave much room for individuals swayed by humanitarian sentiments, individuals who are unable to shake off superstition and who therefore attempt to endow it with noble hues. Regardless of the moral dimension of this phenomenon, it would be improper and lacking common sense to equate these irrational impulses with an act of charity. The silence of the Pope, the Vicar of Christ, regarding this and other matters is, in any case, telling enough.

The struggle against anti-Semitism that awaits the new Polish democracy—and democracies in other countries—is a struggle against the darkest manifestation of reaction; it must be conducted decisively and judiciously. Above all: influence must be exerted through all educational channels—the press, schools, books, and lectures. Veiling this dishonor with silence—and it screams too loudly for that to happen—is not going to make things any better. The problem is not easy because our journalists do not have pens that are truth-loving and passionate enough, because our writers prefer to avoid topics that are too drastic, and because our schools do not feature ranks of teachers inspired by the true spirit of democracy and human brotherhood.

Who will teach the principles of democracy and brotherhood to our youth, demoralized by the criminal occupier for so long and often compromised by their home environment as well? This tremendously significant and extensive problem reaches far beyond the issue we have broached here because it is a question of restoring human proportions to the savage face of the world.

The influence of Nazism on our society had to have far-reaching consequences. It was exerted directly for nearly six years and it burrowed its way less directly into the souls of Germany's neighbors for many years prior.

The task before us is immensely difficult because teachers themselves are not free from the influence of the fascist virus. What kind of mentorship can be offered by a teacher who—in private conversation—expresses the unfortunately commonly held view that "by murdering Jews, Hitler did the dirty work for us."

It would be a mistake to think that most teachers believe this. It is the thinking of ignorant individuals who turned barbarian, drawing inspiration from Hitler. And one has to state—not to justify their ignorance, but to objectively express the truth and make it more powerful—that even in countries with greater resistance to the influence of superstition, countries with a different social structure, in which shadows of past eras have disappeared, or so it seemed, that even there phantoms of the past have started to emerge from the depths.

Literature must employ the powerful weapon of words against Nazi propaganda, which has been active for years. Apposite old and new works must be introduced into school reading lists and textbooks—and there is no shortage of these. Emphasis should be placed not so much on the sentimental aspect of the problem as on facts.

Jews who took part in the Polish national uprisings and in the resistance movement during the German occupation, those who joined the ranks of the People's Army and the Home Army during the 1944 Uprising, Jews in the Polish Army, proclamations made by Polish organizations about the Jewish tragedy, and General Żymierski's orders—all this should find its way into the curriculum.[8]

We must not delay. We must not delude ourselves that a front of national cooperation will be easier to build if we remain silent about an issue unpopular among our countrymen. State officials have already emphasized this by commemorating the anniversary of the Warsaw Ghetto Uprising.

Let us remember that the unenlightened majority (which also includes part of the so-called intelligentsia) is docile rather than fanatical; it simply succumbs to opinions that are too widespread, and which, under certain circumstances, become almost reflexive. People are strongly affected by fear of making original judgments, unwillingness to oppose truths recognized by friends and neighbors, fear of being ridiculed, and desire to be "fully Polish"—since in some social circles anti-Semitism is seen as an inseparable quality of Polishness. For a long time, inheritors of feudalism in Poland saw defense of Jews as an activity directed against the state; rational arguments were considered inappropriate in these circles where hatred reigned. Delayed social development in our country, longevity of the landed aristocracy, which imposed its ideology onto the bourgeoisie and intellectual circles, and the general situation in yesterday's Europe—all this contributes to the current complicated, multifaceted reality, which will not be easy to change despite transformed circumstances. Though it has outlived its initial meanings, the residue that lies deep within people's souls, a residue more durable than the ground on which it first formed, will maintain itself stubbornly for years to come. A feudal relationship to man is more deeply entrenched in the mentality of an average intellectual than we realize.

Complete lack of understanding of historical realities that prevails among many intellectuals and members of the new bourgeoisie, hopes that either England or an archangel will come to our aid, negation of obvious facts, and susceptibility to surreptitiously whispered rumors that parade as news from heaven—all this encourages the lush blossoming of all kinds of superstition and dismal myths that only bring us to ruin.[9]

Słowacki's deeply true adage about the "heart, where thought does not dwell even for an hour" is confirmed once again.[10]

All prudent men in Poland, all adherents of progress and democracy— and there are, fortunately, not so few of them—should desire to have their sober voices heard in Poland and abroad; they should make sure their voices are not drowned in the din of intellectual rabble or overwhelmed by the blind or befuddled bourgeois majority. But we know well that in Poland moral courage is more difficult to find than heroism in direct combat and magnificent bravery and nobility on the battlefield.

In Poland, the war was won because of the valor and sacrifice of thousands of brave people; we will certainly not win the peace by cowardly silence about sensitive issues, by leaving them for later, or by flirting with ignorance. The best traditions of the great eras of our history are on our side.

Editors' Notes

1. Jastrun is referring to the phrase "Hostes dum vulnerati fratres" (When enemies are wounded, they become brothers).
2. The "second fire" and "second smoke" refer to the Warsaw Uprising in August 1944. The Warsaw Uprising, organized by the Polish military underground and the citizens of Warsaw, ended in total defeat and a nearly complete destruction of the city by the Germans.
3. Żoliborz and Praga are districts of Warsaw. Underground educational initiatives were widespread in Warsaw and other cities during the occupation. Some students met with teachers in homes, others came to classes organized in the backrooms of shops and workshops; this allowed many to obtain high school and college diplomas during the war.

4. This is a reference to Julian Tuwim's "We, Polish Jews," which is reproduced in this volume on pages 63–68. Tuwim's essay was first published in September 1944 in the London-based *Nowa Polska* (*New Poland*), but it seems that Jastrum was unaware of this publication when he wrote his essay for *Odrodzenie* in 1945.

5. Adam Mickiewicz (1798–1855) was Poland's most influential Romantic poet. His messianism is discussed briefly in "Poles and Jews in the Nineteenth Century" in the Introduction.

6. In 1848, when revolutions broke out throughout Europe, Mickiewicz was in Rome and formed a military unit, which he called the Polish Legion. The unit was led by Colonel Aleksander Fijałkowski, had 200 soldiers, and fought alongside Garibaldi. It was broken up when it attempted to make its way into Hungary to aid the Hungarian revolutionaries. Its manifesto, called "Skład zasad" (Principles), was written by Mickiewicz and embodied the spirit of democratic idealism. One of the principles reads, "To Israel, an older brother, [we extend] respect, aid in his path toward earthly and eternal Good. Rights equal in all respects."

7. Jastrun is referring to Jerzy Zagórski's occupation-era poems, Stefan Otwinowski's 1946 drama *Wielkanoc* (*Easter*), and Flora Bieńkowska's drama *Wiosna 1944* (*Spring 1944*).

8. The Home Army was the largest Polish military underground organization active during the German occupation. The communist People's Army was a successor of the People's Guard. In July 1944, the People's Army was combined with Polish military units organized (and largely commanded) by the Soviets to create the Polish Army. General Michał Rola-Żymierski joined the Polish Workers' Party (PPR) in 1943; he became the commander of the People's Army in January 1944, and the commander of the Polish Army when it was formed in July. It is not clear which of his often controversial orders Jastrun had in mind. For more about the Polish military underground's relationship to Jews during the war, please see "Poles and Jews during the Holocaust" in the Introduction.

9. Throughout the war, many Poles hoped that England would liberate Poland from the German occupation. Jastrun also mocks the turn to religious beliefs and hopes for divine deliverance, which was common among Catholic Poles during the war.

10. Juliusz Słowacki (1809–1849) was one of Poland's most influential Romantic poets, second only to Adam Mickiewicz. He is best known for his dramas and his mystical view of world history articulated in the prose poem "Genezis z Ducha" (Genesis from the Spirit, 1846).

8

The Problem of Polish
Anti-Semitism

JERZY ANDRZEJEWSKI

Editors' Introduction

Jerzy Andrzejewski (1909–1983) was a novelist, publicist, and screenwriter. Born in Warsaw to a Catholic family, he studied Polish philology there. In the 1930s he became associated with National Democratic circles and published in the nationalist weekly *Prosto z mostu*. He broke with the nationalists in 1938, joining those intellectuals who were organizing support for Jews in Zbąszyń, a Polish town on the border with Germany. In October 1938, the Nazi authorities rounded up several thousand Polish Jews living in Germany and deported them to Zbąszyń on a train, leaving them without any food or provisions. A number of Poles formed committees to organize help for the deported, and their efforts were immediately attacked by the nationalist press.

During the war, Andrzejewski joined the Polish cultural underground, offered help to hide Jews, and wrote the novella *Wielki Tydzień* (*Holy Week*) about the destruction of the Warsaw Ghetto. After the war, he supported Poland's new government and joined the Communist Party (PZPR). He left the party in 1957 along with Mieczysław Jastrun and others who protested against government restrictions on creative expression. During the following decades, Andrzejewski became an outspoken critic of the government and a symbolic figure in the Polish democratic opposition movement. He signed the 1964 letter against censorship; in 1968 he was one of the few who publicly condemned the invasion of Czechoslovakia by Warsaw Pact forces; and in 1976 he joined the Committee for the Defense of Workers (KOR), formed by Warsaw intellectuals to support workers imprisoned by the government after protests in June of that year.

In his books Andrzejewski wrestled with the central questions and issues facing Poles in the twentieth century: fascism, communism, historical identity, and the role of religion in public life. His most important books available in English include *Holy Week: A Novel of the Warsaw Ghetto Uprising, Ashes and Diamonds, The Inquisitors*, and *The Gates of Paradise*. The text reproduced here was first published in the progovernment weekly *Odrodzenie* (*Rebirth*) on July 7, 1946, in Krakow. The Kielce Pogrom took place on July 4, 1946, but Andrzejewski submitted this essay, which explores the broader problem of persistent anti-Semitism in Polish society, before the Pogrom. For the wider context of anti-Jewish prejudice and violence in Poland in the immediate aftermath of the war, please see the Introduction.

I

Despite wartime experiences, the problem of anti-Semitism has not lost its relevance in Poland. Polish anti-Semitism did not burn itself out in the rubble and the smoldering ruins of the ghettos. It turned out that the death of several million murdered Jews was not terrible enough to crush Polish habits of thought and emotion. The Nazi school of contempt and hatred was evidently not an urgent enough warning. It is difficult to speak about this, but this is how things are. The futility of all the casualties, destruction, and anguish suffered by the Jewish people throughout Europe, and especially in our country, is one of the most bitter lessons (not the only one, alas!) Poles should learn from the war. How much more calmly could one think about the millions murdered in camps, prisons, gas chambers, and city streets, about all who died fighting, if their death had been a moral shock to those who survived. I don't mean a sense of calm concerning the dead and the murdered. One cannot be calm about them. But for six years, in the most cruel of all battles in the history of the world, humanity—let us use this grand word—fought for freedom, justice, and human dignity; and woe to the nations unable to draw the right conclusions from this experience. Hatred, contempt, and racial prejudice are certainly not the right conclusions.

We write much about anti-Semitism here, and we say even more about it. It is a painful and shameful issue. It does not win us friends abroad. It aggravates and inflames the atmosphere at home. It disgraces the morality of the Polish nation, and casts a dark shadow over our sociopolitical maturity. Was it on our banners that we used to write "For Your Freedom and Ours?"[1]

The press typically presents manifestations of anti-Semitism as an aspect of social and political reaction. Polish Jews, when addressing these issues, use similar language. I recently came across the text of a memorandum, which the Central Committee of Polish Jews wrote in the name of the entire Jewish community of Poland to the Anglo-American Committee of Inquiry. In the memorandum, the Central Committee claims that "the entire Jewish community, regardless of political differences, is united in the demand that Jews be granted the right to free and unimpeded emigration to Palestine." The first three of the four reasons given to justify this demand focus mostly on psychological issues. Of the 3.5 million Jews who lived in Poland before 1939, survivors numbered no more than 100,000—or fewer than 3 percent. Approximately 160,000 Polish Jews are temporarily staying in the Soviet Union. But those in Poland and those waiting to return are mostly people who lost their families—they are survivors who will find it difficult to lead a normal life in a place where their loved ones perished. Everything in Poland reminds them of the tragedy of Polish Jews. Hence the understandable desire to start a new life in an entirely different place, and especially in Palestine, where many Jews who survived the massacre have relatives who had emigrated from the country before the war.

Only in the final paragraph does the Central Committee refer to the current conditions in Poland. In its entirety the paragraph reads as follows:

> It is an undeniable fact that murders now still take place once in a while, and attacks are launched against democratic activists, secret police headquarters, and the Jewish population. These actions are incited and executed by reactionary underground groups, which maintain uninterrupted contact with the reactionary General Władysław Anders in Italy, and with what remains of the former London-based Government-in-Exile. The same criminal hand that carries out anti-Semitic actions also strikes at activists from democratic parties, officers of the Polish Army, and so on. State authorities and democratic parties are combatting anti-Semitism, which has taken root here during the tsarist era, and which was reinforced during the German occupation through racist Nazi propaganda. The Decree on Summary Proceedings calls for the death penalty for terrorist actions motivated by national, racial, or religious reasons, but anti-Jewish incidents continue to take place nonetheless.
>
> We strongly emphasize, however, that manifestations of anti-Semitism are not the main cause of emigration aspirations, as some foreign commentators mistakenly believe. As we have shown, the causes lie deeper—they are objective, ideological, and psychological.

I purposely quote this argument in its entirety because its message fully overlaps with what gets written about anti-Semitism here. Reaction! Unfortunately, over the course of this past year the concept of reaction has become a bag into which people throw—often too quickly and impulsively, and certainly chaotically—all the deficiencies and maladies of our present situation. The bag is enormous and capacious, a sort of modern version of Dante's hell. General Władysław Anders and metaphysics reside in it side by side, and in its bowels wartime looters and members of the National Armed Forces bump into psychological analyses found in novels.[2] Calling someone a "reactionary" today could mean so many different things that sometimes it means nothing. The word "reaction," while preserving the militant character of a catch phrase, a generality, has suffered an incredibly fast devolution of meaning over this last year; this is neither strange nor unexpected, given the fact that official propaganda has been overly zealous in its efforts to falsify the concept of reaction and to make it repulsive. Besides, most Poles, betraying their childlike character, prefer to name things and phenomena rather than trouble the mind with analysis. It is difficult, however, to delude oneself into thinking that trivial propaganda could help elucidate many entangled and complicated issues. On the contrary, when observing our life, one increasingly has the impression that from all sides—from the left, from the right, from the top and from the bottom, with various voices and various accents placed on the same words—many people are shouting, but they do it in the dark, blindly, often in an atmosphere of outright lies.

The conundrum of anti-Semitism in Poland seems to be one of many problems that get confounded, rather than explained, when they are squeezed into the confines of a generality. Anti-Semitism is reaction? Fine! Should one fight anti-Semitism? Of course! The worst aspects of fascism manifest themselves in anti-Semitism? Granted! But where does this leave us? It means more or less as much as saying that "the atomic bomb is a threat to humanity," or that "tuberculosis is an illness that brutally decimates the country's population." By describing anti-Semitism as reaction and fascism, we do not explain it in any way. We only get a certain social, political, and moral classification. But what is Polish anti-Semitism? Where did it come from? How does it manifest itself? Why does it take certain forms here and not others? A whole series of urgent, necessary, essential questions.

II

The problem of Polish anti-Semitism has been troubling me for quite some time. While traveling in nationalist youth circles a few years before the war, I had occasion to learn about it in its most exacerbated, brutal, and ruthless form. The experience I gained during those years extends beyond the question of Polish-Jewish coexistence. I understood then that when one witnesses the denigration of another person, one is forced not only to defend those who are unjustly scorned but also to reach deeper—into the very system of social and economic relations; because all the noblest human feelings of mercy, compassion, and fraternity will remain meaningless if they do not result in efforts to create forms of life and establish concepts capable of guaranteeing the individual's right to justice, freedom, and respect.

I encountered many Jews during the war. I knew the most honorable individuals and complete reprobates. I met Poles who hid Jews in their homes, risking their own lives and the lives of their families. Never refusing to help, they acted in deeply humane ways. I also encountered lowlifes and cowards, I saw opportunism, and people who turned a blind eye to death, which was still someone else's, but which could at any time eliminate any of us from the ranks of the living. During the first liquidation of the Ghetto, in the fall of '42, I lived in the immediate vicinity of the walls. Those days and nights, filled with the sounds of gunshot salvos and spurts of machine gunfire, were the most difficult moments of the entire occupation. Only the following Easter, and the Warsaw Uprising,[3] surpassed them in bitterness, shameful helplessness, and loss of faith in the meaning of Poland and Poles.

For all honest Poles, the fate of the perishing Jews must have been exceptionally painful. Innocent people were dying, and our nation did not have the right to look them in the eye with a clear conscience. The Polish people could look straight in the eye of the Polish men and women who were dying for freedom. But they could not do the same when it came to Jews fighting in the burning Ghetto.

But Jews took up arms to defend their dignity. Members of the Jewish resistance who survived are right to emphasize that the Uprising in the Warsaw Ghetto was not an act of despair. A handful of fighters did the fighting, and, given their extensive contacts with Polish organizations, almost every one of them could have escaped the Ghetto through the sewers and could have come out alive. If they remained with the multitude of their helpless compatriots, it was to protest against barbarity and violence. Military victory was out of the question. The Uprising was defeated because it had to be. Those Jews who did not die fighting went to their death in the gas chambers of Treblinka, Majdanek, and Auschwitz. The Warsaw Ghetto was razed to the ground and made into a barren desert. And yet beyond its walls, from the moment the first shot was fired, this insurrectionary impulse became the Jews' great victory. Facing inevitable destruction and death, from the depths of most painful humiliation, the loneliest of all who fought during those years, Jews fought for the same truths and values that other nations defended on all fronts and battlefields during the six years of war: freedom, justice, respect for man, and a better social and political order in the world. This was exactly what Poles fought for.

The third anniversary of the Jewish Uprising in Warsaw just passed. Today, when we evoke the somber and lofty meaning of those days in a land that is already free, and where shadows of fallen Jews stand side by side with shadows of fallen Poles, bearing witness to a brotherhood of arms and a community bound by truths worth dying for, today, when after so much suffering, after such unspeakably difficult years filled with so much bitterness, anti-Semitic propaganda still functions in our country, defying good sense and fundamental human dignity—how much must one strain one's voice, and what words must one use to stir consciences that have not been shaken from their stupor by six years of war? When the Warsaw Ghetto was fighting, we, Poles, could not have a clear conscience. Three years have passed, and the anniversary of the Uprising cannot, unfortunately, become merely a solemn commemoration for us. This anniversary of Jewish heroism still bleeds. Pangs of conscience? How much easier it is to have a sensitive and vigilant moral instinct than to act on it no matter what! Only actions have the power to heal. We would pay due homage to the Warsaw Ghetto only by passionately defending our own dignity and fighting against everything in our relations with Jews that casts a dark shadow over our honesty, morality, and our sense of freedom and human solidarity.

III

After everything that happened, the number of Poles willing to openly propagate anti-Semitism is certainly small. Those who disgrace Poland's honor and murder Jews are even fewer. Public opinion in the country condemns them—and this is no doubt genuine. Polish opinion is against anti-Semitism, if one equates it with Nazi methods of fighting Jews. Does that mean that there is, indeed, no anti-Semitism in Poland? That its infrequent, lurid manifestations are, in fact, only minor and degenerate blemishes on a healthy body? Has the history lesson not gone to waste, after all?

How I wish I could honestly answer: "Yes! Anti-Semitism is dying out in Poland, the Polish nation has learned what it needed to learn." Unfortunately—after many years of thinking about this problem that still festers like an open wound on our body, considering everything that went on in Poland before the war, during the war, and now, listening to people from the most diverse circles and with various levels of intelligence, observing their often entirely unconscious reflexes and reactions, and seeing how these automatically lead to certain words and gestures—I cannot reach any conclusion other than that the Polish nation—with all its strata and in its entire intellectual cross-section—had, and after the war continues to have, an anti-Semitic orientation. This aversion to the Jewish people, which is universal here, takes on most varied forms and accents: from the almost-friendly and seemingly warm laughter at Jews, from jokes and mockery, to the so-called sensible criticism of Jews, which simultaneously disavows any ties to anti-Semitism, all the way to open and brutal proclamations of aversion and hostility. We currently encounter this last attitude least frequently because even the staunchest anti-Semites in Poland, if they have not lost all remnants of decency, are somewhat ashamed of their feelings. The war years are still very fresh in their memory; they find it uncomfortable to speak about Jews and relations with them with the same license they used without compunction before 1939. All our conversations about Jews tend to be rather convoluted and obscure, full of oblique statements and inhibitions; they are burdened by the shadows of Majdanek and Treblinka. But just let someone, in any group whatsoever, tell a Jewish joke, an anecdote, or employ an intonation mimicking the Jewish accent—and what sudden liveliness disperses even the most dismal atmosphere!

I recall a certain recent situation. I was at a large gathering where certainly no one could be accused of being either reactionary or anti-Semitic. There were only progressives, leftists, and reform supporters there. Intellectuals, writers. The hour was rather late, everyone had persevered through a long celebration in honor of a great actor, and the atmosphere at supper was not the liveliest, not to say somewhat dull. Our guest (we were in Krakow) was one of our acquaintances from before the war, currently a high official in the Department of Culture. Before the war, this dignitary had distinguished himself through his exceptional storytelling abilities, and he was very well known and popular in Poland as an actor, presenter, and parodist. It turned out that his old skills did not get lost among his new titles: when at one point he told us a few Jewish jokes, using mimicry and the characteristic accent for emphasis, the intellectuals suddenly became quite animated. The evening, which promised to be rather tedious, turned out to be very funny and carefree, as everyone listened to the dignitary's lavish anecdotes.

Someone will say: Fine, but where is the anti-Semitism here? These intellectuals would probably be equally amused by well-told jokes about Scotsmen, Russians, Poles, or Englishmen. Of course, there is no doubt they would laugh; and who knows if jokes about their own countrymen, if they were good, would not get the most laughs. The problem, though, is that

Poles laugh differently at the Scots' proverbial penny-pinching than at jokes about someone named Rappaport.[4]

I've often thought about what Polish anti-Semitism actually is. What intellectual and emotional elements comprise this particular aversion of Poles to Jews? I purposely use the word "aversion" because it does not seem to me that we should evoke the greater intensity of "hatred." Even though it is said that Poles are explosive and volatile by temperament, their feelings actually tend to be lukewarm and moderate rather than passionate and fierce. One neither loves nor hates here. Poles like or dislike. Nothing commands their wholehearted commitment. If they like to have great men among them, they simultaneously like to do everything they can to ridicule and undermine them; and when they don't like Jews, they still like buying from them. Poles are, however, natural-born conservatives, and since they think unwillingly, they tend to be very stubborn in their addictions to certain "likes" and "dislikes." They are traditionalists, but unfortunately in the negative sense of the word. When history forces them to revise their previous ideas and customary norms, the brave souls who take up the challenge face a veritable flood of obscurantism, indignation, and distortions.

If one observes the incredibly diverse ways in which Poles react to Jews, and, through a process of gradual selection, seeks to isolate some fundamental features from the multitude of grudges, aggravations, grievances, criticisms, and the like, one finally arrives at two basic qualities. They seem to contradict each other, but both can be fully explained by our history, and by our country's particular configuration of Polish-Jewish relations in social, economic, and moral realms. Anti-Semitism in Poland, despite what the memorandum of the Central Committee of Polish Jews says, did not "take root during the tsarist era." Its traditions reach further back into history, as it developed in the context of social relations much earlier than those brought by the nineteenth century.

One set of hostile reactions exhibited by Poles toward Jews is clearly anchored in the Polish sense of superiority. At the same time, the sense of inferiority Poles feel in relation to Jews seems to be, just as clearly, at the core of another category of feelings and arguments. As a result, every manifestation of anti-Semitism in Poland can be shown to belong to one of these two categories; in fact, Polish reactions to Jews most often result from the intermixing and mutual penetration of both these feelings. Take, for example, the characteristic and variously inflected claim: "Jewish mentality is degenerate and threatening to Polish culture and it should therefore be eradicated." This is a typical manifestation of Poles' simultaneous sense of superiority and inferiority. Contempt for Jewish mentality, combined with fear and anxiety of people who feel threatened by a force they perceive as dangerous. One could find many similar obfuscations and entanglements. Here Polishness, as in many other cases, throws us into a whirlpool of contradictions, into a circle where, without stopping to think, impatient and imprudent voices simultaneously shout: yes! and no!

Stanisław Wyspiański's symbolism does not speak to me.[5] But whenever I think about the ending of his *Wesele* (*The Wedding*), I am always overcome by bitter and oppressive sadness. One world war has blown through the country and a second, a hundred times worse, has shaken the world; the wheel of history has been turning among the darkest human sufferings, wrongs, and sacrifices; thrones, systems, truths, and illusory hopes have been destroyed; what the mind can barely fathom became reality; nations were covered with infamy and blood, they witnessed the blossoming of heroism and tumbled into abject poverty and degradation. But in Poland—saved from bondage for a second time—among so many hopes and longings, anxieties and torments, in this land, destroyed like no other and filled with shadows of the dead—Wyspiański's Strawman still plays his fiddle for the minds.

IV

Poles' sense of their own superiority to Jews encompasses a vast range of incredibly diverse responses: from patronizing and almost friendly mockery, jokes, and carefree humor, through ridicule, satire, and sarcasm, all the way to openly hostile attitudes of dismissal, contempt, and disgust.

One of the traditional figures in Polish nativity scenes is an amusing village Jew in a long black coat—most often represented, by the way, as a rather sympathetic figure. A Jewish accent is the object of jokes and mockery among all strata of Polish society. The Jewish way of speaking amuses the peasant and the intellectual, the child and the frail old man. Poles find the long black coat and Galician side-curls hilarious. They've decided that Jews are cowards, and this, too, seems very amusing. Archetypal Jewish figures that appear in nineteenth-century Polish novels—leaseholders, middlemen, petty merchants, and traveling salesmen—all tend to be rather entertaining. At this level of their relationship to Jews—still patronizing and, as I already mentioned, almost friendly and often even filled with sentimentality—everything about Jews seems funny to Poles. Matzah and the old Jewish matron's wig are funny, so is "Ma Yofus," gefilte fish, circumcision, attachment to money, predilection for trading and business, Shabbat, Sukkot tents, Jewish cunning, rabbis, dirt, the desire to assimilate, Jewish servicemen in the military . . . in a word, everything that Poles—rightly or wrongly—have identified as Jewish traits and qualities. I think I won't be far from the truth if I say that there is not a single Pole who—to a greater or lesser degree—does not have this sense of amusement in his relation to Jews, and this element derives from his sense of superiority. What's more, this tendency to ridicule Jews and mock them is taken over from the Poles with extreme ease by Jews who, having overcome the dire poverty of the Ghetto, join the property-owning classes, or who, coexisting with Poles, embark on the path of assimilation. Everybody knows that the best interwar jokes about Jews were created by Polish writers of Jewish descent.

Is this anti-Semitism? Perhaps we might even be inclined to claim that it is not because recent years have accustomed us to seeing anti-Semitism as something that refers to phenomena incomparably more dangerous than jokes and anecdotes. I do not believe, however, that we should underrate or dismiss those distortions of human relationships which—it is true—resound with innocent laughter today, but which could resound with the sharp call of disdain and hostility tomorrow. Whoever ridicules someone else can easily, under the right circumstances, kick him or beat him with a stick. The path from ridicule to punches is neither long nor arduous.

Laughter is certainly a healthy thing—so long as it is humor. But true humor comes from human solidarity, and scornful jokes and ridicule have no need for such a strong and stable basis. They typically glide around life's surface, indifferent to any hierarchy of values. True humor is rare. It accompanies people who know what they want and value moral judgments. The weaker and meaner people are, the more easily they succumb to ridicule, jokes, and laughing at someone else's expense. Snickering is the revenge of the weak, or the weapon of those who artificially elevate themselves.

There are therefore many reasons for serious reflection when—through jokes and mockery—a collectivity as large as a nation betrays stunning unanimity in one realm of life. Are Jews really that funny? But what nation or what person doesn't have amusing features? Jews certainly have their share of oddities. But the laughter and derision directed at Jews is all too often akin to the kind of amusement that strikes at disability and handicap.

When one jokes and derides the Jewish accent, the name Rappaport, and the red-haired wig, one doesn't have to think about the dire poverty of the Jewish proletariat, and all the humiliations and suffering that Jews have to bear upon their shoulders. Ridicule tends to be a good sleeping pill for conscience. During the German occupation, jokes and macabre laughter sometimes also surrounded train cars that carried Jews to Majdanek and Treblinka.

We should not go as far as to say that people who told Jewish jokes during that time wanted Jews to die, or approved of Nazi crimes. Most of them certainly condemned the German madness. But even when they did not sympathize with brutality, even when they risked their own lives as they rushed to help Jews, Poles—the best and most vigilant of them—did not shake off the traditional Polish attitude toward Jews. Frequently, and in all kinds of settings, the intellectual exploded with the Polish nobleman's laughter at his leaseholder, and the simpleton evoked his rural ancestors by an involuntary word and gesture. Such strange moments they were, when shadows of a long-gone history slipped over the Ghetto walls, into fire and death, into the depths of the darkest pits of degradation and suffering. These shadows suddenly became animated even in the voices of people who were willing to condemn much in their nation's history, since they considered it necessary to organize life in accordance with new social and economic laws.

The funny Jewish accent and the Jewish matron's red-haired wig have their own long history. What did life look like in the countryside? To the nobleman in his manor, the Jew was a convenient creature—persistent, dedicated, and industrious—who facilitated sales and deliveries, and made all financial trans-actions and loans easier. The "Jew-boy" (Żydek), even when he was liked, was ultimately only a funny and insignificant figure, an object of disrespect and disdain, or, at best, an object of jokes and typical Polish sentimentality—which does not necessitate action and absolves one of all wrongdoing. Ah, this Polish sentimentality, this strange little monster that makes it possible for people with no heart or reason to fool themselves into thinking that they have both. The Pole is easily moved, and he is quick to shed a tear. When he sheds two tears, he feels that he is the noblest person in the world. Nineteenth-century Polish literature is full of such cheap and philo-Semitic accents; it delves deeper into essential values of human coexistence only rarely and only in the works of the noblest and wisest writers. Poles like to talk about fraternity, and thus in daily life they readily see it in the least effortful, apparently impressive, but ultimately meaningless behaviors.

It is easy to be misunderstood here in Poland, and I do not want that. I do not wish to slander my own nation. Every single one of my bitter words about Poles strikes at me as well. I am sharing my thoughts, and what life on this earth has taught me. I desire only one thing: to urge my countrymen to think about this issue, which, like a focusing lens, brings together so many of our defects, faults, flaws, and deficiencies. We will not be free from the long and grasping tentacles of our own history so long as we do not overcome within ourselves all the distortions that this history has instilled in us. The scope and importance of the problem of Polish anti-Semitism extends beyond the problem of how Poles relate to Jews. It is an aspect of human relations in general, an aspect of how we relate to human values, and to ideas, which were subjected to so much abuse recently, but which, despite so many persisting aggravations and misunderstandings, are today once again blossoming with new values like justice, freedom, and respect. Our responsibility is greater than that of the future generations, which will grow up under new social conditions and with new customs; ideas about human coexistence that will shape them will be far more perfect than our own. Living at a turning point and laying down the very first foundations for tomorrow, we have to be vigilant so we do not fill new social forms with the content of old habits. The shaping of our own minds and hearts seems to be just as momentous and pressing as the formation of the socio-economic order. Without recognizing and affirming life's inviolable values, we will offer nothing but ossification and a deceitful illusion of life to even the most perfect of legal systems.

We can only understand and assess the problem of Polish anti-Semitism against the backdrop of history. Detached from this foundation, it must look like an incomprehensible oddity. In our country, anti-Semitism arose from specific class relations, and from all the mental and emotional habits which, thanks to these relations, have shaped Polish mentality and Polish customs. I already mentioned the conditions that obtained in the countryside, and the characteristic mental-emotional relation that emerged between the manor and the Jewish population in the countryside and small towns. And for peasants, whose responses were often the same or at least very similar to those of the landed gentry, the Jew who was a middleman, a shopkeeper or an innkeeper—as someone landless and disrespected by the landlord, and someone with different customs and a different religion that was hostile to Catholicism—was also an amusing figure. He could be kicked around but only so long as he remained poor enough not to become dangerous. Precisely: dangerous, menacing!

In Poland, so long as Jews were weak and impoverished, so long as they could be exploited, they were funny and amusing, sometimes even pleasant, like the traditional village or small-town Sruls.[6] This could be observed in both the countryside and the cities. A Jew selling secondhand goods in the backyard is a rather pleasant and amusing figure. Like the petty shopkeeper, or someone who makes pennies at the stock market. But as soon as a Jew frees himself from dire poverty and aspires to a higher, more responsible position, becomes a capitalist, or gains recognition in the artistic-intellectual hierarchy, Poles' sense of superiority toward him is very quickly shaken. It gets transformed into a nagging inferiority complex. At this level of experience, one rarely hears carefree laughter. When a Pole laughs at a minister, a banker, or an eminent writer with a Jewish background, his laughter is entirely different from the laughter directed at a leaseholder or a merchant selling secondhand items. If disrespect still resounds in this laughter, accents of aversion, hostility, envy, and a sense of danger are incomparably stronger and sharper now.

We still clearly remember the arguments spewed out by militant prewar Polish anti-Semitism. In this rabid and noisy propaganda, Jews in Poland became a dark and menacing power hanging over our entire life, poisoning and distorting it, and becoming a cause—if not the sole cause then at least one of the most important ones—of all the weaknesses of our statehood. Jews supposedly whittled away and brought about the degeneration of allegedly healthy Polish morality. Jews hostile to Poland concentrated industry and trade in their hands; Jews came to control all capital; Jews set the tone in art and literature; Jews held the largest number of management positions; and Jews, finally, were responsible for the allegedly anti-state and revolutionary communist handiwork. One cannot deny the fact—and there is no reason to hide it—that Jews indeed played a significant role in our economic and cultural life in the interwar period. This, however, is not what determines the tone and symptoms of Polish anti-Semitism. It is characteristic for our anti-Semitism to separate Jews from the body politic as a whole, and treat them as a destructive and dangerous element, while simultaneously separating individual facts from the totality of ongoing social, economic, and moral problems.

An enormously large percentage of Poles—succumbing blindly to anti-Semitic propaganda that skillfully takes advantage of aversion against Jews that is traditional here—hardly realized that Jewish capitalism, in both its structure and methods of action and struggle, was no different from Polish capitalism. Most Poles saw the banker, the industrialist, and the factory

THE PROBLEM OF POLISH ANTI-SEMITISM

owner with a Jewish background as dangerous and menacing. Meanwhile, if the same capitalist was a Pole, the general public perceived him as neither menacing nor socially destructive. The most obvious social fact—namely, that analogous social conditions give rise to human types with many similar psychological predispositions, regardless of their racial or national identity—slipped unnoticed among anti-Semitic aggravations and irascibilities. Yet above all local differences, which should not be underestimated, there exists a strong class bond that erases boundaries between nations and races and creates similarities across social groups throughout the world—the gentry, clerks, bankers, rentiers, peasants, and workers.

Must we enumerate all the faults and vices ascribed to Jews by Polish anti-Semitism? From time to time these included rightful accusations; but there were also ones that were superficial or outright false and unfair. Many traits considered by Poles to be specifically Jewish turned out to be completely unimportant when these Jews emigrated from Poland and took up new duties in the Palestinian land. We know that a new generation of physically and morally healthy Jews grew up there—a generation of people who worked the land with enthusiasm, a generation of excellent sportsmen with bold and captivating features, hardly resembling the sickly children from poor basement tenements of the Jewish proletariat or the arrogant bon-vivants of the Jewish plutocracy—sons of bankers and industrialists who exchanged lavish amounts of gold for landed estates, and who married their daughters off to impoverished Polish aristocrats. Unfortunately, people in Poland tended to turn a blind eye to this.

Most of the Jewry's glaring vices that arise from class relations—cynicism, arrogance, impudence, the tendency to exploit, or materialism—were separated from their natural socio-economic basis here, and judged solely in national categories; and these are always erroneous and unreliable when seen as allegedly belonging to some undefined, eternal, and irrational spirit of the nation or race, a spirit that stands beside or above history. By disparaging the Jewish pariah with mockery and jokes we consolidated and strengthened within ourselves an anti-humanist attitude toward Jews, an attitude not yet dangerous when it relied only on the shallowness of minds and the parochialism of hearts, but inhuman when there was a need to respond to truly significant and urgent human problems. Meanwhile, we burdened all those Jews who held any significant positions—and who surpassed us with energy, dexterity, abilities, diligence, and professionalism that far outstripped our dilettantism—with a particular collective responsibility, with that "spirit of the nation," which exists beyond time and history, and which is mystically associated with the fate of the Jewish people. We claimed that Jews were the enemies of Polishness, and, giving up the search for causes of evil among other strictly historical reasons, we created for ourselves a false image of a dark and hostile power.

Many Poles most likely think that their anti-Semitism is based on rational claims, that it is logically derived from reality. How wrong they are! Polish anti-Semitism is permeated by irrationalism. It makes false and anti-historical claims, and it supports and expands them only by recourse to emotion: fits of passion, prejudice, and uncontrolled reflexes.

V

Today's realities confirm precisely this and no other assessment. It would seem that if a nation of 20-some million people wants to avoid a glaring denunciation of common sense, it cannot feed on rumors about Jewish danger when out of 3 million Polish Jews barely 100,000 survived. But it turns out that Poles, having imbibed the irrational notion of a "Jewish spirit," are unwilling to recognize the puzzling significance of numbers. Once again, notions like the idea that all important job positions in Poland have been taken over by Jews, are circulating among us, they are passed along with hushed voices, entangled with falsehoods and inaccuracies, and fueled by ill will. Who among well-known people in today's Poland has not been labeled "Jewish" in one context or another! Jews are still accused of pushing their way to get high-ranking positions. Pushing their way? When they have the right qualifications and their work serves Poland? Are they not Polish citizens? Do Poles, who went through so much themselves, think that the few surviving Jews do not have a right to a full, normal life? At a time when we talk so much about democracy, Jews should vegetate shamefully in hiding somewhere? On the contrary, do we not owe respect to Jews who found enough fortitude, strength, and will to take up work despite such horrible experiences, despite so many years of disgrace and suffering? What measure, finally, are we to apply to assess people's worth? Should it not be, among other things, their resilience in the face of violations, cruelty, and disdain? What right do we have to speak about our own suffering and losses when we do not understand, do not wish to understand, and prefer not to understand another nation's equally unjust suffering and losses, and we choose to cover these with shameful silence? Suffering does not justify one in the eyes of future generations. History passes over suffering that leads to depravity and stunted development; it passes over such suffering with a cruelty well-deserved by malice and moral blindness. Only those wounds become significant which serve the cause of rebirth as they close and heal.

Indeed, Polish citizens of Jewish descent hold quite a few notable positions in today's Poland. This was caused by several factors. Although Jewish intelligentsia suffered huge losses during the occupation, when one looks at percentages, their losses were lower than those suffered by the proletariat. Thanks to financial reserves and a more extensive network of connections with Poles, Jewish intellectuals had greater chances of surviving than thousands of the Jewish poor. In addition, a significant number of Jewish intellectuals found themselves in the eastern territories in September 1939. They later survived by hiding in the depths of Russia. Furthermore, Jewish intellectuals were generally much more leftist than their Polish counterparts before the war. In today's Poland, most of them are not neophytes. They do not have to proselytize to testify to their convictions and social radicalism.

On the other hand, today, just as before the war, there are Jews who hold certain posts, and who, like many Poles, cannot give proof of having adequate moral and professional qualifications. Jews who have not learned anything from the war harm both Jewish and Polish aspirations. And if one has the right to revile the depravity of Poles here, in this land, which is starting the reconstruction process in the midst of daunting difficulties, one must also have the same ruthless right with respect to those Jews who transgress against social solidarity. Unfortunately, all too often the struggle against anti-Semitism in Poland is driven by a false sense of shame felt toward Jews, and people prefer to pass over facts that could put certain Jewish intellectuals in unfavorable light. Perhaps this attitude comes from noble motivations, but it disregards the psychological state of Polish society, and more often than not, it has dreadful consequences. Last year in April, for example, two posters should never have been put up side by side on the walls amidst Warsaw's ruins: the first read: *Long live the heroic defenders of the Ghetto* while the second declared *Shame on the Home Army fascist lackeys*.[7] Such messages, and various similar facts, are a crime against both Poles and Jews. True struggle against anti-Semitism grants equal rights to Poles and Jews, but it imposes similar duties on both groups. True struggle puts an equal sign between Jews and Poles, but it recognizes that this principle must have far-reaching consequences, based solely on truth and justice. Jews should understand that Majdanek and Treblinka in no way redeem those Jewish individuals whose actions deserve condemnation. This is not just a Jewish issue—it is something that concerns our shared homeland and state. And Poles must once again understand that the flaws or crimes of Jewish individuals cannot incriminate Jews in general, nor can they serve as testimony to some imagined "Jewish spirit." Let us speak the truth to each other, and let us demand the right to speak the truth—right now, this is more important than bringing up martyrdom and sacrifices, and it is certainly much more significant than affirming current aggravations by evoking bygone years.

If the Polish nation wished to shake off its traditional habits of anti-Semitic thinking and perception, if it saw the true historical dimensions of the Jewish problem in Poland, and soberly assessed everything this problem encompassed in the past and presently, the problem would cease to exist here.[8] It would die out naturally because the Jewish community is not numerous enough to be a partner, and the current configuration of class relations could not possibly pull surviving Jews into a socio-economic order like the one that had existed before September 1939. Today, the Jewish problem has only one dimension—a moral one. I mentioned above that "the scope and importance of the problem of Polish anti-Semitism extends beyond the problem of how Poles relate to Jews" because "it is an aspect of human relations in general, an aspect of how we relate to human values." That is precisely how it is.

It would be unjustly hurtful to accuse the Polish nation of having no respect for freedom and justice. These lofty concepts—which are eternally alive, and which, despite all evil, keep offering hope to humanity—have always evoked, and continue to evoke, ardent responses in Polish hearts. But in the context of Jewish issues, the idealism cultivated on Polish soil—an idealism that makes spectacular, though sometimes unnecessary death easier than living just a single day sensibly and honestly, an idealism that evokes the noblest human voices and uses them to absolve laziness and carelessness—relegates the concepts of freedom and justice into a realm far too high above everyday reality. Polish ideals very often lack strong roots. They grow from misty longings and heroic, lofty dreams rather than real foundations. While we love and worship justice and freedom, we rarely give them the affirmation they deserve in our daily lives. What's more, we do not always realize that we thoughtlessly tread on and demean the very concepts that we have put up on our banners.

Over the course of the past six years, we have witnessed a degradation of man that has no precedent in history. Even without turning back to look, we can see the cemeteries that hide our loved ones in their depths, we see the empty and motionless death camps, the charred remains and ruins where smoke still rose yesterday, and where blood is not yet dry. During these dark years, we had to live through experiences that have no parallel among Europe's earlier generations. We came to know the limits of human criminality and suffering beyond words.

The initial tallies of wartime losses are already available. Foreign sources provide the following numbers: 14 million killed, 5 million murdered, three million killed in bombardments, 11 million murdered in camps. Altogether— 33 million. And 30 million disabled veterans.

These numbers are certainly not exact. Even if they were exact, they are, unfortunately, not final. Though the war is over, there are enough conflicts around the world to ensure that the year-long peace still comes at the price of many human lives. To the 33 million dead, we will have to add many thousands of those who became victims of fratricidal murders when peace was instituted. Polish, Greek, and Spanish lands know all too much about this bitter toll.

These numbers are far too important and frightening to blot them out from memory. I do not think there is a single honest man anywhere in the world today, who, so long as he lives, could bracket or cross out the war years and their toll. The war concerned the fate of humanity and the world, but the peace that followed will be even more powerfully and permanently decisive for human history. We have been spared by fate. Who, if not we, is to give meaning to the thirty-three million dead and murdered? Who, if not we, has the power to ensure that their death was not in vain?

These questions, which demand answers and actions more urgently than all other questions of our time, should also confront anti-Semitism. I will not say "without love," for this word has suffered too many defeats, and perhaps it points to something that humanity cannot reach. But I will say this: in light of the recent years, a nation does not have a right to be esteemed if it remains without respect for humanity, without serious reflection about man, and without solidarity with truths for which millions gave their lives.

Editors' Notes

1. "For Your Freedom and Ours" was a phrase used by nineteenth-century Polish insurrectionaries who fought in various revolutionary movements throughout Europe, especially during the "Spring of Nations" in 1848.

2. The National Armed Forces and the Home Army are discussed in "Poles and Jews during the Holocaust" in the Introduction.
3. "The following Easter" refers to the Uprising in the Warsaw Ghetto in April 1943.
4. Rappaport was a typical last name among Polish Jews.
5. Stanisław Wyspiański (1869–1907) was an influential playwright and painter. His 1901 play *Wesele* (*The Wedding*) is still among the most frequently staged plays in Polish theater. It explores the divisions and inertia that plagued Polish society during the final years of the partitions period, and ends with a scene where Poles forfeit a chance to win national independence. In this scene, the wedding guests move slowly, spellbound in a lethargic dance, while the Strawman, the play's central symbolic figure, plays his fiddle and keeps them imprisoned in their stupor.
6. Srul is the Yiddish nickname for the name Yisrael.
7. "Last year in April" refers to April 1945, the second anniversary of the Warsaw Ghetto Uprising. The poster "Shame on the Home Army fascist lackeys" was a piece of communist propaganda, which unfairly equated the Home Army with fascism, despite the fact that the Home Army was the main Polish underground military group that fought against Hitler. Here Andrzejewski protests against the injustice of praising Jewish fighters while simultaneously denigrating Polish fighters.
8. This is the only paragraph in this essay in which Andrzejewski uses the phrase "problem żydowski," which is, accordingly, rendered here as "the Jewish problem." For more about the functioning of this phrase in Polish anti-Semitism, and in Polish debates about anti-Semitism, please see the final part of the Introduction.

9

With Kielce in the Background

STANISŁAW OSSOWSKI

Editors' Introduction

Stanisław Ossowski (1897–1963) was a sociologist and cultural theorist. Born in the town of Lipno in central Poland, which was under Russian rule until 1918, he studied philosophy at the University of Warsaw, fought in the Polish-Bolshevik War of 1920, and then studied again in Paris and Rome. In the interwar period, he affiliated himself with leftist anti-fascist circles, and in 1935 he went to study with the anthropologist Bronisław Malinowski at the London School of Economics. He fought in the Polish Army in 1939 and spent the Second World War in Lviv and Warsaw, where he taught underground classes and became an active participant in the Council to Aid Jews (Żegota). After the war, he taught sociology in Łódź and Warsaw, but in 1951 the communist government banned him from teaching for his anti-Stalinist views. Ossowski regained his post in 1957, in the aftermath of de-Stalinization and changes in the Communist Party (PZPR) leadership in October of 1956; he enjoyed great respect among both students and intellectuals.

In his research, Ossowski was most interested in the mechanisms of social transformations, racism, the relationship between class and social consciousness, and various models of social order. In his writings, he maintained a left-leaning perspective and opposed racist ideologies and all forms of nationalism. His most important books include *Więź społeczna i dziedzictwo krwi* (*Social Bonds and the Heritage of Blood*, 1939), and *Struktura klasowa w społecznej świadomości* (*Class Structure in the Social Consciousness*, 1957; available in English, Routledge, 2013).

The essay reproduced here was originally published in the progressive cultural weekly *Kuźnica* (*The Forge*), in Łódź, on September 30, 1946; it is Ossowski's reaction to the Kielce Pogrom that took place on July 4, 1946. Before the war, the town of Kielce was home to approximately 24,000 Jews, who accounted for about a third of its population. Nearly all of them perished in the Holocaust, and by 1946 around 200 survivors returned to live in Kielce. On July 1, a nine-year-old Gentile, Henryk Błaszczyk, went missing for two days. A blood libel rumor spread, and the Jewish Committee on Planty Street was accused of kidnapping the boy and confining him in the basement (the building, it later turned out, had no basement, but the rumor took on a life of its own). On July 4, local police went to the Jewish Committee's building to investigate, and the proliferating rumors about ritual murder brought hundreds of Poles, including a large group of workers from the Ludwików steel mill, to the site. The police entered the building and started beating and shooting at the tenants, and then dragged them out into the street. Those fleeing were attacked by the angry mob outside. The massacre went on for several hours before the military was finally able to restrain the crowd. Meanwhile, brutal attacks were perpetrated against Jews in various other locations in and around Kielce.

The total number of victims was never fully established, but at least forty-two Jews were killed and at least forty others were injured just at the main site of the Pogrom. A few dozen perpetrators (including both police and civilians) were arrested in the days that followed, and a hasty judicial investigation started on July 9. Nine of the defendants were found guilty and executed on July 12, and three others received long prison sentences. The remaining defendants were either cleared of all charges or received brief prison terms. The communist government accused the anticommunist military underground of provoking the Pogrom, though there was no evidence to suggest that this was the case. The opposition Polish Peasants' Party (PSL) suspected that both police and some security service officers were responsible for the Pogrom and called for the creation of a special investigation committee. The government, however, refused to comply.

On Sunday, July 7, priests throughout the Kielce diocese read an episcopal letter that called the Pogrom "sad" and "a misfortune" but did not use the words "Jews," "anti-Semitism," or "blood libel." It took the Częstochowa bishop, Teodor Kubina, to condemn the Pogrom in unambiguous terms and state that belief in Jewish ritual murder was an expression of "criminal fanaticism and unjustified ignorance." The Kielce Pogrom was not an isolated anti-Jewish incident in the years immediately after the war. It took place in the wider context of violence and prejudice, which were often driven by the canard of "Judeo-Bolshevism"—the belief that Jews were secretly acting on behalf of the Soviet Union to undermine Poland's independence. In this context, the Kielce massacre convinced the few returning Polish Jews that Poland was not a safe place to live and contributed to the large postwar exodus of Shoah survivors from Poland.[1]

The Interwar World

It is relatively easy to identify the economic and political bases of prewar anti-Semitism in Poland. The coexistence of two unassimilated ethnic groups with different class and professional structures easily breeds antagonism, especially when professions successfully practiced by the ethnic minority become the object of aspirations of the group whose members see themselves as autochthons and the country's hosts; or when the ethnic minority has a relatively strong presence among the country's economic elites.

Polish-Ukrainian antagonism was exacerbated by the distinct class and professional structure of the Polish minority in the eastern borderlands. Poles were not just people with a different religion and language. Poles were masters. A squire was a typical Polish figure. And wealthy merchants and big-bellied bankers were seen as typical Jewish figures, though when it came to Jews, the key economic conflicts actually played out in petty bourgeois spheres. In any event, the economic background of conflicts was very different in these two cases.

The Ukrainian population felt its disadvantages in relation to Polish landlords and administrative officials; but Ukrainian villages, with their relatively developed local cooperative organizations, had no economic reasons for envying Polish villages, if we disregard the military borderland settlements. In contrast, anti-Semitism of Polish petty bourgeoisie fed on the greater (prewar) sophistication of its Jewish counterpart—religious and racial prejudice added an electrifying flourish to economic motivations.

The political basis of anti-Semitism was also not unique to Poland. In nearly every country where there is even a small percentage of Jews, nationalism and reactionary or anti-humanitarian tendencies typically rely on anti-Semitism for support. At times, anti-Semitism was used intentionally as a powerful tool for unifying nationalist groups, in line with the notion that shared hate unifies more readily than shared affection. Here and there, anti-Semitism functioned as a stopgap against waves of revolutionary feeling, and, above all, supplied easy arguments in various struggles against hostile ideological currents: one could always make the accusation that these currents were Jewish handiwork, or that they served Jewish causes, and a few specific names of activists with Jewish backgrounds could always be conjured up as empirical proof.

People who stayed in Nazi Germany for an extended period of time and returned to Poland in the final years before the war said that anti-Semitism among the Polish population was harsher and more prevalent than in

Germany—despite all the propaganda of the government and the party there. But this fact, too, can be explained without appealing to any unique qualities of Polish national character or Polish mentality. The percentage of Jews in Poland was ten times greater than in Germany or France, and a few times greater than in Czechoslovakia; and since the large Jewish population in Poland was also not as culturally assimilated—differences included not only religion but also language, lifestyle, and even dress—the perceived distance was greater, and encounters with Jews as a foreign group were much more frequent than in other countries of Central and Western Europe.

The unusually large Jewish small-town petty bourgeoisie, as competition for its Polish counterpart, had no equivalent in these other countries. And when we also take into account Polish petty-bourgeoisie's intellectual level and their religious practices, then—even disregarding certain historical circumstances, such as the mandatory immigration of Russian Jews to the Polish Kingdom before the First World War—we will have rich material indeed for explaining the causes of prewar anti-Semitism in Poland.

And when it comes to the frighteningly barbaric manifestations of anti-Semitism that took place at Polish universities in 1937 and 1938—barbaric in the context of the prewar era and the academic milieu—domestic causes were augmented by foreign influences: there was the influence of Nazi culture, and allegedly some influence of Nazi funding as well.

A Thought Experiment

I do not, of course, claim that these cursory remarks constitute an analysis of a phenomenon as complex as anti-Semitism. I only want to point out that someone familiar with the demographic, economic, and political conditions that existed in Poland could deduce the existence of prewar Polish anti-Semitism.

But those conditions changed radically during the war. What if we tried to deduce something about postwar Polish-Jewish relations? Let us imagine that in 1939 we were told about both the unfathomable destruction of the Jewish population that would take place in Poland between 1940 and 1944, and the political and economic changes in Poland and Europe immediately after the war. Let us imagine we were asked to start with these premises and make inferences about relations between the Polish population and remnants of the Jewish community in 1945 and 1946.

Basic human empathy for the unparalleled suffering of the dying multitudes, horror at the elaborate death camps, hatred for a common enemy and blood spilled together in various situations, the shock of liberation, reactions against the ideology of the defeated occupier, a sense of justice which demands that some kind of restitution be made to the survivors (even if only in the form of human kindness) and finally, the sudden reduction of the size of the Jewish population and disappearance of the economic foundations of prewar anti-Semitism—we would probably find these arguments sufficient to infer that anti-Semitism would be impossible in postwar Poland as a social phenomenon.

But someone more far-sighted, more cynical, or more willful, someone who had access to better or perhaps just different historical knowledge, might have reminded us even back then that compassion is not the only reaction to the misfortunes of others, that people whom the gods have singled out for annihilation easily become loathsome to others and tend to be eliminated from human affairs, that the inhabitants of Fiji murder shipwreck survivors, and that men condemned Oedipus because he was subjected to an undeserved curse. Perhaps this far-sighted man might point out that if someone's calamity benefits someone else, the beneficiary often feels the need to convince himself and others that the calamity was morally justified. And owners of shops that had belonged to Jews, or those who had harassed their Jewish competitors, would find themselves in precisely such a situation. Perhaps he would predict that the skillful policies of the occupiers, their division of the conquered population into higher and lower strata, into more and less persecuted and endangered strata—together with appeals to human egoism, the egotistical "glad it wasn't me"—would not allow for attitudes of solidarity to emerge, and, by imposing a caste system, these policies would eventually awaken tendencies characteristic of caste systems. And perhaps, pointing to a series of historical examples, he would voice doubts as to whether reactions against the defeated Nazi ideology would root out the less perceptible influences of the Nazi spirit, influences which seeped in over the course of a few years, and which, in any event, relied on habituation and managed to stop certain slogans from offending human sensibilities.

One would probably have to be somewhat cynical to make such predictions in 1939. But during the final years of the war predictions like these began troubling people who were not cynical in the least. Reality unfolded precisely along these lines.

Another political motivation for anti-Semitism emerged after the war. The stubbornness of German suggestions that identified Jews with Bolshevism (and which already had a longer tradition in Poland), the conviction that Jews support government policies because they are afraid of anti-Semitism, that they take over various management positions that allow them to directly influence these policies, and finally, the old custom of identifying all radical and progressive actions as Jewish handiwork, caused anti-Semitism to become associated with an oppositional stance directed against the government and the alliance with the Soviet Union.

A far-sighted man could thus have predicted even postwar anti-Semitism. But he would have to have been a cynic of the highest order, or a psychopathic misanthrope, to predict that—in liberated Poland—there would be a tendency to continue the Nazi system of murder, murder which is not a form of barbarian combat because its victims include men, infants, and frail elderly women.

The Kielce Experience

Kielce was not the only place where this terrible legacy became manifest. Before then, something like a few hundred Jews rescued from the Germans were killed in liberated Poland only because—like shipwreck survivors in Fiji—they escaped universal annihilation.

But Kielce events must have been an even greater shock for those who were normal in the prewar sense of the word, and especially those who undertook the conscious effort of building a new Poland. Kielce must have nonetheless been something new for them. Previous crimes could have been blamed on the degeneration of partisan fighters whose very way of life put them outside society, or on the equally socially isolated urban vagrants whose presence during the war cannot be surprising. In certain other cases, the circumstances of the crime or the assassination were unclear; they could be interpreted in one way or another, or information about what happened could have aroused various types of doubts.

What took place in Kielce, however, was neither a partisan attack nor a crime surreptitiously committed by vagrants. The action lasted almost six hours—six hours in the city with a population of tens of thousands of people—excitement seized broad segments of the population, and pogrom enthusiasm spilled out beyond city limits. The city's inhabitants were passive participants in the Kielce crime.

The events that played out in Kielce must direct our attention to three categories of facts:

The existence of people who—as we can surmise—are willing to intentionally and treacherously attempt inciting criminal actions that follow someone's program.

The ease of finding those ready to execute such plans, or, to put it differently, the existence of a relatively large number of people habituated to blood and murder, and susceptible to this type of criminal agitation.

Weak reactions of various social groups; indifference or ambivalence based on aversion toward Jews. People condemn the crime out of a sense of duty but they do not actively try to oppose it. This lack of distress in the face of crime is largely an effect of wartime practice: murdering Jews ceased to be extraordinary. Why should these people be distressed by the death of forty Jews if they got used to the idea that Hitler was killing Jews by the millions?

Besides showing barbarity on the one hand, and indifference on the other, the Kielce events also demonstrated widespread susceptibility to the most fanciful and unbelievable rumors. The agitation of the crowd, at least in part, was not caused directly by either racist propaganda or political motives; according to the reports, medieval beliefs about ritual murder actually played a part in these events. This frightening gullibility was soon confirmed by attempts to provoke anti-Semitic incidents in Częstochowa and Kłodzko. It turns out that there are still places in Poland today where persecution of Jews can be motivated by the belief that they murdered Jesus Christ, that they want to stab Christian children to death in order to have blood for making matzos, and that they want to control the world and transform Christians into their servants.

The Bequest of Nessus

The events in Kielce caused waves of protest in various social circles—among both organized workers and intellectuals. As voices of indignation and dismay, assembly resolutions and proclamations published in the press are an understandable reaction—the simplest collective reaction under the circumstances. The character of the individual protests, however, is peculiar: signatures condemning a crime were collected. Condemnation of a crime by moral or intellectual elites can be a troubling sign of the times. Some cultural workers therefore signed these proclamations with a sense of embarrassment: how can one sign a protest against a crime? A protest against psychosis? As if these were phenomena open to argument, as if they were questions where a written protest could be an adequate answer.

But throwing lofty condemnations around is not the most important thing. We know that neither these proclamations nor the gallows erected by judiciary authorities for the captured perpetrators will remove the malevolence; we realize that it is necessary to undertake much deeper educational work in various arenas.

Today, I will not consider the difficult question of "re-educating" society. I do want to, however, point to certain issues concerning the atmosphere in which this re-education is to take place, an atmosphere which is largely the responsibility of none other than the intellectuals.

According to a Greek myth, the mortally wounded centaur Nessus poisoned Heracles, his vanquisher, by a venomous transfer of blood into Heracles' shirt. After periods of great struggle, it is good to remind the victors of this myth and help them stay vigilant in their self-understanding, especially in cases when there was a confrontation of two ideologies, two worldviews, two conceptions of social life.

The situation that emerges after great political, economic, or cultural upheavals can be treated as a synthesis, or merely as unharmonious coexistence, of two processes: reaction against and inheritance of what came before. Opposition and bequest—such is the complex result of victory. Opposition is conspicuous because it organizes the victorious collectivity's symbolism and its entire vocabulary. The legacy of what came before is less perceptible, and one sometimes has to exert significant effort to detect how vibrantly this legacy pulses in the minds of those who disavow it.

And today it seems to me that in anti-fascist, democratic Europe, far from the recesses of crime and hidden currents of fascism, fumes from Nessus's brown shirt still hang in the air; their subtler traces can be found in realms uncontaminated by any contact with his tribe.

National Slogans

A few days before the Kielce events, the monthly *Myśl Współczesna* (*Contemporary Thought*) published E. St. Rappaport's article entitled "Polska jako państwo jednonarodowe" (Poland as an Ethnic State). Already in his opening remarks, the author expresses the opinion that "from now on, from the very moment of establishing international and inter-state relations after the Second World War, the concepts 'Pole' and 'Polish citizen' must—both for us inside the country and for foreigners outside—become indisputable synonyms when applied to Poles permanently residing in Poland." The author posits that "the new postwar Polish Constitution" will give "final form and a legally precise framework to this fundamental image of the Polish state's ethnic character." "For now,"—the author continues—"we have to ensure that all possible means are used to bring about the reality of having a single nation within the Polish state."[a]

Although the text later describes these means in detail, when I read these passages almost immediately after announcements about Kielce, they sounded macabre. I am not blaming the author for this. A coincidental turn of events gave an unexpected edge to his awkward, or perhaps somewhat rashly formulated, phrases. But was it necessary to wait for the events in Kielce to perceive the influence of recent years in this call for the use of all means necessary to transform Poland into an ethnic state as quickly as possible? No one questions the claim that a state whose population is ethnically uniform has, ceteris paribus (all other things being equal), far fewer problems than one with a nationally mixed population. But fierce propaganda that makes a single nation into a dominant principle of domestic policy threatens certain values within national culture—values whose loss cannot be compensated for by the realization of the single-nation principle.

I chose Mr. Rappaport's article because it appeared in *Myśl Współczesna* (*Contemporary Thought*), a serious representative organ of the progressive camp in Poland. But this article is not an isolated case. When it comes to national relations, there is greater harmony in our press than one might suppose—from the left all the way to the right. By praising the idea of an ethnic state, we learn to look at man through the prism of national identity, and grasp all human relations in us-versus-them categories. Numerous essays, declarations, and speeches given at various public celebrations create a climate favoring old nationalism, a climate with weakening resistance against the tendencies that enabled the Kielce Pogrom.

To appreciate the danger, one has to realize that such essays and speeches are often received enthusiastically, and their educational reach is frequently much greater than their authors might wish. This is because for five years the differentiation between Jews and non-Jews was decisive in matters of life

---

[a] *Myśl Współczesna* (*Contemporary Thought*), July 2, 1946, 202.

and death; classifications like German, Ukrainian, Goral, or Pole determined people's degree of safety and the size of their food rations.[2] Hierarchically arranged lists of nationalities have not ceased to have all kinds of biological and social consequences, only the hierarchy has been reversed. Processes associated with incorporating the western territories into Poland occupy an important place in today's reality.[3] This whole realm of images—regardless of nationalist propaganda—exponentially increases people's susceptibility to view diverse social phenomena in national categories. The wartime émigrés who returned to Poland a few months ago say that in some dining halls run by the State Repatriation Office, there were separate lines for Poles and Jews.

In examining the westward shift of the territory of the Polish state we should go beyond thinking only about Poland's future security and domestic affairs. This shift could play a momentous role in the evolution of Central Europe's social life; it could bring about a turn in the great historical processes in these territories. Germany's loss of its eastern provinces, where Prussian power had been consolidated, will perhaps close the period of Prussian domination in German life, and thereby facilitate Germany's internal transformation. In Poland, as some rightly suppose, territorial changes—combined with the loss of old Polish cultural centers in the east—will facilitate deep social transformations and open new possibilities for coexisting with neighbors; these changes will close the great chapter of history when life in Poland was dominated by the gentry.

Taking into account the great significance of these transformations but retaining awareness of the difficulties involved in building a new political system and dangers that threaten young statehood, we have to recognize that arguments in support of the compulsory expulsion of Germans are correct, without, however, giving in to nationalist propaganda. Treating this compulsory process as a massive surgical procedure from which we will have to heal as quickly as we can, we have to protest against equating temporary policing needs with cultural norms.

The so-called higher realms of culture have also not proven to be immune to German models. At the end of last year, for example, Professor Suchodolski's brochure, dedicated to the analysis of the German soul in light of German philosophy, received an enthusiastic review in the Bydgoszcz-based cultural monthly *Arkona*.[b] By claiming that professor Suchodolski

[b] *Arkona*, 1945, nos. 1–2.

undermined the value of German philosophy "in an unusually apposite and effective manner," the author of the review expressed the hope that this work will be followed by two subsequent parts of the trilogy, where German music and German poetry will be trounced in a similar way. This currently common attitude toward the entire culture of a defeated nation is rather familiar to us from German wartime periodicals and speeches, which included frequent ultimate judgments about the souls and cultures of other races and nations.

In the process of social transformation, the fatherland ceased to be a class commodity. Patriotism and the national tradition ceased to be a class privilege. We now appreciate the significance of these values for the masses of workers and peasants. But we have to be careful to ensure that they do not fall prey to degeneration. Patriotism in the Polish People's Republic could easily evoke old traditions of the brotherhood of nations. But it could just as well degenerate into democratized nationalism, which, though deprived of a class basis, will be no less dangerous for the development of culture and human relations than prewar bourgeois nationalism. It seems to me that today's economic and political conditions invite both possibilities. The role and responsibility of the intellectuals is therefore that much greater.

The Criteria of Power

When I spoke about a climate in which immunity against the Kielce virus is declining, I was thinking about something more than just postwar nationalism. I was also thinking about the general attitude toward humanity, regardless of national categories.

Humanitarianism, disregarded by the Polish government during the Bereza Kartuska period,[4] and despised and suppressed by the Germans, has not been fully rehabilitated after the war. It often seems that the worship of "the strong"—people indifferent to the blood and suffering of others—is still an aspect of the spirit of our time. German models are used in staging public executions in front of thousands of spectators; these are exploited by the popular press, while the organizers are not concerned, it seems, whether such spectacles might give rise to inclinations that could find expression in pogroms.

Public executions, and the staged execution of the Stutthof criminals in particular,[5] were attended by isolated voices of criticism, and they were recently condemned by the Minister of Justice.[c] It is significant, however, that while opposing the transformation of executions into public spectacles, one of our eminent journalists seems to be concerned he might be accused of being too soft-hearted or of wishing to weaken the feeling of revenge among the masses: "We are not concerned," he explains, "and we should not be concerned about the criminals' experiences in the final moments before their death (. . .). Hatred for the Germans is an important social value. The striving to punish a crime is an important moral value." Elsewhere, this writer expresses an aversion to inquiring into what motivates human actions, but he nonetheless juxtaposes the need for cruelty "which we must condemn" against the feelings of revenge, which, as he says, "we must respect."[d]

This is not an isolated case. In progressive periodicals, which seek to forge a way forward for Poland, we find articles which, in the name of sober thinking, express disdain for "humanitarian softies," or which, in their struggle against evil, express concern about people's psychological attitudes while also supporting the execution of criminals. Perhaps some of these statements result from misunderstandings, and from illusions about what constitutes weakness and strength. At the turn of the century, a previous generation succumbed to Nietzschean illusions of the power of the "overman." If we judge strength only by external toughness, we might privilege mollusks over vertebrates, since the body of a creature endowed with a spine cannot measure up to the hard shell that hides an oyster.

Motives for condemning the Pogrom have also been varied. I met one person who was genuinely saddened by the Kielce crimes: "We shouldn't do these kinds of things"—she said fervently—"it creates the wrong impression abroad." This woman, with her political reasoning, was certainly no "humanitarian softie."

The Scope of Responsibility

The richness of Poland's cultural life and the flamboyance and diversity of its manifestations after terrible wartime losses arouse admiration and give profound encouragement. But it would be worthwhile to pay closer

[c] See Ewa Szelburg-Zarembina: "Nie jesteśmy narodem morderców" (We Are Not a Nation of Murderers), *Kuźnica*, no. 47; St. Śreniowski: "Trzeba się na coś zdecydować" (A Decision Must Be Made), Ibid.; J. Kott: "Kropka nad i" (Dot the i), *Przekrój*, no. 67.
[d] J. Kott in the aforementioned article.

attention to the traces of the occupation in people's emotional dispositions and ways of thinking.

Polish society's attitude toward Jews suggests that the liberation was not a sufficient shock, that evidently a longer process of purification is needed. In the realm of cultural life, traces of a foreign inheritance are still striking. One would wish for a more radical change in attitudes toward humanity and human dignity.

The protests against the Kielce crimes that were signed by intellectuals should be binding in some way. They should not be a substitute for more difficult forms of action. Those who want to build a new Poland, who want to build socialism as the "kingdom of freedom," must attend to the atmosphere which shapes the psyche; they must carefully select means appropriate for long-term action. We should recognize that there are no isolated phenomena in social life—and this greatly extends the scope of our responsibility.

Editors' Notes

1. For more about the Kielce Pogrom see Jan T. Gross *Fear: Anti-Semitism in Poland after Auschwitz: An Essay in Historical Interpretation* (Random House, 2006); and *Kielce, July 4, 1946: Background, Context and Events* (Polish Educational Foundation in North America, 1996). See also Adam Michnik, "The Kielce Pogrom: Two Examinations of Conscience," in *In Search of Lost Meaning: The New Eastern Europe* (UCLA Press, 2011), 173–203.

2. A Goral is a person from the Polish mountain region. During the Nazi period, there was a category of people called Goralenfolk, collaborators who received special privileges in exchange for informing on their neighbors; they were told they were better than the surrounding Slavic population.

3. For the historical context of the moving of Polish borders after the war, please see "Anti-Semitism in the Polish People's Republic" in the Introduction.

4. This refers to the period between 1934 and 1939, when a detention camp for political opponents of the Sanacja regime was established in the town of Bereza Kartuska in northeastern Poland (today's Belarus). Inmates were imprisoned in the Bereza Kartuska facility, often described as a harsh concentration camp, without due process; they included Communists, far-right activists, Ukrainian nationalists, and others whom the government designated as a threat.

5. The Nazi Stutthof concentration camp was located near Gdańsk; between 1939 and 1945, around 110,000 people were imprisoned there, and 65,000 of them died. It became a site of systematic extermination of Jews in July 1944. The Nazi officials who had been in charge of Stutthof were put on trial in Gdańsk in April 1946, and eleven of the fifteen defendants were sentenced to death. The public and highly publicized execution attracted over 200,000 spectators.

IO

Our Part (A Pessimist's Voice)

WITOLD KULA

Editors' Introduction

Witold Kula (1916–1988) was a historian specializing in Polish socio-economic history and historical methodology. Born in Warsaw, he studied history and economics there. During the war, he joined the Home Army, the main Polish underground military organization, and he taught history seminars to fellow resisters in Warsaw. After the war, he was a professor in Łódź and later Warsaw, where he also joined the Polish Academy of Sciences. He introduced the French Annales School of historical methodology—which stresses long-term social influences rather than political or diplomatic history—to Poland and lectured throughout Europe. His most important books include *Teoria ekonomiczna ustroju feudalnego: próba modelu* (1962; *An Economic Theory of the Feudal System: Towards a Model of the Polish Economy 1500–1800*, Verso, 1987), *Problemy i metody historii gospodarczej* (1963; *The Problems and Methods of Economic History*, Ashgate 2001), and *Miary i ludzie* (1970; *Measures and Men*, Princeton University Press, 1986). His book *Rozważania o historii* (*Reflections about History*, 1958) includes one of his most important essays, "Gusła" (Sorcery), in which he analyzes the mechanisms of Stalinism.

The essay reproduced here was written in the immediate aftermath of the Kielce Pogrom, which took place on July 4, 1946.[1] Kula wrote it for the leftist weekly *Kuźnica* (*The Forge*), but it was not published during his lifetime. It first appeared in print in 2002, in English translation, in *Gal-Ed*, the journal of the Tel-Aviv-based Institute for the History of Polish Jewry and Israel-Poland Relations, with an introduction by Marcin Kula.[2] The Polish text was originally published in Marcin Kula's 2004 book *Uparta sprawa. Żydowska? Polska? Ludzka? (An Intractable Issue: Jewish? Polish? Human?)*. We offer a new English translation here.

A month has already passed since the Kielce incidents. There was a trial, and sentences were meted out to a few hapless individuals who, unlike several thousand others in the crowd, were unlucky enough to fall into the hands of security officials who woke up much too late. Liable security apparatus leaders were arrested, and progressive circles received this news with relief. A wave of more or less originally formulated protests against the Kielce episode rumbled through the press, and voices opposing the sentences given at the trial have now died down in factories, offices, trolleys, trains, and street gatherings. . . .

At present, the center of gravity of the matter has shifted to other realms: on a national level, there is a conflict with reactionary members of the Church hierarchy; on an international level, we are awaiting the Pope's response to the parliamentary petition addressed to him.

It is worth noting that those who orchestrated the Kielce Pogrom—with a fatalism befitting defenders of a collapsing world—have contributed to a series of events that can benefit the new Poland. Above all, they showed the world the fascist face of our opposition—both the partisan fighters in the forests and those gathered around Church leaders. For its part, the wave of Jews that is spilling out throughout the world—and whose departure from Poland has taken on the character of a panicked flight—will reinforce the world's notions about the power of Polish reaction, about its fascist character and brutality. This, in turn, will contribute to persuading even those in the West who are hostile to the Polish People's Republic that the Provisional Government of National Unity (TRJN),[3] together with the affiliated parties, is an indispensable guarantee against the revival of fascism in Central Europe. This improvement of our government's standing in the eyes of Western public opinion was certainly not part of the plan of the architects of the Kielce incidents.

The political struggle will go on. The Kielce episode itself will fall ever more deeply into oblivion. The only thing we might still expect is news about the outcome of disciplinary proceedings against the arrested security apparatus functionaries, including information about their sentences.

Have we thus said everything that can be said about the largest post-Nazi pogrom perpetrated against Jews anywhere in the world? And, more important, have we done everything that can be done? Have we drawn all the necessary conclusions?

My conscience does not let me acquiesce to the falling silence (dear Mr. Żółkiewski, I hereby give empirical proof that the voice of conscience exists!).[4]

Cries of "Long live!" and "Down with" have resounded enough times. If I speak about these matters it is to understand (or possibly to initiate a discussion that would lead to the realization of) what is to be done, and specifically, what we, leftist intellectuals, can do.

Things are clear for the weekly *Tygodnik Powszechny*:[a] we have to teach our children to tell the truth. Because the whole thing started with a ten-year-old telling a lie!

But right now, I do not wish to speak to people who, coerced by the pressure of public opinion, ultimately opted for ambivalent protest (since they make ambiguous accusations). I want to reflect about the problem with people who truly have a conscience, who truly feel a sense of social responsibility. In their honest company, I want to consider what can be done. What can we do?

I call my voice a "pessimist's voice" because it seems to me that the tasks ahead are great and the means are limited. I would be happy if someone would prove me wrong.

Animating Forces and a Reservoir of Power

When it comes to incidents like those in Kielce we have to differentiate between two factors: the clearly perceptible activity of the instigators on the one hand, and, on the other, an accumulated reservoir of social forces ready to respond.

The instigators prepare the ground, determine the right moment, orchestrate the outbreak, and oversee the course of events—intensifying action when it is developing and enlivening it when it is dying out. But all their activity would be futile if it did not fall on fertile ground, if it was not the proverbial spark that ignites the gunpowder. It was not a decision of the command center of the National Armed Forces (NSZ) that caused the outbreak and the success of the Kielce Pogrom;[5] it was the willingness of the Kielce community.

In discussions about the Kielce Pogrom there was much talk and writing about its driving force—the National Armed Forces command center. I do not deny its importance.

---

[a] No. 72: 8.

But people have said and thought much too little about the reservoir of accumulated energies that were ready to heed the insinuations issuing from the center.

I will not write about the Pogrom's driving force here. Primarily because others have already written so much about it. And, above all, because the goal of my essay is strictly practical—and the fight against the leadership of the National Armed Forces is not our fight. It lies fully within the purview of the state security apparatus. Society is only supposed to create a favorable atmosphere for the authorities to take action, and then assess their accomplishments.

Meanwhile, there is the problem of the hundreds of thousands of potential pogrom participants—people whom we constantly encounter in the streets, with whom we ride the trolleys and speak on the trains, whom we meet in factories, offices, or universities, people who merely express contempt or hatred today but tomorrow could tear out rods from railings to crush the skulls of our brothers, our friends, our students, our teachers, our writers, or ultimately anyone whatsoever, even insignificant people, but nonetheless people, people like us. This problem

1. is even more important than the problem of the National Armed Forces command center,
2. has been undervalued in discussions that have taken place so far, and
3. is a problem whose solution—not within the purview of the security authorities—is precisely up to us, Polish leftist intellectuals.

The Scope of the Phenomenon

According to provisional census results, approximately 49,500 people live in Kielce. According to prewar data,[b] children under fourteen and older inhabitants over fifty together accounted for 44 percent of the population. (Today, after the decimation of the mid-range age groups by the war, this percentage is certainly not smaller.) When we combine these data, we can surmise that Kielce had about 27,500 inhabitants between the ages of fifteen and fifty. From this let's subtract the military garrisons, prisons, hospitals, the sick, and people with jobs they could not leave, and we will ultimately get slightly over 20,000 people. Let's juxtapose this number against the terse

[b] *Mały Rocznik Statystyczny* (*Concise Statistical Yearbook*, 1939), 18.

wording of the official communiqué which mentioned "a crowd of several thousand people" gathered at one of the action points—while other groups were active in other city locations (the train station and other places). It would therefore probably not be an exaggeration if we assumed that one-fourth of Kielce's inhabitants took an active part in the Pogrom. And would we exaggerate if we assumed that for every active participant there were two others who, not finding enough courage to go out into the streets, stayed home and followed the incidents with satisfaction, or at least with indifferent approval?

And one more thing: we are by no means viewing Kielce as having some sort of specificity that predestined it to play this disgraceful role. Quite the opposite. The leadership's choice of Kielce was probably arbitrary. What took place in Kielce could have taken place in many other cities. It could have happened precisely because in those cities, too, there is that accumulation of "potential willingness." Sadly, we must therefore regard the approximate calculations of the extent of this "willingness," which we carried out on the Kielce example, as representative.

The current scope and intensity of Polish anti-Semitism surpass the dreams of even the boldest prewar National Radical Camp (ONR) leaders. And this is happening at a time when the Jewish population has been reduced to 3 percent of its previous size! Do we need any better proof of who caused the current upwelling of anti-Semitism? Do we need more proof of the nationally foreign sources of this "nationalist" movement?

But that is not important. Let us return to our main problem.

If anti-Semitism was so much less pervasive before the war, when right-wing circles enjoyed full freedom in formulating their claims, than it is today, when approximately 100,000 Jews of the 3.5 million remain—isn't this in and of itself the best testimony to the fact that this movement is completely irrational?

The present situation in Poland is intolerable for Jews. I was recently on a train from Łódź to Wrocław. Next to me there was a Jewish family. I am truly not exaggerating when I say that fifteen minutes didn't pass before I heard some sort of snide remark, joke, comment, admonition, or sarcastic mimic of a supposedly Jewish accent coming at them from one direction or another. . . . I looked at them when they got off at the Wałbrzych station. I saw how the man straightened up and moved his hand across his forehead. Nine hours! I wonder—when criminals in the Middle Ages were sentenced to whipping, how many hours did it last?

Jews are escaping from Poland. Hochfeld is right when he says that we are full of admiration and gratitude for the fortitude of those who, disregarding everything, are ready to stay with us.[6] But on the other hand, we have no moral right to demand this kind of heroism from anyone. We have no right—primarily because we have no way of guaranteeing personal safety for these people, and also because, even if the appropriate institutions were able to guarantee such safety—we, Polish leftist intellectuals, are unable to guarantee a decent moral climate for them. We do not realize that a Jew in Poland cannot travel by car and that he rides on trains reluctantly. That he is afraid to send his child to summer camp; that he does not dare show up in some small village; and that he aggregates only in the largest cities, because even in midsize ones he cannot walk the streets in peace. Only a hero could live in this climate after six years of torment.

Choking on our shame, we say our farewells to Jews who are escaping Poland—and we know we have no right to ask them to stay.

We also know very well that the irrationalism of the phenomenon has reached such proportions that even if three-quarters of the Jews currently living in Poland were to leave, anti-Semitism would not abate.

Żyd and Żydek: Jew and Little Jew

Do we need a more subtle analysis of how Poles relate to Jews than what Andrzejewski has recently offered us in the weekly *Odrodzenie* (*Rebirth*)?[7] With exactitude, he described two alternatives: hatred and contempt, each with a whole range of hues—and *tertium non datur* [no third possibility].

I, too, recently understood that this is exactly how things are—in one characteristic moment, which I'd like to describe.

I was leading a seminar. The student giving a paper about a few historical figures mentioned a certain Nosek Majerowicz, and, by way of clarification, added the words "some little Jew" (Żydek).[8] The clarification itself was appropriate, but I did not find the form acceptable and decided I should correct it. So I asked whether he had information suggesting that this individual was short. The student was silent. Then, after waiting out the disoriented silence that descended upon the entire room, I added: "So why did you say 'little Jew' (Żydek) and not simply 'Jew' (Żyd)?" The student and the other seminar participants burst out laughing.

And in this laughter was a tone that suddenly made everything clear to me. The student used the word "Żydek" and not "Żyd" because he assumed I was not an anti-Semite. He used the word he considered to be more affectionate (Żydek), to avoid using what he saw as the more offensive word (Żyd). The class saw my remark as a display of anti-Semitism, and that is why they liked it. I was, after all, demanding that the student use the offensive word instead of an affectionate one! This precisely is the Polish meaning of the words "Żyd" and "Żydek" (and the equally affectionate feminine diminutive "Żydóweczka"). Poles' relationship to Jews vacillates along the line that stretches between the contempt and hatred expressed in these words. So where are we to seek mutual understanding?

In the June issue of the Catholic journal *Esprit*, the leading French Catholic intellectual Emanuel Mounier describes how in various conversations—including ones with eminent Catholic Church figures in Poland (and we know whom the group of French intellectuals visited!)—whenever the Jewish issue comes up, "the interlocutor's eyes turn ruthless and cold," and all possibility of understanding disappears. Neither the scorned "Żydek," nor the hated "Żyd" can expect humane treatment in Poland.

I will venture the claim that Polish anti-Semitism will not abate any time soon. It will diminish significantly only after many years, and this will follow the outcomes of social and, above all, economic reconstruction that is currently underway.

Draconian punishments for sowing racial hatred are as indispensable as draconian punishments that are imposed in the context of postwar demoralization for bribery, stealing public property, abuse of power, and so on. However, bribery, theft, and similar crimes will eventually disappear not as a result of these punishments but of improvements in the administrative apparatus of state and local government, public control, better standards of living, and so on. Likewise, even the harshest punishments for anti-Semitism, though indispensable, will not change much—we can expect actual change only as a consequence of the structural reconstruction on the verge of which we only find ourselves now.

But this will not suffice to clear our conscience. Arguments about the deterministic character of ideology and activist orientation of the socialist movement now belong to the history of socialist thought. We have to understand what we still need to do in this regard. What is ours to do. And we have to do our part as well as we can.

Let us leave it up to the appropriate authorities to worry about the leadership of the National Armed Forces. Let us also leave it up to them to worry about the rational application of the system of currently available legal punishments.

Our work involves the hundreds of thousands of potential criminals.

The task of the authorities is to put out the burning fuses ready to set off the accumulated gunpowder.

Our task is to empty the gunpowder warehouses.

The authorities' weapons are the machine gun, the statute, and the court.

Our weapons are words.

We only have to make it clear to ourselves what we should say, and to whom.

Willing Ears

The ears and not the mouth determine how a conversation unfolds.

Do you doubt it?

The war has shown us both the power and the weakness of propaganda.

We have seen the worst rubbish that found its way into listeners' ears— and wisest truths that bounced right off.

If today we read in a periodical published in Bavaria that there are 334 elementary schools in Poland, and teachers have to subscribe to eleven ideological and professional periodicals "a number of which are written in Russian—the language shared by all Slavs,"[c] someone could say that an "iron curtain" is at work here.[9] But it would be a cheap way of dismissing a more serious problem. One can feed people rubbish and outright lies because these correspond to their fundamental a priori attitudes, because they want to hear such things. When at an academic conference in Krakow, held under the aegis of the Polish Academy of Sciences and Jagiellonian University, Rector Przychocki publicly advances the thesis that it was easier for Polish researchers to contact their foreign peers during the Nazi occupation than it is now—we can no longer talk about an "iron curtain." Those who were in the room knew very well what the actual situation was, perhaps even better than the speaker himself, who—assuming our information is correct—did not have firsthand knowledge about life in the General Government. And despite this, we did not hear any voices of protest against

[c] *Słowo Polskie*, year II, no. 5–47 (Feb. 1946): 5.

this open lie, this obvious calumny. The audience accepted this nonsense because they want a respected figure to denounce current Polish realities.

The ears decide.

The ears are against us.

All the social strata deriving from the landowners and capitalists are against us. The entire petty bourgeoisie is against us. Most of the peasants are against us (the wealthy for ideological reasons, the poor because of ignorance). Some of the workers are against us as well. And the entire unskilled white-collar intelligentsia—so numerous in Poland—is against us.

A handful of the better informed peasant activists and, above all, worker activists are with us; as are a handful of progressive intellectuals.

And so we must speak to unwilling ears.

Everybody knows: people think in clusters of ideas. The entirety of one's attitude toward reality amalgamates into a single entity and determines one's reactions to particular words.

Everybody knows: people's reactions to what they hear are determined more by who speaks than by what is said.

Meanwhile, everyone also knows that the Church, which has considerable standing in precisely those social strata with which we are concerned, has basically refused to weigh in with its voice. A large number of teachers have also recently succumbed to anti-Semitic propaganda.

All government propaganda is burdened by those clusters of ideas. People who dreamt for six years about the postwar period would like better wages and more efficient administration—and their grudges against the government close off the path of even the most objective and most rightful arguments advanced by government propaganda.

It is easy to criticize the government.

To do our work we, progressive members of Polish intelligentsia, will have to rely on ourselves.

What Are We to Do?

(1) Above all, we have to start talking to the people we want to reach. So far, many wise and subtle things have been said in discussions about the Jewish issue. We remember the voices of people like Jastrun, Żółkiewski, Szymanowski, Boguszewska, and Andrzejewski.[10] But these voices are, after all, preaching to the choir. I am by no means negating their value. They

deepened our understanding of the phenomenon, provided us with arguments and food for thought, and gave each of us the feeling that we are
not so completely alone after all. But there remains the task of speaking to
people who can be reached by at least some voices capable of penetrating
the covers over their ears. The weekly *Kuźnica* is read by either avowed
enemies or avowed supporters. But *Pamiętniki Szpilmana* (*Szpilman's
Memoirs*),[11] published in 200,000 copies in *Przekrój*, and appealing to simple
human compassion, has certainly done more than even the most insightful
comments in *Kuźnica*, as did Boguszewska's unassuming novellas broadcast
on the radio.

And so we have to start speaking directly to the people we want to reach—
at meetings, mass readings, on the radio, and in *Przekrój*—even all kinds of
minor popular newspapers must receive submissions from writers and other
intellectuals. This demand is not easy to meet. But can we afford not to
meet it?

(2) The second demand may be easier: we have to train leaders. I am
thinking, above all, about the rank-and-file of democratic parties. Personally,
I do not belong to any party, but I am, of course, talking about all parties
that stand for democracy. We all know that things are not going well when it
comes to awareness-raising among the rank-and-file in all parties. Six years
of war, all the underground organizing work, the fact that the best people
were sent to fight against the enemy, and today's pressing reconstruction
tasks—all this does not favor internal party work, deeper ideological education of the rank-and-file, and so on.

Now we must find the time and space for this work, and progressive
Polish intellectuals must help in this work. In this realm, we have to extend
a helping hand to all parties.

When *Kuźnica* publishes one more article about the Jewish issue today, it
is not to initiate another general discussion but to start a discussion about a
specific question: What are we to do?

The argument just presented reveals a somber picture: one of weakness,
limited opportunities for action, and results that will become noticeable
only in the long run.

We will be satisfied if discussion brightens this picture, if it leads to the
identification of sources of power and opportunities which we have overlooked, and if someone shows the possibility of getting results faster.

It does not matter whether we always have sufficient energy to devote to the task, whether results can be obtained immediately or over the long haul—it is necessary to devise a plan of action quickly, and to act.

We have to do our part.

Editors' Notes

1. For a description of the Kielce Pogrom, please see the introduction to Stanisław Ossowski's essay "With Kielce in the Background" reproduced in this volume on pages 114–115.

2. Marcin Kula, "A Leftist Intellectual on the Kielce Pogrom," *Gal-Ed* 18 (2002): 101–117.

3. In the immediate postwar years, Poland was dominated by the Soviet Union. Between June 1945 and January 1947, the Provisional Government of National Unity (TRJN) was established under Moscow's influence. It brought together communist leaders and leaders of the opposition parties, who realized that they must reach a compromise with the Communists. The government included the communist Polish Workers' Party (PPR), the Agrarian and Democratic Parties (SL and SD), and opposition parties including the PPS, the Polish Peasants' Party (PSL), and the Workers' Party (SP). For the wider historical context of the postwar years in Poland, please see "Anti-Semitism in the Polish People's Republic" in the Introduction.

4. Stefan Żółkiewski (1911–1991) was an influential cultural and literary critic, a historian, and a politician. He was among the founding members of the PPR and was later active in the Communist Party (PZPR). Between 1945 and 1948, he was the editor of the weekly *Kuźnica*, for which Kula wrote this essay.

5. The National Armed Forces and their relations with Jews during the war are discussed in "Poles and Jews during the Holocaust" in the Introduction.

6. Julian Hochfeld (1911–1966) was a sociologist. Between 1945 and 1948, he was active in the PPS and he later joined the PZPR, serving as a deputy in the Polish Parliament between 1948 and 1954.

7. This refers to Jerzy Andrzejewski's essay "The Problem of Polish Anti-Semitism" in this volume on pages 95–112.

8. The derisive word "Żydek" is best rendered as "Jew-boy," and that is how it is translated throughout the volume. Here, we chose to keep the literal meaning, since it plays an essential part in Kula's argument.

9. On March 5, 1946, i.e., a few months before Kula wrote this essay, Winston Churchill gave his famous speech at Fulton, Missouri, in which he used the image of the "iron curtain" that divided Europe.

10. Mieczysław Jastrun's and Jerzy Andrzejewski's essays on anti-Semitism are reproduced in this volume on pages 87–92 and 95–112, respectively. Zygmunt Szymanowski (1873–1956) was a physician and professor who belonged to the PPS during the interwar period, and, like other members of this party, publicly condemned anti-Semitism. Helena Boguszewska (1886–1978) was a writer and social activist who worked on behalf of impoverished and disabled children in the interwar period.

11. Władysław Szpilman (1911–2000) was a pianist and composer. In 1940, the Nazis forced him and his family into the Warsaw Ghetto. In 1942, his family members were deported to Treblinka, and a year later he escaped the Ghetto and survived the war. He wrote the book *Śmierć miasta. Pamiętniki Władysława Szpilmana 1939–1945* (*Death of a City: Memoirs of Władysław Szpilman 1939–1945*), which was originally published in Warsaw in 1946. Szpilman's ordeal became the subject of Roman Polanski's 2002 film *The Pianist*.

PART V

1956–1957: The Anti-Semitism of Kind and Gentle People

11

Anti-Semites

Five Familiar Theses and a Warning

LESZEK KOŁAKOWSKI

Editors' Introduction

Leszek Kołakowski (1927–2009) was a philosopher, essayist, and historian of ideas. Born in Radom, he studied in the underground school system during the war and enrolled to study philosophy at Łódź University in 1945. He moved to Warsaw in 1949, and he later taught at Warsaw University. As a young man, Kołakowski was a communist and joined the Polish Workers' Party (PPR). In 1956 he became the leader of the intellectuals who rebelled against Stalinist doctrine and dictatorship. He was expelled from the Communist Party in 1966, after delivering a lecture in which he criticized the persistent repressiveness of the communist system. Deprived of his chair at Warsaw University two years later, in the wake of the March 1968 events, he left Poland for a visiting professorship at McGill University. He later taught at University of California, Berkeley, and finally settled at All Souls College, Oxford, as senior research fellow; he was also a visiting professor at Yale and professor on the Committee on Social Thought at the University of Chicago.

Kołakowski was the author of perhaps the single most important analysis of Marxism, presented in his three-volume *Main Currents of Marxism: Its Rise, Growth and Dissolution* (1978). He also explored diverse philosophical themes and figures in books like *The Individual and Infinity* (a study about Spinoza, 1958), *The Philosophy of Existence, the Defeat of Existence* (1965), and *Husserl and the Search for Certitude* (1975). In addition, he wrote seminal books on the history of Christianity, including *Religious Consciousness and the Church: Studies in 17th Century Non-Denominational Christianity* (1965).

The text reproduced here was originally published in the weekly *Po Prostu* in Warsaw in May 1956. *Po Prostu* was the leading anti-Stalinist periodical of young intellectuals during "the thaw" after Stalin's death. When the government decided to dissolve the weekly in 1957, it signaled a turn away from political liberalization. When Kołakowski wrote this text, he embraced an anti-Stalinist, reform-oriented form of Marxism, which official propaganda designated as "revisionism" at the time. His ideological position is perceptible in both his conceptual vocabulary and language—he embraces communist ideals but criticizes the way in which they have been distorted in both the Soviet Union and Poland. He points to anti-Semitic attitudes in Polish society and warns against the instrumental use of anti-Semitism by Stalinist and anti-democratic activists in the Communist Party. The Introduction to this volume provides a fuller explanation of the historical context of de-Stalinization in Poland, and the anti-Semitic campaign that took place within the party and in wider social circles during and after the Polish October in 1956.

They come in all shapes and sizes, like annoying insects: some study leaflets on ritual murder and demand that Jews be slaughtered, some talk of lower races, others of "cultural otherness," and others still are content with an animosity that is often difficult to capture and readily manifests in everyday life without any help from theories.

Nevertheless—and this is my first thesis—*differences among various types of anti-Semitism are only a matter of quantity, of degree.* A fundamental precondition for bloody anti-Jewish pogroms, massacres, and atrocities has always been an emotional climate of tolerance for anti-Semitism, even in its mildest and most watered-down forms. Wherever crimes eventually materialized, initially there had been a system of discrimination and distrust, however seemingly innocuous; it always cumulated reservoirs of destructive social energy that fed and raised criminals. The restrained, bureaucratic anti-Semitism of the interwar Sanacja regime, even when limited to the "economic boycott" of Jewish merchants, sustained and fueled an atmosphere in which people like the Falanga, Fr. Trzeciak, future Gestapo informants, and blackmailers could flourish.[1] The Nuremberg Laws, as we know, did not contain a program for exterminating Jews but only the principle of racial inferiority. When horse-drawn trolleys were introduced into the Warsaw Ghetto, an article was published in a Nazi-controlled newspaper "proving" that this sought to bring conditions in the Ghetto in line with the spirit of the Jewish race, since horse-drawn vehicles are better suited to the nature of the East than electric trolleys. The Nuremberg Laws celebrated their dreadful triumph with the liquidation of the Warsaw Ghetto at Easter 1943 and behind the barbed wire of Majdanek. But pogroms and slaughter cannot go on incessantly. The dissemination of anti-Semitic attitudes in society creates a reservoir of reactionary attitudes, a warehouse of social dynamite capable of exploding at just the right moment; this is where, for centuries, political leaders of reactionary obscurantism diligently sought to concentrate all negative social tensions—to prevent them from exploding in the appropriate places.

In this way, kind-hearted anti-Semites beget anti-Semitic thugs, mild anti-Semites nourish anti-Semites armed with brass knuckles and knives, and passive and restrained anti-Semites give rise to organizers of pogroms. Under the right circumstances, scattered particles of anti-Semitism, each seemingly harmless and by itself feeble, can be brought together in a flash to create an explosive mixture that detonates in an atrocity. Which is why tolerating even the faintest manifestations of anti-Semitism today is tantamount to tolerating the pogroms of tomorrow. We must seize and wipe out the shadow of anti-Semitism before it becomes flesh. I mention this only because the existence of hotbeds of anti-Semitism in our time is an open secret that needs no telling.

Yet unorganized anti-Semitism is often elusive. It is elusive because—and this is my second thesis—*anti-Semitism is not a theory*. And this is not just because it is discredited in intellectual circles, where theories are born. It is mainly because—like most intellectual phenomena that arise in the struggle against progress—anti-Semitism is in essence irrational, and therefore absolutely resistant to criticism, relentlessly vacuous and completely uncritical. It is not a doctrine subject to criticism; it is an attitude whose social roots are such that it is not obliged to seek justifications. It cannot be confronted with arguments: it is inevitably associated with the type of reaction to which arguments, as a way of thinking, are foreign and inimical. It is anti-culture and anti-humanity, anti-theory and anti-science. This is clear to anyone who has had occasion to conduct hopeless discussions with an anti-Semite—an activity that always resembles trying to teach a foreign language to an animal.

Just as the sounds animals make are not a different language but not human language at all, so anti-Semitic attitudes are not simply a different worldview—every worldview can be an object of critique—but at most an ostensible verbal articulation of irrational states that need no justification. The opposite of anti-Semitism is not a rational theory, but the very habit of rational thinking, not science but a human attitude. Can one explain to anti-Semites that there is something highly puzzling about the very concept of Jewishness understood as a racial rather than a religious, social, or national affiliation? That even the Nuremberg definition of a Jew is a vicious circle ("A Jew is someone who has four fully Jewish grandparents"—Hitlergesetze XIII, IIIb, 2), as a result of which, in Nazi practice, Jewishness came to function as a religious rather than an anthropological concept? Such subtleties are too intricate for anti-Semitic minds. Can one evoke countless examples, in various countries, of persecution of national minorities where the same crude educational procedure is always applied: only negative qualities are attributed to the minority nation, on the basis of examples that are always readily available, while counterexamples are omitted?

Can one point out that people of Jewish extraction who emancipated themselves from the superstitions of Judaism have included such shapers of modern culture as Spinoza, Heine, Marx, Einstein, Ehrlich, and Picasso, as well as such geniuses of great mistakes as Freud, Bergson, and Husserl? Can one point to Proust, to Tuwim, to Chagall? For the anti-Semite this merely provides a reason to hate these names. Can one say that the roots of Christianity (and anti-Semites tend to be good Christians) lie in Judaism? Or that, on the other hand, Christians were persecuted by the Roman imperial authorities with the same, unchanging, centuries-old slogans that contemporary anti-Semitism employs? That Jewish racism is no less mindless, cruel, and primitive than anti-Jewish racism, and that Judaism is just as superstitious and alien to rational thinking as Christianity? The effort would be in vain. Anti-Semitism is not a result of any conviction concerning Jews; it is content to seize on any crumb of a thought, any semblance of a crumb, any inanity, for its imperturbable support—support which is no justification, only a sanction.

It is true that sometimes anti-Semitism seeks quasi-theoretical support and that its effects may be seen in the works of certain—sometimes eminent—scholars (Tadeusz Zieliński's *Hellenizm a judaizm* [*Hellenism and Judaism*], for example); but such cases are examples of a destructive sabotage of irrationalism within scholarship rather than with the rationalization of anti-scholarship, which is what anti-Semitism is. Anti-Semitism is a component of social life to the degree to which social life is anti-intellectual; it is inevitably a weapon of social reactionaries, not only because of its political vocation, but also because of its radical anti-intellectualism, well armored against reason's every design.

Precisely because of this, anti-Semitism, when it is not a political program, is often a disease that is difficult to detect. It can assume surreptitious shapes, avoid programmatic declarations, take murky paths and poison the moral atmosphere with a characteristic mixture of stupidity, cruelty, fanaticism, and hatred. No one becomes an anti-Semite through reflection: typically, one is an anti-Semite by upbringing, from earliest childhood, and its later effects are therefore immensely difficult to surmount. The inertia of tradition exerts its influence even when the primordial sources that had summoned that tradition to life are extinguished—but contemporary anti-Semitism does not rely solely on the power of tradition: wherever reactionary obscurantism fights against the pressure of social progress, anti-Semitism will be fueled and cultivated. It will be one of the centuries-old forms in which crime uses ignorance as its tool.

For—and this is my third thesis—*anti-Semitism is a means of producing a social symbol. Fighting Jews is rarely an end in itself.* From the perspective of its broadest social function, hatred for Jews is to be a focus of irradiation that extends its influence onto the real object of the fight, which the orchestrators of anti-Semitism try in various ways to associate with Jewishness in the social consciousness. Slogans in the fight against Jews are often also linked with other slogans—slogans which embody the real, political meaning of the fight. History offers an abundance of such associations, where the struggle was waged, for example, against Jews and Christians, Jews and Communists, or Jews and democrats.

Political reactionaries need to sustain anti-Semitism especially when they aim to focus people's attention on imaginary sources of social ills, in order to avert it from the real ones. The history of anti-Semitism often reveals its roots to lie in direct economic interests: anti-Jewish pogroms, which drenched dozens of towns in medieval Germany, Spain, and France in blood, much like mass expulsions of Jews from a number of European countries at various times, were driven in part by the simple lust for robbery, perpetrated against Jewish merchants and bankers. And there was no lack of such motivations in Nazi anti-Semitism—a perspective Feuchtwanger explores in his novels—or in Polish fascism. In both countries, property envy and conflicts around commercial and industrial competition were exploited.

But this is not what determined the essence of the movement. The main social mission of anti-Semitism is to create a universal symbol of evil; attempts are then made to tie this symbol in people's minds to phenomena one wants to combat in politics, culture, or scholarship. Jewishness is to become an insult that can be used to brand everything destined for annihilation; it is to be a carrier not of a specific evil, but of evil in general—an abstract negative symbol that can be attached to any situation whatsoever that one wants the world to see as something negative. Anything one wants to denigrate or make into an object of hatred in culture, politics, or any sphere of life, can be presented as a Jewish product; this, however, requires the maintenance of the maximum possible amount of anti-Semitic irrationalism in society. Under such conditions, anti-Semitism creates a social system that functions on the basis of magic: anything that can somehow be presented as tainted by a touch of Jewishness becomes forbidden and treif. And there is no obstacle in the fact that in the process utterly contradictory qualities get attributed to Jews, and to Jewishness as such, since it is in the nature of magic to disdain the principle of non-contradiction.

In his opening lecture at the first Polish Philosophical Congress in 1923, Wincenty Lutosławski claimed that the Jewish spirit is characterized by a tendency toward determinism and a herd mentality in which there is no room for freedom and individuality. In his *Gog*, Papini presented Jewishness as a carrier of perverse individualism, ever on the lookout for opportunities to overturn all socially recognized values. The anti-capitalist demagogy of the fascists regarded plutocracy and the workers' movement as a Jewish tool; Jews were accused of murdering infants and destroying the national spirit through a doctrine of "rotten humanism"; Jews were the creators of bourgeois liberal democracies and Bolshevism. In each case, Jewishness functions as an abstract symbol that can be effectively attached to any content whatsoever, so long as it itself, in its naked symbolic form, is made into an object of abstract hatred. Hence the incalculable value of anti-Semitism for reactionary movements, especially at times of tense social conflicts or cataclysms and misfortunes that affect large masses of people: the great medieval epidemics, which, as we know, were represented as Jewish handiwork, also gave occasion to pogroms; for it is impossible to conceive any absurdity concerning Jews that would be too absurd for anti-Semites.

Historical circumstances made it truly difficult to find a better candidate than the Jews to play the role of this kind of symbol. Scattered throughout the world, they were most readily imbued with qualities of universal and international evil. Everywhere a vulnerable minority, they could most easily become victims of cruelty and crimes. Glaringly different in customs, religion, and language, culturally isolated and therefore estranged from their surroundings, they permitted the quickest overcoming of any scruples and humane feelings; and they were easiest to pick out and point out. Even partial emancipation intensified the Jews' symbolic influence: assimilated into all kinds of milieus, nations, classes, political parties, professions, worldviews, and cultures, they always provided an abundance of examples in any fight whatsoever; any social phenomenon to be combated could be unmasked as the fruit of Jewish work with the use of appropriate examples: Jew-Communists, Jew-anarchists, Jew-liberals, Jew-racists, Jew-factory-owners, and Jew-labor-leaders. Moreover, there was a period when historical circumstances pushed a large part of the Jewish population into professions that easily draw public aversion—commerce and money-lending. Need we describe the benefits that flowed from presenting a Jewish money-lender as a Jew and not a money-lender? Need we recall those countryside tavern-keepers from the Polish-Lithuanian Commonwealth, whose existence was easily exploited by anti-Semitic propaganda whose influence was visible even among otherwise progressive writers like Staszic?[2] Anti-Semitism was a concept perfect and unrivaled in its simplicity, priceless for the ease with which it could become a program, assimilated and understood without a moment's thought, and at the same time applicable to all circumstances and all social situations; it could settle everything.

But with one caveat. Although the universality of the Jewish people's living conditions made it possible to deploy them as a symbol in any struggle, that struggle—whatever its target—could only be waged from the position of reactionary obscurantism, from the right. And this is my fourth thesis— *anti-Semitism can only be a tool of reaction. It might seem that a mythological symbol with such universal application can be used in any political struggle.* In reality this is, of course, impossible, when one realizes that this symbol contains premises whose consequences are radically opposed to the historical tendency of the workers' movement: the assumption of intrinsic inequality among people, the assumption of a biological—and thus insurmountable— conflict between ethnic or national groups, and glaring irrationalism. Hence the tradition of the revolutionary movement includes the struggle against all forms of discrimination and national persecution, also when these are aimed directly at certain elements of the bourgeoisie and the petty bourgeoisie. The Dreyfus Affair is one example. In his *Histoire Contemporaine (Modern History)*, Anatole France cites workers' discussions about it. A Mr. Roupart, a carpenter, describes a socialist meeting where the following sentiment was voiced:

> Let the capitalists fight each other. Stand back and wait for the anti-Semites. . . . When it comes to expropriating capitalists, why shouldn't we start with the Jews?" "And then the comrades let their fists fly. . . . because it seems to me that socialism, which is truth, is also justice and goodness. And everything that is good and just is born without miracles, like apples on the apple tree. There is no double-dealing. It seems to me that to fight against injustice is to work for us, proletarians, who bear the burden of the whole world's injustice.

Here France articulates the principle of the existence of the proletariat as a class, which, to use Marx's words, "is the total negation of man, and it can thus possess itself only by fully repossessing man."

There is no form of oppression, or national or racial discrimination, which is not also a negation of the very core of communism. For the workers' movement, national problems are about suffering discrimination and violence. The principle of "national unity" can work for socialism when it is directed against external attempts at national oppression; "national unity" achieved through discrimination and national hatred is only a tool of counterrevolution, a means of mystifying real social relations and authentic conflicts. It is a product of distorted social consciousness. In socialist education, the struggle against racist superstition will never cease to be a daily task as long as shadows of its tradition continue to poison collective life. . . .

The rabble is the main agent of anti-Semitism. This word is, admittedly, far from unambiguous, but it is packed with dynamic emotional meaning. Anti-Semitism would, of course, become superfluous if it did not muddy the consciousness of people whose real interests are contrary to its social tasks. "Through a collective suggestion, racist ideology can appeal to groups or individuals who have no rational reasons for 'racial' antagonisms. Ideology inflamed by economic conflicts can become a force whose action is independent of the issues that gave rise to it in the first place."[a]

The rabble is the agent of anti-Semitism. The rabble is not same thing as "superfluous people" in Stefan Czarnowski's sense of the word, that is, those who have a defined place in the social order—even if only negatively. The rabble's composition is not determined by class, but its social tasks are. It can arise out of the most diverse social elements. The rabble comes into being in a mass of people; when dispersed it maintains no sense of solidarity but only a vague readiness to renew that bond which is based on neither class nor nationality, and which is not a permanent bond at all, but a circumstantial one, with volatile meanings. The bond established by the rabble is incapable of constructing a distinct program; it is purely negative and destructive, necessarily devoid of class consciousness. It gives collective expression to disoriented discontent and it is therefore incapable of rationalized reactions; it is categorically opposed to discussion, subject to only the most primitive suggestions, submissive in the face of demagogy, and invaluable as a tool of crime perpetrated in someone else's name.

The rabble is the accumulation of negative collective tensions—tensions which are unaware of their sources and therefore susceptible to the imposition of almost any direction of development, so long as it is sufficiently simple and concrete, not requiring reflection or independence, and capable of releasing all inhibitions stemming from both rational arguments and the existence of fundamental rules of universal human morality. The rabble can act against the most obvious interests of the majority of its participants, but in general it is consciously directed from outside—because it is incapable of

[a] Stanisław Ossowski, *Więź społeczna i dziedzictwo krwi* (*Social Bonds and the Heritage of Blood*).

independently deciding on or organizing its actions, and because one of the principles of its existence is the negation of internal social discipline.

It was the rabble that tore the learned Hypatia to pieces on the streets of Alexandria; the rabble became active on St. Bartholomew's night, in Polish attacks on people of other faiths, and in anti-Jewish pogroms. The rabble can only be a tool of political reaction. It acts only when there are clear prospects of immediate success and only when it outnumbers the enemy; it retreats only before power. Anti-Semitism is the favorite form that can be imposed onto its dim consciousness.

These five theses are not new. Nor are they, unfortunately, all that outdated. Let us not delude ourselves: the parasitic aggression of anti-Semitism resists the propagandists' carefree writings about the results of a socialist upbringing. Closing one's eyes to it does not make it go away.

And in conclusion—a warning: whenever so much as the faintest shadow of anti-Semitism slithers by the gates of our homes, Beware! The canaille is just around the corner, counterrevolution is baring its fangs.

Editors' Notes

1. The National Radical Camp (ONR) was founded in 1934, and a year later it split into two factions: ONR-ABC and ONR-Falanga; the latter was led by Bolesław Piasecki and opted for an openly fascist program, modeled on Mussolini's movement. Rev. Stanisław Trzeciak (1873–1944) was a Warsaw priest known for his extremist anti-Semitic views and writings.

2. Stanisław Staszic (1755–1826) was an Enlightenment writer and social activist who advocated the modernization of Poland. He played an important part in Polish constitutional debates in the early 1790s and warned of the deleterious influence of the dominance of the gentry and nobility in Polish political life. Some of his writings contain anti-Semitic elements.

12

From National Democrats to Stalinists

KONSTANTY A. JELEŃSKI

Editors' Introduction

Konstanty Aleksander Jeleński (Kot) (1922–1987) was an émigré essayist and literary critic. Born in Warsaw, he left Poland after the Nazi invasion in 1939 and enlisted to fight against Hitler's army in France. He decided not to return to his native Warsaw when Poland became communist in 1945, eventually settling in Paris, where he spent the rest of his life. For over three decades, he worked closely with Jerzy Giedroyc's monthly *Kultura*, the most important journal of the Polish émigré community during the communist period. He also wrote for various leading newspapers and periodicals, including the French *Le Monde*, the German *Der Monat*, the Italian *Tempo Presente*, and the American *New Republic*. Jeleński was an outspoken opponent of totalitarian communism, a critic of anti-Semitism in Poland, and a defender of the autonomy of the art world from government incursions. His most important book is a collection of essays about culture and politics entitled *Zbiegi okoliczności* (*Coincidences*, 1981); he also edited the 1970 volume *History and Hope: Tradition, Ideology, and Change in Modern Society*, which was a publication of the Congress for Cultural Freedom.

The essay reproduced here was originally published in *Kultura* in September 1956. In February of that year, Stalin's successor, Nikita Khrushchev, delivered the "Secret Speech" at the Twentieth Congress of the Communist Party of the Soviet Union. As he sought to bolster his own and the party's legitimacy, Khrushchev criticized Stalin's abuse of power and proposed that the "cult of personality" that had developed around Stalin was responsible for the party's mistakes; without Stalin, the party could now return to the rightful course originally set by Lenin during the Bolshevik Revolution. Khrushchev's speech was a crucial moment in the process of de-Stalinization, or "the thaw," in the USSR and its satellite countries—it invited the search for relative pluralism and democratization within communism. In the months following Khrushchev's speech, an intense factional struggle emerged in the Communist Party (PZPR) in Poland, in which liberals advocated reform while hardliners sought to preserve the status quo. As discussed in the Introduction to this volume, the hardliners resorted to anti-Semitic arguments and unleashed an anti-Semitic propaganda campaign that spilled out beyond the confines of the Communist Party and contributed to the emigration of approximately 50,000 Jews from Poland in 1957 and 1958. The liberal faction gained dominance in October 1956, and Władysław Gomułka became the new first secretary of the Communist Party. Jeleński's piece was published shortly before this important breakthrough. The title of his article evokes the vehemently anti-Semitic interwar Polish National-Democratic Party (SND), and he examines the process of de-Stalinization in Poland from abroad, identifying anti-Semitism as the common denominator of both fascist and communist anti-democratic tendencies.

No one has raised the problem of anti-Semitism in the Polish press for nearly ten years since the Pogrom in Kielce on July 4, 1946. If it were not for stories told by Jews emigrating from Poland to Israel, or for the unsettled voices of visiting Poles, one might think that anti-Semitism has ceased to be a problem in Poland.

Since April 1956, however, a whole series of extremely alarming articles about manifestations of anti-Semitism have appeared in Polish dailies and weeklies. The facts described are few, but they are horrifying.

—The monument to fighters who fell in the Warsaw Ghetto Uprising was ruthlessly desecrated (Gustaw Kaden's radio show, Warsaw, June 13, 1956).

—Jewish graves are deliberately plundered and profaned. Here is what Jerzy Broszkiewicz wrote about it in *Przegląd Kulturalny* (*Cultural Review*) on June 7, 1945:

> There are hyenas in Poland. They feed at cemeteries. They do not feed equally freely at all graveyards, however. Even though the number of remaining Jewish cemeteries is minuscule, that is precisely where they feed most readily, finishing the work so honorably initiated by SS-men, Vlasov's men, the Lithuanian Special Squad, or members of the National Armed Forces.[1] Sometimes even hyenas start something brand new. Thus, for example, at a Jewish cemetery in Wrocław there are Jewish graves that have been devastated *only after 1945*. The graves of Lassale, and Graetz, the historian. . . .[2]

—There are even more ominous facts. Anti-Semitism is penetrating schools, and teachers often support it. In the June 6, 1956 issue of *Trybuna Ludu* (*The People's Tribunal*) Antoni Czałbowski talks about little Helenka, whom her teacher willfully calls "Hinda." During a break, her peers—*seven-year-old children*—surrounded her in a circle and mocked her in a choir of voices: "Hin-da-the-Jewess, Hin-da-the-Jewess." And in the article I just mentioned, Broszkiewicz gives an example of "Jew-benches,"[3] which are making a return to Poland eleven years after the demolition of the gates of Nazi concentration camps:

> She's the only one in a class full of nine- and ten-year-olds. She sits alone at her desk; none of her peers want to sit next to her. Only once did it come to open cruelty, yelling, and throwing mud and small stones. She ran away from her tormentors. It wasn't until she got home that she broke down crying. But she did not want to say why. She also did not tell the teachers who it was. Maybe she was afraid. In any case, it did not happen again. Day-to-day, there is only alienation, mean words, hair-pulling, and ridicule. Perhaps the tormentors know that they should avoid yelling and hitting—or perhaps someone mature, wise, and sensible, someone "tactful" simply gave them such advice. After all, small thorns should suffice. They will certainly suffice if they prick often enough.

In the radio show cited earlier, Kaden described how teachers participate in this harassment of Jewish children and this poisoning of Polish
children's souls:

> Bringing shame to her profession, a teacher in a Warsaw school tells a little girl
> to sit at a separate desk, and explains to the class that she did this because the
> girl is Jewish. . . .

On May 20, 1956, Hanka Szwarcman's shocking "Kartki z pamiętnika"
(Diary Pages) appeared in *Po Prostu.* After the war, this young Jewish woman
returned to Poland from France, where she spent her entire childhood. She
does not have a "Semitic" appearance, and this is probably why, over and
over again, her peers and acquaintances made anti-Semitic comments in
front of her. Her life was poisoned by "remnants of cannibalism and the
Middle Ages."

For ten years, the "iron curtain" was a curtain of lies. Communist propaganda fought against racism, but focused on countries that were criticized by Soviet imperialism. The indignation of local "liberals" focused on
the problem of Negros in America, and racial segregation in South Africa.
They preferred not to write about homegrown racism—indeed they did
not dare write about it. In any event, lies of the propaganda men from the
"socialist country" fell on fertile ground. Even Polish liberals and democrats, even Poles who see anti-Semitism as something utterly inimical and
alien, are inclined to pass over issues that seem to be too shameful. How can
one admit to oneself that Polish anti-Semitism survived the Nazi occupation, that the sight of the greatest mass murder in the history of the world
did not move Poles to a massive response of solidarity with the Jewish
population? As if reaching for a life vest, Polish liberals and Christians turn
to well-known examples of Poles who put their own lives on the line to
save Jewish friends or children. But these *exceptional* episodes (the number
of Jews who survived the war testifies to their rarity) cannot compensate
for the passive responsibility for the destruction of three million people
that weighs on the Polish nation. . . . I was not in Poland during the Nazi
occupation, but from eyewitness accounts given by both Poles and Jews I
know of episodes far more repulsive than passively watching "how Hitler
eliminates the Jewish problem in Poland." I am thinking about blackmail,
about "refuge" provided to Jews who paid huge sums of money for it, gold
coins demanded for glasses of water that Poles sold to Jews deported from
Holland on "death trains," exploits of the "blue police" in the Ghetto, or

"actions" of the National Armed Forces. . . . Stories about how Jews jubi-
lantly welcomed the Soviet Army's entry into eastern Poland figure among
Polish anti-Semites' favorite arguments. "They waved those red sheets, yes
sir, and they yelled, sir, such rabble." A more natural reaction would be hard
to find. After all, this impoverished Jewish community, persecuted for years
but still hanging on to life, would have been *sentenced to death* if the German
and not the Soviet Army had entered their village. No wonder they were so
joyful in welcoming—not the system and not the people—but the miracle
that was about to save their lives. . . . The fact that Jews died together with
Poles with whom they were deported to Soviet gulags, just as they died
together with Poles in Auschwitz—is a different matter. In any event, given
the fact that Polish anti-Semitism survived the Nazi occupation, when it
should have been completely destroyed by a simple human response, not
to mention a Christian one, it is no wonder that the Soviet occupation
only inflamed it. This time Poles found a *pretext*: the significant percentage
of Jews and people with Jewish backgrounds among party dignitaries and
in the security apparatus. But let us think about it. Isn't it understandable
that in a country in which the tradition of anti-Semitism spans at least a
hundred years, the Jewish population would gravitate toward a party and
a system that theoretically eliminates the entire problem of anti-Semitism?
Some explain Jews' predilection for communism by invoking their logical,
philosophical temperament and thirst for a universal doctrine. This interpretation is perhaps not without some merit—similar factors make other
Jews inclined toward Catholicism. But it is absurd to throw accusations of
"collaboration" at Polish citizens whose "collaboration" with communism
can be explained by the need for self-preservation: communism would not
be as appealing to Jews if Poland had not pushed them away for so many
years. And besides, who is loudest in making such accusations? The ideological comrades of people who metamorphosed from members of the Falanga
or the National Radical Camp (ONR) into not so much "collaborators" as
agents of the communist regime.[4] We have seen enough examples of Polish
"nationalists" and local anti-Semites who shower the Communists with
repugnant flattery to know that the argument about Jewish "collaboration"
with communism is untenable.

Recent articles about anti-Semitism in the Polish press suggest something more dramatic. Many of them contain allusions that seem difficult to
understand individually but which acquire rather ominous meaning when
one brings them together: there is not a single article that does not mention

anti-Semitic tendencies within the Communist Party (PZPR). The allusions are discreet, authors make them in passing, but they recur so often that it is difficult not to attach significance to them; it is difficult not to suspect that their message crosses tacitly respected boundaries.

In *Przegląd Kulturalny* (*The Cultural Review*) from June 7, Jerzy Broszkiewicz writes:

> I cannot vouch that the shadow of anti-Semitism has not set foot in any of the party committees.

And further down:

> The penetration of party ranks by each thought and each tendency that negates the basic premises of the workers' movement, and which is hostile toward the laws and principles of communist morality . . . could become the only truly serious danger. . . . There are cases when party members succumb to the pressure of alien and hostile tendencies, when . . . obscurantist, nationalist, and medieval tendencies are smuggled in under the banner of national unity.

And here is a passage from the polemics that followed Hanka Szwarcman's article in *Po Prostu*:

> In Poland, we are dealing with a historically rooted triple nationalism based on anti-German, anti-Russian, and anti-Jewish feelings. The first two manifestations of this nationalism appear in propaganda and in the upbringing of children and youth. . . . *But when it comes to Jews . . . there is obligatory silence.* (my emphasis—K.J.).

In *Dziennik Polski* (*The Polish Daily*), May 24, 1956, Ignacy Krasicki does not hesitate to point out the causes of this "silence" and writes that the "tragic crimes" resulting from "the cult of personality" (a more easily decipherable euphemism is hard to come by today) cast a dark shadow over the problem of anti-Semitism, and the repulsive anti-Semitic overtone of so many of the trials was a fundamental element of "Beriaism" (another form of the euphemism).[5]

Similarly, in the April 12 issue of *Przegląd Kulturalny* (*The Cultural Review*), Arnold Słucki writes:

> Could the Doctors' Plot not become a peculiar prelude to a special type of mystification that will have far-reaching social consequences? We should not pass over these matters in silence. Anti-Semitism, August Bebel once said, is the socialism of the stupid. We should consider whether, under the wings of Beriaism, a variant of communism for idiots was not perhaps being tested.

And Stanisław Jerzy Lec puts the same idea even more directly (*Przegląd Kulturalny* [*The Cultural Review*], May 10):[6]

August Bebel said that Anti-Semitism is the socialism of the stupid. Will we yet have to say that anti-Semitism is the communism of the stupid?

Edmund Osmańczyk (*Świat* [*The World*], May 20) clearly suggests that there is an anti-Semitic group among the Communists:

He who respects the USSR and our party, but tolerates racist, and specifically— in our situation—anti-Semitic prejudice around him and in his own psyche, is not a progressive man.

Before attempting a closer analysis of these allusions, let us move on to other information about anti-Semitism in the Communist Party—information that obviously cannot appear in the Polish press. According to Seweryn Bialer, a former official in the Communist Party's Central Committee who himself has Jewish roots, and who recently escaped Poland, the first anti-Semitic purges in the party took place at the end of 1953 and the beginning of 1954. The following people with Jewish backgrounds were fired from posts they held at the time: Oskar Kluski, director of the Central Committee's international subcommittee; Artur Starewicz, director of the propaganda subcommittee; his deputy Teodora Feder, Stefan Staszewski, director of the press subcommittee; Leon Kasman, editor of *Trybuna Ludu* (*The People's Tribunal*)—and many others. Strong anti-Semitic tendencies are said to exist in Rokossovsky's party and in his army.[7] At about the same time as the above purge, several thousand officers with Jewish backgrounds were retired from the army without any official explanation. Kazimierz Witaszewski, Rokossovsky's righthand man, undersecretary of state in the Ministry of National Defense and director for political education in the army, is said to be a vicious anti-Semite. He was recently made a general, and currently heads the Internal Security Service. People tell the following story about him: At a meeting of the Warsaw Dzierżyński Academy (a military political education institution), Witaszewski was criticizing Hilary Minc and his economic policy and alluded to Minc's Jewish background several times.[8] During the discussion, one of the officers protested and said that one can attack Minc's economic policy, but he doesn't see how it is connected with his Jewish background. Witaszewski asked this intrepid officer for his personal background, thinking that "Jewish solidarity" was at play. But it turned out that the officer was not a Jew, and the audience applauded him.

Rokossovsky and Witaszewski are said to be "hardliners" (as the French press calls them) and opponents of Poland's "new course," much like Edward Ochab and Wiktor Kłosiewicz[9] (a new member of the Political Bureau and head of the syndicates), both of whom are also known as anti-Semites. People say that at a party rally in Łódź, someone from the audience passed Ochab a piece of paper with a question (a custom established after the Twentieth Congress of the Communist Party): "Why do Jews hold the best positions in the party, the government, and the administration?" Ochab allegedly berated the anonymous questioner for his anti-Semitism and said that it is contrary to communist ideology, but, characteristically, added that "the government will audit how certain positions are staffed."

Ochab is particularly unpopular among party intellectuals—especially artists and writers. He never concealed his unease and dissatisfaction with the turn "the thaw" has taken in Poland. There is no shortage of Jews among writers and journalists who were first to fight for greater freedom, and who did it most bravely. Primitive minds—whether fascist or Stalinist—were always suspicious of Jews as propagators of murky liberal tendencies. In none other than *Życie Warszawy* (*Warsaw Life*), in the May 31 issue, we can find a stunning sentence, provided as the opinion of a certain faction of Polish anti-Semites: "*Jews are characterized by a fondness for bourgeois liberalism.*" What kind of anti-Semite, if not a Stalinist one, can speak this way today? As we can see, the notion of "Judeo-Bolshevism" has been replaced by the idea of "Judeo-liberalism."

To sum up: the many pieces of evidence reaching us from Poland make it possible to reconstruct the following picture of the situation. A "Stalinist group" in the Polish Communist Party, opposed to reform and all changes to the existing status quo, is largely anti-Semitic. Anti-Semitism is the platform that makes it possible for any Polish government to get the approval of the most backward part of society. Dropping the earlier policy of terror at the Kremlin's command, and being thus forced to look for somewhat broader social support, the regime unhesitatingly sacrifices a group of people who have been loyal to it: the Jew is always and everywhere an ideal scapegoat. Because authentic liberal tendencies are represented inside the party by intellectuals, among whom there is no shortage of those with Jewish roots, this is the Stalinists' way of laying the groundwork for a conflict with the "liberal" opposition.

The fact that the anti-Semitism of Polish Stalinists mirrors that of their Moscow patrons makes this argument all the more likely to be accurate.

Ochab is said to enjoy Khrushchev's confidence. In the West, in general, Khrushchev is said to have anti-Semitic tendencies. Western opinion was troubled by the fact that Khrushchev's speech did not include a condemnation of crimes perpetrated against Jews during the Stalinist era. Even the American communist periodical, the *Daily Worker*, published the following sentence on June 6, 1956:

> We are also concerned about the fact that the long list of crimes mentioned in the speech does not include crimes perpetrated against Jewish culture and Jewish cultural products.

Everyone also knows that people from Western circles—especially socialist ones—have intervened about this issue several times in talks with Soviet leaders, and that Khrushchev dismissed them by saying that there is no anti-Semitism in the USSR. The June 16 issue of the Swiss *Neue Züricher Zeitung* cites this kind of conversation between Khrushchev (who went to visit London with Bulganin) and the leading British socialist Hugh Gaitskell; it also cites a discussion between Khrushchev and the delegates of the French Section of the Workers' International in Moscow. When asked about the fate of Jews in the USSR, Khrushchev is said to have claimed that Jewish intellectuals have played an important role during the Revolution, and were therefore given important positions in the party and the administration. This was necessary at the time because Russian intellectual forces were lacking. But conditions have changed. Bolshevism has educated its own administrators and intellectuals, and it no longer needs to rely on Jewish intellectuals. Khrushchev announced, finally, that Jewish cultural organizations themselves attach no importance to their own culture, and wish for the quickest possible "Russification" of the two million Jews living in the USSR. These announcements contain a hefty dose of anti-Semitism, even if it is unconscious. And the thesis that Jews played a leading role in the October Revolution is ultimately identical to that advanced by the Black Hundreds.[10] But Khrushchev is much more direct when he speaks in "people's democracies" than in his talks with Western democrats. At a meeting of the Central Committee of the Polish Communist Party that took place after Bolesław Bierut's death in 1956, Khrushchev munificently talked with the delegates in private, patting them on the back. Here are a few of his statements concerning the Jewish issue: (looking at the list of delegates) "You have too many Abramoviches here." Or, like an "older brother" passing out friendly advice: "If you have to choose between Kowalski and Rosenblum, and Kowalski is not a complete idiot and hoodlum, while Rosenblum is a genius, always choose Kowalski. . . ."

Soviet anti-Semitism is, by the way, well-known in Poland. In June 1956, a trip to the USSR was organized for representatives of the Polish collective farms. At the last minute, all Jews, including the dignitaries, were crossed off from the list of delegates.

Communists' exploitation of anti-Semitism is nothing new in Poland. Today, we know that the 1946 Kielce Pogrom was provoked by the local—rather than Russian—security officials.[11]

In light of this information, the aforementioned Polish articles with their allusions to anti-Semitic tendencies within the Polish Communist Party take on special significance.

Over the course of the last ten years, the traditional deep Polish anti-Semitism has not lost any of its intensity. But—as one of the Polish journalists said—there was *obligatory silence*. Only since April 1956, as a result of "the thaw"—in its rather advanced phase—did people start talking about anti-Semitism in Poland again. It is an interesting coincidence that the same newspapers and journalists who were first to raise this issue were also first to dare wage the struggle—on the pages of Polish papers—for broadly defined liberalization.

They have to realize that this liberalization is threatened by Stalinists, "bigwigs," administrators who hold privileged posts, and eternal Polish parochial reactionaries. These journalists realize that Stalinists and reactionaries can forge an alliance that targets Jews. And this is why they are taking advantage of the current climate to warn us against this double danger. As a result of a tragic irony of fate, anti-Semitism, which inflicted so much harm in Poland and on Poles, is once again becoming a present danger. Poland's current oppressors can exploit it, just as its yesterday's oppressors did.

Editors' Notes

1. Andrei Vlasov (1901–1946) was a Soviet general who collaborated with Nazi Germany. In 1944, he formed a military formation called the Russian Liberation Army, which briefly fought alongside Nazi Germany against the Red Army. The Lithuanian Special Squad was an execution squad formed by the occupying Nazi government in Vilnius. Its members were primarily Lithuanian volunteers; they participated in perpetrating the massacres in the Ponary Forest near Vilnius. The National Armed Forces was a Polish underground military organization; it is discussed in "Poles and Jews during the Holocaust" in the Introduction.

2. Ferdinand Lasalle (1825–1864) was an influential German-Jewish socialist leader; Heinrich Graetz (1817–1891) was a pioneer in the field of Jewish history.

3. The phrase "Jew-benches" refers to the "ghetto benches," or segregated seating areas for Jewish students in university lecture halls in interwar Poland; they are discussed in "The Interwar Years: Polish Independence and the Crisis of Democracy" in the Introduction.

4. The National Radical Camp (ONR) and its Falanga fraction are discussed in Editors' Note 1 to chapter 11 and in the Introduction.

5. Stalin unleashed an anti-Semitic campaign between 1949 and 1953. In January 1953, Soviet propaganda began promulgating the idea that there was a group of doctors who were plotting against the life of Stalin and other high-ranking Soviet leaders. Nine innocent doctors, six of them Jewish, were arrested and tortured in prison; two died, while others admitted guilt. When Stalin died on March 5, 1953, the doctors were released, and their innocence was publicly announced. Lavrentiy Beria (1899–1953) was the chief of the brutally repressive Soviet secret police (NKVD); the term "Beriaism" (*beriowszczyzna*) appeared frequently in the Polish press in 1956 and 1957 and suggested that Beria was responsible for the Soviet anti-Semitic campaigns that took place during Stalin's final years in power.

6. Stanisław Jerzy Lec (1909–1966) was a Polish poet from a Jewish family from Galicia.

7. Konstantin Rokossovsky (Konstanty Rokossowski, 1896–1968) was an influential Polish-born Soviet military commander during the Second World War; he is most famous for leading the Red Army to victory against the Nazi forces during "Operation Bagration" in the summer of 1944. He served as Poland's minister of defense between 1952 and 1957.

8. Hilary Minc (1905–1974) was one of the three most powerful government officials during the Stalinist period in Poland. The other two were Bolesław Bierut (1892–1956), who served as president of the Polish Republic and secretary general of the Central Committee of the Polish Communist Party (PZPR) between 1948 and 1956, and Jakub Berman (1901–1984), who served as the minister of public security and was in charge of the brutal secret police. Minc served as deputy prime minister for economic affairs and minister of industry and commerce.

9. Eward Ochab (1906–1989) succeeded Bolesław Bierut as the first secretary of the Communist Party (PZPR) in March 1956; he served in this capacity until October 1956, when he was succeeded by Władysław Gomułka.

10. The Black Hundreds was a Russian ultranationalist movement that became active around the time of the Russian Revolution of 1905; it was known, among other things, for violent anti-Semitism and pogroms.

11. For other views about the role of the communist officials in provoking the Kielce Pogrom, see for example, Krystyna Kersten's and Aleksander Smolar's essays in this volume on pages 193–225 and 232–270, respectively.

13

Anti-Semitism

JERZY TUROWICZ

Editors' Introduction

Jerzy Turowicz (1912–1999) was the editor of the Catholic weekly *Tygodnik Powszechny*, one of the few independent intellectual forums in communist Poland. Born in Krakow, he studied machine construction at the Lviv Polytechnic and philosophy at Jagiellonian University. In the 1930s, Turowicz joined the Catholic student group Odrodzenie (Rebirth), and during the war he worked with a Catholic underground cultural organization and published in various underground journals. He cofounded the weekly *Tygodnik Powszechny* and became its editor in 1945. *Tygodnik* recognized the authority of Poland's communist government, but it maintained an independent voice, claiming a realm of freedom for religious thought. In 1953, Turowicz and the editorial board refused to publish a government-sponsored Stalin's obituary, and *Tygodnik* was closed down. It was reopened a few months later, but the editorial board passed into the hands of progovernment Catholic activists. In the wake of de-Stalinization in 1956, *Tygodnik* was returned to Turowicz and his colleagues, and he remained its editor until his death in 1999. During the March 1968 events, and in all conflicts between democratic opposition activists and the communist government in the 1970s and 1980s, Turowicz and *Tygodnik* defended civil rights and liberties, and criticized government abuses. In 1989, Turowicz was a delegate at the Round Table negotiations between Solidarity and the government.

In his articles and essays, Turowicz embraced the open-minded and tolerant Catholicism advocated by the Second Vatican Council. He enjoyed great respect among Catholic intellectuals throughout his life, and he was among the harshest critics of anti-Semitism among Catholic Poles. The essay reproduced here originally appeared in *Tygodnik Powszechny* in March 1957, when anti-Semitism was widely discussed in the wake of the 1956 anti-Semitic campaign within the Communist Party.

I was leaving Warsaw on April 19, 1943. That day, the airplanes in the sky above the city were circling more intensely than usual; you could hear the crackling of machine guns and explosions. When I was already on the train, I found out that an Uprising had broken out in the Jewish Ghetto, that the SS squads which attempted to liquidate the Ghetto had encountered armed resistance. People who had practically no chance of saving their lives were fighting against Hitler's fascism. They were not fighting for their lives; they were fighting to salvage their dignity.

The Uprising in the Warsaw Ghetto was a culmination of the Jewish people's fight against Nazism. The years between 1939 and 1945 were a time of greatest tragedy in the history of this nation. Of the three-and-a-half million Polish Jews, over three million perished in gas chambers and execution fields. During the same period, several million Jews from other European countries perished as well. Meanwhile, Poles were perishing in concentration camps and prisons for resisting the German occupation, for fighting against Nazism. Jews perished primarily just because they were Jews.

That community of people who were persecuted and who fought and suffered changed Polish-Jewish relations in our country in a rather fundamental way. Traces of anti-Semitism disappeared in much of the Polish population, and were replaced by a sense of solidarity; the will to help the persecuted appeared, and it was transformed into action. During the Ghetto Uprising, these feelings were augmented by admiration for a nation which fought until the very end in such a hopeless situation.

I thought then, as did many people in Poland, that future Poland would be free from anti-Semitism, that this murky phenomenon was relegated to the past once and for all. And not simply because there would be very few Jews in Poland after the war.

Yet today, in 1957, that conviction seems like an illusion. For some time now, an intense campaign against anti-Semitism has been underway in the Polish press.[a1] So there is anti-Semitism. And we have to examine its scope, character, and sources.

I maintain that there was basically no anti-Semitism in Poland during the postwar years. Admittedly, in 1946—if I'm not mistaken—there was an anti-Jewish Pogrom in Kielce, and it was widely publicized throughout the world. I believe, however, and many people in Poland think this

---

[a] The press campaign focused on anti-Semitism has good and bad sides. Since manifestations of anti-Semitism do exist here and there, it is right for the press to point them out and fight them. On the other hand, especially for a foreign observer, this campaign could create the impression—untrue and harmful to Poland's interests—that anti-Semitism in Poland is a universal and dangerous phenomenon.

way, that the circumstances of that Pogrom have still not been properly clarified. During the years that followed, all the way until 1956, people did not write about anti-Semitism, nor did we hear about its manifestations. In today's Poland there are no groups, no political or ideological formations that advocate anti-Semitism. In this regard, great changes have taken place in Polish mentality since 1939. We can claim that—as a programmatic stance—anti-Semitism has been surmounted in Poland.

An enormously large percentage of the small group of Jews living in Poland today—a group of probably no more than 100,000 people—is leaving Poland, or plans to leave. They say that 20,000 to 25,000 Jews have applied for foreign passports. The foreign press discusses this extensively and comments that these departures are a result of Poland's rampant anti-Semitism. Things are not that simple. In recent years, many Jews wanted to leave Poland for Israel or other countries because they see Israel as their new homeland, or they have families in other countries, and they would like to be reunited with them. They could not leave Poland in previous years and now they can, so they are leaving. But it is also undoubtedly true that anti-Semitism—actual anti-Semitism or fear of future anti-Semitism—is one of the reasons for their departure.

Given today's domestic situation in Poland, I see this fear as unfounded. During the occupation years, Polish anti-Semitism was surmounted and has become less infectious. I am, however, far from being dismissive about anti-Semitism that manifests itself here and there. One has to fight these manifestations, and this is why we write about them in *Tygodnik Powszechny*.

Unfortunately, anti-Semitism has a rather long tradition in Poland; before the war, a relatively large part of society fell under its sway, and today, too, a certain susceptibility to anti-Semitic slogans remains among the less-advanced social strata whose thinking is more primitive.

The sources of anti-Semitism include the fact that Jews are separate from the societies in which they live, that there is an ethno-cultural Jewish community that has existed for 2,000 years despite, or perhaps to some extent thanks to, the diaspora, thanks to the situation caused by dispersal. And frequently even whole generations of assimilation could not undermine this community. Anti-Semitism—which is, by the way, typically tied to nationalism—takes advantage of this separateness of the Jews, ascribes various negative traits to them as a social group, and accuses them of having a destructive impact. In its extreme form, anti-Semitism takes on the features of an irrational, magical-mystical outlook, which ascribes responsibility for all evil to Jews, accusing them of a worldwide conspiracy against the whole non-Jewish part of humanity, a conspiracy that aims to rule the world. Anti-Semitism leads to aversion, hostility, and hatred toward Jews, and to attempts to isolate them from the life of the society with which they coexist, which, in turn, leads to boycotts, pogroms, and crimes.

We will not conduct a detailed polemic against anti-Semitic theses here. First, anti-Semitism does not exist in Poland today in its elaborated form— as an ideology. And second, polemics against its theses have been undertaken many times before, and exposed the senselessness and baselessness of its claims. Many have argued that one of the greatest losses anti-Semitism inflicts on every society is the fact that by mythically explaining all evil as Jewish handiwork, it turns attention away from actual causes of evil, which usually lie in distorted social structures, or deformed configurations of social, economic, or political relations. Anti-Semitism thereby relieves people of making a conscious effort to eliminate the actual causes of evil.

Here, I would only like to point out two issues: Jews' place in Poland, and the relationship between anti-Semitism and Catholicism.

The first issue: anti-Semites claim that Poland belongs exclusively to Poles, and Jews are a foreign and harmful element here; their influence on life in our country should therefore be limited to a minimum. They forget, however, how Jews arrived in Poland. They forget that Jews came to Poland several hundred years ago because they were persecuted elsewhere, and Poland was rightly famous for its hospitality and tolerance. But today one should no longer evoke hospitality and tolerance when talking about Jews' rights. After several hundred years of coexisting with Poles in these lands between the Tatra Mountains and the Baltic Sea, Jews have the rights of co-hosts here. Regardless of whether there are 3 million or 100,000 of them, Jews have played their part in our country's history, economy, and culture. Anti-Semites say that Jews' participation in these realms has been bad and harmful. There is no basis for such a general statement. Of course, sometimes their influence was bad. As was the case with Poles. Both are human.

Recently, on the anniversary of Julian Tuwim's death, we published a poem dedicated to his memory in *Tygodnik Powszechny*.[2] We received a series of letters from readers who were displeased, because Tuwim was a Jew and wrote immoral poems. Julian Tuwim did, indeed, write a number of poems which we cannot endorse from the perspective of Christian morality. But many Polish poets with "Aryan" backgrounds also wrote immoral poems, and somehow no one holds it against them—because they were not

Jews. And, as a matter of fact—regardless of what anti-Semites might wish for—Julian Tuwim belongs to the history of Polish literature. While I value Tuwim's poetic craft, I am not an admirer of his poetry and believe there were greater artists in both his and the following generation. But this does not change the fact that Tuwim's place in Polish culture is undeniable—it is not determined by race and blood but by a writer's rootedness in the living flesh of culture.

Let us now turn to the question of the relationship between Catholicism and anti-Semitism. In both distant and more recent history, anti-Semitism was often rampant among Catholics. But this is not a general rule. In Protestant America, anti-Semitism is typically connected with anti-Catholicism (and with racism aimed at Negroes), and neopagan Nazism was directed against both Jews and Christians. Moreover, the Church often condemned anti-Semitism; in prewar Poland there were Catholic circles that opposed the wave of anti-Semitism, while during the occupation years Catholics, and underground Catholic organizations, played an important role in helping Jews; a number of Jewish children survived the years of degradation hidden in Catholic monasteries.

But because today, as before the war, anti-Semitism makes itself known among Catholics, we have to say clearly: anti-Semitism and Catholicism cannot be reconciled; anti-Semitism is pagan in its essence.

Anti-Semites sometimes use a rather primitive religious motivation: one should hate Jews because they put Christ, the God-Man, to death on the cross. Yes, but the Crucified, as man, was also a Jew, and His mother Mary was a Jewish woman. Peter—the rock on which the Church was built—was also a Jew, as was Paul of Tarsus—the apostle of nations—a true, fierce, and passionate Jew. The apostles and Gospel writers were Jews, and Christianity's holy books, the Old and the New Testaments, also belong to the national treasures of Jewish literature. Connections between Christianity and Judaism are direct and much deeper than the average anti-Semite supposes. Hatred directed at Jews is also an indirect strike at Christianity.

It is also a strike at Christianity because anti-Semites have no understanding of the actual meaning of what took place at Golgotha 2,000 years ago. The "Chosen People" were chosen to represent all humanity. In the name of humanity, this nation rejected and crucified the Messiah. One can say that in a certain sense it was not Jews but all of humanity that crucified Christ; he was crucified by the fury of the world, in which every person plays his part.

Jews do, too. Christ thus died on the cross for everyone. From this perspective, the diaspora can be seen as a historical consequence of the crucifixion, but there is no place for anti-Semitism here.

Jacques Maritain says that Christians can be anti-Semites only by obeying the secular spirit of the world and not the spirit of Christianity. One can say more: a Catholic who is simultaneously an anti-Semite is *not* a Catholic insofar as he is an anti-Semite. It is, therefore, a sort of mutilated Catholicism.

Anti-Semitism cannot be reconciled with Catholicism because anti-Semitism is hatred for a human being because he is Jewish. Catholicism allows and demands that we hate evil, but it does not allow us to hate people. Christianity's main commandment concerned with human relations is an injunction to love one's neighbor. And this neighbor is every person, regardless of race, skin color, or convictions.

Catholicism proclaims the principle of the equality of all people. People—both individuals and social groups—differ from one another, of course, in terms of their level of culture, awareness, morality, and so on. But no deterministic principles apply here. Every person was granted free will and reason, everyone is called to develop his personality and to do good, and everyone thus deserves fundamental rights that flow from his nature.

This leads to the universalism of the Catholic outlook. Humanity is one; all humanity, by its collective efforts, constructs the edifice of culture and history. If mankind's history includes antagonistic divisions, these divisions are an unavoidable affliction of human historical existence, but they must not be elevated to the status of law. Solidarity and universalism are the law.

Finally, Catholicism is personalist.[3] It treats each person as a self-contained whole, rational and free, with a duty to seek the truth and to do good. Each person has inalienable rights that elevate him above the collectivity, each person carries within himself a limitless potential for good and evil, and each person is, ultimately, responsible for his own actions, and only for his own actions.

Along with nationalism and racism, anti-Semitism belongs to categories of thought that negate both universalism and personalism. Anti-Semitism negates universalism because it divides humanity into antagonistic groups; it divides the world into higher and lower races, good and bad people. Contrary to what anti-Semites proclaim, or subconsciously think, the boundary between good and evil does not run between people. The separation of the good from the bad, the wheat from the chaff, will take place at some point in the future on Judgment Day, according to criteria different from our human ones, at a point when the shape of each personality, and its final account of good and evil, will be closed. Here, on earth, the boundary between good and evil runs through the center of each of our souls—Jew or non-Jew, Catholic, infidel, or pagan.

Anti-Semitism is anti-personalist because in place of a person's responsibility for his own actions it establishes some sort of collective responsibility of a nation, race, or social group, enclosing the human person within a combination of materialist determinism and a magical, irrational interpretation of the world.

There is thus no agreement between anti-Semitism and Catholicism. If many reconciled these two attitudes within themselves in Poland before the war, this only testifies to the intellectual weakness and superficiality of much of Polish Catholicism; it testifies to the lack of understanding of Christianity's essence. Luckily, this was not a universal phenomenon.

Today, when anti-Semitism is by no means—I emphasize this again—a mass phenomenon in Poland, there are signs suggesting it could be revived here and there, and one has to speak out, if just preventatively, to forestall attempts to reconcile things that cannot be reconciled.

Perhaps this last part of our reflection will not be entirely clear to all our readers. It is necessary, however, for every Catholic in Poland to clearly understand one thing: all anti-Semitism is contrary to the injunction to love man.

Some of our periodical's friends and readers will probably not like the views expressed in this article. I can say one thing to them: these views are not anything new here; they are neither opportunistic nor a response to a favorable situation. Those who created *Tygodnik Powszechny* and who manage it today have been proclaiming these views for many long years, also before 1939. These views are the only logical consequence of our entire worldview. We proclaim them because we believe they are right, regardless of whether people like them or not. *Amicus Plato, sed magis amica veritas* [Plato is my friend but truth is a better friend]. We repeat: it is not possible to simultaneously be an aware and conscientious Catholic and an anti-Semite. One has to choose.

Editors' Notes

1. For a different analysis of anti-Semitism and the Polish press in 1956, please see Konstanty Jeleński's essay "From National Democrats to Stalinists" in this volume on pages 153–161; we discuss Polish anti-Semitism during the war and in its aftermath in "Poles and Jews during the Holocaust" and "Anti-Semitism in the Polish People's Republic" in the Introduction.

2. Julian Tuwim's essay "We, Polish Jews" is reproduced in this volume on pages 63–68.

3. Personalism was a philosophical current, often associated with the French Catholic thinker Jacques Maritain (1882–1973); at its heart is the notion that the human person is irreducible and should be the center of philosophical reflection.

14

The Anti-Semitism of Kind and Gentle People

TADEUSZ MAZOWIECKI

Editors' Introduction

Tadeusz Mazowiecki (1927–2013) was a Catholic intellectual and Poland's first prime minister after the fall of communism in 1989. Born in the city of Płock in central Poland, he studied law at the University of Warsaw. In 1948, he joined the progovernment Catholic organization PAX led by Bolesław Piasecki, but he left the group in 1955 after protesting against Piasecki's authoritarianism and excessive loyalty to the government. A year later, Mazowiecki cofounded the progressive Club of Catholic Intellectuals (KIK), and in 1958 became the editor of the newly founded Catholic monthly *Więź* (*Bond*), a forum for Catholics who supported the spirit and reforms of the Second Vatican Council, convened by Pope John XXIII in 1962. Between 1961 and 1971, Mazowiecki served as a deputy in the Polish Parliament, and in 1968 he joined the anticommunist democratic opposition movement. In August 1980 he became an expert adviser to Lech Wałęsa's workers' strike committee at the Gdańsk shipyard, and he was imprisoned by General Jaruzelski's government when martial law was announced in Poland in December 1981 to clamp down on the increasingly powerful Solidarity movement. Mazowiecki was a Solidarity delegate to the 1989 Round Table talks with the communist government, and he became Poland's prime minister in August 1989, after Solidarity won a landslide victory in the June 1989 elections.

In his writings, Mazowiecki advocated liberal and tolerant tendencies in Catholicism; he wrote many books and essay collections, the most important of which was *Rozdroża i wartości* (*Crossroads and Values*, 1971). The essay reproduced here is the text of a 1960 talk he gave at the KIK in Krakow on March 24 and in Warsaw on April 8. It was first published a month later in the Warsaw-based *Więź*. Mazowiecki gave the talk because he felt that Polish Catholicism must confront anti-Semitism within its ranks.

The greatest tragedy of Jews is not that the anti-Semite hates them, but that the good, gentle people say: "He is a decent man, even though he is Jewish."

—Ludwik Hirszfeld, *Historia jednego życia* (*The Story of One Life*)[1]

I have to admit that I was initially seized by doubts when the initiative to discuss this problem was proposed. Isn't it pointless to discuss anti-Semitism in Poland today—or worse—aren't the effects the opposite of what one intends? In a word, I worried if this might not be a way of fomenting trouble, of unintentionally arousing passions that, in this case as in no other, should finally fall silent.

After all, this problem appears to be quite different in Poland today than it was in the interwar years. And this is the first general claim that is impossible to ignore when setting out to analyze this issue. The phenomenon of open, militant anti-Semitism has disappeared from the surface of our life. There are no organizations that programmatically proclaim racism and anti-Semitism. The state has taken a different stance and treats both these ideologies as hostile to humanity and forbidden by law. The social situation looks different. We have the experience of war behind us. We have also done much authentic educational work, which had direct or indirect effects on a deeper, nonmechanical transformation of human attitudes.

But, though the situation is different in every respect, one cannot run away from taking up this problem—because the problem exists. There is no open, militant anti-Semitism, but there is still anti-Semitism that enters the battlefield with its face concealed. Its reach and meanings are different, but it has not disappeared altogether. And, most important, a subtle anti-Semitism exists and is still prevalent in our society—as disdain preserved at the bottom of one's heart, or simply an anti-Jewish myth, which, like a flickering ember, is not that difficult to rekindle, and is sustained by many newly accumulated complexes.

The process of surmounting anti-Semitism thus remains incomplete. Not long ago, we were reminded of this in a very drastic way. Rudolf Buchała published in *Więź* an article about neo-fascist centers throughout the world, discussing, among other things, the problem of well-known anti-Semitic brawls that recently took place in West Germany and other countries. The article was based on a talk he gave in the Club of Catholic Intellectuals (KIK) in Warsaw, and it was at that discussion that the audience suggested an initiative to explore the problem of anti-Semitism. A few days after the publication of Buchała's article, the editors of *Więź* received a letter, signed with a cryptonym and resembling old, most unsophisticated anti-Semitic enunciations. The author of the letter blames Jews for all the evil in the world and in Poland; in his opinion *Więź* brought eternal shame upon itself by publishing an article that fights anti-Semitism.

One could shrug one's shoulders and say: here is a person who hasn't been cured, a crypto-fascist. And yet, are the arguments he uses not still in circulation? There is, of course, no point in having a discussion with a man who burns with the desire to cut off Jewish heads. But let us not reduce the problem to the statement that there are still some fanatics who have not been cured in Poland, people always ready to turn their dreams about pogroms into reality. There is, above all, the issue of a context that still nourishes such phenomena. Namely, the problem of the sociopsychological climate still marked by a deep residue of anti-Semitism. This is precisely why I address these reflections not to fanatics and heirs of fascism, and not to militant anti-Semites, a discussion with whom is pointless. In our circumstances, their attitude is not, in any case, the "central trope" in the depiction of this problem. Much more significant is that residue of anti-Semitism from the past, which has persisted in ordinary attitudes, or which has been deposited anew, making itself known from time to time. I therefore write this with ordinary people in mind, the kind and gentle people who say, "He is a decent man, even though he is Jewish."

Sociologists sometimes say that certain relations between social groups are governed by the categories of superiority and inferiority. These qualities can emerge in social relations for a variety of reasons. In the case of class differences, they emerge, above all, on the basis of fundamental differences in socio-economic circumstances and the resulting system of dependence. They can also have their main source in the set ways in which one group perceives the qualities of the other. Anti-Semitism is this kind of phenomenon.

Its international reach is testimony to the fact that it is different from typical national conflicts. It cannot be contained in the framework of hostility toward national minorities. For instance, in interwar Poland conflicts between Poles and Ukrainians, Poles and Czechs, or Poles and Germans, had a different tone than anti-Semitism. Even artificially fueled national conflicts obtained their justification by appealing, first and foremost, to concrete problems and difficulties of coexistence and not to qualities ascribed to these nations in general. In a certain specific sense anti-Semitism is also classless: it turns against Jews in general, regardless of their social position;

and it appeals to anti-Jewish solidarity while bypassing contemporary social stratification. These qualities of anti-Semitism already suggest what role generalities and a priori premises play in this phenomenon, and what role is played by actual social conflicts. It is an attitude of hostility toward Jews, or toward people with Jewish backgrounds, deriving not so much from the accumulation of concrete social conflicts, as from the attribution of certain qualities to Jews or Jewishness in general.

I do not want to say that Jews—scattered throughout various countries, overcoming obstacles to maintain the distinct identity of their culture, language, and customs over the course of many centuries, and often surrounded by social ostracism—have not, as a community, also acquired negative traits. There is also Jewish fanaticism. But neither militant nor subtle anti-Semitism is based on rational critique of negative qualities that emerged among Jews over the course of their historical development. The anti-Semite does critique—as one might critique flaws in the national character of Poles, Germans, Russians, Frenchmen, or Englishmen. The anti-Semite typically not only exaggerates Jewish flaws but, most important, also treats them as immanent qualities of Jewishness—universal throughout space and immutable in time.

Thus regardless of the grounds on which it grows in any given case, anti-Semitism itself introduces the categories of superiority and inferiority into social relations. They are, moreover, in principle impossible to subvert, since Jewishness in general is, in itself, a negative quality.

Value judgments made by anti-Semitism are based on either racial premises or socio-economic arguments. It is probably unnecessary to go into detail about the nature of racism here. Admittedly, as problems Blacks face make clear, racism still cannot be said to be a phenomenon of the past, but besides the Union of South Africa no country openly proclaims it as the dominant ideology or even one that deserves to be on par with others. Contemporary scholarship has utterly discredited the intellectual lie of racism. It is worth taking this occasion to emphasize the contributions made by Polish scholarship in this regard, and mention the names of Professor Czekanowski, an anthropologist, Professor Hirszfeld, who investigates blood types, and Professor Ossowski, a sociologist. The attribution of value to distinctive biological characteristics is groundless. Racial qualities are not imprints that predestine some individuals—or some societies—to be fully human and play exceptional historical roles, while denying such destiny to others. Racist arguments belong with simplifications based on unscientific myths whose consequences we know well. Contemporary science also emphasizes the extensive racial intermixing which has taken place, especially within the realm of European culture. Against this background, the problem of "racial purity" or "the purity of blood," accentuated so strongly by Nazism, turns out to be pure nonsense. Professor Ossowski writes: "It is a well-known fact that, anthropologically speaking, the Jewish population is very diverse and its racial profile differs from country to country; these differences, moreover, are correlated with the anthropological profiles of the surrounding populations. . . ." And Prof. Hirszfeld provides a table that shows the percentages of different blood types among Jewish and non-Jewish populations of various countries; he notes that his research has led him to conclude that "blood-type profiles of Jewish communities tend to become similar to the profiles of nations among which they live."

Socio-economic arguments constitute the second motivational source of anti-Semitism. These are based on the claim that Jews and people with Jewish backgrounds are a parasitic and destructive component of societies in which they live. In the interwar period, when anti-Semitism became intensified, economic arguments often took center stage. They seized the imagination of many, but they were astonishingly primitive and limited. Poland's civilizational backwardness did not derive from the large number of Jews who lived there before the war, but from socio-economic structures that existed at the time. The ease with which economic arguments put forward in support of anti-Semitic tendencies were accepted, however, can be explained by the fact that they fell on fertile ground. If there is little bread to go around, it is easy to argue that one's hardship results not from the scarcity of bread, but from giving what little there is to those who could be denied the right to it for one reason or another. The Polish bourgeoisie, or rather petty bourgeoisie, was just beginning to assert itself during this time, and anti-Semitism thus fell on the ground of rivalry. Trade was the main area of the Jewish population's activity, and it was generally not very strictly organized. It was therefore uniquely capable of facilitating—against the background of actual shortages and anomalies—the emergence of the stereotype of the swindling Jew as a symbol of evil that oppresses Poland. And besides, the fact that trade—especially at the "province" level, in dealings with the most primitive and underprivileged lumpenproletariat from small towns and villages—was mostly in Jewish hands in some parts of Poland, put Jews in a very specific social position in the wider framework of underdeveloped Polish capitalism; it also created a certain psychological aura around them. For Jews often found themselves playing the role of those refusing to extend shop credit, lending "at interest" before the harvest, etc. This led to reflexes of aversion, which were exacerbated by differences in custom and religion; it led to subsuming all Jews under the same rubric, heedless of the fact that their own coreligionists also fell victim to larger and smaller Jewish capitalists. The primitive nature of the socio-economic anti-Semitic arguments was characterized by the fact that anti-Semitism did not differentiate between Jews who were capitalists, and those who were employees, shopkeepers, or proletarians—it glossed over social stratification and all its consequences for the evaluation of social phenomena.

Today, the arguments put forward to justify and support anti-Semitism are of a different kind. Before we turn to these, it is first worth thinking about some of the more general causes of anti-Semitism's popularity and about the function it serves. One could ask what makes it possible for social justifications of anti-Semitism to appear under various historical circumstances, and, despite their limited intellectual content, encounter a psychological climate that favors their acceptance and persistence.

Here, I'd like to refer to a thesis proposed by Leszek Kołakowski who says that "anti-Semitism is a means of producing a social symbol." "Fighting Jews"—Kołakowski writes—

> is rarely an end in itself. (. . .) Slogans in the fight against Jews are also often linked with other slogans—slogans which embody the real, political meaning of the fight. History offers an abundance of such associations, where the struggle was waged, for example, against Jews and Christians, Jews and communists, or Jews and democrats. (. . .) The main social mission of anti-Semitism is to create a universal symbol of evil; attempts are then made to tie this symbol in people's minds to phenomena one wants to fight in politics, culture, or scholarship. Jewishness is to become an insult that can be used to brand everything destined for annihilation; it is to be a carrier not of a specific evil, but of evil in general—an abstract negative symbol that can be attached to any situation whatsoever that one wants the world to see as something negative.[2]

Indeed, one only needs to pick up any of the classics of Polish anti-Semitism to see the myriad qualities and aspirations that have been attributed to Jews, and learn about the countless groups who allegedly served these aspirations. Individualism and collectivism, the French Revolution, the Russian Revolution—all these are Jewish ideas and handiwork. Louis Barthou and Franklin Roosevelt, Edvard Beneš, Bible Students, Rasputin, Kerensky, and Lenin—these are only some of the many tools of Jewish world politics. But take, for example, the conclusion of a work which takes

200 pages to demonstrate concordance between Jews' aspirations and the *Protocols of the Elders of Zion*—a book whose authenticity is put into question by even the most intransigent anti-Semites who simultaneously rely on it to ascribe the most repugnant qualities to Jews. The conclusion is unswervingly unambiguous:

> Jews must leave Poland because they are the nation's misfortune. And therefore: given the dangers of the current situation and the dangers of the coming era, Poles must create a single, cohesive national camp. . . . Great ideals need to be reinforced in the entire nation, the sense that the governing authorities are just and impartial needs to be strengthened, noble national feelings and not merely a sense of loyalty to the party must be awakened; because at the present time in Poland, in the face of rapidly escalating revolutionary tendencies, there can only be two parties for the future: a national party or a revolutionary one. . . .

Anti-Semitism has always served to cover up real social conflicts. And there is a characteristic regularity: anti-Semitism, as means of creating a social symbol, has always served to impede society's development. It grew and intensified when either the preservation of existing social structures was at stake—and there was a need to resist social pressures aimed at changing or repairing these structures—or when the imposition of totalitarian tactics on society required a certain protective cover. Anti-Semitism is as convenient for turning attention away from real sources of difficulties and social conflicts as it is for directing society's dissatisfaction toward a universal symbol of evil. This regularity was confirmed in various social conditions, wherever anti-Semitism has appeared: in fascism where it reached its nadir, in the liberal system, and also under diametrically opposed social conditions, as evidenced by Beria's methods and the Doctors' Plot.[3]

The fact that anti-Semitism can be used to deceive society and turn its attention away from actual problems and social conflicts is rather obvious. The causes that make this possible seem less obvious. But anti-Semitism is an irrational attitude. It speaks to the imagination with primitive but suggestive arguments. And by appearing over a long period of time in various circumstances it created susceptibility to the kind of arguments it uses. One could say more: that it managed to create a social habit that facilitates uncritical reception of anti-Semitic messages. This kind of habit persists more easily when elements of confusion, darkness, and misinformation exist in social life, when people cannot or are unable to discover the true mechanisms of social and political life. This habit of seeing the Jewry as a universal coefficient of various kinds of social evils is more durable than the periods of intensification of open, militant anti-Semitism. It is also decisive in the undying possibility of the resurgence of anti-Semitism, despite, or rather because of, its irrational character.

And yet—some ask—does anti-Semitism not have some basis in reality? Does it not have such a basis in our circumstances in particular?

Refusing to take up this question when discussing this topic would be a way of "dodging" the issue. Running from explaining problems that must be posed in a touchy way does not serve the cause of solving them, but rather preserves hidden traumas and misunderstandings. This, in any event, clears the way for anti-Semitic views. And so instead of sidestepping arguments occasionally posed today to justify anti-Semitism, let us instead try to take up this aspect of the problem as well, and, having set emotions aside, attempt to consider it calmly also from this point of view. These arguments can be reduced to two claims: (1) that something like a Jewish mafia is functioning in the political power structure, and (2) that Poles of Jewish descent often turn out to be cosmopolitans, and their connection with Poland is illusory.

Causes of the fact that in 1945 a large number of Poles with Jewish roots found themselves in the political power apparatus—often holding responsible positions—should be sought in the historical situation of that time and not in some eternal qualities of Jewish character, or, worse, in the plans of world Jewry. These Poles belonged to the assimilated or still assimilating intelligentsia that had Jewish origins. They either already had ties to the communist movement earlier, or they became associated with it particularly strongly after the hellish ordeal they endured during the war. They saw the premises of this movement, which was, after all, the engine of the army that defeated fascism, as a durable barrier against the possibility of the resurgence of racism and anti-Semitism. This doubtless influenced their attitude toward the new, revolutionary government. Meanwhile, the overwhelming majority of traditional Polish intellectuals opposed this government in one way or another. Today, people easily forget these facts when they seek to determine "ethnicity proportions" and use these to argue for the alleged correctness of anti-Semitism's claims in our circumstances.

Another argument centers on the fact that people of Jewish descent working in the state or economic apparatus form something like a mafia or a clique. In order to move from the sphere of generalities to concrete details, or rather from myth to reality, this claim, too, needs to be broken down into its basic components. When are we dealing with anti-Semitism? Not in cases of specific criticism but when common reasoning begins to incorporate characteristically anti-Semitic generalities. Those generalities are the real sting of anti-Semitism.

We will not negate the fact that groups whose members support one another often form in various enclaves of the state or economic apparatus. Sometimes this turns into cliquishness. And, by the way, the greater the level of democratic control and professional competence in our social life, the less room there is for such phenomena. When one criticizes these phenomena, however, one cannot lose sight of or negate the simple fact that they appear among both Poles who have Jewish roots and those who do not. And if one frequently observes reflexes or special tendencies toward solidarity among people with Jewish backgrounds, one should not see these as some sort of proof of their—allegedly typical—foreignness from the rest of society. What one should see here is nothing other than a consequence of anti-Semitism and all the durable effects it creates in our sociopsychological atmosphere. This is because anti-Semitism is characterized by the fact that it creates a sense of threat. The contemporary era—in which it made its appearance and left enduring traces in the life of societies—accustomed people with Jewish roots to worry that unexpectedly, at any time, their social position and situation could be threatened solely because of their origin.

Obviously, the accusations we are discussing can always be supported by pointing to some example, or a person with a Jewish background who did one thing or another, or a group of people who make their own lives easier without concern for anything else. Encouragement to track down evil no matter who its carrier is, however, is not a distinguishing characteristic of anti-Semitism. Instead of calling evil by name—regardless of whether it is perpetrated by people with Jewish or non-Jewish backgrounds—anti-Semitism subsumes the phenomena it criticizes under a general Jewish symbol. This is because generalization is its typical methodology; it draws the "kind and gentle" person into the orbit of claims that make a Jew into an all-encompassing cause and carrier of evil. At this same time, it is not always easy to decipher the fact that anti-Semitism is only a pretext and a veil for pursuing other ends.

The same method of generalization as a way of thinking that characterizes anti-Semitism is also at work when accusations of cosmopolitanism get generalized. To point out that there are also cosmopolitans among other people or to recall the number of eminent Poles who had Jewish backgrounds would have the aura of participating in an auction—one conducted on the playing field delineated by anti-Semitism. That's why we will not stop to consider an accusation stated in such general terms. Indirectly, however, this touches upon an important and complicated problem that deserves close attention. I have the question of national integration in mind.

Anti-Semites have tended to put the matter this way: Jews are strangers in Poland, they are foreign and harmful, and so they should leave Poland; in any case, they have no basis to claim the right of co-hosts here. Meanwhile, insofar as Jews faced the problem of choosing a homeland, this problem did not take the vulgar form typically portrayed by anti-Semites. Those Jewish groups that lived with full awareness of their national and intellectual distinctiveness had a sense of having two homelands: a past and a future Jewish one, which, by the way, they often idealized, and a second, chosen one, in which they lived and with which they also felt connected—there is no lack of examples in Polish history to prove this. Those who assimilated, on the other hand, Poles of Jewish descent, thought of themselves as simply having a single homeland. They, too, however, faced the problem of choosing a homeland when circumstances put them in a position where they became convinced that the homeland they considered their own was pushing them away. In any case, after centuries when Jewish communities lived in Poland, centuries marked by both good and evil, and, above all, centuries of co-creating Polish culture and national heritage, Jews' right to feel as co-hosts here cannot be questioned, and no one has the right to artificially reopen the problem of choosing a homeland.

Thus when I speak about the problem of choosing a homeland, I am referring to people in whose experience this could be a problem—either because they already had a Jewish national identity or because they faced this choice by encountering people who questioned their Polish nationality. This problem was posed in a new way, in a certain sense, when the state of Israel was founded. Strictly speaking, in our context, it appeared practically together with the appearance of political circumstances where such a choice could actually be made. While heretofore affiliation with the Jewish national community was primarily centered on culture, customs, and spirituality, since the founding of the state of Israel, it can also be expressed more fully, as it were, in a material way, and it can overlap with belonging to a state. Thus if this choice was either unsettled or open for any Jew or Pole of Jewish, he could make it in two ways. One option was to either go to Israel or remain in Poland, and see oneself as a member of a national minority. The other was to opt for Polish national integration. People have been choosing between these two options, and they continue to do so. Clearly, when it comes to such a subtle issue, any external disturbances distorting the freedom of this choice are exceedingly harmful.

Here, we are primarily interested in the problem of national integration. Not because I wish to disregard the question of organizing Poles' coexistence with the small Jewish national minority. That is a narrower problem which, by the way, derives from the general social atmosphere. Meanwhile, the problem of relations between Poles of Jewish and non-Jewish descent is related to the general social climate in an important way.

I am purposely speaking about integration and not assimilation. This is because the concept of assimilation has elements of the notion of illegitimate adoption in it. As one opposes anti-Semitism, it is important to avoid a different kind of simplification or mistake. Sartre points this out when he describes the typical attitude of French liberal democrats—opponents of anti-Semitism. His observations, however, seem to be an accurate portrayal of a certain broader problem. They concern the attitude of those who, wishing to eliminate any sort of Jewish problem as quickly as possible, and basing their thinking on an individualistic concept of man, propose that Jews assimilate into the culture and nation in which they live, on the condition, as it were, that they dispose of their Jewishness as something that could and should be rejected, either because it makes life more difficult, or because there are no Jews, Frenchmen, Russians, or Poles—there is only man as such. "Between his enemy and his defender," Sartre writes, "the Jew is in a difficult situation: apparently he can do no more than choose the sauce with which he will be devoured."[4] People with Jewish roots often learn that they are different from the rest of the society in which they live only because of manifestations of anti-Semitism and the entire atmosphere it creates. At a certain point in their lives, society makes them feel as if they have some flaw that classifies them, in one way or another, as worse, not fully valuable. There comes an awareness of being flawed, of having a flaw that determines one's value and assigns a specific place in society. That is precisely why the sense of distinctiveness created by anti-Semitism is not healthy, creative, or normal— the way a diversity of traditions and cultural values introduced into social life is healthy and normal. That is because awareness of this distinctiveness is accompanied by a sense of inadequacy, alienation, and danger.

On the other hand, the proposal to assimilate, as it is sometimes understood, is a proposal to deny one's roots and cultural traditions. Assimilation understood this way is a proposal to agree to view "Jewishness" as a flaw, as something that really is humiliating. One should not wonder at the bitterness of people whose sense of affiliation with the Jewish community might be very faint, and might consist solely in shared awareness of having this "flaw," but who do not want to agree to that understanding of assimilation which proposes that they throw off the mark of being Jewish as a condition for receiving the full status of being human. A Pole of Jewish descent who is utterly involved in Polish life and culture would still feel that he belongs to a somehow contaminated category; he would have to justify his connection with Poland by showing how far he has traveled on the way from being a Jew to being a man in general, and from being a man in general to being a Pole.

In contrast, national integration is a much more complex process. Above all, it is essential to notice that this process does not just encompass people with Jewish backgrounds, but rather characterizes a permanent phenomenon in the life of modern nations—the phenomenon of expansion, mixing, and enrichment. It is a continuous process, which can be more or less extensive, but which takes place in every nation. If this process is to unfold normally, it cannot allow for special categories, around which an atmosphere of inadequacy and threat is created. If it is to be meaningful, integration has to increase a man's rootedness in the society in which he lives; it cannot take place in an atmosphere that demands embarrassed denial of one's Jewish roots or the rejection of the Jewish cultural heritage, as if it were something humiliating. On the contrary, for the process to be normal it must be clear that it is a process of mutual enrichment and expansion, a process that unites and not one that destroys values. Under current civilizational conditions, a nation unable to open itself to these kinds of processes sentences itself to being trapped in fanaticism; it shuts itself off from the normal influx of elements that would enrich its life and culture.

Here, a certain disintegrating function of anti-Semitism appears with full clarity, regardless of the form it takes. Anti-Semitism, which is anachronistic from the perspective of the contemporary concept of a nation— where the coexistence of people with various ethnic backgrounds is normal—not only creates artificial barriers to a nation's enrichment, but also divides it and cuts off people who grew up and remain in the nation. It is the residue of anti-Semitic ideas functioning in society—rather than any specific qualities of these individuals—that takes away their sense of equal worth and sentences them to living with complexes and a sense of being threatened.

There is one more aspect of the problem of anti-Semitism that cannot be left untouched. I am thinking of what is sometimes designated as a specifically Christian type of anti-Semitism, or religiously motivated anti-Semitism.

Catholic doctrine and moral judgments are clear and unambiguous regarding this matter. Any current or tendency that sows hatred among people, based on the claim that Jews are a lower race or an all-encompassing primordial cause and carrier of evil is not only contrary to Catholicism, but it is also imperative for Catholics to fight it. This is because it attacks basic moral principles. Jerzy Turowicz was right to claim that "a Catholic who is an anti-Semite is not a Catholic insofar as he is an anti-Semite."[5]

I will not discuss filiations that appeared between numerous, though by no means all, Catholic circles and anti-Semitism in Poland in the past. Clearly, the source of such filiations should be sought not in the Catholic worldview itself, but in the superficiality of Catholic attitudes, and in the entire sociological picture of society at various historical moments. I will also not describe how change took place both during the war and thereafter. This change is clearly perceptible, and I don't think anyone would deny it.

However, from the perspective of the problem we are addressing here—the problem of tracking down traces of anti-Semitic messages that still remain in people's attitudes (and this applies equally to Catholics)—it is necessary to overcome what gets designated as religious anti-Semitism. This term should be applied, above all, to those phenomena and influences in Christian upbringing which favor anti-Semitism and create or magnify social susceptibility to its bacilli.

We could call it the Jesus and Judas problem in Christian upbringing. I use this expression to denote a certain mystification to which we sometimes succumb. Theology teaches us that all of our sins contribute to the tragedy in which Judas was a vehicle; we also know that the fruits of Salvation are granted to all. But the mystification consists in the fact that very often we, Christians, claim an exclusive right to Jesus' legacy while leaving Judas' legacy to Jews. As a result of being used to certain images and interpretations, in the eyes of a Christian a Jew is someone who is particularly stigmatized by Judas' sin. Just as all people are marked by the sin of Adam and Eve, for many, Jews also carry, as it were, an additional original sin, the sin of belonging to Judas' people, a mark that differentiates them from us.

In the writings of Jules Isaac, an eminent French historian who devoted many years of work to this problem, I recently found an attempt to determine what factors came together to form a deposit of various anti-Jewish residues in Christian upbringing. He analyzed these causes in a paper he gave at the Sorbonne; large fragments were recently published in the weekly *Express*. He believes that the aberration is serious and reaches back to the split between Christianity and Judaism. According to him, the aberration appeared primarily in the fourth century, under the pressure of certain necessities. Evangelization among pagans necessitated a maximally emphatic explanation of why Jews negated Christianity—an explanation of the fact that Christianity did not take hold in the country where Christ was born. At the same time, Christianity faced the challenge of explaining to recent converts how it differed from Judaism, which was still very influential. It was then, according to Jules Isaac, in the context of polemical and—as we would say today—propaganda fervor, that theses which humiliate Israel and represent Jews as a degenerate, God-killing, and rejected nation began to function in Christianity. "Let us not be surprised"—Isaac writes—"that these theses, created in the heat of merciless polemics, overstepped both the Holy Scriptures and historical knowledge in every possible way. But when one reflects on the fact—and we should reflect on it—that these teachings were proclaimed for entire centuries, from generation to generation, by hundreds and thousands of people, often most emphatically, and often as offensively as possible, it is truly not that surprising that in the end they became imprinted in Christian mentality, that they formed and shaped this mentality down to the very depths of the unconscious."

Let's leave the determination of the formation and size of these residues to people who are appropriately qualified—historians and biblical scholars. We should emphasize that systematic efforts are underway to eliminate these residues within the Church. During the last two decades, mutual interest between Christianity and Judaism has increased significantly, resulting in a series of initiatives intended to create a better atmosphere between them.

We should, however, state a fact that can be observed and confirmed sociologically: these residues are still largely present for the average person. We accepted the image of the Jew as Judas's descendant—an image formed under the influence of these residues—and we are passing it down to coming generations like a relay baton. As a result, a Jewish child, or a child whose parents have Jewish roots, learns about the stigma that hangs over him from a slur heard from his peers—and he gains bitter awareness of alienation and humiliation this way. Earliest complexes begin to take shape in one group, while anti-Semitism begins to take root in the other—and some complaisant gardener can cultivate it later without our continued participation. This is why, if we want to remove anti-Semitism from social life, it is not enough to cut off its roots, but we must also make it impossible for them to grow back. The question of upbringing is thus most important.

Christian religious upbringing has a central role to play in this task because of its influence on the formation of moral attitudes, and also because it will always touch Jewish issues. "It is impossible to teach the Christian religion without speaking about Jews"—Father Démann once wrote in a brilliant article reprinted by *Homo Dei* at some point. "We have to speak about Jews. But here is the whole problem. To speak in a Christian way means to speak 'with dignity': according to truth and justice. Without distorting facts. Without generalizing. Without accusing the innocent. Without finding unwholesome satisfaction in humiliating others. . . ."

There are no anti-Semites among us. No one, except for one or two fanatics, would own this label today. And in any case, kind and gentle people have always said, "I am not an anti-Semite, I condemn this type of attitude . . . but those Jews."

And so there are no anti-Semites among us. But is there no anti-Semitism? How frequently can one still encounter the workings of anti-Semitic generalizations in people's reasoning, with a tendency to substitute generalizing stereotypes for the effort to understand all kinds of difficulties that have other and more complex sources. Does everyone understand that the expression "he is a decent man, even though he is Jewish" contains as much nonsense as the expression "he is a decent man, even though he is Polish"? In many circles, the word "Jew" continues to function as an insult, it often replaces arguments and gets hurled at opponents like an abusive epithet.

One could say that this happens in petty-bourgeois and reactionary circles. It's only that this does not solve anything. This is because petty bourgeoisie and reactionaries are not just sociological categories. These terms also describe a type of mentality, an attitude that can appear among people with scholarly titles just as likely as among shopkeepers.

It is not my intention to exaggerate and sound an alarm. Much has changed in Poland. But we should not become complacent and believe that the problem is disappearing by itself. The state and law can forbid anti-Semitic propaganda, but they cannot eliminate it altogether by themselves. It will not disappear so long as the very core of social life does not undergo an ultimate revision of attitudes and concepts, making it impossible for bacilli of anti-Semitic messages to implant themselves in it.

This is precisely why I claim that the main problem lies with the attitude of the "kind and gentle people." In any case, committed and militant anti-Semitism has always been the work of a small handful of fanatics, but its chances of success are determined by the level of awareness of "kind and gentle people."

It is not enough to return to this issue when an alarming event takes place. We should speak about it precisely when such a reason does not exist, when overcoming anti-Semitism is accompanied by a calm atmosphere, and when substantive arguments are more likely to succeed than demagogy.

This overcoming, by the way, will not be accomplished by periodic and exclusively moral appeals. Without dismissing moral arguments whenever they are necessary, we should see this overcoming as a long-term and all-encompassing educational process. Its method must consist in showing the intellectual groundlessness of anti-Semitism, and then, only against this background, revealing the moral falsehood it contains and the social evil it brings. A man intellectually inoculated against anti-Semitism is also a man educated to participate in social life in a way that will enable him to move beyond chauvinisms and particularisms. The eradication of remaining anti-Semitic residues can take place in the process of social education when it is simultaneously supported by an appropriate general atmosphere that eliminates social obfuscation and misinformation, a climate of transparency in public life, favoring everyone's awareness of the real springs of social and political life and proper recognition of its mechanisms.

The meaning of the struggle against anti-Semitism is profound and multifaceted. Socially, it is a struggle against one of the most dangerous phenomena that interfere with the process of integration. At the same time, it is a struggle against the possibility of concealing actual problems behind a false universal symbol of evil. Morally, the struggle against the climate that favors anti-Semitism is also a struggle for human dignity. But—it is worth adding—whose dignity? Outwardly, a Jew, or a Pole with a Jewish background, is the one who is humiliated. But in reality the person who succumbs to anti-Semitism and heeds such groundless and false arguments in the twentieth century is the one who humiliates himself.

This is why the struggle against anti-Semitism is not an accomplishment or a humanitarian gesture of mercy; neither is it simply a struggle to defend the dignity of Jews. It is just as much a struggle for everyone's dignity. And that is because the tendency to generalize, which is at the heart of anti-Semitism, can lead us to cross the threshold of moral precepts—a threshold which man must not cross if things are not to fall apart.

Editors' Notes

1. Ludwik Hirszfeld, *Historia jednego życia* (1946); citation from Marta A. Balinska's English translation: *The Story of One Life* (University of Rochester Press, 2010), 341.
2. This quote is from Leszek Kołakowski's essay "Anti-Semites: Five Familiar Theses and a Warning" in this volume on page 146.
3. Lavrentiy Beria and the "Doctors' Plot" are discussed in Editors' Note 5 to Konstanty Jelenski's essay in this volume on page 161.
4. Jean-Paul Sartre, *Anti-Semite and Jew*, trans. George J. Becker (Schocken Books, 1948).
5. This quote is from Jerzy Turowicz's essay "Anti-Semitism" in this volume on page 167.

PART
VI

1967–1969: Expulsion
from Poland

15

March 1968 and the So-Called Jewish Question in Poland after the Second World War

KRYSTYNA KERSTEN

Editors' Introduction

Krystyna Kersten (1931–2008) was a historian specializing in twentieth-century Polish history. Born in the city of Poznań, she studied history at the University of Warsaw, where she later taught for several decades. Between 1954 and 2001, she also worked for the History Institute at the Polish Academy of Sciences. She joined the Communist Party in 1956, when de-Stalinization seemed to promise greater political openness and pluralism. She left the party in 1968 to protest the invasion of Czechoslovakia by the Warsaw Pact army and was active in the democratic opposition movement in the 1970s and 1980s. Kersten published widely, and her works enjoyed great popularity in the anticommunist underground. In December 1981, shortly before General Jaruzelski introduced martial law in Poland, Kersten published the first detailed Polish analysis of the Kielce Pogrom ("The Pogrom of Jews in Kielce on July 4th, 1946," available in English from the Digital Repository of Scientific Institutes). In her research, she explored the origins of the Polish People's Republic, diplomacy before and after the Yalta Conference, population transfers in Eastern Europe during and after the Second World War, Polish intellectuals under communism, and Polish-Jewish relations. Her most important books include *Narodziny systemu władzy. Polska 1943–1948* (1985; available in English as *The Establishment of Communist Rule in Poland, 1943–1948*, University of California Press, 1991) and *Polacy, Żydzi, komunizm. Anatomia półprawd 1939–1968* (1992; *Poles, Jews, Communism: The Anatomy of Half-Truths, 1939–1968*).

The essay reproduced here comes from this book; it was written twenty years after the anti-Semitic campaign and student protests of March 1968. It is one of the most comprehensive analyses of what transpired in Poland in the spring of 1968. In the immediate aftermath of the March events, and for more than a decade afterward, the subject of anti-Semitism became taboo in Poland, and it was not until the early 1980s, when the emergence of Solidarity contributed to a new political climate of relative openness, that Polish-Jewish relations became a subject of public debate, despite the introduction of martial law in December 1981. Kersten's essay examines the 1968 wave of anti-Semitism in the context of the entire communist period; it was first published in an abbreviated version in *Res Publica* in Warsaw, on March 5, 1988; some of Kersten's detailed bibliographical footnotes have been omitted.

More than twenty years have passed since March 1968, and anniversaries inspire thinking in terms of the *longue durée*. This is how I would like to look at everything that adds up to March '68 as a symbol: student protests, state militia actions, and the brutal campaign of poisonous words and actions directed primarily against people selected according to a formula whose anti-Semitic essence could not be concealed by either ideological camouflage or the smokescreen of "Zionism." These actions were directed against Jews according to a criterion of birth and not individual self-identification, and thus—however much this was masked—according to a racial criterion, a criterion of blood, a Nuremberg criterion. Jewishness was ascribed to people who were being stigmatized in the press, at rallies, mass gatherings, and meetings organized throughout Poland; they were called "instigators and organizers, provocateurs," scholars who saw "great opportunities for themselves in covering up murky political arguments with patriotic emotions," "cynical rabble-rousers" and "politicos." These people were exposed and unmasked by the appropriate authorities, and their alleged Jewishness was signaled by apt allusions or by the word "Zionist," which replaced the word "Jew"—a word that could not be used openly without revealing the anti-Semitic character of the ongoing campaign. When on March 11 *Trybuna Ludu* and *Słowo Powszechne* published a list of names of student "instigators of the incidents" at Warsaw University, the commentary claimed that behind these students hid "instigators known to the authorities, hailing from among a diverse group of politically discredited individuals." Meanwhile, the main paper of the PAX Association also emphasized that these instigators are "Zionists" who serve West Germany's "anti-Polish policies."[1] That same day, Józef Kępa, first secretary of the Warsaw Committee of the Communist Party (PZPR) picked up this theme of "Zionism" in his talk at a meeting of the Committee's sociopolitical subcommittee when, while attacking Stefan Staszewski and Roman Zambrowski, he said: "We are not anti-Semites, but we will not tolerate masked Zionists."[2] That Monday, a rally at the FSO automobile factory—the first of many rallies throughout the country— was organized under slogans like "Students to the Classrooms, Writers to Their Studies" and "Purge Zionists from the Party." Banners at other rallies read: "Away with Israeli Saboteurs," and "Yes to Students and Intellectuals, No to Zionists and Revolt." And a satirical student song included the line *"Tokarz Buła się odcina: Syjonistów wina"* (The worker replies with the claim: Zionists are to blame). "Zionists" was a code everyone understood; very few in Poland knew what Zionism actually was. This was picked up in a Warsaw joke in which one editor asks another: "Tell me, how do you spell the word 'Zionist?'" The other replies: "I don't know, but before the war it was spelled with a 'J.'"

Years later, we can see that 1968, a year inscribed so powerfully and permanently into the lives of tens of thousands of people, was a crucial moment in Polish society's most recent history. Yes—the history of Polish society, not just the history of Polish Jews, Poles of Jewish descent, or Polish-Jewish relations. In any case, perhaps no one doubts that what we have been referring to as the Jewish question after the Second World War has been—and remains—an essential fragment of Polish reality and its moral, psychosocial, and political dimensions.[3] What took place in 1968 cannot be reduced—as is commonly done—to the political tactics or social engineering exercised by Mieczysław Moczar's coterie in the context of intraparty power struggles.[4] On the contrary, March '68 was a consequence of processes rooted in both distant and more recent past, processes shaped by the situation in which Poland found itself after the defeat of Nazi Germany.

A few general remarks to start. Everyone knows that issues bearing on Polish-Jewish relations constitute a field where nearly every move can provoke defensive-aggressive reactions. This field is not easy to enter because we encounter obstacles in the form of deficiencies in both our language and conceptual apparatus. When confronted with emotions and phobias—either conscious or unconscious—words, definitions, and simple claims lose their unambiguous character, and cease being useful tools for describing reality. This was doubtless also influenced by a sui generis pact of silence around Polish-Jewish issues, a pact broken only a few years ago, and only partially. I am not just thinking about official silence, but also, and perhaps above all, about how Jewish issues are treated in relationships among people, even within one's own family. Silence, however, does not eliminate the problem. On the contrary— when it is passed over in silence, stifled, and pushed aside, the problem grows more powerful and more dreadful; its effects become poisonous.

I agree with Roman Zimand when he writes that we do not have the kind of language that would allow us to talk normally about Polish-Jewish matters.[a] This applies to the very concepts of Jews and Poles. These concepts only seem to be clearly defined. Yet bringing order here by creating little compartments and rigid pigeonholes of terms and definitions is a risky undertaking, one that leads to simplifications, misunderstandings, and sometimes either intentional or unintended mystifications. At the same time, this lack of intellectually

---

[a] Zimand, *Popiół i piołun* (*Ashes and Wormwood*), (Warsaw, 1987).

unambiguous and emotionally neutral terms burdens simple claims with ideological content, favoring the emergence of all kinds of tensions.

When I say "Poles" I am thinking about all those who identify as Poles,
and so both those whose forefathers belonged to the Polish community as
well as those who, having other roots, chose Poland and Polishness as their
fatherland, not only in the sense of a civic bond with the Polish state, but
also in the form of a mental bond with the cultural community, leading
to national identification. Analogously: a Jew is someone who feels a bond
with the Jewish people. We have to remember, however, that the principle of
self-identification has a Janus face: on the one hand, it means that a person
chooses his identity by himself; on the other hand, however, in a system of
national monoculture, it often serves as means of enforcing identity. As early
as 1918, when the principle of self-identification was celebrating its triumphs,
René Johannet, conscious of its dangers, wrote that there will come a time
when this principle will occupy "an honorary place in a museum of passé
ideas, with an epigraph which I dare not express in any other words:

Phaselus ille quem videtis hospites,
Ait fuisse navim celerrimus."[b]

That sail-boat you see there, visitors,
Claims to have been the speediest of ships."[5]

But in reality the path from Jewish to Polish identity is a two-way street;
and it is full of dramatic turns. People's bonds with the Jewish world were
often revealed only in the face of discrimination, in the name of basic
human dignity or as a result of identifying with a community threatened
by Polish anti-Semitism. Already before the war, for obvious reasons during the war, and especially after 1945, Jewishness was often imposed on
people whose integration into Polishness was so powerful that the word
"assimilation" is too weak to express it. Sometimes things were different but
equally awful: in some ways, Poles of Jewish descent lost the right to their
natural bond with the world of their grandfathers and their fathers, and
sometimes also with the world of their own childhood or youth. The pressure of their milieu was so strong that often consciously, and less commonly
unconsciously, they acquiesced to this mutilation or decided that this was an
inevitable price they had to pay if they were to enter the mental world of

[b] Johannet, *Le Principe des Nationalités* (Paris, 1918).

Polishness. Something natural was replaced by artificiality, and simple matters of genealogy became shameful.

Within this complex reality, how is one to reconcile the principle of self-identification with the fact that both a large proportion of Poles and many Jews see Jewishness as something one is endowed with at birth, something inalienable? How is one to avoid imposing a Jewish identity on people who have grown profoundly connected to Polishness, and simultaneously avoid denying the right to maintain a separate religious or cultural identity and a bond with the Jewish people to those among them who, while living in Poland and having a deep bond with the Polish soil, desired (and desire) to have this Jewish identity and this bond? This is basically an unsolvable dilemma.

One could date the prehistory of 1968 to the end of the eighteenth century—to the intensification of the process of modern nation-building. It was at that point that the juxtaposition Pole-Jew, rather than Christian-Jew first appeared in Polish texts, and a national rather than religious opposition began to function in general awareness. During a feud concerning a Warsaw settlement called New Jerusalem (1775–1776), and involving the elite of magnates and noblemen, Christian bourgeoisie, and the Jewish community, "in 1775, perhaps for the first time, Warsaw bourgeoisie, which aspired to social prestige, replaced the opposition 'Christians vs. infidels' with the opposition 'the Polish nation vs. Jews' thereby undermining the concept of the 'gentry nation' and recognizing themselves as part of the Polish nation."[c]

Nation-building processes caused new, more dynamic, and more rapacious bonds to arise alongside traditional ones. Most often these two spheres of belonging—national and religious—overlapped and reinforced each other. Polishness and Catholicism started to interweave into a cultural community. Being a Jew, in turn, signified belonging to the Mosaic religious community.

But most often does not mean always. The national idea is not the only notion created by the eighteenth century—its heritage also includes secularization of public life and culture. This brought about the process of severing religious identities from national ones, which created the conditions for the opening of communities which had heretofore been surrounded by double walls. In Poland, however, only narrow gates were made in these walls. Both communities guarded their integrity—the Jewish community treated "deserters" with aversion, not to say hostility, and the Polish community

---

[c] K. Zienkowska, "Spór o nową Jerozolimę" (The Feud about New Jerusalem), *Kwartalnik Historyczny (Historical Quarterly)* no. 2. (1987).

did not admit "others" and "intruders." In 1915, Leon Wasilewski described the Jewish question as the most difficult and complex social and political problem that is specific to Poland and does not appear in a similar form in Western Europe. In Polish lands, Jews not only maintained their religious identity but were also not absorbed by the emerging modern Polish nation, as was the case in France, Germany, or England.

A number of causes resulted in the failure of programs focused on the emancipation of Polish Jews; the size of the Jewish population together with the weakness of the Polish bourgeoisie and the underdeveloped state of capitalism were crucial in this respect.[d]

From the beginning, the Polish nation, emerging without statehood and threatened by Russification and Germanization, had an incredibly strong inbuilt defensive mechanism coupled with aggression against "others." This reaction, stemming from a sense of weakness, was largely responsible for generating anti-Semitism that had two basic forms: it targeted Polonizing expatriates from the Jewish community and the Jewish community itself. One form of this anti-Semitism expressed itself in tracking down Jewish ancestors, while the other found an outlet in pogroms, slogans like "Do Not Buy from Jewish Stores," Jew-benches, and National Radical Camp (ONR) fighting squads. Often, especially in the second half of the 1930s, when radical nationalist movements grew in strength, the two forms became intertwined. Both before and after the war, a significant number of voices in Polish public opinion disapproved of anti-Semitic brawls, and until the Holocaust the Polish population related to Jews with a particular mix of otherness and familiarity, aversion and sympathy, prejudice and curiosity, fear and aggression. But resistance against Jews who were taking on a Polish identity, or even those who have been living with it for a generation of two, was (and continues to be) rather universal.

Nationalisms that took center stage in post-Versailles Europe—Polish nationalism among them—shattered the hopes of those Poles and Jews who, at the dawn of regained independence, deluded themselves into thinking that when Polish society has the option of taking things into its own hands, "independent Poland will call upon its Jewish citizens to contribute to the country's development," and people will create civil—if not national— conditions for integration.[e] The Second Republic was reborn as a state

---

[d] L. Wasilewski, *Die Judenfrage in Kongress-Polen. Ihre Schwerigkeiten und Ihre Losung* (Vienna, 1915).
[e] Ibid.

whose character was national even though its population was nationally mixed. For most citizens—both Poles and non-Poles, the words "We, the Polish People," which open the preamble of the 1921 Constitution, did not mean "We, Citizens of the Polish State." The prevailing conceptual cluster Pole-Polish citizen, and the interchangeable use of the words "Pole" and "citizen" in both everyday speech and official documents, were not so much an expression of the recognition that there is a supra-ethnic civil nation, as a symptom of the nationalist tendency to disregard national minorities. Even the wisest programs and efforts of people like Tadeusz Hołówko, Leon Wasilewski, or Henryk Józefski remained in the realm of intentions and partial undertakings.[6] Full of vacillation and inconsistent, these efforts were no match for dynamic nationalisms. Since the beginning of the 1930s, the Republic was taking swift steps to become a nation-state, the state of a nation—an ethnic community. National Democrats (SND) saw this community as tightly sealed off to Jews, while the Piłsudski-affiliated Camp of National Unity (OZN) was ready to open it only to "particular individuals of Jewish descent, whose life and proven service to the Polish Nation have shown that they are Poles, and they thereby belong to the Polish national community."[f]

We can simplify and say that the reality of Polish-Jewish relations existed between two extremes defined by different approaches to assimilation and national integration. For those on one end of the spectrum, it was about equal rights for Jews as Jews; the central focus was on guaranteeing that the Jewish people had opportunities for free, unhindered economic, cultural, and religious development; there was emphasis on respecting equal rights guaranteed by the Constitution and the 1919 treaty on protecting minorities. The opposite was true for those on the other end of the spectrum—for them what mattered most was the right to assimilate, to be a Pole. In both cases, essentially the same thing was at stake: a person's fundamental right to maintain and freely develop his national and cultural identity. Both expatriates from the Jewish community who chose Polishness as their spiritual homeland and Poles who called for the national community to have an open form spoke out against barriers that made assimilation either difficult or impossible. This struggle was not between Poles and Jews but between nationalism and a democratic, liberal idea of the nation. Poland was not the

---

[f] See "Deklaracja ideowo-polityczna OZN" (The OZN Ideological-Political Declaration), February 21, 1937, and Council Resolutions from May 21, 1938.

only place where this struggle unfolded, but it took on a particularly dramatic form here.

Unlike the conflicts and tensions between Polish and Jewish communities, the pushing away or outright rejection of assimilating Jews by the Polish collectivity had an almost exclusively irrational basis, even though people sometimes attempted to attach pseudo-rational justifications to it. This rejection was controlled mainly by emotions stemming from a sense of threat, from uncertainty, weakness, and ingrained phobias and superstitions.

Characteristically, social groups whose position was weak and uncertain showed greater tendency toward fighting Jews and manifested both forms of anti-Semitism differentiated earlier. Ksawery Pruszyński pointed to this aspect of Polish anti-Semitism when after Roman Dmowski's death he wrote about him in *Wiadomości Literackie*, emphasizing the fact that Dmowski had been born in Kamionek.

Perhaps some will say that geniuses were not born a dime a dozen in Żułów either, but that will not be particularly insightful; it was precisely in towns like Żułów—scattered from Połąga to the estuaries of that sea about the existence of which we have completely forgotten today—that all things wonderful and disdainful that created and destroyed Poland were born over the course of several centuries.[7] In fact, they were born there and nowhere else (. . .). In such towns, the confrontation was not between landed noblemen's sons and innkeepers but between workers' sons and merchants. And that is a different kind of confrontation. Finally, one has to reimagine that somber, rich Warsaw, with its majority that was not Polish but Russian-Jewish. It created aversion. One has to remember that there were onion domes of Orthodox churches in Staszica and Saski Squares, there were *baryshnyas*, officers, *soldats*, and Russkis—and all this morally enslaved the population.[8] And, finally, one has to remember that Jews who lived there were not even Jews from the Nalewki district, in their long black coats, but Litvaks, who had only recently arrived from Russia and either remained in the ghettos or became Russified. It was not their fault that Warsaw's Polish traditions must have been as foreign to them as Aztec traditions had been to immigrants arriving in America from Europe. (. . .) Behind Russians there was the tsar, behind Jews there was money. What could Dmowski have to back him up in that Warsaw from only forty years ago?

Polish-Jewish relations, inflamed after twenty years of Poland's independence, were subjected to a test imposed by Nazism during the last war. Poles were given the role of helpless witnesses of the annihilation of the Jewish community, which had lived on the same soil with them for centuries. Though this role was forced on them, they accepted it largely passively and without rebelling because people who were first in line for German death sentences were separated from their neighbors by a barrier of religious and cultural otherness, a barrier cemented by prejudice and resentments. And this otherness sometimes brought out reactions that led to incomprehensible and outright pathological behaviors among Poles. Pre-existing stereotyped ways of viewing Jews were overlaid with Poles' and Jews' different situations, determined by the occupier's policy.

Those different fates left traumatic traces in the awareness of both groups. Jews rescued from the Holocaust kept memories of the indifference of their surroundings, an indifference sometimes filled with compassion and sorrow, but often tinged with aversion or a sense of superiority. Some of the responses sent to a contest announced by the Czytelnik Publishing House in 1948 are characteristic in this respect. Here is what a nineteen-year-old peasant from around Bielsk Podlaski wrote about hiding Jews:

> The Jew was undiscriminating. He would eat a potato or a piece of bread, he sat in dampness, in stench, and had a handful of straw for a bed; and this Jew-boy (Żydek) didn't need anything else, he only asked the farmer not to tell anyone he was still alive. Once, in late fall, a Jew-boy we knew came to us to get a bite to eat. It was after sunset when he came, and he says to my father: "Nu, Pioter, I'm alive, and you know, Pioter, you're a good man, give me something to eat. You have no idea how hungry I am. I've been sitting in a haystack in the field since morning and I've had nothing to eat." And how could you not give this Jew some food, he's a man, too, he doesn't have a home, and he wanders and wanders throughout the world.

Everything is here: compassion for a suffering man, a sense of otherness, a dose of disdain mixed with a sense of one's own superiority. Few sources from that time convey this type of mentality in such undiluted form; and this mentality was not unique to the countryside.

Jews who escaped the Holocaust by hiding or using the so-called Aryan papers, have memories of loneliness, humiliation, and fear—not just of Germans, but, even worse, also of their Polish compatriots. In Polish memory, in turn, dominated as it was by Poles' own suffering and resistance, there was no room for the tragedy of Polish Jews. If it was brought up, the point was most often to reveal the enormity of German crimes and—typically in a defensive fashion—to show what Poles did to rescue Jews. By using half-truths, people created a construction to replace the truth about reality too difficult to confront directly. The role of witnesses—the majority of them passive—of the extermination of a nation with whom they had lived on the same soil for hundreds of years caused moral unrest among Poles, an unrest which, by the way, did not always enter conscious awareness. People therefore tried to negate or cover up this witness role; on the one hand, they pointed to the help Poles offered Jews, while on the other they evoked the myth that equated Jews with carriers of evil, a myth that lingered in the Christian tradition, and was later also inscribed into the tradition of extremist nationalism.

The end of the war opened up a new field of tensions. Once again, history assigned antagonistic roles to Poles and Jews. The government established by the Communists seemed to the one group as imposed and hostile, while the other saw it as a guarantee of safety and a chance for equal rights. Postwar realities overlaid on history generated phenomena inimical to Polish-Jewish coexistence.

Hopes for a rebirth of the Jewish community in Poland turned out to be in vain. With more or less open support from authorities and silent applause of the society, a significant proportion of Jews who survived in Poland or repatriated from the USSR left Poland: between 1945 and 1948 this took place in illegal but tolerated ways, and between 1949 and 1951 it happened by means of organized transports to Israel.

The drive to emigrate from Poland was so strong that it had to be taken into account even by Jewish Communists who programmatically claimed that the Jewish population should remain and become productive. Their attitude toward emigration was ambivalent and reflected the situation that resulted from the clash of various political and ideological orders, first and foremost among which were a negative stance toward Zionism and dependence on Stalin's policies concerning the Palestinian question. As a result, they oscillated between opposing emigration and giving in to the prevailing atmosphere. In the fall of 1945, one of the participants at a meeting of the Polish Workers' Party (PPR) faction of the Central Committee of Polish Jews (CKŻP) said:

> Emigration tendencies now exist among Jews everywhere. In Poland, there are currently opportunities for Jews to make it their home and anti-Semitism can be curtailed. There were symptoms of anti-Semitism in the USSR as well, but when the authorities took appropriate steps these symptoms disappeared. (. . .) Arabs are hosts in Palestine. The USSR wants to win over the Arab world. Our stance cannot be Zionist. Jews should be taught how to work just as they are taught to work in the USSR (. . .). Our orientation should go in

the direction of supporting the most active possible participation in the life of democratic Poland.

Other speakers, however, pointed out that aspirations to leave the country resulted from difficulties Jews faced in finding a place for themselves in Poland; they emphasized that freedom to emigrate should be safeguarded, and claimed that Jews must have the right both to live in Poland and to leave it. Michał Mirski announced: "We are basically not proponents of Palestine. We must, however, have a positive stance toward a national home. Jews want to live gathered together and we have to take that into account. (. . .) For Zionists, emigration is tied to growing pogrom tendencies. We should have a positive stance toward Palestine not because of anti-Semitism but because we want the rebirth of Jews as a nation." The leadership of the Polish Workers' Party (PPR) had a similarly ambiguous stance. In 1948, after the declaration of the establishment of the state of Israel, the Political Bureau claimed that

> the departure of PPR members to Palestine to fight for a Jewish state and a people's democracy does not contradict the ideological principles of our party. However, in light of the fact that all necessary conditions for a complete solution of the Jewish problem exist in our country, the Party does not recommend and does not organize departures; it only shows individual support for those comrades who decide to leave.

We do not have access to accurate statistics on postwar Jewish emigration, but even incomplete data make it possible to say that more than half of those rescued from the Holocaust emigrated.[g] To over 200,000 people who left between 1945 and 1955 one should add all those who never returned to Poland: from the West—by their own choice, from the USSR—primarily because they were unable to. According to international statistics, in 1948 the Jewish minority in Poland was 88,000 people, and many of them emigrated between 1949 and 1951. During this time, nearly 28,000 left in organized transports to Israel.

---

[g] See M. Proudfoot, *European Refugees 1939–1945: A Study in Forced Population Movements* (London, 1957), and *International Migration 1945–47*, ILO (Geneva, 1959). According to these statistics. 5,800 people left Poland in 1946; 7,700 in 1947; 32,200 in 1948; 26,500 in 1950; 3,500 in 1951; 600 in 1952; 200 in 1953; 300 in 1954; 400 in 1955; 0 in 1956; and 25,500 in 1957. Moreover, tens of thousands left in 1945. See K. Kersten, "Migracje powojenne w Polsce. Próba klasyfikacji i ogólna charakterystyka zewnętrznych ruchów ludności" (Postwar Migrations in Poland: An Attempt at a Classification and a General Characterization of External Population Movements), in *Polska Ludowa (People's Poland)*, vol. 2 (Warsaw, 1963). The number of survivors can be estimated to have been over 300,000.

Emigration was paralleled by the stifling of the Jewish community's national, religious, and social life. Actions and initiatives that sought to save even the small fraction of the Jewish community that survived on this soil were consistently and effectively paralyzed. Only façades that functioned as alibi were allowed to stand, and they were entirely subordinated to the state government and the party.

After 1945, the Jewish problem in Poland did not really apply to the Jewish cultural and religious minority. This minority basically disappeared from the Polish horizon in the first five years after the war. What remained was a real problem faced by Communists and non-Communists, Poles of Jewish descent and Jews who identified as Poles and who had already distanced themselves from the Jewish world.

The political determinants of the Polish-Jewish problem were very complicated and reached far beyond Poland's borders. They were determined by rivalry among great powers, bound up as it was with the USSR's changing policies that first supported the creation of the state of Israel and later opposed it. The influence of these policies on the Polish government, which was entirely subjugated to Moscow in this respect, is unquestionable. What I want to emphasize in the first place, however, is a syndrome that arose as a result of linking the Jewish question to the system of government imposed in Poland. In a truly surrealist way, this syndrome mixed together real and mythical worlds, rationality and phobias, political morality and political pragmatism, manipulation and elemental spontaneity, past and present, as well as nationalism and Communism. It encompassed attitudes functioning in society and government circles, among elites and masses, and among Poles and Jews.

The following phenomena (already referred to several times) were particularly important in defining reality:

1. The perception—by most of the society, especially during the earliest postwar period—that the government was foreign and a threat to national existence, especially in its spiritual dimension; this was combined with associated defensive reactions. Among these reactions, efforts to "nationalize" the imposed order, particularly once it proved permanent, played an important role.

2. The presence of people with Jewish backgrounds in the state apparatus—including departments responsible for repression. Among them were prewar Communists, people who became involved in the Union of Polish Patriots (ZPP) or who found themselves in the ranks of the army formed in the USSR after the departure of General Anders's army.[9]

3a. The fact that it was quite common for Jews and people with Jewish backgrounds to camouflage—not entirely of their own choosing—their Jewish origins by changing their last names and sometimes also their first names, including their parents' names. Aware of the negative attitude of a large part of society toward Jews and the government, Communists made Isaacs into Jans, and Miriams into Marias while tossing around national slogans and proclaiming that the renewed Polish state would be national. This camouflage was intended to legitimate the national character of the order that was being created, and counter the more or less crassly understood myth about the rule of Judeo-Bolsheviks. At the same time, government authorities who were looking for adherents of the new order—and who were convinced that their social backing was weak—turned to people with Jewish roots in their personnel policies. From the very beginning, these issues were surrounded by special hypocrisy. They were one of many elements of a façade intended to mask reality, though this particular element was exceptionally destructive to both society as a whole and people ordered to cover up their roots, and de facto deny the legacy of their ancestors and their connections with the Jewish world—as if these ruled out belonging to the Polish world.

3b. Covering up external signs of one's Jewish origins was not, of course, something done exclusively by Communists. And it was not, as Jews sometimes claimed, only a way of hiding a Jewish identity out of fear of Polish anti-Semitism. It was not uncommon for it to be a natural behavior of people who, having lost a sense of connection with the Jewish community and identifying as Poles, sought to avoid markers that would make them Jews in the eyes of society. For the most part, this category of people survived the war in Poland, often by using the so-called Aryan papers. They would have experienced a return to their former names as an intentional choice of Jewishness, with which they no longer had, or did not intend to have, any points of contact. Because they considered themselves Polish they—rightly—viewed instances of others' pointing to their Jewish origins as symptoms of racism, anti-Semitism, or nationalism.

4. The Jewish question was used instrumentally in the political struggle that played out on two levels: between the ruling camp and forces hostile to it, and within the ruling camp itself.

From the moment when Communists first established their rule, the Jewish question was a very important component of political life—either out in the open or as an undercurrent. It had its real referents, but it was also reducible to a fairytale world where the Jew was a menacing figure, to be avoided if one wanted to save one's soul. This mythologized approach was not simply a characteristic of primitive minds and psyches: its fragments penetrated collective mentality like ice crystals penetrating Kai's heart in Hans Christian Andersen's tale about the Snow Queen. Many educated people shared the conviction that Jews threatened Polish traditions, culture, or even Poland's spiritual fabric—though, of course, theirs was a sophisticated version of this conviction. And the threat allegedly issued from among people inside the Polish community—from Jans and not from Isaacs. It was thus Jews who wore Polish national garb and not those who remained closed within their religious and cultural communities—Jews *extra muros*— who were viewed as the greatest threat; they were the object of distrust, hostility, and aggression.

Until the middle of the 1950s, the presence of the Jewish question in the political sphere was primarily, though far from exclusively, a derivative of the dominant conflict between the ruling camp and society. This is an important caveat because within the ruling camp, and even at the very pinnacle of its hierarchy, there were people hostile toward Communists with Jewish backgrounds.

Analogously, among those who opposed the authorities there were many critics of the ruling camp who were entirely free of the anti-Jewish complex and immunized against anti-Semitism in its every mask and form. Yet among the majority of the population the cliché cluster that equated Jews with government authorities was widespread, just as in the governing circles there was a conviction that linked anti-Semitism with the oppositional attitude. Speaking at a countrywide meeting of the Jewish activists of the Polish Workers' Party (PPR) in October 1945, Edward Ochab[10] said:

> by using the argument of Catholicism, the Polish Peasants' Party (PSL) aims to concentrate reactionary elements around itself (. . .). So far, the Party has underestimated the danger of anti-Semitism and the gravity of this issue has become clear only recently. The problem of fighting against anti-Semitism is bound up with the general process of fighting to consolidate the gains of Polish democracy.

A similar situation was causing extraordinary sensitivity to the Jewish issue. For opponents of the new order the link between Jews and government authorities strengthened the sense of distance toward both Jews and the authorities by providing proof of the government's anti-national countenance. This link was so deeply entrenched in collective consciousness and its social potency was so great that it survived the fall of communism. Like a lens, it focused old resentments and new anxieties, new complaints, and new frustrations that give rise to that aggression which traditionally found an outlet in attacks on real or imagined Jews.

For the Communists, the implications of this situation were more complex and their activities were therefore both multidimensional and ambiguous; this resulted, in no small measure, from a collision of two inherently antagonistic ideological orders: communist and national. In line with doctrinal premises, the ruling camp proclaimed struggle against anti-Semitism, and it often used the accusation of anti-Semitism to discredit opponents, especially before the world's public opinion. Yet at the same time, the authorities pragmatically assumed an anti-Semitic point of view, so to speak, by resorting, for example, to the already mentioned camouflage operation or to a sort of *numerus clausus* policy in some government departments as early as the first half of the 1950s. A specific pathological atmosphere was emerging in which the issue of connections—past or present, or even family related—to the Jewish world (most loosely defined) was becoming shameful, touchy, and sometimes outright offensive. This atmosphere was poisoned even more by the fact that awareness of hushed-up "Jewishness" remained ubiquitous among both Communists and their opponents, both Poles and Jews, but no one could talk about it out loud. Let me just point to the storm that broke out around Zenon Nowak's speech at the Seventh Plenary Meeting of the Central Committee of the Communist Party (PZPR) in July 1956,[11] when he started enumerating comrades with Jewish roots in the Military Political Council (GZP), the Military Prosecutor's Office, the Ministry of Foreign Affairs, the State Commission for Economic Planning (PKPG), and the already dissolved Ministry of Public Security (MBP). Nowak's speech was, as it were, a harbinger of March '68, and the sharp reaction it provoked was certainly justified—except it was not Nowak who came up with the problem of an "excess" of Jews in the above institutions. Appropriate personnel departments silently took this up much earlier—and it was tied straight to directives flowing from Moscow. Whether of his own initiative or by acting in accordance with a preapproved plan, Nowak pulled this card out only to use it in the political game.

Thus during the first postwar decade, from the point of view of the authorities, *being a Jew*—whatever this was supposed to mean for each specific person—was a double-edged qualifier: both positive and negative. It was negative because of the already described stance of the society, which could not be disregarded. It was negative especially when it came to high-visibility offices or people who stood out because of their looks, accent, and comportment. Many reports show that these factors were taken into account in personnel decisions—also in cases when the person making the decision had a Jewish background himself. Jakub Berman *as a Jew*—as he would refer to himself in an interview with Teresa Torańska—was sentenced, also in his own eyes, to play the role of no more than a gray eminence. Unlike in Czechoslovakia or Hungary, the Polish Number One had to have Aryan ancestors. Being a Jew was negative, finally, when Stalin, and later his successors, turned to anti-Israeli policies and started eliminating Jews, especially from the military and the Foreign Service. Anti-Semitism that emanated from the Kremlin, by the way, showed its face very early on in the trials of communist leaders in Czechoslovakia, Romania, and Hungary, among other things. With the Slánský trial, the Western world, and Jewish circles in particular, began to realize, even if slowly and with resistance, "that in both the satellite countries of Central Europe and Soviet Russia itself Jews are again being treated as members of a suspicious minority; they are persecuted and used as scapegoats to hide the crimes and failures of a discredited regime."[h]

Paradoxically, however, from the point of view of government authorities the aversion of such a large part of Polish society against Jews was simultaneously one of the more important aspects of the positive character of *being a Jew*. The barrier of prejudice, perceived by both Poles and Jews, made Jews a useful instrument for Stalin's policies. He relied on this instrument with full awareness, appreciating opportunities for taking advantage of tensions that existed between Poles and Jews to strike against both groups. I agree with the opinion expressed a few years ago in the essay "Żydzi a komunizm" (Jews and Communism) where the author hiding behind the pseudonym Abel Kainer wrote:

> Instead of looking for evidence that Jews were the ones who organized such dreadful terror, it is necessary to explain why it [the security apparatus—K. K] employed Jews or Poles of Jewish descent. Here is the natural answer: this crucial nexus of the system, the political police, had to have the most trusted people, and thus ideally prewar communists, among whom there were many

---

[h] P. Meyer, B. Weinryb, E. Duschinsky, and N. Sylvain, *The Jews in the Soviet Satellites* (Syracuse University Press, 1953).

Jews and people with Jewish roots. But that is not all. Because there were, after all, not that many of the old trusted comrades, anyone who could be expected to be completely loyal would do. This potentially loyal person was someone as isolated as possible, someone without the backing of family and neighbors. Someone drawn to socialism, for whom the party would become a primary reference point.[i]

As the totalitarian system expanded, and in proportion to the progressive enslavement of society, the political context of Jewish issues moved from the juxtaposition between society and the communist government to the only political entity endowed with agency at the time—the party-state. Jews were becoming an important element in intraparty struggles. And the so-called Jewish question, or rather anti-Semitic tendencies, were largely a product of these struggles. This became most clearly perceptible at critical moments—in 1956 and 1968: each time in a somewhat different way.

In 1956 and 1968 anti-Semitic impulses—issuing from specific government circles—appeared when society (which had never been fully subjugated) became active. At rather regular time intervals, every ten to twelve years, there appeared waves of protest capable of threatening the existence of the system of total power. As it entered public life, every successive generation expressed its opposition against the government, and this opposition combined national, social, and economic motives. Unextinguished resistance against the oppressive order erupted periodically with mass protests. But in all these rebellions, revolts, or uprisings, as some historians call them—in June 1956 in Poznań, in October of that year throughout Poland, in 1968, in 1970 on the coast, in 1976, and in 1980—there did not appear, except for sporadic instances, any grassroots-generated slogans that would fuse Jews with government authorities. One could encounter a veiled form of this fusion in party newspapers but not on protest banners, in strike documents, or student resolutions.

This does not mean that over the course of the ten years that separated June or October 1956 from the Kielce Pogrom there was a miraculous radical restructuring of Poles' collective consciousness. In 1956, in the wake of "the thaw," active anti-Jewish behaviors were revived in Lower Silesia, where a large number of Jews repatriated from the USSR were settled in 1956.

[i] *Krytyka*, no. 15, 1983.

Articles taking up the theme of Polish anti-Semitism with great concern appeared in *Tygodnik Powszechny, Po Prostu, Nowa Kultura*, and other socio-cultural weeklies. Leszek Kołakowski and Jerzy Turowicz were among those who addressed this issue.[12] Maria Czapska wrote in *Kultura*: "Today, revenge for the lies and depravity of communist Poland's recent years once again threatens Jews—the eternal scapegoat, eternal wanderer among nations." Pointing to Turowicz's article, which she found too restrained, she asked: "Is there still time to prevent a new disgrace, and will the Catholic Church in the country, stronger and livelier than ever before, intentionally take up the fight against growing anti-Semitism, with a sense of its Christian responsibility?" At the same time, Jerzy Giedroyc initiated a poll about Polish anti-Semitism in *Kultura*, and its results offer food for thought. Discussing them in the name of the editorial board, Konstanty Jeleński observed:

> Out of twenty four letters sent in by émigré readers, four admit that Polish anti-Semitism is a dangerous and a nearly pathological phenomenon. Today, it is not easy for a 'Pole who idealizes his nation to bring himself to criticize it so sharply. Fourteen émigré readers put things rather symptomatically (with different inflections): they claim that Polish anti-Semitism does not exist. Unfortunately, these readers are inclined to ascribe nearly all faults in Polish-Jewish relations to Jews—something that is practically tantamount to anti-Semitism. Only one letter condemns Polish anti-Semitism, treating it as a fragmentary phenomenon that does not warrant conclusions about the entire nation. (. . .) The lack of responses from some, a minority who sharply criticize their own nation, and a majority who negate the existence of anti-Semitism: is Rafał Malczewski right, perhaps, in claiming that Polish anti-Semitism is a collective psychosis? The reflexes of people suffering from individual psychosis are no different: avoidance of the problem, avid negation of the very fact of psychosis, and cruelty toward oneself as soon as the psychosis is recognized.

Today, it is impossible to determine—in any way that could even approximate rigorous scientific standards—how society's attitudes toward Jews or Poles of Jewish descent evolved in the 1950s and 1960s; how attitudes of indifference, hostility, and sympathy were configured in different milieus and generations; how the concept of the Jew functioned in social consciousness; and whether any significant changes were underway in regard to these issues. It is also difficult to separate spontaneous attitudes and reactions from those brought about, or provoked, by intentional activities. Basically, statements that can be made about this subject with certainty come down to two obvious claims: first, society was replete with still rather large reserves of aversion, prejudice, and hostility—potential rather than active, slumbering, and ready to manifest under favorable circumstances; and second, people in government circles knew about the attitudes of aversion against Jews. Responding to Nowak at the Seventh Plenary Session, Józef Cyrankiewicz soberly claimed:[13] "The tone of this speech gave it [i.e., this issue—K.K.] new dimensions, and these different dimensions threaten to transform themselves [!] into something qualitatively different, especially beyond the confines of this room. (. . .) And in Poland, once you let the snakes of anti-Semitism out of Pandora's Box, it is not that easy to lock them back up."[14]

This was the background of the role the Jewish problem was to play in the political theater of 1956.

The government crisis, growing since Stalin's death and intensified after the Twentieth Congress of the Communist Party of the Soviet Union, made it necessary for the Polish Communist Party (PZPR) to look for new instruments of rule. Most generally speaking, three more or less crystallized conceptions clashed within the party. The first—let us call it conservative—sought to overcome "the mistakes and deviations of the former period," while simultaneously retaining the doctrinal principles of communism, liberalized perhaps and adjusted to existing realities; the second—associated with the names of young Central Committee secretaries Władysław Matwin, Jerzy Morawski, and Jerzy Albrecht—proclaimed the need to democratize and create "a likable socialism"—that's a Poznań worker's phrase, often quoted by Matwin; and the third—most closely tied to the Soviet sovereign—assumed the need to suppress the crisis by means of force coupled with populist and crypto-anti-Semitic demagogy, using, among other things, the tried and true method of a scapegoat to fool society. The link between Jews and Stalinist crimes was intended to channel social emotions into the anti-Semitic riverbed, supplanting the postwar cliché that linked Jews with government authorities.

In Poland, Stalinism had a fundamental flaw: even though it attempted to put on national colors, it was not perceived as national. The coterie I'm referring to sought to correct this flaw by activating those reserves of social consciousness on which the actions of extremist nationalist and totalitarian movements were based just before the war, and by appealing to the tendency—present in society—to "nationalize" the Communists' rule, all the while maintaining an unchanged totalitarian form of the system and Poland's non-sovereign status. Bolesław Piasecki, who enthusiastically supported the group representing these tendencies in the leadership of Communist Party, probably did not do it simply because of his "contract" with the NKVD General Serov, which he had signed in a prison cell in 1944. The suggested proposals to eliminate some persons with Jewish origins from government posts served to confirm the Polish national character of the authorities, while at the same time diverting attention from important internal problems. An alliance of totalitarian communism and National Radical Camp (ONR) type of nationalism was appearing on the horizon.

This way, the Jewish question, largely artificially created and somewhat mystifying, became a spectacular tool in the struggle of the feuding party factions. In this clash, proponents of actual democracy, but also some of the conservatives, commonly referred to as Pulavians, stood against the Natolin faction. The former had an unquestionably better position, and not just because they had the backing of mass media (which, by the way, they managed at the time), or because they were supported by the majority of party intellectuals, students, workers, and a significant part of the party apparatus. Their activities were facilitated by the fact that it was easy to denounce one's opponents as anti-Semites, while open proclamations that Jews are responsible for Stalinist crimes or that "there are too many comrades with Jewish backgrounds in the government" were still impermissible. One had recourse to cafés and intentionally spread rumors. Poland was buzzing with stories that either denounced someone's anti-Semitism, or quite the opposite, pointed out someone's Jewish ancestors or his former last name.

It is difficult to determine to what extent the use of camouflaged anti-Semitism by one of the party coteries reflected cynical manipulation; it is also difficult to say how accurately it expressed the mentality and views of a current within the party which was soon to find its leader in Mieczysław Moczar. And we do not know how Soviet factors played into the situation. At the time, in the aforementioned article, Konstanty Jeleński wrote that Polish anti-Semitism manifested itself on two levels.

> One of these levels is the murky ground of the national and peasant subconscious (. . .). The second consists of Soviet pressure, Soviet influences, and activities of both Soviet agents and Polish Stalinists. Anti-Semitism in the USSR is taking on frightful dimensions. (. . .). At a time when Poland is gradually breaking away from the Soviet Union—through the unity of the whole society and the prudence of the political leadership—it is a sad fact that the connection between anti-Semitism and Soviet influence in

Poland has not yet sufficiently penetrated the nation's awareness. The Natolin Targowica advocated anti-Semitism[15]—and continues to advocate it—almost as if it were one of its main slogans. (. . .) Incidentally, writers and journalists with Jewish backgrounds have made a great contribution to the destruction of the total lie of Stalinism, and to the liberalization and democratization of Polish life. Unfortunately, even when they admit this, Poles still use concepts with recognizable remnants of the National Radical Camp's myth about "Judeo-Bolshevism."

In 1956, anti-Semitic attitudes in the party-state establishment were generally not given the floor. They did not, however, remain without consequence. Another wave of Jewish émigrés left Poland—about 40,000 people left, half of whom were Jews newly repatriated from the USSR on the basis of the 1957 agreement. A large part of the Jewish population of Lower Silesia left at that time. Many Communists left as well. Those leaving were people who lost all faith in the possibility of leading a normal existence in Poland—whether as Jews, or as Poles with Jewish backgrounds—without exposing themselves to the anti-Semitism of their surroundings. They were failed by the government and the party to which—aware of the presence of anti-Semitism in society—they tied their hopes and their life opportunities. The wave of anti-Semitism that welled up within the party turned out to be the last straw for many. After 1957, there were probably 25,000 to 30,000 Jews remaining in Poland. It all depends, in any case, on what criteria one wishes to apply.

Tendencies held back but not destroyed in 1956 manifested themselves in all their horror twelve years later.

Those twelve years between October and March are typically associated with *our little stabilization*.[16] Yet the period can be clearly divided into two phases. In the first phase, Gomułka's post-October government managed to contain the crisis effectively. Social aspirations were blocked so that they neither threatened to dissolve the system nor infringed on the total rule of the Communists. At the same time, there was a generally perceptible loosening of the reins that had constrained the lives of millions of people. The Church, artistic circles, scholars, and peasants gained small extensions of freedom, which were quite significant, however, when compared to previous years. There were clear improvements in people's material circumstances. The Great Fear of the former decade gave way to little anxieties—these were easier to bear, though no less spiritually damaging, leading to moral conformity and the ubiquitous appearance of extreme opportunism.

But already at the beginning of the 1960s it turned out that the little stabilization would not be, as Kazimierz Wierzyński wrote in his "Black Polonaise," either great capitulation or even great resignation. The poet was wrong when he sketched a hopeless image of Poland:

Wszystko się jakoś zabliźni
W naszej pijanej ojczyźnie,
Na ranach pajęczyna
W dziurawych ścianach mech . . .

Scars will cover everything
In our drunken fatherland,
There are cobwebs on wounds
Moss on cracked walls . . .

It is true that in the early 1960s social discontent was still far from that critical point beyond which the smallest impulse suffices to create an explosion. Yet already in 1961, in an analysis sent to Gomułka, Władysław Bieńkowski warned: "The most striking thing is the continuous worsening of the "social atmosphere" over the last few years, the so-called feelings of large masses of society, feelings which have been manifesting themselves as discouragement or outright irritation during this last year. Something most accurately described as a crisis of trust in the government is growing in broad segments of social consciousness."[j] Slowly, with fading memories of the peak of the Stalinist period, and the maturation of a new generation that did not experience the first postwar decade, a sense of dissatisfaction was gaining ground—dissatisfaction which grew along with the increasingly acutely felt inability to satisfy basic needs, both economic and psychological. Disillusionment was becoming deeper—the hopes of October remained unfulfilled. Outlines of another crisis of the system were becoming perceptible, and this time, in the international context the crisis was coupled with the accumulation of democratizing processes in Czechoslovakia.

Special tensions became perceptible among intellectuals affiliated with the party-government configuration, intellectuals who had played such an important role in 1956. Ideological ferment was intensifying, many intellectuals were leaving the party, and others were dismissed after accusations of

---

[j] *Socjologia klęski* (*The Sociology of Defeat*) (Paris, 1971).

"revisionism." Feuding camps emerged and their roots reached back to the divisions created in 1956. One of the fields in which various currents and groups clashed was the realm of national tradition and national values, and, more broadly speaking—the concept of Polishness and its form. This field was neither new nor created ad hoc. Wrestling with the *form* of Polishness is an important element of our national culture, which spans the spectrum from Henryk Sienkiewicz to Witold Gombrowicz.[17] This was precisely the field where much of the March 1968 scenario played out.

Scenario? This word suggests activities prepared ahead of time, intentionally aimed at a specific goal, bearing the marks of a provocation. Indeed, one can see this type of activity in the 1968 events, though it is still impossible to point to evidence that proves this. It was a seemingly simple, not to say primitive, scenario that duplicated well-known patterns from the past—including the prewar period. National Democrats had behaved very similarly when in the early 1930s they attacked the ruling camp and *used the Jewish dimension as one of their strongest battle and propaganda trump cards.* With the accompaniment of a media uproar, parliamentary speeches, street riots, and university brawls, the government was accused of philo-Semitism with the intention, as an author of a Jewish column in *Sprawy Narodowościowe (Nationality Matters)* wrote, "to take advantage of anti-Semitic feelings of certain social strata in the fight against the May government."[k] Professor Roman Rybarski's article "Polityka żydowska" (Jewish Politics) printed in *Gazeta Warszawska* served as a signal. The author claimed that Jews "are today the main backbone of the Sanacja government, from Jewish intellectual circles all the way to the Tzadikim in provincial towns." In 1968 it was impossible, of course, to advocate anti-Semitic slogans openly, but the essence of the sociotechnical manipulation remained unchanged. Whoever prepared and led it used partly authentic themes; brought up the hot subject of national values that were being deprecated by the Communists; played on emotions, obsessions, and prejudices; took advantage of myths rooted in Polish consciousness; skillfully mixed half-truths and falsehoods; created

---

[k] "Mniejszości narodowe w Polsce. Żydzi" (National Minorities in Poland. Jews), *Sprawy Narodowościowe (Nationality Matters)* 5, no. 6 (1931). Representing OZON in a parliamentary debate about the 1939/40 draft budget, S. Skwarczyński claimed: "But as we discuss the Jewish question, we cannot not touch upon another side of this problem. For some in Poland, the Jewish question is becoming an instrument in partisan quarrels among Poles and a source of anarchy in Polish civil life. We adamantly oppose this way of treating the issue, which becomes more dangerous because it demoralizes youth and damages our noble spirit." Fifth Sejm, Parliamentary Stenographic Record no. 3.

deformed contexts; and appealed to national feelings and anti-Jewish resentments—without passing over some very concrete interests of strong lobbies within the framework of the establishment.

In 1968, however, it was not just about the struggle between two competing political camps or the political form of Polish life. As in 1956, the Communist Party faced the problem of preserving the system of rule with all its basic elements. As is well known, this was not only an internal problem, but also—given that real sovereignty was lacking—an object of interest and direct interference of the Soviet sovereign. One should therefore view March 1968 not as a result of conflicts among coteries who fought for a place at the top, but rather as an outcome of a growing crisis of the system, whose regulatory mechanisms, intended to ensure a minimum of internal balance necessary for survival, were seriously weakened. It was a pragmatic reaction to phenomena taking place in society and capable of threatening the existing order. Gomułka's ossified government was helpless against these, unable to act in a way that would either respond to society's aspirations or effectively suppress them. All the clashing party cabals (to use this old Polish term) were aware of the growing threats but drew different conclusions about them. In the years leading up to March, Gomułka—who had been terrified by the growing activation of society, which had threatened to escape the party-state's control already back in October 1956—feared that discontent caused by the worsening standards of living and a lack of opportunities, along with ferment among intellectual elites, could turn into what he considered a "counterrevolutionary" eruption, rife with unpredictable consequences. In this regard, Gomułka did not have any illusions similar to those of the party "liberals" and "democrats;" his political instinct and his intuitions about Polish society told him that allowing Poles to voice their aspirations would activate an avalanche reaction, creating mortal danger for the system and—he was fully convinced of this—for Poland. Which is why he was ready to resort to drastic means to suppress all seeds of "revolt," whether it was the distribution of *Kultura*, the "Letter of the Thirty-Four," Jacek Kuroń and Karol Modzelewski's "Open Letter to the Party," or the activities of the Ruch (Movement) group.[18] Milieus and activities which still remained, at least in part, within the framework of the system and evoked Marxism and socialist ideology were fought particularly ardently because they were the only ones that mattered on the political scene at the time. At a Politburo meeting on April 8, 1968, Cyrankiewicz said: "Above all, already back in December, after the outbreak of the incidents in Czechoslovakia,

we should have realized that they would find an echo on the ground prepared by Kołakowski and Brus. In March, we were essentially threatened
by counterrevolution, we were threatened by blood, and it would have
been necessary to pay a heavy price."[l] And on December 19, 1970, Zenon
Kliszko claimed:[19] "currently, the situation will unfold differently than in
1956 because today the Home Army soldiers are well prepared. We will face
a situation in which we will have to call the Red Army for support."[m]

Looking at it from the perspective of time, the party coteries that emerged
on the eve of March (their configuration, by the way, is very unclear, and
the division into Moczar's "partisans" and "Gomułka's men" seems much
too simplistic) appear to be the *two pianos* to which Ochab referred in his
interview with Torańska. First Secretaries in "garrison countries"—as he
put it—who refuse to cooperate, or (let us add) are insufficiently effica-
cious, are kept in check by being forced to play "a second piano. To frighten
them and to have other alternatives. Since under normal circumstances the
first secretary has to start defending himself (. . .)."[n 20] For keen observers,
by the way, it was obvious already in 1968 that the melody—regardless
of which piano was being played, and variations notwithstanding—would
essentially remain the same. Today, we are unable to decipher Moscow's
role in the prehistory of March, though there is much to suggest that the
anti-Semitic current that characterized these events had its inspirations
also (if not primarily) in the USSR. Appealing to anti-Jewish phobias was
a tried and true method of reacting to danger in this country, and the great
revolt of the second half of the 1960s, which encompassed our entire civilizational realm, did not stop at the Elbe or even the Bug River. The seed of
independent public opinion was planted in the Soviet Union, and national
aspirations intensified in its republics. Reform tendencies were gaining
ground in the protectorate states. Descriptions of March often underesti-
mate its affinity with the Bierut era; Stalinist notions were eclipsed, so to
speak, by nationalism and anti-Semitism. And yet even the March version
of nationalism and anti-Semitism was more reminiscent of Stalinist than
National Radical Camp (ONR) precedents. Michał Głowiński showed this
emphatically in his analysis of March propaganda and the creation of the

---

[l] "Biuro Polityczne pproponuje" (The Political Bureau Makes a Proposal), a note from the discussion at the Political Bureau meeting on April 8, 1968, Agenda Item no. 5—Personnel Issues,
Polityka (*Politics*), no. 23 (1991).
[m] As cited by B. Seidler, Kto kazał atrzelać (Who Gave the Order to Shoot) (Warsaw, 1991).
[n] Teresa Torańska, *Oni* (Warsaw, 1985).

figure of the enemy.[21] In Poland, where anti-Semitism of the Stalin and Khrushchev eras appeared in a diluted form (it was probably blocked by Polish leadership), the prewar experience became the point of reference. It seems, however—without taking due "credit" away from Piasecki and without underestimating the significance of homegrown anti-Semites— that the anti-Jewish operation of 1967–1968 was largely rooted in the Russian-Soviet tradition, and it was a reflection of anti-Jewish activities taking place in the USSR.

Government authorities were unable to meet the growing wave of social unrest in Poland with a realistic program for improving people's living conditions—and thus only violence and demagogy remained. These were also used in 1968 and 1970—that is, during both phases of containing the crisis of the late 1960s. Although no blood was actually spilled in March 1968, the brutal demonstration of force at the University of Warsaw on March 8, and the later actions of the Citizens' Militia (MO) and the Security Service (SB), accompanied by a massive propaganda attack, led to the activation of fears encoded in social consciousness. Let us note that the reaction to society's increasingly feverish mood took place before it reached the thresh-old of explosion, and when intellectual circles affiliated with the establish-ment were ideologically and politically divided. Moreover, this time, unlike twelve years earlier, as a result of Gomułka's policy of removing revisionists who represented the democratic orientation within the party, the strong-est position at the various levels of government belonged to an extremely anti-democratic and anti-liberal group. With the help of many national and populist slogans, this group appealed to aversions and emotions rooted in social consciousness, skillfully activating the irrational strata of individual psyches and collective awareness. This orientation partially expressed the mentality and aspirations of a new generation of Communists—careerist forty-year-olds, who were educated after the war, and who could not wait to take their place in public life. In those Polish realities, the process of gen-erational change, normal in a healthy system, took on the degenerate form of reckoning with "national nihilists, cosmopolitans, masked Zionists, feudal lords in scholarship," and so on.

Let us return to the word "scenario." It is conceivable that it emerged spontaneously, as a result of the tense social situation. After all, in the atmo-sphere of excitement that existed in Warsaw's intellectual and political circles and among some students at the end of 1967, no Machiavellian plotting was necessary for the audience to react enthusiastically to Mickiewicz's *Dziady*

(*Forefathers' Eve*), and in their anxiety about this, the authorities first limited the number of shows, and then banned them altogether. Both reactions were in line with their respective behavioral models. Things were similar in subsequent events: the youth's march to Mickiewicz's monument, the collection of signatures under the petition to the parliament, the meeting at the Polish Writers' Union, and repressions aimed at student activists all fit into the natural—so to speak—order of things. It is also difficult to estimate the length of preparations for the operation opened by the brutal breaking up of the student rally on March 8, 1968.

Much seems to suggest that the idea of pulling out the anti-Semitic card reaches back to at least 1967. It was then that purges in the military and other institutions intensified, under the pretext of removing those who rejoiced at Israel's victory. We do not know, and we probably will not know, where the idea was born. And it was not about the few Communists with Jewish backgrounds who still remained in offices, committees, institutes, hospitals, or editorial offices. The goal was different. The campaign directed against Jews was an instrument utilized to defuse the rising liberation movement. It was also used in intra-party conflicts. Their mechanism was laid bare by recently published notes from the Communist Party's Politburo meeting on April 8, 1968.

It seems that in the genesis and mechanism of March there was a double provocation: first, there were intentional activities aimed to provoke a social reaction—a reaction that would provide a pretext for countrywide repression; and second, there was an exaggerated reaction—typical of all police states—to a situation perceived as a threat. It is likely that when it came to *Dziady*, both forms of provocation were present, while the March 8 police action was a purposeful, planned step, intended to increase tensions and provide a pretext for a crackdown on specific communist establishment circles. In turn, later actions against the student revolt that overstepped the framework of the scenario had a different character; they were an expression of the perception of being threatened by "reaction," "counterrevolution," and "anarchy," which was ingrained in the minds of communist authorities from the very beginning. Fear of "anarchy" accompanied Gomułka from October to December, and it was not unfounded.[22] He understood that allowing for the expression of social and national aspirations would activate an avalanche that would threaten both internal and external dimensions of the existing system at its very foundations.

A rich arsenal of national and populist slogans was activated in front of a mostly disoriented society; these slogans were saturated with anti-Semitic connotations and coupled with activities directed against people who were within the framework of a broadly understood establishment, and who were sympathetic to democratization processes. Insinuations evoking archaic obsessions and resentments were used to activate old clichés in social consciousness: Jews and the Comintern, Jews and communism—and the new edition: Jews and Stalinism; Jews as those who are not real Poles, cosmopolitans without a fatherland, or the opposite, Jews as Israeli patriots and Zionists. That last equation appeared in 1967, when Israel's success met with approval in Poland—not just among Jews or Poles with Jewish backgrounds.

Many things contributed to the fact that the police operation achieved significant success, even though it probably did not meet all of its intended goals. While there were no radical changes at the top of the party-state hierarchy, at lower levels there was a change of cadres on a scale unimaginable in a different situation. What is more important, the attack on the emerging democratic opposition, carried out in an atmosphere of raging anti-Semitism, inhibited the development of liberation movements and blocked the chances for agreement and cooperation among various social groups for some time—this applied, above all, to workers and intellectuals. Recourse to anti-Semitism made it possible to hold back the efforts—gaining ground in Poland, as in Czechoslovakia—to reform the system in a way that undermined its totalitarian essence. The absurdity and hypocrisy of this campaign made it more dreadful, and magnified its paralyzing effect on the entire society. The producers of the events rightly foresaw that by manipulating fear and demagogy they would subdue most of the society. Anti-Semitic slogans, covered up by various masks and associated with populist and anti-intelligentsia themes, spoke to the compromised strata of social consciousness all the more effectively on account of their patriotic content, and sometimes obvious anticommunist and anti-Soviet allusions. We could point to Moczar's famous sentence that juxtaposed people who came from the East in their gray greatcoats against real Polish patriots from the Polish Workers' Party (PPR).

True, attacks waged against Jews in the party, government, administration, culture, and scholarship did not bring society any closer to the authorities. Foreign observers who saw photographs of the rallies in the press—with hundreds of banners with the words "Zionists" . . . "Away With" . . . "Treason" . . . "Troublemakers" . . . —and claimed that "the party is capable of mobilizing a hundred thousand Poles under the single slogan of 'anti-Zionism'" were mistaken. The mechanism whereby mass rallies express either support or opposition in a system created by Communists is a separate problem in itself, but one thing is certain: those massive demonstrations did not show the actual relationship between the people who attended them and the slogans that were written on banners and shouted from podiums. In 1944, crowds demanded the transformation of the Polish Committee of National Liberation into the Transitional Government, and in 1976 they condemned troublemakers from Radom and Ursus. 1956 was the exception.[23]

The Communist Party's campaign that unleashed anti-Semitism met with disapproval in many circles and among the elites. The Church distanced itself from it. Some condemned this campaign primarily because they were convinced that it undermined Poland's reputation. At a general meeting of the Warsaw section of the Polish Writers' Union, Paweł Jasienica said:[24] "Friends, someone who is keeping his goals secret, is attempting to attach the stigma of anti-Semitism to our nation. Lack of tolerance had already made its mark on Poland's affairs during Voltaire's time, when the question of our religious intolerance was raised. As a historian I know this well—nothing can bring us greater harm today than convincing the world public opinion that we are a nation of anti-Semites."° People responded to him with an ovation that went on for a long time. Others, viewing anti-Semitism as an unconditional evil, were first and foremost terrified not only by the activities of the authorities but also by the reaction of that part of society which responded to the attack on Jews and anti-Semitic propaganda with indifference and passivity, if not approval and acquiescence. Many felt a piercing sense of shame, which was not always expressed in behaviors, public demonstrations of solidarity with those subjected to discrimination, or in clear, unambiguous denunciations of all manifestations of anti-Semitism. To some extent, this was a result of fear of the consequences, but it was also an expression of a defensive reflex, rooted deeply in Polish mentality and expressed in the belief that Poles are not anti-Semites, that there is only hypersensitivity among Jews.

The openly anti-Semitic campaign—the accompanying hypocrisy did not mislead anyone—lasted a dozen weeks or so; on June 24, the censor's office issued the following ruling:

° Statements similar in tone were made, for example, at a staff meeting at the History Institute of the Polish Academy of Sciences (PAN), after Professor Tadeusz Manteuffel's speech that denounced the anti-Semitic and anti-intelligentsia campaign.

The unnecessary emphasis on and accumulation of Zionism-related material in individual issues of periodicals and radio and television programs should be stopped. While discussing the background of the March events, the Jewish origins of their instigators should not be emphasized, and instead there should be a crackdown on revisionism and all kinds of social reaction. (3) While discussing personnel changes, expressions that directly emphasize the Jewish origins of people affected by the changes should be avoided. (4). In court reports, the Jewish origins of the defendants should not be (individually) emphasized.

Point 5 of these instructions gave the order to

eliminate from the press, radio, and television, all nationalistic accents and all elements that deform a class-based approach to the historical evaluation of our nation and the history of the workers' movement. This applies to the evaluation of our interwar period in particular, and to the configuration of political forces during the occupation. All attempts to whitewash right-wing social forces and give tendentious accounts of the past of the revolutionary movement should be eliminated.

But not all papers had participated in the anti-Semitic Sabbath. When one browses through newspapers from the time, the weeklies in particular, the restraint of many papers and journalists is quite striking, as is the sometimes clear criticism of the evocation of National Radical Camp precedents. Stefan Olszowski who was the director of the Central Committee's Press Bureau at the time wrote his master's thesis on the main tendencies in literary and newspaper journalism against the background of the March 1968 events. While praising the great "March" services rendered by *Kurier Polski, Słowo Powszechne, Prawo i Życie, Życie Literackie,* and *Życie Gospodarcze,* he claimed that not all editorial boards *displayed an understanding of the situation.* There were delays and commentaries so enigmatic that they *could not appear in print.* The Press Bureau blocked the first commentary in *Kultura,* Professor Czesław Bobrowski's statement, and Kazimierz Koźniewski's article about the meeting of the Warsaw section of the Polish Writers' Union that appeared in *Polityka.* Commentaries in *Świat* and *Dookoła Świata* did not meet the Bureau's demands, and the attitude of the editorial boards of *Przekrój* and *Argumenty* did not win the Bureau's respect.

This relatively brief witch-hunt—viewed with reserve by large groups of intellectuals with and without party affiliation—was overlaid on experiences from the past. The seemingly extinguished fear, familiar from the interwar and war years, came back to life. The actions of the authorities were often perceived as a harbinger of imminent persecution; what was taking place seemed to be a synthesis of fascism and Stalinist anti-Semitism. It gave rise to the worst kind of associations and evoked fear, which was worse than the actual danger. Yet more important than fear was the protest against humiliation and disdain, which, it turned out, were only seemingly a thing of the past. The brutal purge not only deprived people of their positions and professional opportunities but also attempted to strip them of their dignity. And this was a replication of Nazi and Stalinist models.

There followed yet another—and perhaps final—exodus from Poland. An apparently voluntary exodus, which was in fact forced by situational coercion—as Albert Sauvy puts it—and which was associated with the lawless procedure of having to renounce one's Polish citizenship.[p] Meanwhile, it was obvious that many of those who left had grown to identify with Polishness, and they would continue to live in their Polishness after leaving the country.

The post-March emigration almost fully completed the process of removing Jews from Polish lands. Only a small number remained; they were people who—regardless of the nature of their connections with the spiritual realm of Jewishness and Polishnesss—could not imagine living outside Poland. They were later joined by youth who wished to return to their Jewish roots and recreate—even if only on a micro-scale—Jewish life in the Polish lands. But let us not delude ourselves: even though there is no Jewish community left in Poland and so few people with connections to Jewishness remain— even if we describe Jewishness only in terms of genealogical descent—the specter of the Jew is still haunting the country. The *Jew* as a magical *sign,* nearly entirely stripped of any real referents, is still a signifier of the other, someone who cannot be trusted, who should be avoided, and who can be blamed for one's misfortunes. Someone who does not belong to the collective US, who is not OURS. Or at best—not fully OURS. The specter of the Jew feeds upon fears, uncertain future, chaos, lack of security, and people's disorientation in today's Poland, which is undergoing lightning-fast changes. . . . And it will accompany us until Poland and Poles finally muster the will to become normal.

---

[p] Sauvy, *Theorie Générale de la Population,* vol. 2 (Paris, 1959).

Editors' Notes

1. PAX was a communist-era, progovernment Catholic association created and initially led by Bolesław Piasecki (1915–1979), who in the interwar period had been the leader of the fascist National Radical Camp Falanga group.

2. Stefan Staszewski (1906–1989) and Roman Zambrowski (1909–1977) were both Poles with Jewish backgrounds who worked in the structures of the postwar United Polish Communist Party (PZPR); both had belonged to the interwar Polish Communist Party (KPP).

3. We discuss the cliché *kwestia żydowska* (Jewish question) in the final part of the Introduction to this volume.

4. Kersten's essay includes many historical referents that we discuss in the Introduction. In "The Interwar Years: Polish Independence and the Crisis of Democracy," we discuss topics like the treaty on protecting minorities and Poland's 1921 Constitution; Roman Dmowski and the National Democrats; Piłsudski's 1926 coup d'état (the May coup) and the Sanacja regime, which held power between 1926 and 1939; the National Radical Camp (ONR); "Jew benches" (also known as "ghetto benches"); the *numerus clausus* campaign that sought to limit the number Jewish students at Polish universities; and the Camp of National Unity (OZN, often called Ozon). In "Anti-Semitism in the Polish People's Republic," we summarize the major turning points of Poland's communist period—1948, 1956, 1968, 1970, 1976, and the 1980s; we also discuss Bolesław Bierut, Jakub Berman, and other Stalinist leaders; the Pulavian and Natolin factions within the Polish Communist Party (PZPR), which competed for power in 1956; the Prague Spring; the Polish and Soviet reactions to Israel's victory in the Six Day War in 1967; Mieczysław Moczar; the March 1968 events in Poland; and the pivotal role of the performance of Adam Mickiewicz's drama *Dziady* (*Forefather's Eve*) in the March events.

5. Guy Lee, *Catullus: The Complete Poems,* Oxford World's Classics (Oxford University Press, 1998).

6. Tadeusz Hołówko (1889–1931) was a Polish Socialist Party (PPS) activist, politician, and diplomat; one of his articles on anti-Semitism appears in this volume in the collage of newspaper excerpts collected by Czesław Miłosz ("Jews—the 1920s"). Leon Wasilewski (1870–1936) was also a PPS activist and delegate to Versailles as the minister of foreign affairs between 1918 and 1919. Henryk Józefski (1892–1981) was a pro-Piłsudski politician and the voivode of Volhynia between 1930 and 1938; he is the subject of Timothy Snyder's book *Sketches from a Secret War: A Polish Artist's Mission to Liberate Soviet Ukraine* (Yale University Press, 2007).

7. Roman Dmowski, the leader of the National Democrats (SND) was born in the town of Kamionek, while Piłsudski was born in the town of Żułów. The sea referred to is the Black Sea, which the Polish-Lithuanian Commonwealth had

bordered in the sixteenth century; Połąga is a Lithuanian town on the Baltic Sea, and it is another pointer back to the Polish-Lithuanian Commonwealth.

8. The Russian words *soldat* and *baryshnya* mean "soldier" and "wealthy woman."

9. The Union of Polish Patriots (ZPP) was a pro-Soviet organization created by Polish Communists in the USSR in 1943; it was active until 1946.

10. Eward Ochab (1906–1989) was the first secretary of the Polish Communist Party (PZPR) between March and October of 1956. He continued serving in the Politburo during Gomułka's rule until 1968, and he headed the Polish State Council between 1964 and 1968. He resigned from the government and the party in April 1968, in the aftermath of the March events.

11. Zenon Nowak (1905–1980) was a member of the Central Committee of the Polish Communist Party (PZPR); he belonged to the hardline Natolin group in 1956.

12. Jerzy Turowicz's and Leszek Kołakowski's essays are reproduced in this volume on pages 164–169 and 143–150, respectively.

13. Józef Cyrankiewicz (1911–1989) was a Polish Socialist Party (PPS) activist in the interwar period. He later became a member of the Central Committee of the Polish Communist Party (PZPR) and served as Poland's prime minister between 1947 and 1952. He took part in the brutal suppression of workers' protests in Poznań in 1956, and he carried out Gomułka's directive to use force to quell workers' protests in Gdańsk and Gdynia in 1970.

14. Bracketed notes in this quote appear in the original.

15. In Polish history "Targowica" functions as a synonym for betrayal of national interests and surrender of the country to a foreign power. It refers to the 1792 Targowica Confederation, established when the sovereignty of the Polish-Lithuanian Commonwealth was threatened by Russia, Prussia, and Austria, which had already annexed parts of the Commonwealth's territory in 1772. The Confederation included magnates willing to support Catherine II and opposed to the 1791 Constitution and other reforms that sought to modernize Poland and strengthen it against the aggression of the partitioning powers. The Targowica declaration was followed by the invasion of the Polish-Lithuanian Commonwealth by Russian forces, which led to the abolition of the 1791 Constitution and the second partition of the Polish-Lithuanian Commonwealth in 1793.

16. "*Nasza mała stabilizacja*" (our little stabilization) was used to describe social life in Poland during Gomułka's rule (1956–1970); it refers to the retreat from Stalinist terror, relative loosening of censorship, and the relative improvement in the standard of living.

17. Henryk Sienkiewicz (1846–1916) was a novelist and Nobel Prize laureate, best known for his historical novels that sought to educate and hearten the Poles during the partitions era. Witold Gombrowicz (1904–1969) was a writer and playwright widely considered to be among Poland's most important

twentieth-century figures; he is best known for his irony, willingness to undermine national pieties, and keen psychological analyses of Polish society and
culture.

18. The "Letter of the Thirty-Four" is described in the introduction to Maria
    Dąbrowska's essay. In 1964, Jacek Kuroń (1934–2004) and Karol Modzelewski
    (b. 1937) wrote an "Open Letter to the Party," in which they called on the
    Communist Party leadership to abandon abuses of power and return to com-
    munist ideals, and for which they were both imprisoned for three years. The
    "Ruch" (Movement) group was active between 1965 and 1970; it rejected
    communist rule and advocated democracy and Polish independence from the
    Soviet Union.

19. Zenon Kliszko (1908–1989) worked closely with Gomułka. In 1968, he rec-
    ommended the ban on the performance of Mickiewicz's *Dziady* (*Forefathers'*
    Eve), a decision which became a catalyst for the March student protests. In
    December 1970, Kliszko ordered army units to open fire on striking workers
    in Gdańsk and Gdynia.

20. Kersten is referring to Teresa Torańska's award-winning book, which is available
    in English as *Them: Stalin's Polish Puppets*, trans. Agnieszka Kołakowska (Harper
    Collins, 1988).

21. Michał Głowinski (b. 1934) is a writer and literary historian who published
    many influential studies of the structure and functions of the communist
    "newspeak."

22. That is, between October 1956 and December 1970 when Gomułka was the
    head of the Communist Party and the Polish state.

23. Kersten is arguing that the progovernment mass demonstrations in 1944 and
    1976 were organized by the Communists, and therefore have little value for
    assessing the attitudes prevalent in society.

24. Paweł Jasienica (1909–1970) was a historian and essayist; he signed the 1964
    anticensorship "Letter of the Thirty-Four" and criticized the government's
    decision to stop the performances of Mickiewicz's *Dziady* in 1968.

PART
VII

1970–1989: The Poor Poles Look at the Ghetto

16

Jews as a Polish Problem

ALEKSANDER SMOLAR

Editors' Introduction

Aleksander Smolar (b. 1940) is a political scientist, economist, and chairman of the board of the Stefan Batory Foundation, which supports prodemocracy initiatives in Poland and East Central Europe. Born in the city of Białystok in northeastern Poland, he studied economics and sociology at the University of Warsaw, where he later worked at the Department of Political Economics. He was one of the leaders of the student protests at the university in March 1968, and after his arrest served a prison sentence until February 1969. In 1971, Smolar left Poland to live in Paris; he cofounded the influential émigré quarterly *Aneks* in 1973 and served as its editor-in-chief until 1990. He returned to Poland in 1989 and served as political advisor to Prime Ministers Tadeusz Mazowiecki and Hanna Suchocka. He is currently the vice chair of the Academic Advisory Board at the Institute for Human Sciences (Institut für die Wissenschaften vom Menschen) in Vienna, and a member of the Council of the ECFR (European Council on Foreign Relations).

The Polish version of the essay reproduced here was originally entitled "Tabu i niewinność" (Taboo and Innocence) and published in a 1986 issue of *Aneks* devoted to Polish-Jewish relations. In this text, Smolar refers to a number of essays reproduced in this volume, including those by Borwicz, Wyka, Andrzejewski, Turowicz, and Błoński. He also refers to Krystyna Kersten's analyses of the 1946 Kielce Pogrom and anti-Semitism in the Polish Communist Party (PZPR). This English translation of Smolar's essay initially appeared as "Jews as a Polish Problem" *Daedalus* 116, no. 2 (Spring 1987): 31-73; it is reprinted here with permission from MIT Press.

Until quite recently, and for several decades, systematic attempts were made to eliminate the Jews from Polish memory. The Jews tended to disappear from Polish history, from the landscape itself, from guides for tourists, and, as a particular group of victims, from official publications about war. Still, they kept an important place in the national consciousness; they were present in conversations about those in power, about communism itself, about the prewar era and the war; they were present in neurotic phantasms, and also in rational debates.

Voices from abroad, conscious of the past, evoked (even if not always in a just and balanced way) the problem of moral responsibility for the traditions and consequences of Polish anti-Semitism. The apparent efficiency of official communist anti-Semitic propaganda posed the same problem. Such questions—and more generally, those concerning the Polish-Jewish past—have been posed by more and more young people who do not know Jews, who know almost nothing about their past in Poland, who do not understand the accusations coming from distant places, but who consider the silence itself a moral and intellectual scandal. Since the beginning of the 1980s, particularly in the sixteen months of relative freedom during the Solidarity period, the Jews—their history, traditions, and culture—and the Polish attitude toward them have become a very important matter of discussion in all four major Polish networks: the official, Catholic, underground, and emigration presses. "The Jewish question" in Poland today exists principally as a Polish problem: that of facing history, the burden of moral responsibility, and the difficult questioning of the Polish heroic and tragic self-image, formed in the perpetual fight for freedom, independence, and national survival.

The argument generally invoked by Poles when they are charged with anti-Semitism is that their country has an age-old tradition of national and religious tolerance. Indeed, for hundreds of years, even in the age of the Reformation and the Counter-Reformation, Jews persecuted in other countries of Europe were in the habit of finding sanctuary in Poland— hence, the great concentration of Jews in the lands of the pre-partition Commonwealth. Poles sometimes forget that this is now a rather distant past. The situation of the Jews in Poland began to deteriorate precisely at the time when religious toleration was becoming the rule in Western Europe, when Jews were being given full civic rights. The Polish situation was changing in a very different way, caused by the decline of the nation itself, but also by the growing role of the Catholic Church in maintaining the unity of that nation. The changed position of the Church greatly complicated relations with people of other faiths.

Jews tend to view Polish history as a perpetual process of growing anti-Semitism. In fact, since the end of the last century, traditional anti-Jewish attitudes among Poles, mainly of a religious kind, have been compounded with new forms of anti-Semitism whose roots are various: conflicting economic interests; changes in social structure; budding modern nationalism. A marked deterioration in Polish Jewish relations occurred after the First World War when Poland regained its independence; this became even more conspicuous in the late 1930s. This was a time of radical anti-Jewish ideologies, of anti-Semitic brawls, and of massive discrimination in many spheres: in the economy, in higher education, in the professions. New anti-Jewish legislation came to be prepared. The view that Jews must seek their future outside Poland became more widespread among political elites, and by no means affected only those on the right.

Jews, when pointing to these facts, sometimes neglect to take into account that their misfortunes were part and parcel of a set of dramatic problems facing a country that had recently re-established its independence and unity after a long period of political subjection. The country was locked in a vicious circle of poverty that affected Poles no less than Jews, not to mention other minorities. Also, though anti-Semitism in Poland tended to assume ever more brutal forms, this must be seen as part of a more general tendency in Europe at the time—a rebellion against both democratic and liberal values. We know that in many countries of Central and Eastern Europe in the thirties the situation of the Jews was no better, and indeed was sometimes worse, than it was in Poland.

Poland between the wars was not the chosen land for the Jews. But it was, despite growing antipathies, the land of the largest and the most culturally and politically dynamic Jewish community in Europe. Poles and Jews view their coexistence in different ways, and give different explanations for the growing hostility. Jews speak about intolerance, religious hatred, prejudice, violence in the streets, and pogroms at the moment that an independent Polish state was being created. They also dwell on the economic boycotts that were organized during that period. Poles evoke dramatic images of overpopulation; of Jewish cultural, linguistic, and social isolation; of the role and number of the so-called Litvak Jews, pushed into Polish territory by the tsarist policy. They recall the lack of enthusiasm among Jews for an independent Polish state, and emphasize the influence of procommunist sentiments in the Jewish community. The arguments on both sides, valid in some part, reflect age-old prejudices, and suggest how difficult coexistence has been for two radically different ethnic groups.

Also, it must be remembered that a large part of the Jewish community in the United States, in Western Europe, and in Israel originated in Poland. Mass Jewish emigrations from Poland, which took place in periods of growing economic difficulties and mounting social and racial tensions, have made the image of Poland in Jewish memory a rather negative one. Still, pre-Second World War history is not sufficient to explain the generally hostile and very emotional attitude of many Jews toward Poles and Poland; nor does it explain the role Poles play in Jewish memory, giving rise to stereotypes widely accepted throughout the world. The prewar history of the Jews in Poland was not very different from the history of Jews among many other nations. The particularly tragic elements of the relationship have much to do with events that began in September 1939, when the Second World War erupted.

The War

It is extremely difficult to give an accurate account of Polish attitudes toward Jews during the Second World War, and it is not my objective here to try to do so. What interests me is how the specific conditions of life under the occupation in Poland affected both Poles and Jews, the relations that existed between them, and why the images of this past, as represented by Poles and Jews, are so dramatically different.

It is best to begin by stating a fundamental fact: there was not the slightest chance of saving all three million Polish Jews or the three million Jews of other countries who were doomed to perish on the territory of occupied Poland. A different behavior on the part of the Poles might possibly have saved some more Jews. Individual Jews might have escaped death; the people itself was doomed. Only the Allies could have changed this had they grasped what was going on, had they shown the will to save Jews regardless of cost, had they been able to act. What sealed the fate of the Jews was not so much a lack of knowledge of their plight as a lack of imagination, determination, and the ability to act.

Thus, what is at stake in the continuing controversy between Poles and Jews, at least in respect to the war, is not the ultimate fate of the Jewish

nation. At stake is a moral judgment on Polish attitudes toward the destruction of the Jews. The object of the controversy is immensely important, but
it needs to be seen in proper perspective.

It is possible to distinguish between a dominant "Polish" and an equally
powerful "Jewish" vision of recent history. Both, perhaps, make excessive use
of pure colors: the first uses too much white; the second, too much black.
Characteristic of the "Polish" position is the belief in a historic discontinu-
ity, the insistence that the tragic experience of war brought about a radical
change in the attitudes of Poles toward Jews. Władysław Bartoszewski, a
historian with a commendable record of saving Jews, writes: "Conditions of
the occupation led to a considerable decrease of anti-Semitic sentiments in
Poland as compared to the prewar period. A common fate of the persecuted,
the suffering, and the fighters contributed to a new sense of solidarity and
a will to help those who were perishing."[a] Andrzej Micewski, a Catholic
journalist and close adviser of Cardinal Glemp, says, ". . . when all is said and
done, we as a society and as a nation have no reason to suffer from complexes on account of our attitude toward the Jews."[b] Jerzy Turowicz, an eminent Catholic intellectual and editor-in-chief of the prestigious *Tygodnik
Powszechny*, says, "The commonality of persecuted, suffering, and fighting
people changed quite radically the Polish-Jewish relations in our country.
In a very large part of Polish society the last vestiges of anti-Semitism disappeared to give way to a sense of solidarity, and there appeared the will, very
often effective, to help the persecuted."[c][1]

Jewish memory is very different; it tells a story of historic continuity.
Anti-Semitism is seen to be constant, despite its changing guises or varying degrees of intensity. Three Jewish historians, considering the effects of
prewar anti-Semitism on the attitudes of Poles during the war, offer an
interpretation very different from that of the Poles. Paweł Korzec, a historian who emigrated from Poland after 1968, writes, "We don't think it is an
exaggeration to conclude that the fate that interwar Poland had prepared
for the Polish Jews contributed to the feasibility of the immense tragedy
that befell them under the Nazi yoke."[d]

[a] Władysław Bartoszewski and Zofia Lewinówna, *Ten jest z Ojczyzny mojej* (*He Is from My Homeland*), (Znak, 1969), 17.
[b] Andrzej Micewski, "Tradycje historyczne katolicyzmu polskiego" (The Historical Traditions of Polish Catholicism), *Znaki Czasu I* (1986).
[c] Jerzy Turowicz, "Antysemityzm" (Anti-Semitism), *Tygodnik Powszechny*, March 17, 1957.
[d] Paweł Korzec, *Juifs en Pologne (Jews in Poland)*, (Presses de la Fondation Nationale des Sciences Politiques, 1980), 282.

Toward the end of his *Social and Political History of the Jews in Poland,
1919–1939*, a very balanced work, Joseph Marcus gives an account of the
September 1, 1939, session of the Sejm. He writes: ". . . the government
statement in the Sejm that Poland would fight 'to the last dying breath'
was given frenetic acclaim . . . and the statement by representatives of the
Ukrainian minority, declaring full support and participation in the common defense of the country, was also loudly applauded. But when, in turn,
Deputy Szymon Seidenman made a similar and much more convincing
pledge on behalf of the Jewish people, there was icy silence in the House."
Marcus adds: "It was an ominous silence for the Poles' attitude in the coming months of tragedy during which forty generations of continuous Jewish
history in Poland virtually ended."[e]

Ezra Mendelsohn, an Israeli historian, writes, ". . . when Hitler's soldiers,
aided by Soviet troops, stamped out Polish independence in 1939, Nazi anti-
Semitism, though far more extreme and thorough than the Polish variety, struck
a highly responsive chord among large sections of the Polish population." The
author adds, "In this respect, too, Poland was typical of East Central Europe."[f]

Such contrasting histories—Polish and Jewish—permit one to pass judgment on the behavior of this or that party; they contribute little, however,
to an understanding of the tragic entanglement of human fates that led to
so great a catastrophe in such inhuman conditions. For documentation of
this, one must go to other sources; I shall dwell on two examples that are
too little known in the West.

In August 1942, Zofia Kossak, a novelist and head of a small but very
active Catholic social and educational organization, the Front for the
Rebirth of Poland, issued in its behalf a leaflet entitled "Protest." She wrote,
"He who remains silent in the face of murder becomes an accomplice of
the murderer. He who does not condemn, condones." In the second part of
the leaflet, not usually quoted by Polish authors, she adds:

> Our feelings toward Jews have not changed. We still consider them to be polit-
> ical, economic, and ideological enemies of Poland. What is more, we are aware
> that they hate us more than they hate the Germans, that they consider us to
> be responsible for their misfortunes. Why, on what grounds—this is a mystery

---

[e] Joseph Marcus, *Social and Political History of the Jews in Poland, 1919–1939* (Mounton Publishers,
1983), 433.
[f] Ezra Mendelsohn, *The Jews of East Central Europe Between the World Wars* (Indiana University Press,
1983), 83.

of the Jewish soul, but it is a fact that is being confirmed again and again. The awareness of these feelings, however, does not relieve us of our duty to condemn the crime.[g]

This document, more than any other that measures assistance and betrayal, reveals the tragic complexity of the relations between Poles and Jews. It is significant that Zofia Kossak, having written this appeal, became involved in building the underground organization Żegota that saved the lives of many Jews. A Christian, bound by the divine command to love her neighbor, she was prepared to help the persecuted Jews, whom she considered enemies—who, in her opinion, considered the Poles enemies. It is a fact that many anti-Semites, including some who were notorious as such, did a great deal to help the Jews during the war, for very similar reasons. They included, among others, the well-known fascist Jan Mosdorf, who helped the Jews in Auschwitz, and the equally well-known prewar anti-Semite Father Marcel Godlewski, who cared for Jews in the Warsaw Ghetto. Such a list ought also to include Jan Dobraczyński, a novelist who remains an active anti-Semite today and who is now chairman of the so-called Patriotic Movement of National Rebirth (PRON), created by General Jaruzelski to replace the banned Solidarity movement. Dobraczyński rescued a number of Jewish children during the war. While such individual gestures were not unknown, they ought not to be generalized; helping those whom one does not like is an uncommon virtue, especially if the price to pay may be extremely high.

Those wishing to argue against the conventional Jewish indictment of Poles have often cited the work of Bartoszewski and Lewinówna, *He is of My Country*.[h] This is an impressive collection of documents and testimonies on the care and compassion demonstrated by many Poles toward Jews during the war. It contains three documents on the importance of respecting minority rights in the future. Interestingly, all three are written by Poles in exile; in their criticism of intolerance and discrimination, they reflect Western influence. There is not a single document of this kind that originates in Poland. Because views on the "Jewish question" expressed in Poland by Poles are of course far more interesting than what is said abroad by Poles who are away from home and no longer in the mainstream of

---

[g] The text may be found in Teresa Prekerowa, *Konspiracyjna Rada Pomocy Żydom w Warszawie, 1942–1945* (*The Underground Council to Aid Jews in Warsaw: 1942–1945*), (Państwowy Instytut Wydawniczy, 1982), photograph no. 33.

[h] Bartoszewski and Lewinówna, *Ten jest z ojczyzny mojej*.

Polish life, who did not experience the occupation, it is important to ask why we know so little about this.

Polish attitudes toward the Jewish question, as distinct from attitudes toward individual Jews murdered en masse, provide a fascinating theme. The conspiracy of silence on the subject has recently been broken in a book by Jacek Majchrowski, who tells of the wartime program of the home-based Polish Christian Democratic party called the Labor Party (Partia Pracy), which advocated the removal of Jews from Poland, arguing that the Jewish nation was the product of a religion of conscious evil that encouraged Jews to be parasites on the bodies of other nations.[i]

The conclusion was obvious: only in forced emigration could the problem be solved. A plan was drawn up. The first group to be forced out would be Jews aged eighteen to forty, thereby reducing at once the Jewish birthrate; the rest would be left in Poland to die off. Isolated from Polish society, Jews would enjoy a limited self-government, controlled by the state. They would be allowed to satisfy their more essential current needs, but they would be banned from public office and military service. They were to be prevented from providing goods and services to the rest of the population. Poles who had married Jews were to be similarly ostracized. Only Jews baptized before 1918, and some few others in quite exceptional circumstances, might apply for Polish citizenship, which would be granted by the Sejm. That these were mere words, that the plan was never realized, cannot alter the fact that the idea was more radical than anything contemplated under France's Vichy government or the Horthy regime in Hungary, two governments of the extreme right, allied with Nazi Germany. When one considers that the program was formulated by a Christian Democratic party thought to be moderate rather than radical, and represented in the Polish underground state, it becomes easier to understand the views of Jewish historians who see the wartime attitudes of Poles as simply a continuation of prewar anti-Semitism. However, those who tend to believe this forget or at least minimize the tensions created by the division of Poland, the occupation of the country by both Germans and Russians. For them, there is no break between the rampant anti-Semitism of the late thirties and the Holocaust of the early 1940s. Yet for the Poles there was a memory that rankled; it had to do with Jewish attitudes toward the Soviet invader.

---

[i] Jacek Majchrowski, *Geneza politycznych ugrupowań katolickich* (*The Genesis of Catholic Political Formations*), (Libella, 1984), 69.

Jews under the Soviet Occupation

When war broke out in 1939, Poles faced two enemies at once: Germany and the Soviet Union. That, however, was not the way certain ethnic minorities saw it. For almost all ethnic Germans and Lithuanians who were Polish citizens, as well as for many Byelorussians, Ukrainians, and Jews, the dual onslaught was an occasion for celebration. The reaction of ethnic Germans and the Lithuanians who, for a short time, were to be part of an independent Lithuania, was understandable; one may even understand the reaction of the Ukrainians and the Byelorussians. They were expressing a preference more national than ideological. Given the way that successive Polish governments had dealt with them, they were all alienated. Why, however, were the Jews so accepting of the Soviet invasion? They had no territorial claims against Poland; they were not seeking a state of their own in Eastern Europe. Yet the evidence is overwhelming: large numbers of Jews welcomed the Soviet invasion, imprinting in Polish memory the image of Jewish crowds greeting the invading Red Army as their liberators. How is this attitude to be explained?

The Jewish writers who have chosen to treat the matter have generally given a single answer.[j] In divided Poland, German power and Soviet power were equally hostile to Poles, but not to Jews. For Jews, the danger was Nazi Germany, with its openly declared anti-Jewish policies. The Soviet Union, on the other hand, was seen as a country that allowed Jews full civic rights, or, more precisely, deprived them of rights in the same measure as it deprived others.

This is a weighty argument. If it is accepted, the attitude of Jews in September 1939 can be explained by their own interests, which were inevitably distinct and different from those of Poles. Their attitudes cannot be judged in moral terms. Still, this is not the whole story. In 1939 and 1940, no one foresaw where the radically anti-Jewish policies of the Germans would lead; no one prophesied the "final solution." Still, fears existed; the tales of discrimination against Jews in Germany, the humiliations they experienced, Crystal Night itself had made a deep impression. But it was not universally held. Some Jews, disappointed with the Soviet occupation and wholly

---

[j] Izrael Gutman, "Polish and Jewish Historiography on the Question of Polish Jewish Relations During the Second World War." Speech, Oxford Conference on Polish-Jewish Relations in Modem History, Oxford University, September 17–21, 1984.

unaware of what was in store for them, actually decided to make their way to German-occupied Poland.

In any case, the perception of a German threat—even if widely accepted—cannot explain the enthusiasm with which many Jews greeted the invaders from the East. The explanation may be found in the words of a Polish respondent to a questionnaire circulated by the Paris-based Polish monthly *Kultura* on the subject of anti-Semitism. He wrote:

> The welcome extended to the Bolsheviks was above all a demonstration of a separate identity, of being different from those against whom the Soviets were waging war—from the Poles—a refusal to be identified with the Polish state. We must not pretend that we do not realize this, or fail to admit that it was the result of our own policies and of our anti-Semitism. . . . In the year that war broke out, the alienation of the Jewish community had reached its zenith because of a propaganda campaign that almost amounted to a pogrom, calling for bloodshed. This had alienated even quite assimilated Jews.[k]

A tragic, vicious circle. Many Jews welcomed the invader because they no longer considered Poland to be their country. Shunned and persecuted, the subject of public debates on how they might be evicted, they reacted as a wounded people often will. Still, this is not the whole explanation, and in any case, it only deepened the hostility of the Poles. It confirmed their suspicions about the loyalty of Jews to the Polish state, and indeed to the idea of Polish independence itself.

Straining relations further, many Jews, whether communist or not, educated or not, were given posts in the local administration imposed by the occupiers. They became actively engaged in the consolidation of Soviet power. In some instances, they even helped hunt down Polish officers and members of the deposed Polish administration. The fact that thousands of Jews eventually followed hundreds of thousands of Poles to the most inhospitable parts of Siberia, deported not because they were Jews but because they had become disenchanted with Soviet rule, changed nothing. Soviet power proved itself no less hostile to them than to others. Jews were the "wrong" social class: shopkeepers, artisans, and professionals; many were religious. In any case, the Soviet authorities did not tolerate unofficial associations. It is a cruel paradox that even deportation did not necessarily dampen Jewish sympathies for the USSR. Though exiled Jews suffered no less than

[k] Adam Uziembło, *Kultura* 1, no. 2 (1957).

others, only in their case did the suffering seem to make sense: it gave them at least some chance of survival, which did not exist for Jews trapped in occupied Poland, soon wholly overrun by the Nazis.

Some Poles, according to the Commander-in-Chief of the Polish Home Army, General Grot-Rowecki, greeted the invading Germans in July 1941 as "liberators from the Bolshevik oppression in which Jews had played a great part."[l] Hatred and ethnic tension became manifest in Brest, where a pogrom is said to have taken place, arranged by Poles released from prison.[m] Once the whole of Poland found itself under German occupation, news of the behavior of Jews under the Soviets spread throughout the country, with obvious effects. General Grot-Rowecki's report of September 30, 1941, to the Polish government in London has been quoted often. He wrote:

> Please take it as an established fact that an overwhelming majority of the population is anti-Semitic. Even the socialists are no exception. There are only tactical differences about what to do. Hardly anybody advocates imitating the Germans. German methods provoke compassion, but after the merging of the occupation zones, on learning how the Jews behaved in the east, this is now considerably reduced.[n]

In no other country in Europe did the clash of Jewish interests and attitudes with those of the surrounding population reach such dramatic proportions as they did in Poland under the Soviet occupation of 1939–1941. In other occupied countries, the Jews were in conflict with parts of the surrounding population—with local quislings, for example—but they had behind them the rest of society. In Poland, under the Soviet occupation, the Jews were themselves seen as quislings. This should be borne in mind in any discussion of Polish-Jewish relations.

The Paradoxes of National Unity

There are traitors in every country. In Poland, Poles worked for the Germans for money, out of spite, in fear of blackmail or torture. However, there was no collaboration based on the belief that national interests would be served

---

[l] A dispatch from London of July 8, 1941, cited by Krystyna Kersten, *Narodziny systemu władzy. Polska 1943–1948* (*The Establishment of Communist Rule in Poland, 1943–1948*), (Libella, 1986), 172.
[m] Ibid.
[n] Ibid.

by cooperating with the occupying power. There was no Petain or Quisling in Poland. In any case, the Germans were not looking for cooperation with anyone in Poland. As far as the Germans were concerned, Poland was a nation without a future; and all Poles would eventually share the fate of all Jews. Destroying the Polish elites was only the first step in the process of destroying Poland. All this is well known, but it is significant in any consideration of Jewish-Polish relations.

Poland was unique in another respect: resistance against the invader served to unite organizations and parties that before the war had nothing at all in common. Democrats and totalitarians, liberals and socialists, nationalists and Communists, freemasons and Christians were all engaged in the same struggle. In other German-occupied countries, anti-Semitism was the monopoly of quisling governments and parties. The resistance, as a rule, was anti-fascist, democratic, and anti-anti-Semitic. Anti-Semitism, for them, was part of the syndrome of treason. Only in Poland was anti-Semitism compatible with patriotism (a correlation considerably strengthened under the Soviet occupation in 1939–1941) and also with democracy. The anti-Semitic National-Democratic Party was represented both in the Polish government in London and in the structures of the underground within Poland.

Precisely because Polish anti-Semitism was not tainted by any trace of collaboration with the Germans, it could prosper—not only in the street, but also in the underground press, in political parties, and in the armed forces. Indeed, a thriving political and cultural life existed outside the official underground establishment, especially on the right. The Szaniec (Rampart) group and the Confederation of Independent Poland were eagerly developing their totalitarian nationalist program, envisaging, among other things, a radical solution to the Jewish question. Some Polish poets would have been happy to ostracize poets deemed "alien" to Polish culture precisely because they were Jewish. These "aliens" included men of the distinction of Julian Tuwim, Antoni Słonimski, and Bolesław Leśmian.[°] There were also powerful military organizations on the extreme right: the National Military Organization (NOW), the Lizard Union (Związek Jaszczurczy), and the National Armed Forces (NSZ). Pobóg-Malinowski, a historian, describes the men the NSZ attracted: "hot-headed dynamic youths, mostly town bred, among them many supporters of 'national radicalism,' perhaps not

---

[°] Tadeusz Gajcy, "Już nie potrzebujemy" (We No Longer Need It), *Sztuka i Naród* 11, no. 12 (1943).

quite a kind of nazism, but not unlike it, brutally uncompromising in striving for power and domination, devoted to hard terrorist methods verging on banditry, utterly chauvinistic. . . ."[p]

The patriotic credentials of wartime anti-Semitism allowed it to penetrate far and wide. Some military units of the radical right, while subject to their own political structures, were also part of the official Home Army linked to the London-based government in exile, and this could only affect the atmosphere in the forces. Marek Edelman, one of the leaders of the 1943 Uprising in the Warsaw Ghetto, recently said that after the collapse of the Warsaw Uprising of 1944, in which he took part, he was warned by his commanding officer not to surrender to the Germans in the company of his unit: "I cannot vouch for my soldiers, one of them may betray you as a Jew."[q]

Józef Cyrankiewicz, recalling soon after the war the time he spent in Auschwitz, tells how he would try to explain to prisoners from other countries the anti-Semitic behavior of certain Polish inmates: "Germans, Austrians, and French are all politically well-defined groups, for they are all anti-fascist; there are no fascists in the camps, for fascists work hand-in-hand with their Nazi friends. Only in our camps are we together with our reactionaries. . . ."[r] It is important to realize how this phenomenon, however marginal, helped to shape the reputation that Poles have in the West as incurable anti-Semites.

The Cost of Being a Witness

"I have often found," says Herling-Grudziński, "that man is human in human conditions, and I have always thought cruelly nonsensical the attempts to judge him by the deeds done in inhuman conditions, as if water could be measured by fire, and the earth by hell."[s] A descent into hell can only leave its marks. What indeed are the boundaries of the inhuman

[p] Władysław Pobóg-Malinowski, *Najnowsza historia Polski (Poland's Recent History)*, (London, 1983).
[q] Conversation with Marek Edelman in *Czas* 4, no. 5 (1985).
[r] Józef Cyrankiewicz, *Oświęcim walczący (Resistance in Oświęcim)* cited in Michel Borwicz, *Organizowanie wściekłości (The Orchestration of Rage)*, (Wydawnictwo Ogólnopolskiej Ligi do Walki z Rasizmem, 1947).
[s] Gustaw Herling-Grudziński, *Inny świat (A World Apart)*, (Instytut Literacki, 1965).

world? Extending them too far is dangerous—it dispenses with moral responsibility.

Zofia Kossak wrote in "Protest," "We know how poisonous the seed of crime is. Compulsory attendance of the Polish people at the gory spectacle performed on the Polish soil may well breed moral indifference, sadism, and above all a dangerous conviction that one can murder with impunity." There follows a warning that is surely not empty of rhetoric: "He who does not understand this and dares to link a proud, free Polish future with despicable glee over the misfortune of his neighbor has no right to call himself a Catholic or a Pole!"

No European people was condemned to witness crime in the same measure as Poles, who, living in hell themselves, were forced to watch day by day the ever lower and more horrific infernal circles. In the West, people saw the trainloads departing eastward; they witnessed individual murders, saw the humiliation in the yellow badges worn by Jews, and were certainly aware of the anti-Jewish laws. As for the Germans, for the most part they saw nothing. They might have known or guessed, but apart from those who served in the occupied East and those, of course, who were in any way involved in any stage of the "final solution," they physically saw nothing.

Polish peasants, however, knew of the extermination camps and smelled the stench of burning human flesh. City and town dwellers alike saw the sickening misery of the ghettos, peopled by walking skeletons whose faces resembled more and more the demonic monsters of German propaganda. They read the warning notices on the Ghetto walls: "Jews, lice, typhoid," which induced a conditioned reflex of fear and disgust.

Indifference in the face of horror and crime was steadily growing, as suggested in the writings of Miłosz, Andrzejewski, Rudnicki, and, more recently, of Mrożek.

> What was happening to the Jews was not a cause of amusement but of horror, but this horror was just one factor in the general horror of war and occupation. After all, what the Germans did to the Jews was a matter between Germans and Jews. No concern of ours, no need to stick your head out. A very, very unpleasant business, perhaps even more than unpleasant, perhaps even horrible, but not ours.[t]

---

[t] Sławomir Mrożek, "Nos" (Nose), *Kultura* 7, no. 8 (1984).

When the dominant feeling is one of helplessness, indifference comes to be seen as the most decent form of escape from responsibility.

But indifference was not the only reaction. The image of the Jew underwent a change. Before the war that image had been a combined product of stereotype, prejudice, and ideological commitment; it was also a product of everyday experience. As the popular saying went: "Every anti-Semite has got his favorite Jew." Now this everyday experience no longer existed. The Jew had ceased to be a person of flesh and blood, liked or disliked, respected or despised, as any man may be. Now he became indistinguishable from the stereotypical portrayal of propaganda, and all past prejudices surfaced and became widespread.[u] While German propaganda had some part in this change, more important was another factor: Poles began to feel that the fate of the victim may not have been wholly undeserved. This is a natural reaction, well known to psychologists. It is possible to disdain the myth of a people guilty of deicide, to treat the delirious "Protocols of the Sages of Zion" with a healthy skepticism, and yet to imagine that the Jews cannot be wholly blameless if they have so often been punished by history.

In the face of Hitler's murderous orgy and indescribable horror as a daily occurrence, there was a natural tendency to seek a rational explanation for it all. The sense of outrage very often turned against the Jews themselves. The well-known writer Zofia Nałkowska described the reaction of a simple woman living close to the Ghetto wall. "I can't take it, I can't take it," she would say, adding, "It's better for us if the Germans finish them off. They hate us more than the Germans. . . . Everybody says so. Ask anyone who knows them. Should the Germans ever lose the war, the Jews would murder us all."[v] The poet Mieczysław Jastrun noted the remark of a man in the crowd watching the burning Ghetto: "The Germans have just forestalled a Jewish action against us"; or consider the tale told by a school girl about Poles murdered by the Jews who had managed to escape.[w2] Reactions to all this horror ranged from dislike and fear to indifference. There was also the kind of reasoning described by the critic Kazimierz Wyka, who said: "The Germans have committed a crime murdering the Jews. It is on their conscience, but for us it is a sheer benefit, and in the

---

[u] Borwicz, *Organizowanie wściekłości*.
[v] Zofia Nałkowska, *Medaliony* (*Medalions*), (Warsaw, 1946).
[w] Mieczysław Jastrun, "Potęga ciemnoty" (The Power of Ignorance), *Odrodzenie*, June 17, 1945.

future we shall reap more benefits, with a clear conscience, without blood on our hands."[x][3]

After the shock of the Holocaust, there was silence. People were trying to forget. If the matter was raised at all, it was only to defend Polish honor against unjust accusations. In this overwhelming silence, it is difficult to know how many shared the feelings of Jerzy Andrzejewski:

> For all honest Poles the fate of the perishing Jews must have been exceedingly painful, for the dying . . . were the people whom our people could not look straight in the face, with a clear conscience. The Polish nation could look straight in the face of Polish men and women who were dying for freedom. Not in the face of the Jews dying in the burning ghetto.[y][4]

The Postwar Years

With the end of the war, normal life resumed, though in the abnormal conditions of war's aftermath, and in the abnormal shell of a new political order established over (but not accepted by) the nation. People restored their homes, cleared the rubble, or trekked to the West—to the new western territories of Poland and to the more distant West—as did the Jews. At first there were very few of them, consisting of the small number who had survived the occupation in the homes of trusted neighbors, in the forests, or, occasionally, in camps. Later, they were joined by Jews who returned from Russia. No more than 10 percent of the prewar Jewish community had survived.

One would have expected the war to have cleared away the causes of hostile attitudes of Poles toward Jews. Indeed, this is the dominant Polish interpretation today. Jerzy Turowicz, noted Catholic editor, has written: "I say that in Poland after the war, anti-Semitism was virtually nonexistent."[z] Bohdan Cywiński, an eminent Catholic journalist and historian who has been actively engaged in the democratic opposition to the communist regime since the 1970s, writes:

[x] Kazimierz Wyka, *Życie na niby* (*Living as If*), (Książka i Wiedza, 1959), 199.
[y] Jerzy Andrzejewski, "Zagadnienie polskiego antysemityzmu" (The Problem of Polish Anti-Semitism), in *Martwa Fala* (Wiedza, 1947).
[z] Jerzy Turowicz, "Antysemityzm."

The Nazi occupation affected Polish-Jewish relations through the fact of the Holocaust. The enormity of this fact proved to be a shock for the whole of Polish society, and has since been recognized as the absolute apex of Nazi criminality. At the same time it exposed the depth of the moral depravity; this has sunk deeply into the national consciousness, creating an effective barrier against any possible revival of anti-Semitism.[aa]

Andrzej Szczypiorski, a well-known opposition writer, has said: "The great theoretician of the national question and incomparable friend of mankind [Stalin] was quite wrong. With the experience of war and nazism behind us, anti-Semitism in Poland did not have a great chance."[bb]

While refraining from quoting Jewish assessments of these same postwar years, the contrast is in fact marked. Indeed, Poles, writing immediately after the war, were more divided than these sanguine remarks suggest. For example, Stanisław Stomma, a historian and politician close to the Polish Episcopate, said, "It seemed that the horror of the occupation and the enormity of the crimes committed against the Jews would bring about a radical change of the views on the Jewish question, deepening them and humanizing. The reality is different."[cc] Jerzy Andrzejewski, the author of *Ashes and Diamonds*, writes: "Polish anti-Semitism has not burnt itself out in the ruins of the ghettos. The death of several million massacred Jews was not enough to wipe out Polish mental and emotional habits."[dd] Kazimierz Wyka, a professor of literature and an acute observer, writes, "The only country in Europe where anti-Semitism is still alive, leading to political and moral crimes, is Poland. The country where Jews have been most thoroughly wiped out and where resistance against the occupation was the strongest. And yet it is there that nazism has planted its bastard seed."[ee]

After the 1946 Kielce Pogrom, *Tygodnik Powszechny* published a courageous article by Professor Stefania Skwarczyńska. She noted that while the natural reaction was to deny responsibility, to seek culprits as far away from Poland as possible, she knew, with a heavy heart, that one could not shift

---

[aa] Bohdan Cywiński, "Zagadnienie stosunków polsko- żydowskich w opozycji lat 70-tych" (The Problem of Polish-Jewish Relations in the Polish Democratic Opposition in the 1970s), *Puls* 24 (1985-1986).

[bb] Andrzej Szczypiorski, "Polacy i Żydzi" (Poles and Jews), *Kultura* 5 (1979).

[cc] Stanisław Stomma, "Oskarżenie ze wszystkich najstraszniejsze" (The Worst Accusation of All), *Tygodnik Powszechny* 49, 1946.

[dd] Andrzejewski, "Zagadnienie polskiego antysemityzmu."

[ee] Kazimierz Wyka, "Potęga ciemnoty potwierdzona" (The Power of Ignorance Confirmed), *Odrodzenie*, September 23, 1945.

the blame to others. Even assuming that "alien interests were involved," how could a "healthy society thus be led by the nose?" Calling for an unequivocal condemnation of the crime, she appealed to others to give witness to those Christian attitudes that had been demonstrated during the war. Her appeal was addressed to Jews and others of the German-invented "otherness."[ff]

Tygodnik Powszechny published three replies to this appeal. Each is interesting; each, written by a woman, expresses gratitude to those who, despite extreme danger to themselves, have offered their help. Laura Kaufman responded because she was afraid that "hysterical noises and malicious whispers would drown the calm and truthful voices."[gg] E. Koenowa, while expressing her gratitude, adds, "Antisemitism has not come to an end in Treblinka, Majdanek, and Auschwitz. It is very sad that often the same people who had compassion for the Jews during the war and helped them as much as they could are now unfriendly to them."[hh] Ewa Szmajdlerowa, telling of help she received from fifteen people, says:

> It is a pleasure to relate all this, but I would not dare to mention the names of these people in public, for fear that it would be anything but a service to them. Similarly, I do not dare to display openly the cross which, as a Catholic, I wear under my dress. It does not go with my racial type. Please consider carefully the last two sentences. I am content to add one brief comment: the Germans have taught me contempt for death. The Poles are now teaching me contempt for man, and to be ashamed, terribly ashamed.[ii]

There are other witnesses of this same kind. Michel Borwicz wrote of the curious unwillingness of courageous people who helped Jews during the war to be "exposed" as such after the war.[jj] Maria Hochberg-Mariańska, in the introduction to her book *Children Accuse*, writes: "I wonder whether outside Poland it is possible to understand the fact that having saved an innocent child from the clutches of a murderer may be a cause of deep embarrassment, even infamy."[kk] What is to be learned today from these testimonies and assessments gathered soon after the war?

[ff] Stefania Skwarczyńska, "In Tenebris Lux" (Light in the Darkness), *Tygodnik Powszechny,* August 11, 1946.
[gg] *Tygodnik Powszechny,* September 8, 1946.
[hh] *Tygodnik Powszechny,* October 27, 1946.
[ii] Ibid.
[jj] Letter to the Editor, *Kultura* 11 (1958).
[kk] Ibid.

In the uniformly serene picture of Polish-Jewish relations after the war, sketched by Polish writers today, there is said to be only one exception: the Kielce Pogrom of 1946, which saw civilians go after and kill several dozen Jews. Such an event could not be ignored or glossed over; innocent people were murdered; tens of thousands of Jews were forced to emigrate. But the exception is more apparent than real. The responsibility for the Pogrom is externalized: it is not the Polish population that is considered responsible, but some alien forces. Various political groups identify these forces differently.

According to the authors of a publication about Polish-Jewish relations distributed by the Polish Accord for Independence (Polskie Porozumienie Niepodległościowe, or PPN), an underground association of intellectuals founded in 1976, the Kielce Pogrom was actually part of a long-term Soviet policy in Poland. Once diplomatic relations had been broken off with the Polish government in London in 1943, the Soviets began a propaganda campaign to defame the Polish underground. The Soviets accused the Home Army of collaborating with the Germans, but also of being nationalist and anti-Semitic. "The latter charge was revived in 1946 when, in order to justify the failure of the USSR to honor the obligations it had entered into with the Western powers, the NKVD (Soviet Security Service) and the UB (Polish Security Service) organized the so-called Kielce Pogrom, a mass murder of Jews. Their intention was to represent the Poles as a nation of racists, quite incapable of governing themselves."[ll]

The same view is held by Stanisław Żochowski, ex-chief of staff of the NSZ (military resistance movement of the extreme right), whose political orientation is radically different from that of the PPN. He considers the Kielce Pogrom to have been an indubitable provocation of the Polish Security Service; as he puts it, "Ten years later, in October 1956, the Party announced that the pogrom had been a mistake."[mm] There is in fact no evidence that the party did anything of the kind. The assertion that the Pogrom was the work of the NKVD or the UB appears in many different accounts, but generally without any proof. Among those who have tried to prove it are Krystyna Kersten[nn] and Michael Checinski.[oo]

[ll] Polskie Porozumienie Niepodległościowe, "Polacy-Żydzi" (Polish Independence Accords: "Poles-Jews"), Report no. 23, April 1979.
[mm] Stanisław Żochowski, O Narodowych Siłach Zbrojnych (*The National Armed Forces*), (Brisbane, 1983), 177.
[nn] Krystyna Kersten, "Kielce-4 lipca 1946 rok" (Kielce, July 4th, 1946), *Tygodnik Solidarność*, 36, 1981.
[oo] Michael Checinski, *Poland, Communism, Nationalism, Antisemitism* (Karz-Kohl, 1982), 24–35.

A quite different theory comes from the propaganda of the other side; the Communists and their friends argue that the Pogrom was the work of the Polish government in London, that General Anders and Stanisław Mikołajczyk are in some way culpable. In the confidential minutes of a meeting of the secretariat of the Communist Party's Central Committee, the record of a discussion on "the matter of the pogroms" is interesting to study. Politbureau member R. Zambrowski, discussing aborted pogroms in Krakow, Radom, Miechów, Chrzanów, and Rabka, suggests that these were all centrally planned and organized. Zambrowski is interested more in the political than in the criminal aspects of these events. The Jewish question, he argues, "is for the forces of reaction simply an opportunity to foment hatred and public disorder, to present the government as weak, to create an appearance of great numbers of people being involved." He told his colleagues that in the fight against anti-Semitism ". . . we are assured of the support of the European democracies."[pp]

What is the truth? Who in fact were the killers? Was this mob incited by the UB or by the extreme right of the anticommunist underground? Is it possible that both sides had a hand in it? Today, such questions are impossible to answer, and it may not be useful to pursue them. Still, we know that the Pogrom in Kielce effectively distracted the attention of the West from the scandal of the falsified government referendum. Also, we must ask how it was possible, in the middle of the twentieth century, after a bloody war, for thousands of ordinary people to take to the streets and massacre several dozen other ordinary people, on the charge that the latter were guilty of ritual murder. Those murdered were not, by the way, Communists, security men, or hated dignitaries; they were very ordinary men and women.

It is unnecessary to offer all the concrete evidences of continued hatred and aggression now available to us.[qq] The facts cannot be denied; they must, however, be explained. How could Poland, which had witnessed the murder of three million Poles and six million Jews, become the scene of compulsive hatred? And why is it that forty years after the war, instead of asking such questions, even the best Polish intellectuals seem content to seek refuge in comforting formulas or choose to remain silent? To understand anything,

[pp] *Zeszyty Historyczne* 2 (1973): 141–142.
[qq] A comprehensive journalistic survey is found in a recent book by Marc Hillel, *Le Massacre des Survivants en Pologne 1945–1947* (*The Massacres of Survivors in Poland: 1945–1947*), (Librairie Pion, 1985). The book contains a number of inaccuracies, distortions, and statements verging on the absurd. The main facts, however, are well documented.

the safe ground of standard interpretation must be abandoned. The theory of the purifying effect of war must be rejected, but so also must the theory of endemic Polish anti-Semitism.

Let us consider, for a moment, the changes that occurred in Polish social consciousness as a result of the war. The overall effect, as with other European nations, was a radicalization of the country. Fundamental demands included not only the withdrawal of the invader and the guarantee of independence, but some sort of democracy in the political order, together with far-reaching reforms in the social and economic spheres. During the interwar years, democracy was under attack everywhere in Europe. After the war, democratic values were broadly accepted by all elements in the population except for the Communists.

In Poland, however, with the crushing of the Warsaw Uprising of 1944 and the inevitable approach of the Soviet army from the east, hopes for independence suffered a, traumatic setback. Faith in democratic values gave way to a growing chauvinism, anti-Semitism, and stubborn conservatism.[rr] After the collapse of Germany, the Soviet Union and its Polish allies were the chief enemy, the only enemy of the Polish people. Patriotism came to mean everything that was contrary to the new power structure's programs, which sought to camouflage its real aims in a democratic-populist phraseology and the semblance of democratic reforms.

In the West, the left, led by intellectuals, was morally victorious. Stalinist tyranny, labor camps, the true meaning of communist rhetoric—all this was conveniently overlooked. The traditional ethos of the right, compromised by spiritual kinship—however distant—with fascism, wartime collaboration, and antidemocratic tendencies, was clearly disintegrating. This was not the case in Poland, where the right was in equal parts patriotic, anti-German, anti-Soviet, and anti-Semitic. Poland felt no need to rethink its values. There was no crisis of the rightist ethos under new Soviet-imposed power. The result was the consolidation of two traditional stereotypes, the "Polish-Catholic" on the one hand, the "Judeo-Communist" on the other.[ss] Both seemed to gain credibility as never before. A Polish Catholic was now, as always, a defender of the fatherland—with its tradition, culture, and

---

[rr] Tadeusz Lepkowski, "Myśli o historii Polski i Polaków" (Reflections about the History of Poles and Poland), *Zeszyty Historyczne* 6 (1984).
[ss] Cf. Kersten, *Narodziny systemu władzy.*

religion—against the communist power imposed by the Soviets and exercised on their behalf by the Jews.

The Jews became very visible indeed, especially in the central nodes of power. Popular imagination multiplied their numbers, sensing the existence of Jews under newly adopted Polish names everywhere. For the man in the street, this "Jewish flood" was a shocking new phenomenon, more shocking than certain other more essential and more durable aspects of the new communist reality. It seemed to be a resumption and indeed a continuation of the Soviet occupation of eastern Poland in 1939–1941, but also a continuation of the "cold civil war" between the "Polish element" and the "Jewish element," which in the minds of right-wingers had been waged in Poland even before the war. Official posters, appearing in April 1946, read "Honor to the heroic defenders of the ghetto," and "Shame to the fascist knaves of the AK army [Interior Army]."

To many Poles, it seemed as though the Jews had "won." How humiliating after years of wartime deprivation and heroism, sacrifice and hope, to find Jews—with all their stereotypical attributes—intact. The bloodsuckers and demoralizers denounced in the gutter press of the right, the devil incarnate, the ominous sages of the "Protocols of Zion" who had been reaching for power all over the world, had won! Indeed, their very re-emergence into society was a shock. People had gotten used to not seeing Jews; their absence seemed almost natural. It was a resurrection of sorts—the resurrection of Judas—or so many felt.

The anti-Jewish incidents ended some time in 1947, caused perhaps by an ebb in anti-Jewish feeling, by the radically diminished number of Jews, by the absence of political motivation on the part of those in power, or simply by the marginalization and eventual liquidation of the extreme right wing underground. It is difficult to know why the incidents stopped. However, just as the absence of open political demonstrations does not necessarily mean the acceptance of a particular system by a society, so the end of anti-Jewish demonstrations does not necessarily mean the end of anti-Semitism.

After the Kielce Pogrom, Stefania Skwarczyńska wrote about the horrendous defeat suffered by the "world of ideas," not only the one that happens to be "at the helm today," but also the much older one "which preaches love of man to man, according to Christ." "The latter tells the former: such is the harvest of your rule; while the former tells the latter: this is the achievement of many ages of Christian civilization, the fruit of Catholicism." Neither of the two answers is satisfactory. Nevertheless, the "world of ideas" and its associated institutional structures, both with powerful means at their disposal for shaping collective responses, had a decisive influence on the development of Polish-Jewish relations.

The Church and the Jews

A pastoral letter by Cardinal Hlond, primate of Poland, written in 1936, provides eloquent evidence of the Polish Church's official position on the Jews at that time. The letter says:

> The Jewish problem is there and will be there as long as Jews remain Jews. It is a fact that Jews are in opposition to the Catholic Church, that they are freethinkers, the vanguard of godlessness, bolshevism, and subversion. It is a fact that they exert a pernicious influence on public morality and that their publishing houses are spreading pornography. It is true that Jews are swindlers, usurers, and that they are engaged in fostering immoral earnings. It is true that the effect of the Jewish youth upon the Catholic is—in the religious and ethical sense—negative. But we must not be unjust. This does not apply to all Jews. There are very many Jews who are believers, honest, righteous, merciful, doing good works. The family life of many Jews is healthy and edifying. And there are among Jews people morally quite outstanding, noble and honorable people.[tt]

This reads like a classic statement of traditional Christian anti-Semitism of the kind frequently found outside Poland. Typical of the attitude (other parts of the letter could be cited as well) is a rejection of integral anti-Semitism and racism, together with a condemnation of all anti-Jewish violence. In the context of the Church and its history at that time, the position of the primate could be described as moderate. More liberal and humanistic attitudes, which were undoubtedly there—Catholic personalism, for example, was important—were limited to a small intellectual elite. Of special importance were the center at Laski, near Warsaw, which fostered Father Korniłowicz and his periodical *Verbum*, and the Association of Catholic University Students, Odrodzenie, which was the intellectual cradle of many eminent

---

[tt] Quoted in Bohdan Cywiński, *Z dziejów Kościoła Katolickiego w Polsce niepodległej* (*From the History of the Catholic Church in Independent Poland*), (Niezależna Oficyna Wydawnicza, 1980).

postwar Catholic personalities, including Jerzy Turowicz and Stanisław Stomma. Apart from such small enclaves, the Church was predominantly peasant and nationalist. The powerful nationalist sentiment, associated with an equally strong anti-Semitism, was represented by the Catholic periodical *Rycerz Niepokalanej* and the daily newspaper *Mały Dziennik*.

It is virtually impossible to say anything about the attitude of the Church toward the Jews, or toward the Jewish question more generally, during the war. No documents or pastoral letters were published on the subject. The Church, itself severely repressed and decimated, remained silent. As in other countries, however, the Catholic Church had a magnificent record of saving the persecuted from certain death. This was largely the work of individual priests ready to incur great risks, and of certain religious orders, particularly orders of nuns. Still, the question remains: What was the relation of the Church to the small Jewish community that survived the war, and also to the Jews in the power apparatus?

Krystyna Kersten, in her recent book, suggests that "cases of assaults on Jews were resolutely condemned by the head of the Polish Church." Her evidence is words spoken by Cardinal Hlond to the representative of the Jewish Religious Associations, professor Michał Zylberg. The Cardinal said: "[The assaults] are a source of great sadness to me. Without reiterating the arguments based on Christian principles, in present-day Poland there are no objective reasons for anti-Semitism. It is the madness of those who are still conspiring in the forests. They conceive of this as politics; they think that by assaulting the Jews they are fighting the government. As a Pole and a Catholic, I condemn those activities."[uu] Kersten's interpretation of these words is, in my view, debatable. The cardinal, in the difficult postwar years, did not do what he had done ten years previously—condemn hatred and anti-Jewish violence absolutely. Requests to do so were made to him by many parties, including the Jews, both before and after the Kielce Pogrom. The primate's reply was always the same. In a conversation with a group of foreign correspondents, for example, he said that the deterioration in Polish-Jewish relations was the fault of the Jews:[vv] Anti-Jewish incidents were provoked by the presence of Jews in the structures of power imposed on Poland against the will of Polish society. Hostility to the Jews, then, was

---

[uu] Cf. Kersten, *Narodziny systemu władzy*, quoting from *Gazeta Ludowa*, January 13, 1946.
[vv] Cf. S. L. Shneiderman, *Between Fear and Hope* (Arco, 1947); Kersten, *Narodziny systemu władzy*, 170.

neither anti-Semitism nor racism, but simply a political attitude. There are victims among the Jews, but there are even a greater number of Polish victims. Therefore, the Church cannot specifically condemn anti-Jewish violence; it can only say that it is against all hatred and all violence.

That was the position of many bishops as well. A short time before the Kielce Pogrom, local Jews, sensing the danger, appealed to the local bishop, Czesław Kaczmarek, to issue an appropriate pastoral letter. The bishop refused, arguing against it on reasons similar to those given by the primate. After the Pogrom, a statement was issued which said, inter alia, "No Catholic can refrain from expressing sincere outrage at these tragic and deplorable events." It went on to say, ". . . it is all the more unfortunate that all this happened before the eyes of young people and children."[ww] A frightening ambiguity is raised: young people and children were also among those killed. Was the attitude of the primate, the bishop of Kielce, and, as will be seen, the bishop of Lublin and the future primate, Stefan Wyszyński, typical of the Polish Church as a whole? It is difficult to say. There were certainly eminent churchmen who thought differently.

The aged metropolitan of Krakow, Cardinal Sapieha, for example, agreed to be one of the patrons of the celebrations commemorating the third anniversary of the Warsaw Ghetto Uprising.[xx] In the prevailing atmosphere this was more than magnanimous; it was an act of courage. His was to remain the only significant public gesture of a member of the Polish hierarchy honoring the martyrdom of the Jews until the present primate, Cardinal Glemp, took part in the celebrations of the fortieth anniversary of the Uprising.

The bishop of Częstochowa, Tadeusz Kubina, virtually prevented a pogrom in Częstochowa by cosigning, together with other local dignitaries, a public statement that said, among other things, "*Everything about the alleged ritual murders is a lie.* No member of the Christian community, whether in Kielce, Częstochowa or anywhere else in Poland, has ever been injured by Jews for religious ritual purposes."[yy]

Why, then, did the primate and some other bishops deem it inadvisable or impossible to speak out in defense of the Jews? What prevented them from making a gesture that, at the time, barely a year after the end of the war,

---

[ww] Paweł Jasienica, "Pan Sieradzki dyskutuje" (Mr. Sieradzki Discusses), *Tygodnik Powszechny*, September 1, 1946.
[xx] Cf. Borwicz, *Organizowanie wściekłości.*
[yy] Ibid.

was shocking by its absence? It appears that the justification given by the primate needs to be taken literally. Bishops chose to see the persecution of the Jews only in political terms. This was a civil war—at times hot, at times cold—against the ruling power; it claimed numerous victims from among the Poles, but also from among the Jews, who were paying a price for other Jews being in power.

Another factor may have been even more important. The communist authorities were using the real and imagined anti-Semitism of their opponents to compromise them in the eyes of the public, both at home and abroad. It is not only that those in power were perceived by many as "Jewish"; the power structure, for its part, perversely used the charge of anti-Semitism to compromise both the opposition and those unreconciled elements of Polish society on the international stage. It may even have helped organize the pogroms to that end. In circumstances where the authorities were acting as defenders of the Jews, any gesture along the same lines by the Church might have been interpreted as giving support to the Communists. The Church risked placing itself in a highly ambiguous situation in the eyes of many of the faithful, who were suffering ruthless persecution at the hands of a party and government perceived as predominantly Jewish.

The dilemma was terrible: How to follow the clear logic of compassion in the face of so many diverse victims! It is no wonder that respect for the traditional values of Polish Catholicism seemed to require that love of country be given preference to love of neighbor.

In view of the exceptional position of the primate, Cardinal Wyszyński, in postwar Polish history, it is useful to consider his views on the Jewish question in some detail. In the specific Polish conditions, the voice of Cardinal Wyszyński was the voice of the Church.

After the Kielce Pogrom, two members of the Jewish committee in Lublin, M. Szyldkraut and S. Słuszny, were received by the bishop, Stefan Wyszyński. An account of the meeting found its way into the world press. The bishop was said to have repeated the views of the primate on the causes of anti-Jewish riots. He stressed that "nations were going through a period of postwar depravation," and that this claimed victims among Jews no less than among Poles. His assessment of the contribution the Jews made to Polish life was negative; he suggested that Jews "should strive energetically to acquire a state hood of their own in Palestine and possibly also a colony in South America."[22]

[22] Private archives.

Like the primate, the bishop refused to make a public statement on the Kielce incident. Soon after, however, in September 1946, on the occasion of the "Majdanek Week," he told the faithful: "Fight the Nazi prejudice which, prompted by racial hatred, has tried to obliterate Jewish cemeteries. Let us remember that violence done to the right of the dead to peaceful and decent rest will by its own impact take revenge on us."[aaa] It was, it seems, easier to condemn violence done to the dead than to those who were still alive.

Let us pass over the 1950s, when the primate and the whole Church were fighting for mere survival, and also the early 1960s, with its more confined trench warfare, and concentrate on the March 1968 events and the Church's reaction to them. As in many other parts of the world, this was a time of large-scale protest by students and intellectuals in Poland; such demonstrations were followed by severe reprisals. This was a time of serious attack on Polish culture and science, but also of police provocation; there was a power struggle, great disillusion among reformers, together with a vicious anti-Semitic campaign organized by the communist authorities. This led to a mass exodus of thousands of Jews from Poland.

Two statements regarding these March events were issued by the Polish episcopate. The first stressed the need for a social order that "would respect the fundamental rights of persons and society." It commended to God ". . . all who have suffered much in the last few days."[bbb] The other argued that "no one may be branded an enemy on the grounds of holding different convictions."[ccc] Much attention was given to freedom of opinion, its role in culture and science, and to the need for a pluralist press, with dialogue between people holding different views.

In this same document, after a lengthy paragraph on the baselessness of charges that Poles were in some measure responsible for the Holocaust, two enigmatic sentences appear that on close inspection seem to offer an indirect condemnation of the official anti-Jewish campaign, and, more generally, of anti-Semitism. It reads: "The Second Vatican Council, in the 'Declaration on the Attitude to Non-Christian Religions,' has formulated clear principles which govern the attitude of Christians to, among others, believers in

[aaa] Quoted after Peter Raina, *Stefan Kardynał Wyszyński Prymas Polski* (*Stefan Kardynał Wyszyński, the Primate of Poland*), (Oficyna Poetów i Malarzy, 1979), 155.
[bbb] *Listy Episkopatu Polski 1945–1974* (*Letters of the Polish Episcopate: 1945–1974*), (Editions du Dialogue, 1975), 518–519.
[ccc] Ibid., 525.

the religion of the Old Testament. The Bishops remind all the faithful of the deeply humanitarian meaning of these principles." Reference to the text of the declaration *Nostra Aetate* reveals the thought of the council fathers: "The Church repudiates all persecution against any man. Moreover, mindful of her common patrimony with the Jews, and motivated by the Gospel's spiritual love and by no political considerations, she deplores the hatred, persecutions, and displays of anti-Semitism directed against Jews at any time and from any source."[ddd]

Why such circumspection in condemning a campaign that was being unequivocally condemned all over the world? Before this question is answered, it may be useful to quote from the sermon preached by the primate in the Warsaw Cathedral on Maundy Thursday, April 11, 1968:

> I, Bishop of the Metropolis, suffer greatly because of these "spectacles of hatred." Perhaps I am to blame that as bishop of Warsaw I did not say enough on the law, the obligation of love and of loving, regardless of speech, language, and race, that I did not prevent your being overtaken by the monstrous shadow of a new racism, allegedly in order to defend our culture. That is not the way! Not the way of hatred—We can defend our country only by the way of love.[eee]

These words are deeply moving. At last, what was happening in Poland was being called by its proper name: racism. What is more, the primate had raised the question of the moral responsibility of the Church, not so much its historical responsibility for anti-Semitism as the responsibility of the pastor for his flock, for their deeds and omissions, for the good and evil that make up the human condition.

Adam Michnik, quoting the primate, notes that the authorized text of the sermon, published in 1972, is "somewhat different" from the version originally given. It is useful to compare the two versions. In the published version, the words "speech, language, and race" and "shadow of a new racism" have been replaced by words on the obligation of loving "all, regardless of their views and convictions."[fff] The condemnation of anti-Semitism has disappeared. The statement becomes more careful, less defined. Why? We will probably never know. Some illumination may be gleaned from a

---

[ddd] *The Documents of Vatican II* (Geoffrey Chapman, 1966).
[eee] Cited in Adam Michnik, *Kościół, lewica, dialog* (*The Church and the Left*), (Instytut Literacki, 1977); after *Na Antenie*, November 24, 1968.
[fff] Stefan Kardynał Wyszyński, primate of Poland, *W Sercu Stolicy* (*In the Heart of the Capital*), (Papieski Instytut, 1972), 93–95.

conversation held many years later by a *Kultura* correspondent with "several representatives of the Polish Church hierarchy." The journalist repeated the words of one (or more) of his interviewees:

> [March 1968] was above all a "family quarrel," a contest within the power elite, not a racist campaign. It is true that among the victims of the factional struggle in the party were many who were not directly involved, but in fact those who emigrated did so for economic reasons, since the Jewish community had lost its privileged position. The methods applied in the anti-Semitic witch-hunt, though morally repulsive, are not likely to obliterate the memory of what the priests, Catholic activists, and society in general had suffered in Stalinist times when the apparatus of repression was manned by so many dignitaries and functionaries of Jewish descent, conspicuous for their great zeal. The volte-face effected after 1956 by the Jewish prominents of the Stalinist "ideological front" and of the cultural milieu did not fool anybody. So also the later anti-Zionist purges could not give rise to the conviction that the Jews were being victimized only because they were Jews. The anti-Zionist campaign, under-taken to settle old scores within the party, has done a lot of moral damage and soiled the reputation of Poland as a country with the traditions of national and religious tolerance. . . .[ggg]

This seems to be the dominant perception in the Polish Church of events that ended the Jewish presence on Polish land. Ten years after March 1968, a certain amount of publicity was given to a letter from the primate to an Israeli citizen, Israel Zyngman. In the letter, which thanks Zyngman for a book that he had sent to the primate, there is a passage about the Ghetto that the writer had observed "for a number of months over the wall along Elektoralna Street," and also about the state of Israel, which Wyszyński had thought to be necessary even before the war. The letter also contains a con-cise summary of Polish-Jewish relations: "This common experience [the war] has equaled the historic course of several centuries of coexistence of our two nations on Polish soil. I think that since the time of those terrible sufferings and sacrifices a fuller understanding for [the possibilities of] a new history has developed."[hhh]

This was the first written statement by the head of the Polish Church on Jews and Polish-Jewish relations since the pastoral letter of Cardinal Hlond,

---

[ggg] Dominik Morawski, "Korespondencja z Rzymu" (Correspondence from Rome), *Kultura* 5 (1973).
[hhh] Cited in Andrzej Micewski, *Kardynał Wyszyński Prymas i mąż stanu* (*Kardynał Wyszyński: Primate and Statesman*), (Editions du Dialogue, 1982), 383.

already quoted. How very different are the two statements! The second is a private letter to a Jew in Israel. The primate writes to tell him, for the first time, "I was close, I saw it all." But he also wishes to tell him that the many centuries of coexistence on the same territory have now come to an end.

After the war the Jews ceased to be a socio-economic or cultural problem for the Poles. They were perceived wholly as a political problem, a political group par excellence. They were no longer part of society; they were outside it, either as part of a hostile establishment or living outside Poland altogether.

In recent years a symbolic return of Jews to Polish society and Polish history has begun. In April 1983, on the occasion of the fortieth anniversary of Warsaw's Ghetto Uprising, the highest representative of the Polish Church, Primate Józef Glemp, celebrated for the first time in history a solemn mass for the Jews. By now, the Jews had ceased to be even a political problem. Instead, reintegrated into Polish history, they had become a moral problem for the people of Poland, and also for the Polish Church.

The Power Structure and the Jews

The Jews were part of the communist movement from its very beginning. The utopia of the universal brotherhood of nations was for them a way to escape their own particularism, to emerge from the narrow confines of the Jewish community, to avoid the hostility of the outside world. Stepping outside the Ghetto, they were more likely than other peoples to abandon their faith, to give up the ties of tradition and national identity. In the communist movement, they were welcomed as uprooted people ready to reject their ethnicity. Just as the Bolshevik Revolution draped itself in the clothes of the French Revolution, so the Bolshevik Jewish policy was a caricature of the French program formulated in 1791 by Clermont-Tonnere: "Nothing for the Jews as a nation, everything to the Jews as individuals."

The political position of Jews in postwar Poland was shaped by a number of factors: communist tradition, the policies of the Kremlin, the emergence of the state of Israel, the heritage of Polish–Jewish relations. Long before the end of the war, the political elite of the future People's Poland was selected in the Soviet Union, mostly from among the old Communists, but not exclusively. Once Poland was occupied, the expanding apparatus of domination absorbed anyone willing to cooperate, calling primarily for educated people, who were then in very short supply. Many educated Poles were ready to help in the rehabilitation of their country, restarting the economy and developing education; they were not, however, ready to participate in ruling the country under Communists. The new authorities, for their part, were deeply suspicious of the intelligentsia, a group rich in long and lively patriotic traditions.

The Jewish response was quite different. Grateful to the Soviet Union for saving their lives, emerging from an almost complete isolation, the Jews were culturally uprooted, acutely aware of the distrust felt toward them by the rest of Polish society. Dreaming of brotherhood and equality, and at the same time quite willing to give the "reactionaries" a lesson, they were ideal candidates for the new men in power. Independent of that, many were convinced Communists of long standing.

Under these circumstances, the Jews who decided to remain in Poland—a small minority of the survivors of the Holocaust—and those who, at the same time, decided to break out of the Jewish community and culture—a small minority of those who remained—were caught up by the governing power apparatus. They were funneled into those branches of bureaucracy where loyalty and obedience were of crucial importance: security, the army, the party apparatus, propaganda, international relations. All possible measures were taken to make the presence of Jews in the administration less conspicuous. Gentile features and fluent Polish were important requirements in their recruitment. Candidates were asked to assume Polish names and surnames, and even personal documentation relating to dead family members was altered. These procedures were immensely humiliating. The Polish public, aware of all this, saw it principally as a large-scale deception designed to camouflage the alien character of the new power. Most of these Jews were not simply assuming a Polish exterior while continuing to cultivate Jewish particularities in secret. They were not new Marranos; they accepted their new Polish identities wholeheartedly, with enthusiasm. But it was a very peculiar kind of Polish identity, adjusted to the requirements of official doctrine. And it is by no means certain that these people would have accepted the risks of assimilation as readily in less socially privileged circumstances. Czesław Miłosz, later a Nobel laureate, may have been right when he had one of his characters say: "They can survive only by not being Jews; those who remain Jews will emigrate."[iii]

[iii] Czesław Miłosz, *Zdobycie władzy* (*The Seizure of Power*), (Instytut Literacki, 1953).

There is no doubt that Jews were favored by the new authorities. This policy, however, was prompted by purely pragmatic considerations. Jews were given responsible posts not because they were Jews, but because they were faithful. This, however, could not last. Very soon the authorities felt the need for a new "cadres policy," which meant replacing the Jews with a rapidly trained Polish personnel, a switch made possible by a gradual consolidation of the new system and a broader social base from which to draw. The process of eliminating the Jews from positions of power was greatly helped by the anti-Jewish policies of Moscow. The Cold War created the "iron curtain"; under the circumstances, Jews, with their traditions, culture, and international connections, tended to become suspect citizens. With the emergence of the State of Israel—which at first enjoyed the support of Moscow as part of an anti-British diversion—the situation deteriorated still further for Jews, as it did in other countries of the Soviet bloc. A new, ominous word appeared: "cosmopolitanism."

Anti-Semitic trends were clearly visible in the trial of Laszlo Rajk in Hungary in 1949, and were important in the 1952 trial of Rudolf Slánský in Czechoslovakia. Devoted Stalinists were accused of treason; their treason was increasingly attributed to their Jewish back ground. Prominent *apparatchiks* were not the only ones to fall victim. In 1952, the entire top echelon of Jewish culture in the USSR was liquidated, which, after the devastation of the war, meant the total destruction of high Jewish (Yiddish) culture. Only the death of Stalin prevented a thorough anti-Jewish purge throughout the Soviet bloc.

The Polish "Spring in October" of 1956 was, apart from everything else, a time of enhanced consolidation of the communist power in the country. The old guard was replaced by Władysław Gomułka, only recently released from prison. In an atmosphere of general euphoria and patriotic fervor, those who symbolized (and, at lower levels, implemented) the process of Stalinization were dismissed, among them thousands of Jews. The power structure was being Polonized, not only in ideology, but also in the people who constituted it.

Until then, Poland had been very much like any other country in the Soviet bloc. For example, Poland's power structure included neither more nor fewer Jews than did the power structure in Romania or in Hungary. Everywhere, Jews played the part of the loyal praetorian guard. Now they were being ousted—they had done their job. But in the early 1960s the ruling elite in Poland took a different road from the one taken by other "fraternal parties"—a road that was to lead to March 1968.

According to some observers, the March events in Poland were a natural stage in the evolution of communism. Why, then, was this stage absent in the other countries of the Soviet bloc? Why was there no wave of organized anti-Semitism in Hungary? Surely, after the suppression of the revolution in 1956, Hungarian Jews could easily have been made responsible for the Stalinist aberrations and all the resulting misfortunes: the party leader, M. Rakosi, was a Jew; his short-lived successor, E. Gero, was a Jew; the cultural dictator, M. Farkas, was a Jew; so also was the head of the police, G. Peter. Nine out of twenty-five members of the Central Committee in 1945 were Jews. Why, then, was there no March 1968 in Hungary?

Soviet policy cannot provide a full explanation. While there had been the Six Day War of 1967 and a breaking-off of diplomatic relations with Israel by Moscow, together with a virulent anti-Jewish campaign directed from the Kremlin, other countries did not respond as Poland did. Romania did not break off relations with Israel; there was no anti-Semitic campaign there. Hungary, while adopting an anti-Israeli stance, did not extend this hostility to its own Jewish population. There was, it seems, some room for maneuver within these states, whatever the overall anti-Israeli policy of the Soviet government.

The March events in Poland were, in fact, largely a consequence of the failure of October 1956. October offered Polish society a certain model of coexistence with communism, which stressed national autonomy and the need for internal reforms, together with a widening of the field of civic liberties and a certain democratization of the system. But the movement for renewal—the so-called revisionism—soon collapsed under pressures from Moscow and the local party apparatus. The system rejected a transplant that was wholly contrary to its nature. The sense of frustration in the party, of missed opportunities, combined with a new internal and external configuration, led to the emergence of "moczarism" (named after its ambitious leader, General Moczar), a new and very different program for Polonizing the system. The party, in need of popular support, did not draw from earlier Polish democratic liberal or leftist traditions; it reached instead for a non-democratic national heritage.

Anti-Semitism, once used as a weapon against the ruling establishment, now served as evidence that the establishment had at last rid itself of an alien element. The government was no longer Jewish cosmopolitan; it had become Polish-national. The views and sentiments that found expression in the March events were not all the result of cynical manipulation. They expressed also the authentic needs of frustrated party members, alienated from the rest of society and deprived of plausible perspectives. These were people who had risen to various heights from villages and small towns; they had nowhere to go home to. Their frustrations were in some measure consonant with the more general frustrations and obsessions of the society. It was along these lines that the party sought to reestablish its links with the people.

Did the regime succeed? The general verdict is that it did not. I am inclined to subscribe to the opinion of Leszek Moczulski, who in the late 1970s founded the Confederation of Independent Poland (KPN), a right-wing opposition movement. According to him, the events of 1968 showed that "admittedly only a part, but a considerable part, of society believed that the elimination of a foreign body—the so-called Zionist group—would automatically bring about a radical improvement of the situation."[iii] The bulk of society could not be misled for very long; it was too sensitive to the subterfuges of official propaganda. To be credible to the people, authentic Polish nationalism had also to be anti-Soviet. Moreover, state anti-Semitism, like other state enterprises, was doomed to fail. Bernard Singer, a noted prewar journalist, had said this about anti-Semitism in the late thirties; it was still true in the late 1960s.

During the 1970s, still more Jews emigrated, leaving only a few old men behind, a few "good comrades," together with a number of assimilated young men and women, many of whom were joining the emerging opposition. The rebellion and the ensuing massacre of the shipyard workers in Gdańsk and Gdynia in December 1970 brought the March "renewal" to an end. March 1968 and the Jews are no longer mentioned. The rulers of today are men who came to the fore in 1968 and later; they are not inclined to boast about their role in those days. Anti-Semitic propaganda exists primarily to attack the opposition.

The sixteen months of the legal existence of Solidarity in 1980–1981 saw little change in this respect. It was allowed to condemn publicly the anti-Semitic campaign of 1968, but also to criticize Jews and freemasons. Real change came only in the wake of the imposition of martial law on December 13, 1981. It is now recognized that Jews, having ceased to be an internal problem, have become an international problem for the Polish People's Republic. This does not mean that there is no longer anti-Jewish propaganda for internal consumption, intended to further the interests of the Empire; this still exists. What

[iii] Cited by Adam Michnik, *Krytyka* 1, no. 2 (1978).

is new, however, is the abundance of friendly gestures that have been made, not so much to Polish Jews as to foreign Jews, particularly American Jews. It is for them that the anniversaries of the Warsaw Ghetto Uprising are celebrated, and the expensive albums published, and the Jewish cemeteries restored amid much publicity. Signs of goodwill and friendly intervention are expected in return. The Poles want help in securing new credits; a friendly foreign press is hoped for. The People's Republic wishes to break out of its international isolation; it has already enjoyed some success in this. Jewish leaders, criticized for meeting General Jaruzelski in New York in the autumn of 1985, do not deny that they are not principally concerned with Poland, human rights, or Solidarity. What concerns them, they say, is that the ban on Israel in the countries of Eastern Europe be lifted, and that the rate of Jewish emigration from the Soviet Union be increased. In these matters, Jaruzelski is potentially far more useful than Solidarity leaders like Zbigniew Bujak or Lech Wałęsa. Moreover, as has been reported, the General told these leaders that there was anti-Semitism in Solidarity.[kkk]

A Polish Problem

The history of Polish-Jewish relations has come to an end. Jews in Poland are no more, and never will be again. "We are too late," Andrzej Kuśniewicz writes in his recent novel; "it is impossible to wash this laundry clean. Some individual personal contacts will remain, a method of avoiding rocks and dangerous shoals. Passing by, sliding over, as if nothing had happened."[lll] This is not quite so: something else, far more important, does remain—the heritage of the past as an internal Polish problem. The ugly hump is there, whether or not it is recognized. It is all the more unavoidable since anti-Semitism, notwithstanding optimistic assurances to the contrary, is by no means dead: ". . . anti-Semitic slogans survive in our Polish community, we keep hearing them to this day. . . . It is no use burying your head in the sand. Anti-Semitism is a reality which must not be overrated, but neither can it be neglected," states Father Bronisław Dembowski.[mmm] He is echoed by Tymoteusz Klempski: "I do not say that there never was anti-Semitism in

---

[kkk] *Przegląd Wiadomości Agencyjnych* (*Press Review*), 29 (1985), cited in *Jewish World* 17 (Oct. 1985).
[lll] Andrzej Kuśniewicz, "Nawrócenie" (Conversion), *Twórczość* 10 (1985).
[mmm] "Patrząc na historię w prawdzie," (Confronting Historical Truth) *Więź* 4-6 (1985).

Poland. I shall say more, it exists to this day in the form of a paranoiac relapse, because in fact there are no Jews in this country, since they have either merged into the rest of society or become associated with the party. . . ."[nnn] Finally, "T. S.," an anonymous writer for the Polish underground press, states, "any honest man must admit that in the circle of his acquaintances there is a number of more or less virulent but unmistakable anti-Semites."[ooo] Many such statements can be found to this day in the Polish press: Catholic, official, and above all in the underground. At the same time, it is much more difficult to find descriptions of actual events, or attempts at diagnosis.

The sixteen months of the legal existence of Solidarity provided a unique opportunity to observe the kind of views, attitudes, and behavior that found expression in open public life. The Jewish problem soon became one of the many sources of friction between the union and the authorities. The latter—at least in part—tried to compromise Solidarity by pointing out with glee the number of intellectuals with a Jewish background in the union, greatly exaggerating both their number and the range of their allegedly destructive influence. In turn, union activists criticized the Party for promulgating anti-Semitic propaganda, recalling, among other events, March 1968 and the Kielce Pogrom. Wiktor Kulerski, one of the leaders of the underground Solidarity movement after December 1981, responding to the onslaughts of the openly fascist progovernment association, Grunwald, said: "Realizing who is trying to divide us and why, realizing the cruel and perverse methods applied to achieve this end, aware of the cost of tacit permissiveness in the face of incitement to hatred and prejudice, we must counter these attempts by preserving an elementary sense of human solidarity within our union."[ppp]

There have been other voices as well. Marian Jurczyk, a prominent Solidarity leader, attacked Jews in the Polish government—an incident that caused the union deep embarrassment. A representative of the democratic opposition had drawn a typically paranoid picture of humanity, ascribing all evil in the world to the Jews. Was this an isolated case? It is impossible to say. Bogdan Borusewicz, one of the earliest fighters for a free trade union movement—and, after December 13, 1981, like Wiktor Kulerski, a leader of the underground Solidarity—writes:

[nnn] Tymoteusz Klempski, "'Ich' drogi donikąd" ("Their" Dead-End Paths), *Zeszyty Historyczne* 75 (1986).
[ooo] T. S., "Polski antysemityzm" (Polish Anti-Semitism), *Spotkania* 29, no. 30 (1985).
[ppp] Wiktor Kulerski, "Prawdziwe cele antysemickich wystąpień" (The Real Aims of Anti-Semitic Statements), *AS Biuletyn Pism Związkowych i Zakladowych* 7 (1981).

The movement was beginning to be plagued by all the negative features of the system: intolerance . . . suppression of criticism, primitive chauvinism. . . . There emerged in Solidarity a wing of opinion not unlike Grunwald or *Rzeczywistość* [*Reality*: the paper by the most hardline faction within the party]. There was only one difference: the totalitarian ideology of "true Poles" within Solidarity was of a different color than red. It is quite amazing that it had a considerable following among the workers. At the same time, the so-called liberal elements in Solidarity were being pushed out of the union—first, as a result of the Party propaganda, second, by the "true Poles," third, by the Catholic hierarchy, which was more sympathetic to Solidarity totalitarians.[qqq]

Another source of interesting insight into the various trends within Solidarity is the collective work of a group of French and Polish sociologists under the direction of Alain Touraine.[rrr] These authors agree that while the democratic ethos of Solidarity prohibited the public airing of anti-Semitic sentiments, such sentiments did occasionally surface in private utterances among union activists. It was quite possible for the same individuals to represent one view on a given matter in public and quite another in private. With the increasing tension in and degeneration of the movement, antidemocratic, anti-intellectual, populist, and nationalist elements tended to come to the fore. Private anti-Semitism, at first kept under firm control, began to enter the public arena. It is important not to forget, however, that even in the worst of times, the issue was very marginal in comparison with other far more fundamental problems and conflicts.

What causes the survival of anti-Jewish sentiments in a world without Jews? In order to define at least the direction in which possible answers may be found, we must outline the consequences of the Holocaust for what may be called the Western mentality and for the Polish mentality.

For the West, the Holocaust came as a tremendous shock, incomparably greater than any produced by other cases of genocide in the distant or even quite recent past. The very word "holocaust," meaning a religious burnt offering, has in some ways sanctified the death of the Jews. The shock may be attributed to many causes. One had to do with the behavior of the West at the time of the Holocaust; another relates to the huge disproportion

---

[qqq] In Maciej Łopiński, Marcin Moskit, and Mariusz Wilk, eds., *Konspira (Conspiracy)*, (Spotkania, 1984), 15.
[rrr] Alain Touraine et al., *Solidarite: Analyse d'un Mouvement Social* (*Solidarity: An Analysis of a Social Movement*), (Editions Fayard, 1982); Michel Wieviorka, *Les Juifs, la Pologne et Solidarność* (Editions Donoel, 1984).

between the losses suffered by the West and the fate of the Jews. The Holocaust helped create a sense of crisis in Western civilization. The crime, committed in the center of Europe by a nation that had greatly contributed to the development of Christianity, served as a mirror that twisted all the surrounding images into grotesque distortions. The Holocaust quite abruptly revealed the ugly, irrational side of a civilization built on the premise of technical rationality. Man had become not only the tool but also the raw material of a supremely efficient process of destruction. Perhaps worst of all, as Hannah Arendt has aptly remarked, in the course of it all, evil itself was turned into a banality.[sss]

Another cause of the shock to the West had to do with the religious nature of the offense. The Jews had been singled out for destruction because they were the Chosen People. In the eyes of many Jews, the Holocaust was the crowning event of centuries of Christian hate and contempt; this was the punishment for the alleged crime of deicide, the final consummation of the Gospel's "His blood be upon us and upon our children." This deterministic vision deprived Nazism of its own distinct, murderous dynamics and saw continuity in what was in fact a terrible mutation. More convincing, certainly, was the opposite view: that the murder of the Jews was the symptom of a pagan rebellion against Christianity, its characteristic values and ethical principles.

However, this does not explain the choice of the victim; here, surely, the traditions of European anti-Semitism are very relevant, including the specifically Christian variety, which ascribes to Jews—*perfidis Judaeis*—a definite place in sacred history. That is why so many Christian thinkers and churchmen, while denying responsibility for the Nazi crimes, recognize the special responsibility of Christianity for the fate of the Jews. Pope John XXIII is said to have prayed, "For centuries our brother lay prostrate, weeping and bleeding, through our fault, because we forgot about Thy love."[ttt] The French cardinals, M. Etchejaray and J. M. Lustiger, wrote after a visit to Auschwitz: "On that spot where so many sons and daughters of the Jewish people, the people that had received and passed on to us the command 'Thou shalt not kill,' were led to extermination, we can only think of our responsibility."[uuu] Cardinal Etchejaray said: "We have a mission of repentance

---

[sss] Hannah Arendt, *Eichmann in Jerusalem: A Report on the Banality of Evil* (Penguin Books, 1978).
[ttt] Cited in *Znak* 2, no. 3 (1983).
[uuu] See *Tygodnik Powszechny*, July 31, 1983.

for our secular attitude as regards the Jewish people. . . . We should know how to ask forgiveness of the Lord and of our brothers so often fed with the 'teaching of disdain' and plunged into the horror of the Holocaust. We should commit ourselves to repair what should be repaired."[vvv]

In the West, the consequences of Nazi anti-Semitism have led to an unequivocal condemnation of all forms of anti-Semitism. Sometimes even quite trivial signs of xenophobia are thought to carry with them the menace of a new Auschwitz. By now anti-Semitism, whether religious or political (apart from its peculiarly leftist form, anti-Zionism), social or economic, is in the West more severely ostracized and provokes stronger reactions than many other kinds of religious or racial discrimination.

The Polish reaction to the Holocaust has been quite different. It never caused a shock to the collective Polish mentality. The experience at the time of war and in the immediate postwar period served mostly to strengthen old resentments and revive traditional hostility. Circumstances of the day favored the retention of anti-Jewish stereotypes; anti-Semitic postures were not compromised. According to Polish perceptions, there was no connection between even the radical anti-Semitism of the nationalist right and Nazi German anti-Semitism. On the contrary, both the war and the postwar years confirmed for many the patriotic legitimacy of anti-Jewish feelings.

The enormous loss of life among Poles helped minimize the significance of the extermination of Jews. The Germans killed three million Poles and three million Polish Jews. Why should one group of victims be treated differently than the other? Why should the likelihood of death, the circumstances, methods of selection, and mode of destruction be more important than the fact of death itself?

Great cataclysms provide a sort of protection against smaller cataclysms. In times of war and revolution, for example, suicides are a rarity. The Poles, having suffered much heavier losses than their allies in the West, and entering upon yet another era of foreign domination, have had little time to worry about a crisis of civilization, let alone indulge in Christian-European remorse with regard to the Jews.

With time, however, anti-Semitism came to be seen as unacceptable also in Poland. Meanwhile, history leaves its traces, and continues to have an

---

[vvv] See the *International Herald Tribune*, November 8, 1983.

impact on current Polish thinking. Anti-Semitism is considered to be a matter of opinion, and opinions differ. Indeed, the very meaning of the word "anti-Semitism" is often circumscribed in Poland to allow a greater freedom of definition than is common in the West. One author, for example, argues that advocating an economic boycott on a group of citizens is not proof of anti-Semitism;[www] another holds that anti-Jewish prejudices, stereotypes, and propaganda do not constitute proof of anti-Semitism.[xxx] These are traces of a long tradition, of a certain innocence, of a Polish anti-Semitism that even today remains hardly disturbed by the enormity of the German crimes. On the contrary, it sometimes seems that these crimes have simply fostered the conviction that only open racism or readiness to use violence against Jews can qualify as anti-Semitism. More general anti-Jewish attitudes are often thought, it seems, to be acceptable.

Only quite recently has the problem of anti-Semitism and Christian responsibility for it been raised in the Polish Church. This, no doubt, owes much to the influence of Pope John Paul II. During a mass on the occasion of the fortieth anniversary of Warsaw's Ghetto Uprising, Father Bronisław Dembowski said, "We must admit that the crime of genocide of the Jewish people had its origin in the sin of anti-Semitism."[yyy] For a Westerner this may appear to be a mere tautology; for a Pole, it is not. The preacher was speaking of anti-Semitism in general; he was placing the problem of responsibility in a far wider context than is normal in Poland; it did not concern Nazi Germany alone. Similarly, Jerzy Turowicz, in a recent article, used words that until now have been taboo. He wrote: "Polish Catholics, who witnessed the terrible fate of Jews on the Polish territory and have seen what anti-Semitism can lead to, are bound to make a thoroughgoing examination of conscience as regards the sin of anti-Semitism. I must say clearly, though it hurts me, that in my opinion this examination of our conscience has not yet been thorough enough."[zzz] In an even more open way, and very shocking to many Poles, the problem of Polish responsibility for anti-Semitism was posed recently by Jan Błoński, literary critic and professor at

---

[www] Kinga Strzelecka in a text devoted to Saint Maximilian Kolbe. *Więź* 4-6 (1985).

[xxx] W. W., "Żydzi, Polacy, antysemityzm" (Jews, Poles, Anti-Semitism), *Polityka Polska* 6 (1984).

[yyy] Ewa Berberyusz, "Z grzechu antysemityzmu" (The Sin of Anti-Semitism), *Tygodnik Powszechny*, April 17, 1983.

[zzz] Jerzy Turowicz, "Shoah w polskich oczach" (How Poles See the Shoah), *Tygodnik Powszechny*, November 10, 1985.

the Jagiellonian University in Krakow, in an article entitled "The Poor Pole Looks at the Ghetto."[aaaa] [5] The title paraphrased a well-known poem by Czesław Miłosz, "Poor Christian Looks at the Ghetto," written immediately after the Germans crushed the Warsaw Ghetto Uprising.

In spite of these examples and many others, it is obvious that the examination of Polish consciousness "has not yet been thorough enough." Why was Poland so late in raising the problem of anti-Semitism, in inquiring into its origins, in dealing with issues of moral responsibility? Why the silence of Polish intellectuals, who have occasionally voiced moral protests and made some public condemnation of anti-Jewish postures and behavior, but who have never attempted an in-depth analysis, if for no other purpose than to try to understand their own society?

The answer, quite simply, is that a painful confrontation with the past requires the freedom to confront opinions and assessments—in other words, it implies a free public life. This has never existed in postwar Poland. Another explanation may have to do with the general position of Polish intellectuals. Many of them, especially those most sensitive to discrimination, fanaticism, and anti-Semitism, more or less enthusiastically welcomed the all-encompassing political embrace of the new authorities. One of the motives often evoked then and now by the victims of seduction by the communist power was the nondemocratic, xenophobic, anti-Semitic character of the political right and of the Church. This was, of course, only partly true; in any case, it did not justify the misalliance. When, in the mid-1950s, certain individuals began to free themselves from that deadly embrace, they could not but suffer a feeling of guilt for having betrayed the society they were supposed to serve. It was not becoming for them to moralize from the heights of an authority they no longer possessed.

However, the most important cause lay elsewhere. How, indeed, could one fight anti-Semitism when anti-Semitism had become, tragically and paradoxically, part of the protective wall raised by the nation against the pressures of the new power trying to impose on it a completely alien vision of the past, the present, and the future? The wall was absolutely necessary to survive the cruel bloodletting of the war, the unceremonious postwar amputation of Poland, and the shifting of its frontiers further west; also, the brutal transplantation of millions of people ordered by the Soviet Union, a

[aaaa] Jan Błoński, "Biedni Polacy patrzą na getto" (The Poor Poles Look at the Ghetto), *Tygodnik Powszechny*, January 11, 1987.

virtual civil war in the late 1940s, the red terror, and the disintegration of many traditional social structures. The wall was built of anything that lay at hand in Polish tradition and culture: good and noble materials were used no less than inferior and vile stuff. The state of siege, permanent since 1944, never allowed for thorough reflection or necessary self-questioning. To take only one (though far from trivial) example: Was it possible to analyze critically the shortcomings of the Polish Church, Catholic anti-Semitism, and Christian responsibility when the new authorities were gleefully doing everything to compromise and destroy the Church, the last stronghold of the nation's spiritual independence?

In recent years, the issue of Polish-Jewish relations has been raised in official publications, most wisely and most candidly in the Catholic press, most honestly and without inhibitions in the independent underground press. This has become possible with the coming of age of a new generation of Poles, unburdened by memories of the war and of the immediate postwar years, or of Stalinism itself. Even more important, perhaps, is the unfettering of social consciousness brought about by the emergence of Solidarity. Polish society has become acutely conscious of its strength, but also aware of the spiritual poverty of its enemy. It can now afford to discuss calmly and openly its most embarrassing shortcomings and problems.

Editors' Notes

1. Jerzy Turowicz's essay is reproduced in this volume on pages 164–169.
2. Mieczysław Jastrun's essay is reproduced in this volume on pages 87–92.
3. Selections from Kazimierz Wyka's essay are reproduced in this volume on pages 56–60.
4. Jerzy Andrzejewski's essay is reproduced in this volume on pages 95–112.
5. Jan Błoński's essay is reproduced in this volume on pages 273–285.

17

The Poor Poles Look at the Ghetto

JAN BŁOŃSKI

Editors' Introduction

Jan Błoński (1931–2009) was a historian of literature, literary critic, and translator. Born in Warsaw, he studied Polish literature at the Jagiellonian University in Krakow, where he later taught for several decades. Over the years, he worked with various cultural and literary periodicals in Poland, and his interests were extraordinarily diverse. In the world of literary criticism, he is best known for his elegant and incisive interpretations of Polish and European twentieth-century authors, including Marcel Proust, Samuel Beckett, Witkacy (Stanisław Ignacy Witkiewicz), Witold Gombrowicz, Czesław Miłosz, and Sławomir Mrożek. His most important books include *Widzieć jasno w zachwyceniu. Szkic literacki o twórczości Prousta* (*To See Clearly in Wonderment: A Literary Sketch about the Works of Proust*, 1965), *Forma, śmiech i rzeczy ostateczne. Studia o Gombrowiczu* (*Form, Laughter, and Ultimate Things: Studies of Witold Gombrowicz*, 1994), *Wszystkie sztuki Sławomira Mrożka* (*All the Plays of Sławomir Mrożek*, 1995), and *Miłosz jak świat* (*Miłosz Like the World*, 1998).

Błoński's most influential work—in Poland and abroad—was the essay reproduced here. He published it in *Tygodnik Powszechny* in January 1987, and it initiated a period of fierce debates and deep reflection about Polish moral responsibility during the Holocaust. This English translation was prepared by Anna Zaranko, and it first appeared in *Polin: Studies in Polish Jewry*, vol. 2, edited by Antony Polonsky (1987; reissued in paperback by the Littman Library of Jewish Civilization, 2008; https://liverpooluniver-sitypress.co.uk). It is reprinted by permission of Jan Błoński's estate and the Institute for Polish-Jewish Studies and the American Association for Polish-Jewish Studies. For the historical context of the impact of Błoński's essay and the discussions that followed, please see "Working through the Past" in the Introduction to this volume and Antony Polonsky's edited vol-ume *My Brother's Keeper? Recent Polish Debates on the Holocaust* (Routledge, 1990). The title of Błoński's essay evokes Czesław Miłosz's 1943 poem "Biedny chrześcijanin patrzy na getto" (The Poor Christian Looks at the Ghetto).

On more than one occasion Czesław Miłosz has spoken in a perplexing way of the duty of Polish poetry to purge the burden of guilt from our native soil which is—in his words—"sullied, blood-stained, desecrated."[a] His words are perplexing, because one can only be held accountable for the shedding of blood which is not one's own. The blood of one's own kind, when shed by victims of violence, stirs memories, arouses regret and sorrow, demands respect. It also calls for remembrance, prayer, justice. It can also allow for forgiveness, however difficult this may be. The blood of the other, however, even if spilt in a legitimate conflict, is quite another matter but it also does not involve desecration. Killing when in self-defense is legally condoned, though it is already a departure from Christian moral law: Christ ordered Peter to put away his sword. Whenever blood is spilt, it calls for reflection and penance. Not always, however, can it be said to desecrate the soil.

What Miłosz means here is neither the blood of his compatriots nor that of the Germans. He clearly means Jewish blood, the genocide which—although not perpetrated by the Polish nation—took place on Polish soil and which has tainted that soil for all time. That collective memory which finds its purest voice in poetry and literature cannot forget this bloody and hideous defilement. It cannot pretend that it never occurred. Occasionally one hears voices, especially among the young, who were not emotionally involved in the tragedy, saying, "We reject the notion of collective responsibility. We do not have to return to the irrevocable past. It is enough if we condemn this crime in toto as we do with any injustice, any act of violence." What I say to them is this, "Our country is not a hotel in which one launders the linen after the guests have departed. It is a home which is built above all of memory; memory is at the core of our identity. We cannot dispose of it at will, even though as individuals we are not directly responsible for the actions of the past. We must carry it within us even though it is unpleasant or painful. We must also strive to expiate it."

How should this be done? To purify after Cain means, above all, to remember Abel. This particular Abel was not alone, he shared our home, lived on our soil. His blood has remained in the walls, seeped into the soil. It has also entered into ourselves, into our memory. So we must cleanse ourselves, and this means we must see ourselves in the light of truth. Without

---

[a] As cited by Ewa Czarnecka in *Podróżny świata. Rozmowy z Czesławem Miłoszem, komentarze* (*Conversations with Czesław Miłosz*), (New York, 1983), 119.

such an insight, our home, our soil, we ourselves, will remain tainted. This
is, if I understand correctly, the message of our poet. Or, at any rate, this is
how Miłosz sees his duty, while calling upon us at the same time to assume
this obligation also.

How difficult this task is can be seen from Miłosz's celebrated poem
"Campo di Fiori." At the heart of it, there is the image of the merry-go-
round which was—by chance, but what a coincidence!—built in Krasiński
Square in Warsaw just before the outbreak of the Ghetto rising. When the
fighting broke out, the merry-go-round did not stop; children, youngsters
and passers-by crowded around it as before:

> Sometimes the wind from burning houses
> would bring the kites along
> and people on the merry-go-round
> caught the flying charred bits
> This wind from the burning houses
> blew open the girls' skirts
> and the happy throngs laughed
> on a beautiful Warsaw Sunday.
> (translated by A. Gillon)

Miłosz compares "the happy throng" to the crowd of Roman vendors
who—only a moment after the burning at the stake of Giordano Bruno—
went merrily about their business as before, enjoying their "pink fruits of
the sea" and "baskets with olives and lemons" as if nothing had happened.
He ends the poem with reflections of "the loneliness of dying men," who
have "the poet's word" for their only consolation. It is only the word, the
poet seems to be saying, which can preserve what can still be saved. It purges
the memory by voicing a protest against the passing away and "the oblivion
growing before the flame expired."

The act of remembering and mourning fixes in the memory the image
of the stake in the middle of the market place or that of a merry-go-round
on the grave. The success of the poem itself—which is often quoted and
has been translated into many languages—is a clear proof of that. In its
Hebrew version, the poem may appear as evidence of the hostile indifference of the Poles in the face of the Holocaust. Years later, Miłosz wonders
"whether there really was such a street in Warsaw. It existed, and in another
sense it did not. It did exist, because there were indeed merry-go-rounds
in the vicinity of the Ghetto. It did not, because in other parts of town,
at other moments, Warsaw was quite different. It was not my intention to

make accusations."[b] The poem, he concedes, is too "journalistic," allowing one too easily to draw conclusions. It simplifies truth and, by so doing, soothes the conscience. Worse, the poet discovers that he has written "a very dishonest poem." Why? Because—I quote—"it is written about the act of dying from the standpoint of an observer." So it is; the piece is so composed that the narrator, whom we presume to be the poet himself, comes off unscathed. Some are dying, others are enjoying themselves, all that he does is to "register a protest" and walk away, satisfied by thus having composed a beautiful poem. And so, years later, he feels he got off too lightly. Matched against the horrors of what was occurring at the time, he says, the act of writing is "immoral." "Campo di Fiori" does not succeed in resolving the conflict between life and art. Miłosz adds in his defense that the poem was composed as "an ordinary human gesture in the spring of 1943" and, of course, we must immediately concede that it was a magnanimous human gesture. During that tragic Easter, it saved—as someone put it somewhat grandiloquently—"the honour of Polish poetry." We agree with the poet, though, that the last word on the subject has yet to be spoken.

This agonizing over a poem may perhaps help us to understand why we are still unable to come to terms with the whole of the Polish-Jewish past. Here then I shall abandon literature and draw directly on my personal experience. Perhaps, on reflection, not even very personal, as almost everybody who has traveled abroad, especially in the West, must have had this question put to him at one time or other: "Are Poles anti-Semites?" Or, more bluntly: "Why are Poles anti-Semites?" I myself have heard it so many times, and so many times I have tried to explain, that I could attempt a thumbnail sketch of some twenty or so of such conversations:

"Are Poles anti-Semites?"

"Why do you put your question in this way? There are Poles who are anti-Semites, some others who are philo-Semites, and a growing number who do not care either way."

"Well, yes, of course, but I am asking about the majority. Poles have always had a reputation for being anti-Semites. Could this be an accident?"

"What do you mean by 'always'? Wasn't it true that at a time when Jews were expelled from England, France and Spain, it was in Poland, and not elsewhere, that they found refuge?"

[b] Ibid., 63–64.

"Yes, maybe, but that was a long time ago, in the Middle Ages. At that time Jews were the objects of universal contempt. But at least since the mid-eighteenth century in Europe, there has always been a problem of Polish intolerance."

"But it is exactly at that time that Poland disappeared from the map of Europe!"

"Polish society, however, continued to exist and the Jews could not find their place within it."

"Why?"

"We were under foreign rule; we had to think of ourselves first."

"This is precisely what I mean. Why could you not think of yourselves together with the Jews?"

"They were too numerous. We did not have sufficient resources. We could not provide for their education, judiciary, administration. Jews didn't even speak Polish: they preferred to learn Russian or German. But there were enlightened people among us who advocated the course of assimilation and strove to bring the two communities together."

"But why? Why couldn't Jews simply remain Jews? You were also responsible for pogroms, why?"

"It is not true, the first pogroms took place in Ukraine and they were provoked by the Tsarist police. . . ."

And so such discussions continue:

"When you regained independence, the fate of Jews did not improve. On the contrary, anti-Semitism became even more vicious."

"You can't change society in only twenty years, and besides that, was it not much the same elsewhere in Europe at the time? In the aftermath of the First World War, we received many Jews from Russia, and after 1934 from Germany."

"That may be true, but you still treated them as second-class citizens. During the war you saved too few."

"There is in Israel a place commemorating people who saved Jews during the war. Thirty percent of the names on that list are Polish names."

"But the percentage of Jews who survived the war in Poland is low, the lowest in Europe in relation to the total number of the population."

"In 1942 there were four Jews for every eight Poles in Warsaw. Now, how is it possible for the eight to hide the four?"

"It was indeed the Poles who used to identify Jews and passed them on to the Germans and to the police which was, let us not forget, Polish."

"In every society there is a handful of people without conscience. You have no idea what the German occupation in Poland was like. To hide one Jew meant risking the life of one's whole family, children included."

"Yes, that's true, but there were equally brutal punishments for the underground activities, yet a great number of people were involved in them. Following the war, Jews did not wish to remain in Poland."

"Indeed, it was difficult for them to live surrounded by memories."

"It was difficult for them to live among Poles who did not wish to give them back their houses and shops and threatened and even killed some of them. Have you not heard of the pogroms in Kraków and Kielce?"

"The pogrom in Kielce was a political provocation."

"Even if it was, so what? It did find a response. Ten thousand people besieged the Jewish apartment house in Kielce. Ten thousand people can't be provocateurs."

"Jews were sometimes a target not for being Jews but for sympathizing with Communists."

"In 1968, is it because they were communists that they had to leave Poland?"

And so on, indeed, endlessly. The debates of historians resemble this discussion. The same arguments and events—only more carefully documented—appear time and again. There is a vast body of literature, of both a personal and a documentary nature, of which we have very little idea in Poland. We should, however, know it better, because it also refers to us. It contains a wide range of viewpoints and opinions. There are books whose authors do not hide that they are motivated by hate. We cannot afford to ignore them; they are born of personal experiences whose authenticity cannot he doubted. And, besides, haven't we ourselves produced a literature abounding in pronouncements full of hatred, sometimes hysterical hatred, toward Jews?

There are also many books which are cautious and, as far as is possible, devoid of partisanship. These books carefully remind us of the intellectual as well as the material conditions of Polish-Jewish coexistence. They take into account the terror, unimaginable today, of life under the German occupation and a certain moral degradation of the society which was a direct result of life under this enormous pressure. This, in fact, was not a uniquely Polish experience; it happened also elsewhere.[c] They make a tacit assumption that tragedies of Eastern Europe cannot be measured by the yardstick of, say, the English experience. When the skies are literally falling in, even a kick can be an expression of sympathy and compassion. The truth, however, remains difficult to determine and difficult to accept. Two years ago, I attended a

---

[c] The victim cannot accept that he was not only wronged, but also humiliated and demeaned by his persecutor; that he was unable to stand up to the inhumanity of it all. In the years 1944-1948, Polish opinion was not able to acknowledge the disintegration of all norms and moral debasement among a large part of our society in the aftermath of the war. The drastic treatment of these themes by writers such as Borowski and Różewicz aroused indignation. The readers of this journal (*Tygodnik Powszechny*) took exception to J. J. Szczepański's short story "Buty" (Shoes). It was hard to accept the truth of the "infection with death" (the term coined by K. Wyka). A rather similar attitude was, of course, also to be found among Jews.

discussion in Oxford between some foreign and some Polish specialists and I must confess that it was a distressing experience. For us as well as for the Jewish participants, I suppose. We were a long way from agreeing with each other, but that is not the aim of such conferences. I was continuously aware of what was not being said there and what is the main reason why these discussions—friendly, for the most part—were painful for all concerned. It was later that I came to the conclusion that this was due to the sense of a kind of contamination, a feeling of being somehow soiled and defiled, which is what Miłosz had in mind in the passage noted above.

And that is why I would like to go back once more to the poet. In 1943, Milosz wrote another poem about the destruction of the Ghetto, a poem entitled "A Poor Christian Looks at the Ghetto." It is more ambiguous, perhaps more difficult to understand. It opens with the image of destruction:

> It has begun: the tearing, the trampling on silks,
> It has begun: the breaking of glass, wood, copper, nickel,
>   silver, foam
> Of gypsum, iron sheets, violin strings, trumpets, leaves,
>   balls, crystals,

And later:

> The roof and the wall collapse in flame and heat seizes
>   the foundations.
> Now there is only the earth, sandy, trodden down,
> With one leafless tree.

The city was destroyed, what remained is the earth, full of broken shells and debris. It is also full of human bodies. In this earth, or rather under it:

> Slowly, boring a tunnel, a guardian mole makes his way,
> With a small red lamp fastened to his forehead.
> He touches buried bodies, counts them, pushes on.
> He distinguishes human ashes by their luminous vapor.
> The ashes of each man by a different part of the spectrum.

Who this mole is, it is difficult to say. Is he a guardian, perhaps a guardian of the buried? He has got a torch, so he can see; better, at any rate, than the dead can see. And the poet himself, he is as if among the buried. He lies there with them. He fears something. He fears the mole. It is a striking, startling image:

> I am afraid, so afraid of the guardian mole,
> He has swollen eyelids, like a Patriarch

Who has sat much in the light of candles
Reading the great book of the species.

And so this mole has the features of a Jew, poring over the Talmud or the
Bible. It seems more likely that it is the Bible, as this alone deserves the
name of "the great book of the species," meaning, of course, the human
species.

What will I tell him, I, a Jew of the New Testament.
Waiting two thousand years for the second coming of Jesus?
My broken body will deliver me to his sight
And he will count me among the helpers of death:
The uncircumcised.
(translation Cz. Miłosz)

It is a terrifying poem; it is full of fear. It is as if two fears coexist here. The
first is the fear of death; more precisely, the fear of being buried alive, which
is what happened to many people who were trapped in the cellars and
underground passages of the Ghetto. But there is also a second fear: the fear
of the guardian mole. This mole burrows underground but also underneath
our consciousness. This is the feeling of guilt which we do not want to
admit. Buried under the rubble, among the bodies of the Jews, the "uncircumcised" fears that he may be counted among the murderers. So, it is the
fear of damnation, the fear of hell. The fear of a non-Jew who looks at the
Ghetto burning down. He imagines that he might accidentally die then and
there, and in the eyes of the mole who can read the ashes, he may appear
"a helper of death." And so, indeed, the poem is entitled "A Poor Christian
Looks at the Ghetto." This Christian feels fearful of the fate of the Jews but
also—muffled, hidden even from himself—he feels the fear that he will he
condemned. Condemned by whom? By people? No, people have disappeared. It is the mole who condemns him, or rather may condemn him,
this mole who sees well and reads "the book of the species." It is his own
moral conscience which condemns (or may condemn) the poor Christian.
And he would like to hide from his mole-conscience, as he does not know
what to say to him.

Miłosz, when asked what or who is represented by this mole, declined to
answer. He said that he had written the poem spontaneously, not to promote
any particular thesis. If this is so, the poem would be a direct expression of
the terror which speaks through images, as is often the case in dreams and
also in art. It makes tangible something which is not fully comprehended,

something that was, and perhaps still is, in other people's much as in the poet's own psyche, but in an obscure, blurred, muffled shape. When we read such a poem, we understand ourselves better, since that which had been evading us until now is made palpable. As for myself, I have—as probably every reader does—filled in the gaps in my own reading of "A Poor Christian." I hope, however, that I have not strayed too far from the intentions of the poet.

Here I return to the hypothetical conversation. It is a simplified summary of dozens of arguments and discussions. What is immediately striking here? In the replies of my fictitious Pole one detects the very same fear which makes itself felt in "A Poor Christian." The fear that one might be counted among the helpers of death. It is so strong that we do everything possible not to let it out or to dismiss it. We read or listen to discussions on the subject of Polish-Jewish past and if some event, some fact which puts us in a less-than-advantageous light, emerges, we try our hardest to minimize it, to explain it away and make it seem insignificant. It is not as if we want to hide what happened or to deny that it took place. We feel, though, that not everything is as it should be. How could it have been otherwise? Relations between communities, like the relations of two people, are never perfect. How much more imperfect are relations as stormy and unhappy as these. We are unable to speak of them calmly. The reason is that, whether consciously or unconsciously, we fear accusations. We fear that the guardian mole might call to us, after having referred to his book, "Oh, yes, and you too, have you been assisting at the death? And you too, have you helped to kill?" Or, at the very least, "Have you looked with acquiescence at the death of the Jews?"

Let us think calmly: the question will have to be asked. Everybody who is concerned with the Polish-Jewish past must ask these questions, regardless of what the answer might be. But we—consciously or unconsciously—do not want to confront these questions. We tend to dismiss them as impossible and unacceptable. After all, we did not stand by the side of the murderers. After all, we were next in line for the gas chambers. After all, even if not in the best way possible, we did live together with the Jews; if our relations were less than perfect, they themselves were also not entirely without blame. So, do we have to remind ourselves of this all the time? What will others think of us? What about our self-respect? What about the "good name" of our society? This concern about the "good name" is ever-present in private and, even more so, in public discussion. To put it differently, when we consider the past, we want to derive moral advantages from it. Even when we condemn, we ourselves would like to be above—or beyond—condemnation. We want to be absolutely beyond any accusation, we want to be completely clean. We want to be also—and only—victims. This concern is, however, underpinned by fear—just as in Miłosz's poem—and this fear warps and disfigures our thoughts about the past. This is immediately communicated to those we speak to. We do not want to have anything to do with the horror. We feel, nevertheless, that it defiles us in some way. This is why we prefer not to speak of it all. Alternatively, we speak of it only in order to deny an accusation. The accusation is seldom articulated but is felt to hang in the air.[d]

Can we rid ourselves of this fear? Can we forestall it? I think not, as it lies, in all truth, in ourselves. It is we ourselves who fear the mole who burrows in our subconscious. I think that we shall not get rid of him. Or at least, we shall not get rid of him by forgetting about the past or taking a defensive attitude toward it. We must face the question of responsibility in a totally sincere and honest way. Let us have no illusions: it is one of the most painful questions which we are likely to be faced with. I am convinced, however, that we cannot shirk it.

We Poles are not alone in grappling with this question. It may be helpful to realize this. Not because it is easier to beat one's breast in company. Not because in this way the blame may appear less weighty. Rather because in this way we shall be able to understand it better. To understand both our responsibility and the reason why we try to evade it.

We read not so long ago about John Paul II's visit to the Synagogue in Rome. We are also familiar with the Church documents in which—already at the time of Pope John XXIII—the relationship between Christians and Jews, or rather, between Christianity and Judaism, was redefined, hopefully for all time. In the Pope's speech as well as in these documents one aspect is immediately clear. They do not concern themselves with attributing blame nor with the consideration of reasons (social, economic, intellectual or whatever) which made Christians look upon Jews as enemies and intruders. One thing is stated loud and clear: the Christians of the past and the Church itself were wrong. They had no reason to consider Jews as a "damned" nation, the nation responsible for the death of Jesus Christ, and

---

[d] That is the reason why there are so few literary works that treat the theme of Polish society's attitude to the Jewish Holocaust. It is not only because literature is rendered speechless in the face of genocide. The theme is too hot to handle; writers felt that they came into conflict with their readers' sensibility.

therefore as a nation which should be excluded from the community of
nations.

If this did happen, it was because Christians were not Christian enough.
The Church documents do not state: we "had to" defend ourselves, we
"could not" save Jews or treat them as brothers. They do not attempt to look
for mitigating circumstances (and these can be found). Jews, being mono-
theists, were "beyond the pale" already in antiquity. In the Middle Ages,
what cemented Europe together was religious unity. Let us bear in mind
that the Church was, on the whole, more tolerant than the secular rulers.
None the less, all this does not change the basic situation and must be put
aside. Instead, what has to be stressed is that the Church sustained hostility
toward Jews, thereby driving them into isolation and humiliation. To put it
briefly, the new Church documents do not attempt to exonerate the past,
they do not argue over extenuating circumstances. They speak clearly about
the failure to fulfill the duties of brotherhood and compassion. The rest is
left to historians. It is precisely in this that the Christian magnanimity of
such pronouncements lies.

I think we must imitate this in our attitude to the Polish-Jewish past. We
must stop haggling, trying to defend and justify ourselves. We must stop
arguing about the things which were beyond our power to do, during the
occupation and beforehand. Nor must we place blame on political, social,
and economic conditions. We must say first of all—Yes, we are guilty. We
did take Jews into our home, but we made them live in the cellar. When
they wanted to come into the drawing-room, our response was—Yes, but
only after you cease to be Jews, when you become "civilized." This was the
thinking of our most enlightened minds, such as Orzeszkowa and Prus.[1]
There were those among Jews who were ready to adhere to this advice.
No sooner did they do this than we started in turn talking of an invasion
of Jews, of the danger of their infiltration of Polish society. Then we started
to put down conditions like that stated *expressis verbis* by Dmowski, that we
shall accept as Poles only those Jews who are willing to cooperate in the
attempts to stem Jewish influences in our society. To put it bluntly, only
those Jews who are willing to turn against their own kith and kin.

Eventually, when we lost our home, and when, within that home, the
invaders set to murdering Jews, did we show solidarity toward them? How
many of us decided that it was none of our business? There were also
those (and I leave out of account common criminals) who were secretly
pleased that Hitler had solved for us "the Jewish problem." We could not

even welcome and honor the survivors, even if they were embittered, disorientated, and perhaps sometimes tiresome. I repeat: instead of haggling and justifying ourselves, we should first consider our own faults and weaknesses. This is the moral revolution which is imperative when considering the Polish-Jewish past. It is only this that can gradually cleanse our desecrated soil.

What is easy in the case of words is, however, more difficult in practice. Its precondition is a change in the social awareness of the problem. For our part, we often demand of Jews (or their friends) an impartial and fair assessment of our common history. We should, however, first acknowledge our own guilt, and ask for forgiveness. In fact, this is something that they are waiting for—if, indeed, they are still waiting. I recall one moving speech at the Oxford conference, in which the speaker started by comparing the Jewish attitude to Poland to an unrequited love. Despite the suffering and all the problems which beset our mutual relations, he continued, the Jewish community had a genuine attachment to their adopted country. Here, they found a home and a sense of security. There was, conscious or unconscious, an expectation that their fate would improve, the burden of humiliation would lighten, that the future would gradually become brighter. What actually happened was exactly the opposite. "Nothing can ever change now," he concluded. "Jews do not have and cannot have any future in Poland. Do tell us, though," he finally demanded, "that what has happened to us was not our fault. We do not ask for anything else. But we do hope for such an acknowledgement."

This means for the Polish side the acceptance of responsibility. Here the guardian mole enters for the last time and asks, "Full responsibility? Also a shared responsibility for the genocide?" I can already hear loud protests. "How can that be? In God's name, we didn't take part in the genocide." "Yes, that is true," I shall reply. Nobody can reasonably claim that Poles as a nation took part in the genocide of the Jews. From time to time one hears voices claiming just that. We must consider them calmly, without getting angry, which might be taken as a mark of panic. To me, as for the overwhelming majority of people, these claims are unfounded. So why talk of genocide? And of responsibility? My answer is this: participation and shared responsibility are not the same thing. One can share the responsibility for the crime without taking part in it. Our responsibility is for holding back, for insufficient effort to resist. Which of us could claim that there was sufficient resistance in Poland? It is precisely because resistance was so weak that we now honor those who did have the courage to take this historic risk. It may sound rather strange, but I do believe that this shared responsibility through failure to act, is the less crucial part of the problem we are considering. More significant is the fact that if only we had behaved more humanely in the past, had been wiser, more generous, then genocide would perhaps have been "less imaginable," would probably have been considerably more difficult to carry out, and almost certainly would have met with much greater resistance than it did. To put it differently, it would not have met with the indifference and moral turpitude of the society in whose full view it took place.

A question arises immediately whether this could be said not only of the Poles, but equally well of the French, the English, the Russians, of the whole of the Christian world. Yes, indeed it can. This responsibility is, indeed, our common responsibility. But it cannot be denied that it was in Poland where the greatest number of Jews lived (more than two-thirds of the world's Jewry are Polish Jews, in the sense that their forefathers lived in the territories belonging to the Polish Republic in the period before the Partitions). Consequently, we had the greatest moral obligation toward the Jewish people. Whether what was demanded of us was or was not beyond our ability to render, God alone must judge and historians will continue to debate. But, for us, more than for any other nation, Jews were more of a problem, a challenge which we had to face.

To refer once more to the realm of literature: nobody understood this better than Mickiewicz. The thoughts and the vision of our romantic poet were more far-sighted than that of any of his contemporaries. Unlike the majority of those who were well-disposed to the Jews, Mickiewicz held a deep conviction that Israel, "the older brother," should not only enjoy the same privileges in Poland as everybody else, but also at the same time retain the right to remain distinct in religion and shared custom. This was also Norwid's attitude; as far as we can judge, Słowacki was of the same opinion. So, at the very least, our literary greats stood on the side of truth and justice. The thinking of Mickiewicz was indeed visionary: he seems to have been aware that only such a path could save the Jews (if only partially) from extinction, and us from moral turpitude. It would have been a truly extraordinary path to take and one which would have merited the epithet "messianic" in the proper sense of the word. Reality, unfortunately, took exactly the opposite form to that dreamt of by the poets. It was nowhere else but in Poland, and especially in the twentieth century, that anti-Semitism became particularly virulent. Did it lead us to participate in genocide? No. Yet, when one reads what was written about Jews before the war, when one discovers how much hatred there was in Polish society, one can only be surprised that words were not followed by deeds. But they were not (or very rarely). God held back our hand. Yes, I do mean God, because if we did not take part in that crime, it was because we were still Christians, and at the last moment we came to realize what a satanic enterprise it was. This still does not free us from sharing responsibility. The desecration of Polish soil has taken place and we have not yet discharged our duty of seeking expiation. In this grave-yard, the only way to achieve this is to face up to our duty of viewing our past truthfully.

Editors' Note

1. Eliza Orzeszkowa (1841-1910) and Bolesław Prus (1847-1912) were among Poland's most influential nineteenth-century positivist writers. Both believed that Polish Jews should assimilate.

PART VIII

1989–2000: Toward Description and Diagnosis

18

Polish-Jewish Relations Thirty Years after the Publication of the "Nostra Aetate" Conciliar Declaration

ARCHBISHOP HENRYK MUSZYŃSKI

Editors' Introduction

Archbishop Henryk Muszyński (b. 1933) is a biblical scholar and the primate emeritus of Poland. Born in the town of Kościerzyna in northern Poland, he studied philosophy, theology, and biblical studies in Pelplin, Lublin, Rome, Jerusalem, and Heidelberg between 1951 and 1973; he received two doctorates and studied the Qumran manuscripts, also known as the Dead Sea Scrolls, discovered shortly after the Second World War. In the 1970s and 1980s, he taught at the Catholic Theological Academy (ATK) in Warsaw. He became the bishop of Wrocław in 1987, the archbishop of Gniezno in 1992, and the primate of Poland in 2009, retiring in 2010. Muszyński is known as an advocate of open and tolerant Catholicism, and he has worked tirelessly to improve both Polish-Jewish and Polish-German relations. Between 1986 and 1994, he led the Polish Episcopal Commission for Dialogue with Judaism, and later served on the planning committee for Warsaw's POLIN Museum of the History of Polish Jews. In 1995, together with Bishop Walter Kasper, he edited the joint letter of the Polish and German Episcopates on dialogue, reconciliation, and a shared Christian perspective on the creation of a united Europe.

The text reproduced here is the speech Muszyński gave in 1997 at the Protestant Faculty at the Union of Evangelical Churches (UEK) in Tübingen, when he received the Dr. Leopold Lucas Prize for his work on behalf of Polish-Jewish understanding. The speech was given in German, translated into Polish by Juliusz Zychowicz, and published in Poland in the Catholic monthly *Znak* in Krakow in June 2000.[1] The "Nostra Aetate (In Our Time) Declaration of the Relation of the Church with Non-Christian Religions" was adopted by the Second Vatican Council in 1965. It outlined the Catholic Church's relationship to Buddhism, Hinduism, Islam, and Judaism; called on Catholics not to blame Jews indiscriminately for the death of Jesus Christ; and condemned all forms of anti-Semitism:

> Furthermore, in her rejection of every persecution against any man, the Church, mindful of the patrimony she shares with the Jews and moved not by political reasons but by the Gospel's spiritual love, decries hatred, persecutions, displays of anti-Semitism, directed against Jews at any time and by anyone.[2]

In his talk, Muszyński examines the process of Polish-Jewish reconciliation and emphasizes the need for a three-way dialogue between Poles, Jews, and Germans. He refers to a few essays included in this volume, including those by Jerzy Andrzejewski and Jan Błoński. He identifies some differences between the situation of Poles and Jews during the Shoah, but it is worth comparing his analysis with that offered by Hanna Świda-Ziemba who is acutely aware of the fundamental asymmetry of the Polish and Jewish experiences under the German occupation. Muszyński accentuates the threats brought by the German occupation to the Poles because he believes this helps shed light on the ways in which Poles participated in debates about Polish-Jewish relations during the Holocaust and in its aftermath.

An official guest lecture on Christian-Jewish relations, given at the Evangelical Theology faculty in Germany by a Catholic bishop from Poland, who is receiving the great distinction of the Dr. Leopold Lucas Prize, is certainly no everyday event. It is rather a historical sign of new relations between our Churches and countries.

I feel deeply honored to receive the Dr. Leopold Lucas prize, and I would like to offer my heartfelt gratitude for this honor—especially to you, Mr. Consul General, since you are the sponsor of this prize. I would also like to thank all those who helped bring the recognition afforded by the Dr. Leopold Lucas Prize to my exceedingly modest contribution to the favorable development of Christian-Jewish and Polish-Jewish relations. I am also happy to use this opportunity to extend friendly greetings from Gniezno to all who are present here at this festive moment—greetings from the tomb of Saint Wojciech-Adalbert, from Poland's oldest archdiocese and its first capital.

Polish-Jewish relations have a long history: it stretches over a thousand years and it is as complex as it is worthy of attention. It includes both times of greatness and periods of painful and tragic experiences. As I speak about this history here, I do it from the Polish perspective, and thus from a perspective which—I am fully aware—will perhaps be unusual, and, in any case, certainly different.

In a pastoral letter issued by the Polish Bishops' Conference on November 30, 1990, for the twenty-fifth anniversary of the Second Vatican Council's declaration on relations between the Church and non-Christian religions we read: "A particular bond exists between us Poles and the Jewish people; it has been there since the earliest centuries of our history. For many Jews, Poland has become a fatherland." Indeed, for hundreds of years Jews saw Poland as their new homeland, where they found refuge from the hostility and persecutions they faced in other countries; in all historical periods, we can find more than enough evidence that confirms this experience.

One of the consequences of this history—a history that can be evoked only very generally here—is the fact that, as we read further down in the aforementioned Polish bishops' pastoral letter, "most Jews currently living in the world have their roots in the lands of the former and present Polish Republic." According to conservative estimates, about three quarters of today's Jews are connected to Poland through their parents, grandparents, or great grandparents. Further down in their letter, Polish bishops say that it is therefore all the more lamentable that "this land, regrettably, became the grave of a few million Jews in our century." These facts—the splendid past and its tragic ending—give all Polish-Jewish history a particular and perhaps unique character.

While for centuries one could justifiably view and describe this history as a history of bilateral relations, of mutual relations between Poles and Jews, this situation underwent a fundamental change in our century. Events from the time of the Second World War, on the one hand, and those caused by them in the postwar period, on the other, have so completely obscured bilateral Polish-Jewish relations that the history of these relations today, and also the reconciliation process to which this history emphatically calls us, have gained multilateral dimensions—in the sense that it is impossible to interpret this history without including Germans. And reconciliation between Poles and Jews is unthinkable and unrealizable without German participation. For, as Theo Mechtenberg rightly emphasizes,[3] when we look at the postwar history of Poles and Jews we are dealing "with a history whose questions are admittedly Polish-Jewish questions, but whose prehistory is also, and even decisively, a German history, namely, the history of the German occupation of Poland fifty years ago."[a]

In this lecture, I would like to focus on the two issues I mentioned: the particular, or even completely unique, character of Polish-Jewish relations, and the problem of the multilateral nature of the reconciliation process. Only the combined efforts of Poles and Germans, and Jews' willingness to be open to these efforts, can help this multilateral process move forward and achieve its goal.

The Particular Character of Polish-Jewish Relations

What accounts for the particular, or even completely unique, character of relations between Poles and Jews?

Rabbi Byron L. Sherwin from Chicago, who has been actively engaged in Polish-Jewish dialogue for at least ten years, says that for over a millennium

---

[a] Theo Mechtenberg "Zum Jüdisch-Polnischen Verhältnis—Ist der Antisemitismus eine Unüberwindbare Barriere?" (Toward Jewish-Polish Relations—Is Anti-Semitism an Insurmountable Barrier?), *Orientierung* 52, nos. 10-12 (1988), (reprinted in "epd-Dokumentation," 41/88; and in G. Särchen and L. Mehlhorn, eds., *Schalom dem Schwierigen Dialog unter Entfremdeten Geschwistern. Polen und Juden—Juden und Polen* (Shalom to the Difficult Dialog between Estranged Siblings. Poles and Jews—Jews and Poles), (Magdeburg, 1991) (a special volume of the Anna-Morawska Seminars)—all further citations follow this edition.

Poland was not just a second homeland for Jews but rather their actual homeland. He adds: "Now that Jews are no longer living in Poland, Poland still lives on in the Jewry. For many of us, Israel is our physical homeland, while Poland is the spiritual one."[4] Of course, the life of Jews in Poland was not free from tensions, prejudices, mutual distrust, and various manifestations of hostile acts. Despite this, unlike any other country, Poland—the historic Polish-Lithuanian Commonwealth headed by a king—was considered a *paradisus Judaeorum*, especially in the sixteenth and seventeenth centuries.[b][5] Around the middle of the sixteenth century, Moses Isserles (born circa 1512/30, died 1572), a famous rabbi and great scholar from Krakow, was writing to one of his students in Germany, and, alluding to Proverbs 17:1, he said: "Better a dry crust with peace—as it is here, where there is no fierce hatred—than in the German lands. May it remain this way until the Messiah comes."[c][6]

And a hundred years later, Moses ben Eliezer ha-Cohen from Narol, who made a last-minute escape from the massacre during the 1648/49 Cossack Uprising led by Bohdan Khmelnytsky,[7] and found refuge in distant Metz, composed the following prayer in exile:

Polsko, Ty, która byłaś rajem
Pierwszą byłaś dla nauki i wiedzy
Od dni, w których odpadł od Judy Efraim,
Ty, któraś słynęła wiedzą umiejętną,
Teraz jesteś wygnaną i samotną wdową,
Opuszczoną jesteś przez swe własne syny.
Gdzie jest lwów schronisko, gdzie mędrcy nauki?
Gdzie mocarze, co łaską szczodrzy są bez miary?
Gdzie pisarze miast polskich i cnoty nadzorcy?
Gdzie jest Bóg, który sądzi i krew krwią odpłaca?
Zlituj się nad swym ludem, z rąk nas wybaw zbójców!
Wdziej na się szatę zemsty za dusze niewinne,
Które jak ofiarne barany porżnięto,
Całe gminy zniszczono, jak jednego męża.
Udziel, Panie, pokoju tym duszom nieszczęsnym
W wiecznym życiu, gdzie ptaki śpiewają niebieskie,
Gdzie owoc palmy kwitnie i woń swą rozsiewa
Tam wysoko u siebie, na Abarim szczycie.

---

[b] For an introduction to this history see Haiko Haumann, *Geschichte der Ostjuden* (A History of East European Jews), (Munich, 1990).
[c] As cited by Byron L. Sherwin.

Poland, you were a paradise,
First in knowledge and learning
Since the days when Ephraim fell away from Judah,
Once famous for your skillful knowledge,
You are now an exiled, lonely widow,
By your own sons you are abandoned.
Where is the lion's lair, where are the wise scholars?
Where are the mighty who were generous with boundless grace?
Where are the writers from Polish cities, and guardians of virtue?
Where is God, who judges and demands blood for blood?
Have pity on your people, save us from robbers!
Put on garments of revenge for innocent souls,
Slaughtered like lambs,
Whole communities destroyed, like a single man.
Give peace, oh Lord, to these wretched souls,
In eternal life where heavenly birds sing,
Where the palm fruit blossoms and scatters its scent,
On high, where you dwell, at the summits of the Abarim.[d]

Indeed, for whole generations, Poland was a place of refuge for Jews—especially those who were persecuted and expelled from Western Europe. In an 1889 painting entitled "Przyjęcie Żydów w roku 1096" (The Reception of Jews in Poland in 1096)—which shows an audience of a delegation of (Spanish) Jews with the Polish ruler, Prince Władysław Herman (ruled 1079–1102), and his son and successor Bolesław Krzywousty (ruled 1102–1138) in front of the Płock Cathedral—the Polish painter Jan Matejko (1838–1893), who created an illustrated chronicle of Polish history with his numerous and monumental works, caught, as if in a shutter image, something that took place in Poland a countless number of times over many hundreds of years: the immigration of Jews from Western Europe and the generous welcome extended to them, along with a guarantee of support and safety.

According to a well-known Jewish legend, even Poland's Hebrew name, Polin, comes from a pronouncement made by the Most High; it was certainly not by accident that Schmuel Joseph Agnon (1888–1970) and Alexander Eliasberg (1878–1924) put this legend at the beginning of their *Das Buch von den Polnischen Juden* (*The Book of Polish Jews*), published in Berlin in 1916. It expresses in words what Matejko painted. The authorship of the legend, by

---

[d] The text can be found in M. Bałaban, *Historia i literatura żydowska ze szczególnem uwzględnieniem historii Żydów w Polsce* (*Jewish History and Literature with Particular Focus on the History of Jews in Poland*), 3 vol. (L'viv-Warsaw-Krakow, 1925, vol. 3; reprinted in Warsaw in 1982).

the way, has been attributed to the already mentioned Moses Isserles from Krakow. This is Schmuel Joseph Agnon's version:

> And here is a legend about our fathers who migrated to Poland: Israel saw that there is no end to persecutions, that it keeps suffering ever new catastrophes, oppression grows more severe, and the forces of wickedness bring ever new misfortunes. And so, the sons of Israel stood at a crossroads and asked themselves what road they should follow to find rest for their souls.
>
> And a note fell from heaven: Go to Poland! When they arrived, they found a dense forest, and each tree had a Talmud tractate carved on it—it was the Kawczyn forest [near Lublin]. And they said to themselves: we arrived in a land where our fathers already lived in the past. But why did they call it Polin? Because the community of Israel praised the Holy One there, saying: Lord of the world! Since the hour of our salvation has not yet come, stay with us here during this night of the dispersion of our people, until you lead us back to the land of Israel.[e][8]

Yet by the end of the eighteenth century, Poland's situation changed fundamentally with the partitions. In three phases (1772, 1793, and finally 1795) the "Polish-Lithuanian Commonwealth headed by a king" was divided by its three neighbors, and independent Poland did not exist again until November 11, 1918. For several generations, Poles and Jews lived under Prussian, Russian, and Austrian rule, and their living conditions—and mutual relations that resulted from these conditions—differed from one partition to another. It was only after the First World War that the Polish state regained sovereignty. The reborn Poland was a multinational state,[f] where Jews were the second-largest minority. Until 1939, Poland had the largest percentage of Jews anywhere in the world (around 3.3 million, which was about 10 percent of the population). In many small towns and villages, but also in large cities, this percentage was often much higher and approached up to a third, or sometimes even half of all inhabitants (in Warsaw, for example, there were about 350,000 Jews—as many as in all of France; in Łódź the number was about 200,000—as many as in all of Czechoslovakia), and in some towns Jews were an overwhelming majority.

---

[e] S. J. Agnon and A. Eliasberg, eds., *Das Buch von den Polnischen Juden* (*The Book of Polish Jews*), Berlin, 1916. The legend relies on Hebrew wordplay since the Hebrew word for Poland is Polin. When the two syllables of this word are written separately and one reads them as two words, one gets the Hebrew sentence po(h])lin, which means stay here overnight (with us), as we read in the cited legend.

[f] See J. Tomaszewski: *Rzeczpospolita wielu narodów* (*The Republic of Many Nations*), (Warsaw, 1985).

For centuries, Polish Jewry was not only the largest Jewish community in the world, but also the "cradle of modern Jewish culture."[g] It was here, among Polish Jews that the essential spiritual inheritance of what goes by the name *Ostjudentum* (East European Jewry) came into being. But that is not all. It was here, in the Yeshivas on Polish territory that the foundations of modern Jewish scholarship and education were laid; it was here, among Polish Jews, that Yiddish reached its full development as both a vernacular and literary language; it was here, among Polish Jews that the spiritual and religious currents of modernity were born—starting with modern rabbinical Orthodoxy all the way to Chassidism and its own original spirituality, and later also extending to secular political movements.[h]

Professor Stefan Schreiner writes: "It is impossible to overrate what Polish Jews once meant for the entire Jewish world; and it has often been said that Jewish culture as a whole—in the broadest sense of the word—at least in the modern era, reaching all the way to our own century, was fundamentally shaped by Polish Jewry."[i] And Rabbi Byron L. Sherwin asks: "What spiritual treasures would we have received if Polish Jews had not burned in a pillar of fire? The Jewish people became irrevocably impoverished as a result of this loss. But Poland, too, is poorer because of it."[j]

In the truest sense of the word, nothing remains of the external existence of the (Eastern) Jewish world. Today, this world lives on only in reminiscences. While there are no more eyewitnesses of its life and its rich culture, there nonetheless still remains its spiritual legacy, as if to confirm that old legend, according to which the parchment of the Torah scroll burned but the letters written on it did not—and ascended into heaven. Synagogues were destroyed, holy Torah scrolls were burned, and priceless cultural treasures were taken away. In many of the once blossoming communities and shtetls there was often not a single Jew left alive. Most Polish territories indeed became *judenfrei*. People were murdered, and their culture was murdered along with them. Words, which the Polish writer and poet Antoni Słonimski (1895–1976), who came from a Jewish family, poured into his

---

[g] Schreiner, "Im Schatten der Vergangenheit—zur Geschichte der jüdischen Gemeinschaft in Polen seit 1945" (In the Shadow of the Past—Toward a History of the Jewish Community in Poland since 1945), *Judaica* 46 (1990).
[h] See Byron L. Sherwin, as cited previously.
[i] S. Schreiner, as cited previously.
[j] Byron L. Sherwin, as cited previously.

"Elegia Miasteczek Żydowskich" (Elegy for Jewish Towns) sound like a lamentation:

Nie masz już, nie masz w Polsce Żydowskich miasteczek,
W Hrubieszowie, Karczewie, Brodach, Falenicy
Próżno byś szukał w oknach zapalonych świeczek,
I śpiewu nasłuchiwał z drewnianej bóżnicy.
(. . .)
Nie ma już tych miasteczek, gdzie Biblijne pieśni
Wiatr łączył z Polską piosnką i Słowiańskim żalem,
Gdzie starzy Żydzi w sadach pod cieniem czereśni
Opłakiwali święte mury Jeruzalem.
Nie ma już tych miasteczek, przeminęły cieniem
I cień ten kłaść się będzie między nasze słowa,
Nim się zbliżą bratersko i złączą od nowa
Dwa narody karmione stuleci cierpieniem.

There are no more Jewish towns in Poland, no more,
In Hrubieszów, Karczew, Brody, Falenica,
You'd look in vain for lit candles, or try to catch
The sounds of singing from a wooden temple.
(. . .)
Those towns are no longer where the wind joined
Biblical airs with Polish song and Slavic sorrow,
Where old Jews in gardens beneath the shade of cherry trees
Mourned the holy walls of Jerusalem.
Those towns are no longer, they've passed like shadows,
And these shadows will fall between our words,
Before two nations, nourished by the suffering of centuries,
Will approach each other fraternally and again unite.[9]

The effects of the Holocaust—the extermination of European Jews—were and remain more tragic, and, in a certain sense, more powerfully perceptible in Poland than in any other European country. Immediately after the war, it was impossible to restore any kind of neutral coexistence between Jews and Christians, Poles and Jews—and in the face of the traumatic experiences that befell many Jews in postwar Poland such coexistence appeared simply inconceivable. In retrospect, it is sometimes difficult to resist the impression that these experiences of the early postwar years influenced Polish-Jewish relations so permanently that the entire history of these relations is seen, as it were, from the perspective of these experiences.

On the one hand, there were no active Jewish communities that could contribute to overcoming the tragic past, while on the other, Jews who survived the Shoah, those who returned to Poland from emigration, or who were repatriated after the war, like the 200,000 Jews who had been transported to Siberia after the Red Army occupied eastern Poland in September 1939—were not welcome in postwar Poland. This is borne out by the pogroms from 1945 and 1946, the background and circumstances of which can be openly disclosed only now,[k] and anti-Semitic campaigns in later years (especially 1956, 1968, and 1980/81),[10] when Polish Jews felt the effects of politically instrumental use of anti-Semitism.[l] Arthur Sandauer (1913–1989), a Polish literary critic with a Jewish background, said that anti-Semitism expelled "from the country those whom [Hitler] did not manage to murder. Poland will indeed become 'judenfrei.'"[m] Awareness that "Polish anti-Semitism did not burn itself out in the rubble and smoldering ruins of the ghettos"—as Jerzy Andrzejewski, author of *Popiół i diament* (*Diamond and Ashes*) and the novella *Wielki Tydzień* (*Holy Week*), wrote in 1946—became "exceptionally painful" not only for Jews but also for every ethically sensitive Pole.[11]

On the other hand, as Polish bishops put it in their pastoral letter, Poles experienced "wrongs and injustice perpetrated by the postwar communist government, in which there were also people with Jewish backgrounds."

---

[k] After the opening of the relevant archives; for information about the Kielce Pogrom, see the documentation collected by S. Meducki and Z. Wrona in *Antyżydowskie wydarzenia kieleckie 4 lipca 1946* (*Anti-Jewish Events in Kielce on July 4, 1946*), 2 vol. (Kielce, 1992–1994).
[l] See the aforementioned book by Th. Mechtenberg.
[m] "O sytuacji pisarza polskiego pochodzenia żydowskiego w XX wieku—rzecz, którą nie ja powinienem był napisać...." (On the Situation of the Polish Writer of Jewish Descent in the Twentieth Century—an Essay Someone Else Should Have Written....), Warsaw, 1982.

The bishops added: "We have to admit, however, that the source of inspiration of their actions was certainly neither their ethnicity nor their religion, but rather communist ideology, which, by the way, inflicted much injustice upon the Jews themselves." It is, in any case, impossible to deny that the concept of "Judeo-Bolshevism" has become a common stereotype in Poland as well.[n] It is self-evident that under these circumstances the initiation of dialogue between Poles and Jews was inconceivable. One does not need to be particularly imaginative to understand that in this situation the few Jews who survived the Shoah did not want to, or could not, speak about the nightmares of the past, while the Polish side simply had no interest in initiating a conversation with them.

There is also a further problem, the consequences of which are an object of discussion and often also controversy among both Jews and Poles to this day—both in Poland and beyond its borders. As everyone knows, the great majority of German concentration and death camps, like Majdanek, Treblinka, Sobibór, and, above all, Auschwitz-Birkenau were located in occupied Polish territories. Very often, the geographic location of these sites of extermination is not seen along with its actual causes but gets tied to "proverbial Polish anti-Semitism," which is seen as the alleged cause of the local population's lack of opposition to the death camps, and the basis of an expectation that this population will be ready to cooperate with Hitler's Nazi Reich in exterminating Jews.[o] This insinuation does not gain legitimacy when it is expressed in numerous publications and statements of distinguished figures, or when it is expressed with intensity, as in Claude Lanzmann's *Shoah*, and presented as a historical fact. Few realize that this film is not a documentary showing the historical reality of Nazi crimes, but that it serves to illustrate a certain a priori perspective, and attempts to reinforce a certain ideology.[p]

As a result, in the awareness of postwar generations of Jews, Poland no longer figures as a spiritual homeland of the contemporary Jewish

[n] See P. Śpiewak, "Antisemitismus in Polen" (Anti-Semitism in Poland), in *Deutsche und Polen. 100 Schlüsselbegriffe* (*Germans and Poles. 100 Key Concepts*), ed. E. Kobylinska, A. Lawaty, and R. Stephan (Munich–Zürich, 1992); S. Krajewski, "Problem żydowski–problem polski" (Jewish Problem–Polish Problem), *Więź* 35 (April 1992); see also J. Holzer, "Polacy i Żydzi w polskim tyglu. Spory—polemiki" (Poles and Jews in the Polish Melting Pot. Arguments and Polemics), *Tygodnik Powszechny*, 3, 1991.
[o] See Th. Mechtenberg, as cited previously.
[p] J. Turowicz, *Shoah—mit Polnischen Augen Gesehen* (*How Poles See the Shoah*), in G. Särchen and L. Mehlhorn, cited by Th. Mechtenberg as cited previously.

community but rather as its grave, an immense cemetery. This fact has destructive consequences for both sides—for Jews and Poles alike. When it comes to the Jewish side, the poet Rajzel Żychlińska—who was born in 1910 in the Polish town of Gąbin, survived the Holocaust and returned to Poland, only to leave again in 1948 and go to New York— expressed what many were surely thinking when, like her, they turned away from Poland soon after the war: "One cannot live in a cemetery,"[q] and especially not in a cemetery which was desecrated by the events of the early postwar years. And it is precisely these postwar events—seen by many as continuation of the collaboration I mentioned earlier—that largely shape Poland's image among Jews, and determine their relation to it to this day.

Poles, in turn, feel deeply hurt by the one-sidedness of this perspective; they view the accusations it engenders as unjustified. When, however, they defend themselves against such baseless accusations—and this defense often takes violent forms—their defense is typically seen as confirmation of their anti-Semitism, and, in order to justify the one-sided perspective mentioned, all the more emphasis is placed on the immediate connection—or the supposedly fluid transition—between prewar Polish anti-Semitism and both the racist anti-Semitism of the Nazi period, which was the basis of the genocide of the Jews, and its continuation after the war. By equating prewar Polish anti-Semitism with racist anti-Semitism of the Nazi era (and the politically instrumental anti-Semitism of the postwar period), Poles are pushed from the role of fellow victims of the same racist ideology—which they feel they are—into the role of perpetrators, and thereby, without contributing to it themselves, they become entangled in the realm of responsibility or even joint guilt for the Holocaust. They do not simply experience this blame as unjustified: it also constitutes an impassable barrier, an insurmountable obstacle which makes reconciliation between Poles and Jews impossible. Theo Mechtenberg thus rightly observes that while it is impossible to deny the existence of interwar Polish anti-Semitism and its consequences, and while one can and should speak about it, one should not at the same time overlook the fact that Polish anti-Semitism "never reached the status of an ideology that stigmatized an entire nation," and it is therefore necessary to sternly oppose opinions that "look for direct connections between it and

[q] As cited by S. Schreiner in the previously cited work.

Auschwitz, and—pointing to their traditional anti-Semitism—depicts Poles as accomplices in the genocide perpetrated against Jews."[r]

We must therefore realize that as a result of the Shoah, which took place in the very heart of Christian Europe, the whole shared Polish-Jewish history that stretched over a thousand years became not just overshadowed but completely concealed. The genocide of the Jewish people, its unprecedented scale, and the way in which it was perpetrated constitute a call to deep reflection and the greatest challenge for Christianity. Germans and Poles are, however, entangled in the reality of the Shoah in utterly specific ways, however different these are from each other, and however dissimilar their causes. Yet while both Evangelical Churches in Germany and the German Catholic Bishops' Conference expressed their position in numerous documents, and this position is generally known and respected, the Shoah—as a problem of the Poles—has not yet become, despite all the discussions of the recent years, an object of the kind of attention it deserves.[s] Please allow me, ladies and gentlemen, to present a few reflections about these issues.

The Shoah as a Problem of the Poles

Besides Poland's own numerous victims of the Second World War, the Shoah—the murder of Jews, which took place primarily in occupied Polish territories—is the most tragic of all the tragic elements of the Nazi legacy in Poland; it strains Polish-Jewish relations so much that it often makes any rapprochement and understanding between Poles and Jews impossible. For Poland, this horrific legacy has become an unavoidable fate of the postwar period. For most Jews in the world today, Poland is simply the "country of the Shoah:" "'Today, Jews almost universally see Poland as the 'Egyptian house of bondage,' from which they had to escape to find refuge in the United States or Israel. Those who did not succeed—perished. This perspective informs everything that Jews experienced in our country. One should not, of course, play down the tragedy of the Shoah; but how can dialogue be conducted,

---

[r] Th. Mechtenberg, as cited previously.
[s] M. Chajkowski gave a good summary of the ongoing discussion in "Auschwitz, Défi pour les Chrétiens Polonaise" (Auschwitz, a Challenge for Polish Christians), in *Les Vérités des Uns et Celles des Autres. Points de Vue de Juifs et de Chrétiens sur la Shoah en Pologne* (*One's Own Truth, the Other's Truth. Jewish and Christian Perspectives on the Shoah in Poland*), ed., D. Tollet and M.-F. Baron (Paris, 1995).

how should it be conducted, when, after everything that happened, Poland and Poles are seen as worse than Germans and Nazis?"[t] This concerns not just the Polish-Jewish problem, but the entirety of Christian-Jewish relations. People uncritically accept and repeat stereotypes without checking what truth they contain—often without even attempting to properly access historical truth. As a result, there is no lack of radical claims that repeatedly blame Poles directly—if not for the mass murder of Jews then at least for the scale of this genocide (this is done, for example by people like William Styron, Jack Gardner, Herman Wouk, Gerald Green, and others). And Mark Hillel even believes that most Jews who survived the Shoah hate Poles more than they hate Germans.[u]

People who do not have detailed knowledge of the horrible terror and the limits of what one could do under the German occupation repeatedly blame Poles for having done too little to rescue Jews. Only a handful know that Poland was the only place where rescuing Jews and offering them any kind of help carried the risk of being punished by death, and this punishment was meted out not only to the person who helped but also to their loved ones and entire families. In helpless rage and terror, people often had to look at the death of their own families. This, of course, neither justifies nor provides the basis for justifying the indifference toward the ghastly fate of Jews during the so-called "final solution of the Jewish question"—this indifference, of course, was also a fact. Before making the accusation of general indifference, however, one has to ask (oneself) the question: What could have been done to rescue Jews in that specific situation? Władysław Bartoszewski was once asked who did everything that could be done to rescue Jews,[12] and he answered: Only those who gave up their own lives for them. . . . Tadeusz Mazowiecki gave a similar answer when, as Poland's first noncommunist prime minister, he gave a speech at the World Jewish Congress: "No one can claim to have done everything that could have been done to rescue our Jewish brothers. No one in Europe and no one in America can say that."[v] And perhaps here I might be permitted to remind

---

[t] W. Chrostowski, "Źródła chrześcijańskich oporów wobec dialogu z Żydami i judaizmem" (Sources of Christian Reticence about Dialogue with Jews and Judaism), in *Maqom. Biuletyn Informacyjny IDKJ* (*Maqom. Information Bulletin of the Institute for Catholic-Jewish Dialogue*) 1 (1996).

[u] See S. Gądecki: "Relacje między polskimi Żydami a Polakami—historia i perspektywy" (Relations between Polish Jews and Poles—History and Perspectives), *Studia Gnesnensia* 10 (1995). About anti-Polish resentments, especially among American Jews, see R. F. Scharf, "In Anger and Sorrow: Towards a Polish-Jewish Dialogue," *Polin* 1, (1986).

[v] Text printed in *Gazeta Wyborcza*, no. 132 (1990).

all of us that most of the trees planted in the Avenue of the Righteous at Yad Vashem in Jerusalem were planted by Poles.[w]

Is it only thoughtlessness when the term "Polish concentration camps" is the phrase most often used in the United States and sometimes even in Germany? To Polish ears, it sounds as if Poland is being directly or indirectly blamed and held responsible for all the atrocities and crimes committed there, and sometimes one has the impression that the greater the temporal and geographic distance from concentration camp realities, the more convincingly do these realities appear as the work of the Poles. Clearly, the location of the concentration and death camps in Polish territory occupied by Germans during the war inevitably brings up the question about co-responsibility for the genocide. But does it justify the accusation of shared guilt? And here people most often overlook the fact that there are differences between cooperation, co-responsibility, and shared guilt.

Precisely these issues have been at the heart of a stormy debate in Poland and among Poles since—more than a decade ago—the Krakow-based Polish literature professor Jan Błoński published the article "Biedni Polacy patrzą na getto" (The Poor Poles Look at the Ghetto) in the influential Catholic weekly *Tygodnik Powszechny*—and spoke about the "sin of omission."[x] [13] This is not the place to get into the details of this controversy. Those interested should consult an interim summary, written three months into the discussion by *Tygodnik*'s nationally and internationally acclaimed editor Jerzy Turowicz.[y] Turowicz also gave a detailed description of the problem as a whole.[z] [14]

The claim made in the aforementioned Polish bishops' pastoral letter, according to which the Shoah was perpetrated "without our will, and not by our hands," met with serious criticism among Jews, and this criticism was expressed by numerous voices. This shows, once again, how deeply the conviction that it was the Poles who perpetrated the Shoah is rooted in the awareness of many Jews. I would like to use two examples to show how

[w]For more on this, see the extensive documentation in W. Bartoszewski and Z. Lewinówna: *Ten jest z Ojczyzny mojej. Polacy z pomocą Żydom 1939–1945* (*He Is from My Homeland. Poles Helping Jews 1939–1945*), (Krakow, 1969); and M. Grynberg *Księga sprawiedliwych* (*The Book of the Righteous*), (Warsaw, 1993).

[x] *Tygodnik Powszechny*, January 11, 1987.

[y] "Racje polskie i racje żydowskie" (Polish Reasons and Jewish Reasons), *Tygodnik Powszechny*, April 5, 1987.

[z] The documentation of this discussion is included in A. Polonsky, ed., *My Brother's Keeper? Recent Polish Debates on the Holocaust* (Oxford, 1990).

extensively this problem has dominated all discussions about Polish-Jewish relations.

In early February 1988, an international congress exploring the history and culture of Polish Jews convened at Hebrew University in Jerusalem. And, of course, the problem of Polish-Jewish relations during the Shoah became a subject of animated discussion. While the Polish delegation was ready to admit that they "share the guilt for not doing enough to rescue Jews,"[aa] nearly all Jewish participants of the congress believed that the survival of so few Jews was caused not by the situation created by the occupation, but by Polish anti-Semitism.

In May 1994, also in Jerusalem, there was a meeting of the international Liaison Committee for the Vatican's relations with Jews and Jewish organizations. During this meeting, Professor Hans Hermann Henrix described, among other things, ongoing preparations to create a document about the Shoah.[bb] Although the content of his talk was strictly confidential and intended only for those attending the meeting, the next day the *Jerusalem Post* published an editorial with the headline "Germans and Poles Ask Forgiveness for the Shoah."

These and similar voices make Poles feel not simply misunderstood but deeply hurt and offended. After all, they were the ones who—as a nation—became one of the first victims of National Socialism's racist ideology. It is known that before the approval of the plan of the so-called final solution of the Jewish question in 1942, an analogous plan to exterminate Polish intellectuals was already in existence. And Polish intellectuals were the first victims of concentration and death camps. All these facts have been known for a long time, and they are undisputed among historians. Despite this, inexplicably, we are often assigned the role of perpetrators and executioners.

And here, I would also like to personally testify that during the German occupation our sense of shared suffering with Jews was much stronger than our sense of our shared Christian faith with Germans.

Basically, there were only two categories of people at the time: executioners and victims. Jews and Poles were both on the side of the victims, though not in the same way and not on the same scale, as Pope John Paul II

[aa] J. Turowicz, "O sprawach polsko-żydowskich w Jerozolimie" (On Polish-Jewish Matters in Jerusalem), Tygodnik, no. 9, 1988.
[bb] *L'Osservatore Romano* no. 23 (1994); on this topic see also Th. Krapf: "Fortschritte im Jüdisch-Katholischen Verhältnis. Tagung des Verbindungskomitees in Jerusalem" (Progress in Jewish-Catholic Relations. A Conference of the Liaison Committee in Jerusalem), *Neue Zürcher Zeitung,* June 2, 1994.

emphasized during both his meetings with the small Warsaw Jewish community when he said:

> Be sure, dear brothers, that Poles and the Church in Poland, which saw up close the horrific reality of the Holocaust—this ruthless, planned and executed extermination of your people—experienced it in the spirit of profound solidarity with you. What threatened you threatened us as well. In our case, it did not happen to the same extent, there was not enough time for it to happen on the same scale. One could say that you bore this terrible sacrifice of destruction for others, for those who were also to be destroyed.[cc]

In light of this past shared community of suffering, many find today's antagonism between former victims incomprehensible—this antagonism is at the basis of the years-long conflict about the Carmelite nuns' monastery in Oświęcim, and it has left its mark in that context.[15] Jews rightly emphasize the absolutely unique character of their fate and suffering. But this is precisely what Poles often take as disregard for all those who were killed ruthlessly as *Judenhelfer* or *Judenretter* (people who helped or rescued Jews)—in the context of the same laws, principles of the same ideology, and recourse to the same collective responsibility and collective repressions. Those thousands of people who paid for their willingness to help Jews with their lives are the other face of one and the same Shoah. But only a few are willing to admit this today.

And so when Poles want to use Christian means to honor Jewish victims of Nazism alongside their own Polish victims, Jews see it as an attempt to blur or even erase Jewish memory, or as an outright Christian appropriation and Christianization of the Shoah. At one point, spilled blood made Jews and Poles fight the Nazi terror together: after the last joint appeal made by Jews and Poles before the final liquidation of the Warsaw Ghetto, two flags were streaming side by side—the white and red, and the blue and white with the Star of David.[dd] This blood no longer unites—it divides.

And that is the essence of the tragedy of today's relations between the two nations.

[cc] Warsaw, June 14, 1987 and June 9, 1991; "Jews and Judaism in the Church's Documents and John Paul II's Teachings," Warsaw, 1990; see also *Tygodnik Powszechny*, no. 30, 1987, and no. 25, 1991.
[dd] W. Bartoszewski, "Gedanken zu den Jüdisch-Polnischen Beziehungen" (Reflections on Jewish-Polish Relations), in G. Särchen and L. Mehlhorn, as cited previously.

For this reason, the Polish bishops' pastoral letter, which I already cited several times, expresses "authentic sorrow on account of all anti-Semitic incidents, perpetrated by anyone at any time on Polish soil," and states that "all manifestations of anti-Semitism are incompatible with the spirit of the Gospel and—as John Paul II recently emphasized (during the fiftieth anniversary of the outbreak of the Second World War)—'they contradict the Christian vision of human dignity.'" At the same time, however, the letter laments that "the frequent use of the concept of alleged Polish anti-Semitism as a particularly dangerous form of anti-Semitism in general" is "unjust" and "deeply hurtful"—especially when it gets linked to the racist anti-Semitism of the Nazis.

In a 1936 pastoral letter, Cardinal August Hlond already warned against this "racist anti-Semitism, pagan in origins and imported from abroad." And so we must decisively reject insinuations that these two forms of anti-Semitism, fundamentally different in their essence and sources of inspiration, are directly related to each other. Polish anti-Semitism had various causes that were religious, cultural, political, economic, and also ethnic in nature. It was free, however, from racial hatred and contempt that were at the basis of the National Socialist ideology of someone like the Nazi ideologue Alfred Rosenberg.

"If any form of anti-Semitism still remains in the Catholic Church in Poland today,"—writes R. J. Weksler-Waszkinel—"it is a vestige of the past. It is an infection which must be cured patiently but with great determination (infections are always dangerous)" because "anti-Semitism is anti-Christian, and in every case also anti-Catholic."[ee]

One could probably say without exaggeration that there is no other country in the world where the direct effects of the Holocaust are felt as strongly as in Poland (I do not want to speak about Germany now). According to Lech Wałęsa, Poland is "a land stigmatized by Auschwitz," and it will remain this way for a long time. Elie Wiesel also admits: "The Holocaust has become an essential element of Polish awareness." Today, fifty years after the war, the Shoah still does not belong to the past for us in Poland; it is a reality we confront every day. It is "a wound that has not healed, one that keeps bleeding" (Pope John Paul II).

[ee] R. J. Weksler-Waszkinel, "Juifs et Judaisme dans la Reflexion de Jean Paul II" (Jews and Judaism in the Thought of John Paul II), in *Les Oliviers de Saint Isaie* (*Isaiah's Olive Trees*) 4, (1996).

Please forgive me for evoking these painful and bitter events in my lecture today. I did not do it to bring specters from the past back to life or to open wounds that have not healed. Rather, I wanted to clearly show two things: first, what is meant when people talk about Polish-Jewish reconciliation today, and second, that given the existing situation, the reconciliation process should be framed, understood, and—above all—carried out not as a bilateral process between Germans and Jews on the one hand, and Poles and Jews on the other, but as a trilateral process between Germans, Poles, and Jews. This is by no means easy—but important steps in this direction have already been taken.

How to Find a Way Out Together

In his 1988 article, which I already cited several times, Theo Mechtenberg writes:

> If a German talks about Polish-Jewish relations, and thereby about Polish anti-Semitism, on the fiftieth anniversary of the so-called Kristallnacht, he may do it only on the condition that he does not, in any way, equate Polish anti-Semitism with the anti-Semitism of the Third Reich that aimed at the total extermination of the Jewish people. It is not the Polish but the German nation that bears the responsibility for the genocide of the Jews. This should be said very clearly not just to Jews but also to Poles. Because after the "final solution" was planned, death camps for European Jews were moved to Poland (. . .), primarily to the General Government; we, Germans, share the responsibility for the fact that Polish anti-Semitism is made co-responsible for the Shoah for world public opinion today (. . .). This, however, is by no means the full extent of the harm we inflicted on Poles in their country by the Holocaust: besides oppression, humiliation, and persecution, which they experienced themselves, they became morally implicated in the blame for the extermination of the Jews; this is an aspect of Polish-German relations that has been almost entirely neglected so far.[ff]

These words about German-Polish-Jewish relations are very lofty, brave, and heartening—not only for Poles. I bring them up here with gratitude also because they approach most recent Polish-German history from a new perspective, thereby paving the way for reconciliation in and through full truth.

[ff] Th. Mechtenberg, as cited previously.

I owe this gratitude, by the way, not only to Mechtenberg, but also to all those who—like Günter Särchen and professor Stefan Schreiner—entered this path equally courageously already during the communist period when Germany was still divided; they sought to support "the difficult dialogue between estranged siblings"—as indicated by the title of a 1991 special issue of the "Anna Morawska Seminar" devoted to relations between Jews and Poles, to which I referred several times today. The Protestant working group "Kirche und Israel" (Church and Israel) in Hessen Nassau also deserves the same thanks for publishing a series of articles on Christian-Jewish/Jewish-Christian relations in Poland, a series which familiarizes the broader public with this topic.

Willingness and openness in treating difficult and painful problems of the past deserve recognition and gratitude. In his interesting article "W cieniu przeszłości—o dziejach żydowskiej wspólnoty w Polsce od roku 1945" (In the Shadow of the Past—on the History of the Jewish Community in Poland after 1945), professor Stefan Schreiner writes, among other things:

> Our own history forbids us, Germans, to issue appraisals or judgments about the past and present of Polish-Jewish relations. As those seeking Christian-Jewish and German-Jewish dialogue, we should be open to both sides and show understanding toward both sides, or at least show our desire and attempt to understand; this should apply to both the small Jewish community with all its anxieties and problems, and to Poles, who are wrestling with their own history. We should do what we can to help facilitate the removal of obstacles that stand in the way of Polish-Jewish understanding and reconciliation, obstacles for which Germans bear considerable blame.

When I raised this issue during a meeting of representatives of German and Polish Bishops' Conferences in 1990 and pointed to obstacles that hinder Polish-Jewish understanding and reconciliation, my words were (still) received with surprise and astonishment by some of the participants. But today, as a result of ongoing brotherly dialogue and better and deeper mutual understanding, both sides are willing not only to admit and confess their own guilt, however difficult this is, but also to decisively reject wrong attributions of collective guilt and the already mentioned unjustified blaming of others.

While in recent years significant progress has been made in the reconciliation between Germans and Poles, there is still no Polish-Jewish reconciliation. In light of the history which I discussed here, this reconciliation could be reached and realized only through the joint efforts of Poles and Germans. In 1990, the Arbeitsgruppe Fragen des Judentums (Working Group for Questions Concerning Judaism) of the German Bishops' Conference, led by Assistant Bishop Karl Reger (Aachen), and the Polish Bishops' Committee on Dialogue with Judaism, led by Assistant Bishop Stanisław Gądecki (Gniezno), established a joint working group, which meets regularly at least once a year in order to discuss current topics in the broadly defined field of Christian-Jewish relations. In addition, there is also a German-Polish group of the German and Polish Bishops' Conferences, led by Bishop Walter Kasper (Rottenburg) and myself, the archbishop of Gniezno; it focuses on all other problems of German-Polish relations. The joint episcopal letter of the two Bishops' Conferences issued on December 13, 1995, to celebrate the fiftieth anniversary of the end of the Second World War is a result of this group's work.

A similar document called "Germans and Poles—Poles and their Eastern Neighbors. Contributions of Churches to European Reconciliation" was also recently published on the Protestant side by a group that brings together the Polish Ecumenical Council and the Protestant Church in Germany. In the context of unification processes in Europe, it talks about a "reconciled plurality," with emphasis on "the impossibility of European unification without reconciliation."

Unfortunately, an attempt to prepare such a joint Polish-German document for the fiftieth anniversary of the liberation of the Auschwitz concentration camp failed. The only cause was concern that many could take a joint statement by Germans and Poles made on this occasion as admission of Poland's shared guilt for the crimes perpetrated in Auschwitz. But the words spoken in this context by Bishop Karl Lehmann, director of the German Bishops' Conference, were, and remain, completely unambiguous. In a speech given for the fiftieth anniversary of "the liberation of prisoners of the Auschwitz-Birkenau concentration camp on January 27, 1945," broadcast on Polish Radio on January 27, 1995, Bishop Lehman said, among other things:

> The National Socialist regime also stained another country, which it took over by force, by its atrocities. Many Jews lived in Poland. There was the desire to hide death camps in Poland, which was situated some distance away from the center of Eastern Europe. It is beyond doubt, however, that these crimes were planned in Germany, and Germans are to blame for them. There should be no suspicions toward Poland here, since Poland was incapable of halting the diabolical machine of destruction in its lands.

> Although today's Germans are not the perpetrators of these crimes, and although many things will remain incomprehensible to future generations, we do not wish to sidestep the responsibility that flows from the effects of these atrocities. We ask the Polish nation to forgive us for the many victims among its own ranks, and for the dishonor that cast its shadow also on this country, where these crimes were committed. We know that we cannot right everything that was done.[gg]

And a statement made by German bishops for the same occasion on January 23, 1995 also adds: "At the same time, this day reminds us of the fact that Auschwitz also has its place in the history of Polish suffering and it burdens relations between Poles and Germans."[hh]

Brave and certainly also painful words, like those I just cited, mean a lot to Poles. They are an important step toward "liberation and reconciliation through truth," and they are also an invaluable contribution not only to Polish-German reconciliation but precisely to Polish-Jewish reconciliation, which can take place only in full truth and—I repeat—requires the involvement of the Germans.

Reconciliation is always simultaneously a process of teaching and learning. It is a constant give and take, a readiness to forgive and accept forgiveness. In the realm of German-Polish reconciliation a great turning point has taken place in this regard. "German-Polish relations have clearly improved in recent times (. . .) but full German-Polish reconciliation"—as Bishop Karl Reger said—"can be reached only when together we deal with relations between Christians and Jews in Poland."[ii]

Polish-German reconciliation is much easier for two reasons. As Christians, we share the belief that "we were reconciled to [God] through the death of his Son" (Romans 5:10, NIV). And besides, in this context, the victim and the perpetrator were unambiguously clear. The Christian perspective is not there when it comes to reconciliation with Jews. The extermination of Jews during the Nazi period is seen in exclusively Polish-Jewish categories,

---

[gg] Citation from the original, which was graciously made available to me by the office of the episcopal curia in Mainz; the broadcast Polish version was published in *Maqom. Biuletyn Informacyjny IDKJ* (*Maqom. Information Bulletin of the Institute for Catholic-Jewish Dialogue*), 1 (1996).

[hh] "Słowo biskupów niemieckich w wwiązku z 50. rocznicą wyzwolenia obozu zagłady Auschwitz-Birkenau" (German Bishops' Statement on the Fiftieth Anniversary of the Liberation of the Auschwitz-Birkenau Death Camp), *Maqom. Biuletyn Informacyjny IDKJ* (*Maqom. Information Bulletin of the Institute for Catholic-Jewish Dialogue*), 1, 1996; see also *KNA–Informationsdienst* (*Catholic News Agency Information Service*), January 26, 1995.

[ii] Interview for *KNA–Informationsdienst* (*Catholic News Agency Information Service*) January 13, 1994.

and this makes the reconciliation process much more difficult. For Poles, in turn, memory of the wrongs and crimes of the communist regime, which included many people with Jewish roots in its ranks (commonly simply referred to as Jews) is still very fresh, and the cliché association of Jews with communism (Judeo-Bolshevism), which I already mentioned, is still deeply entrenched; it places a significant burden on mutual relations. Władysław Bartoszewski is right when he says: "Poles feel that they are completely wrongly perceived when they are made responsible for mass murders in which they themselves were also victims. Similarly, Jews are offended when the crimes of Stalinist police are attributed to them only because Jews held a few of the high-ranking positions in the party's terror machine."[ii]

Everything I said here today, sometimes in necessarily abbreviated form, shows how complex, painful, and charged Polish-Jewish relations have been historically, and continue to be today. It is therefore particularly heartening to see that despite this, the difficult "dialogue between estranged siblings" keeps bringing gradual effects and shows certain signs of progress that warrant hope.

On October 6, 1996, during a celebration of the quadricentennial of the "Colloquim Charitativum" in Toruń, there was a seminar entitled "Brotherly Conversation between Christians and Jews," and it was attended by Jews, Germans, and Poles. The words "brotherly conversation" were not simply a polite expression but part of an authentic reality experienced there. All participants were honestly trying to support this brotherly conversation and serve the multilateral process of reconciliation, which poses equally great demands to all sides. The great extent of mutual understanding and the serious joint involvement and determination present in this conversation are—despite all the difficulties that still arise on the path to reconciliation—a good and heartening sign that the new Europe's better future will be free from hatred and alienation. Here, where—as Elie Wiesel put it—"hope had its terminus," despite everything that happened and everything that still divides us, we have to testify, ceaselessly and together, that "humanity is worthy of hope."[16]

Editors' Notes

1. Excerpts from this talk are available in English at http://www.notredamedesion.org/en/dialogue_docs.php?a=3b&id=20.

[ii] W. Bartoszewski, as cited above.

2. See   http://www.vatican.va/archive/hist_councils/ii_vatican_council/docu-
   ments/vat-ii_decl_19651028_nostra-aetate_en.html.

3. Theo Mechtenberg (b. 1928) is a German Catholic theologian who spent much
   time in Poland, maintained a relationship with the weekly *Tygodnik Powszechny*
   in the 1960s, and brought groups of German youth to Poland to visit sites of
   Nazi crimes and perform community service work.

4. Byron L. Sherwin, *Duchowe dziedzictwo Żydów polskich* (Oficyna Wydawnicza
   Vocatio, 1995), 53. This original edition was expanded and updated, and
   appeared in English as *Sparks Amidst the Ashes: The Spiritual Legacy of Polish
   Jewry* (Oxford University Press, 1997). Muszyński used the Polish version of
   Byron's text in his talk, and since the two versions are not identical, we could
   not locate his exact quotes in the OUP edition; they are translated from Polish.

5. Available in English translation published by Central European University
   Press in 2003.

6. The translation of the beginning of the proverb follows the Hebrew-English
   Tanakh, 2nd Edition (Jewish Publication Society, 1999).

7. The Khmelnytsky Uprising and the associated pogroms are described in
   Editors' note 6 of the first chapter in this volume.

8. This is one of at least three possible interpretations of Poland's Hebrew name.
   Gershon Hundert translates Polin as "dwell here," while another tradition parses
   Polania (the other Hebrew word for Poland) as Poh lan Yah—"Here dwells the
   Lord," see Gershon Hundert, *Jews in Poland-Lithuania in the Eighteenth Century*
   (University of California Press, 2006), 7–8.

9. Translation from *Stranger in Our Midst: Images of the Jew in Polish Literature*,
   Harold B. Segel, ed. (Cornell University Press, 1996), 363.

10. We discuss these campaigns in "Anti-Semitism in the Polish People's Republic"
    in the Introduction.

11. See this quote in Jerzy Andrzejewski's essay "The Problem of Polish Anti-
    Semitism" in this volume on page 98.

12. Władysław Bartoszewski (1922–2015) was a Polish politician, diplomat, activ-
    ist, journalist, and historian. During the Second World War, he fought in the
    Home Army (AK) and was among the founding members of the Warsaw-
    based Council to Aid Jews (Żegota); he is honored at Yad Vashem as one of the
    "Righteous among Nations." After 1989, he served various political functions
    and worked on behalf of improving Polish–Israeli relations.

13. See Jan Błoński's essay "The Poor Poles Look at the Ghetto" in this volume on
    pages 273–285.

14. Also see Turowicz's essay "Anti-Semitism" in this volume on pages 162–169.

15. For a description of this conflict, please see the Editors' Introduction to Hanna
    Świda-Zięba's essay "The Disgrace of Indifference" in this volume on pages
    313–314.

16. As cited by Lech Wałęsa in *The Struggle and the Triumph: An Autobiography*
    (Arcade 1994), 132.

19

The Disgrace of Indifference

HANNA ŚWIDA-ZIEMBA

Editors' Introduction

Hanna Świda-Ziemba (1930–2012) was a sociologist and member of the Presidium of the Polish Academy of Sciences. Born in Vilnius (which was then in the territory of the Second Republic of Poland), she studied sociology in Łódź. She taught at the University of Warsaw and participated in the March 1968 protests there. In the 1980s, she became a Solidarity activist and was imprisoned for a few days when General Jaruzelski introduced martial law in 1981. Between 1991 and 1993 she was a member of the State Tribunal of the Republic of Poland. In her research, she was especially interested in the analysis of totalitarian systems and in the sociopolitical attitudes of successive generations of Polish youth. She authored the best available analysis of the attitudes of her generation toward Stalinism and "the thaw"—*Stalinizm i społeczeństwo polskie* (*Stalinism and Polish Society*, 1991).

The essay reproduced here was first published in the daily *Gazeta Wyborcza* in Warsaw, on August 17, 1998. It was Świda-Ziemba's reaction to the persistent conflict about the erection of crosses near the Auschwitz death camp. In 1983, a Carmelite monastery was built in the immediate vicinity of the extermination camp in Auschwitz, and the local priest soon insisted on erecting crosses there to commemorate Polish victims of Nazism. Despite sharp protests from Jewish organizations around the world, the crosses were erected and the conflict remained unresolved for over fifteen years. After the Polish government announced in February 1998 that the crosses would be

removed, fundamentalist Catholic groups staged several months of aggres-
sive protests, which included vigils, crude anti-Semitic statements, hunger
strikes, and the erection of more crosses. Despite these protests, in late 1998
the government ordered the removal of all but one cross, and this was done
in May 1999. The site of the conflict became known as Żwirowisko, from
the Polish word *żwir* (gravel) around the walls of Auschwitz.[1]

The conflict about the cross at Żwirowisko in Oświęcim is not, in its essence, religious. It concerns a place that is the grounds of a terrible concentration camp for Poles, and the grounds of the Holocaust for Jews. This conflict is entangled with events from the Second World War and the subsequent fate of Jews in Poland.

Evaluating it precisely from this perspective, I want to defend the claim that Jews should be granted primary rights to their symbol of the Holocaust—even though many Poles also perished in this place.

By a decree of history, the Holocaust took place mostly on Polish soil. Poland is also the location of an immense cemetery of Jewish victims. What is most important, however, is that during the war, Polish and Jewish tragedies took place SIDE BY SIDE, and—despite all Polish suffering—the situation of the two nations was not symmetrical: we, Poles, were in a privileged position. I think that this fact, a consequence of Hitler's politics, was the first ember of contemporary Polish-Jewish misunderstandings, including those expressed in the Oświęcim conflict.

Wartime Ethics

I think that Jews, as well as some Poles, are not right when they identify the real "culpability" of the Poles with their characteristic indifference in the face of the Holocaust, and with their fears about providing help. Experiences which befell Poles during the Second World War (or perhaps war experiences in general) hugely numb one's sensitivity to crimes, cataclysms, and other people's tragedies. Often even to one's own tragedies. Exposure to danger, helplessness, and the body's psychological self-defense are at the source of this numbing. A characteristic indifference tends to become a condition of survival in abnormal situations.

One should also remember that the attitude designated by the term "indifference" today concerned not only the fate of Jews but also of Poles— who were imprisoned, executed by firing squads, and deported to Russia. It extended to one's own fate and the fate of one's closest relatives. After a brief period of shock and sorrow, there came a psychologically understandable process of pushing experiences out of consciousness; this enabled people to maintain psychological balance—however false and shaky—and the readiness to fight for survival.

Let me resort to my own reminiscences. When the war broke out, I was not quite nine, and when it ended—barely fourteen. But war experiences accelerate the process of growing up, and they greatly sharpen one's sense of observation. In Vilnius, where I was born and where I spent nearly the entire war, the Holocaust took place almost under our very eyes. The Ghetto was liquidated right outside the city, in the Ponary Forest. This was a shock to people I knew at the time—they were not indifferent. They talked about it, some women wept. But the shock did not stop everyday life from going on. It did not even stop birthday parties. After a few weeks, events became characteristically blurred; one no longer returned to the subject. But at that time people reacted similarly to Polish tragedies, even collective ones—such as the great transport of people deported to Russia, executions of hostages, and mass arrests.

Sometimes war triggers impulses of surprising solidarity—this happens when it is possible to offer help, and especially when it does not threaten one's own existence. But when there is actual danger or helplessness, war neutralizes sensitivity and creates attitudes of harsh inner ruthlessness.

It should therefore not be surprising that (given the size of the population) relatively few Poles participated directly in rescuing Jews. Natural fear for one's own life and the life of one's family intervened into people's attitudes and behaviors. In human collectivities, typically only a small minority of people are brave and heroic. This extraordinary attitude was displayed by Poles who altruistically rescued Jews and put their own life on the line. And again—if one takes into account what I just said—their number was not that small.

I think that awareness of these realities causes Poles to treat accusations of "co-responsibility" during the Holocaust—made in some Jewish circles—as unjustly untrue or as outright calumny; and this gives fresh impetus to anti-Semitic attitudes.

The anti-Polonism and grudges, which some Jews bear against Poles, however, do not arise exclusively from "innocent" Polish behaviors. During the war, there also appeared behaviors where culpability was grave—some Poles, for example, preyed on the Jewish tragedy by treating it as occasion to enrich themselves. And I am not talking about the *schmaltzovniks* (blackmailers); such hyenas function in every community, and they become visible in borderline situations. As a matter of fact, Polish *schmaltzovniks* sought to profit by turning in to the Germans not only Jews but also members of the Polish underground.

I am, however, thinking about citizens who derived benefits from helping Jews.

I am also thinking about certain right-wing underground groups, whose anti-Semitic attitudes were not extinguished even by the Holocaust. And about the National Armed Forces (NSZ).[2] During the war, people in my parents' circles used to say with horror—so it is not just communist propaganda—that members of the National Armed Forces were murdering Jews who were hiding in the woods.

In light of these circumstances, it becomes psychologically easier to understand that from the point of view of the Jews—who were being so ruthlessly exterminated—even natural and "innocent" Polish attitudes could have appeared as ruthlessness and cruelty. In her moving book *Zagłada i pamięć* (*Holocaust and Memory*), Barbara Engelking writes:

> Jews expected nothing but persecution, insults, and terror from Germans. They wanted to see Poles, however, as companions, or fellow citizens united against oppression which affected both groups. They thought that they and the Poles were on the same side of the barricades, and expected empathy and solidarity.

The clash between these expectations and reality must have brought feelings of sorrow, disappointment, anger, and even aggression—and these could have given rise to the anti-Polonism found in certain Jewish circles today.

The Uniqueness of the Holocaust

I nevertheless believe that the fundamental source of contemporary conflicts and misunderstandings lies in the fact that—to this day—most Poles have not integrated the essence of the Holocaust into their awareness; it has not become a traumatic shock that encourages reflection and shapes attitudes and behaviors.

Years ago, I was painfully surprised by this. Today, I believe there are reasons that explain it to an extent. Poles had tragic experiences of their own suffering behind them, and many families were affected. There was also the traumatic experience of the end of the war, which many could have perceived as an irrevocable defeat that resulted from "abandonment" by powerful allies; a defeat—despite so many sacrifices. In addition, for many, the period between 1944 and 1955 did not bring an end to danger and suffering.

Communities preoccupied with their own tragedies are typically not inclined to reflect about the situation and experiences of "others" who are not directly involved in their group's tragedy at the moment—even if those "others" are citizens of the same country, acquaintances, or neighbors. In addition, there were prewar Polish-Jewish economic, cultural, and religious conflicts, and prewar Polish anti-Semitism, which was fueled with arguments from Stalin's postwar politics. But we should note that the role played by Jews in postwar Poland was similar to that played by Turks in Bulgaria, or Poles in the Republic of Lithuania.

All this notwithstanding, today—after so many years, in a free country—nothing excuses the attitudes of many Poles toward Jews. Nothing excuses that self-important, egocentric blindness regarding the Holocaust, a blindness we also encountered in the Oświęcim conflict.

And this is why I would like to encourage at least a few people to engage in reflection that will make it possible to think differently about both relations with Jews, and the conflict about the cross.

What was the Holocaust? Without question—even though many terrible mass-scale crimes have been perpetrated in the human world—it was a unique and extraordinary crime. It was the scandal of twentieth-century Europe. It was incomparable.

And I am not just talking about the number of victims (perhaps the number is comparable to something), but about the PRINCIPLE according to which the crime was perpetrated. A principle which weighed on the experiences of those who perished, the awareness of those who survived, and the awareness of others whose nationality or roots are Jewish and whom the Holocaust bypassed because of where they lived or when they were born.

It is important to emphasize that Jews were not only massacred but also—and this is essential—stripped of their humanity. "The final solution of the Jewish question" was treated like an "urban rat extermination project." It was not an act of crushing real or imagined enemies, it was not a result of either war or revolution, nor was it revenge in the context of a massive battle. The extermination of Jews ("racially" understood) was perpetrated "in cold blood," systematically, with the use of all modern technological means. The act of stripping Jews of their humanity was expressed in the "equality" of everyone who had "a drop of Jewish blood" in their veins. Their nationality did not matter, neither did their beliefs or their relationship to religion; it made no difference whether they were wise or foolish, evil or noble; their worldviews, attitudes, judgments, lifestyle, age, and gender

were unimportant. Everything that makes us human—our biological existence, our cultural background, and our ability to make SUBJECTIVE
CHOICES, which is the very essence of our humanity—was invalidated.

In this sense, defense was not an option. "Jewishness" was tracked down
the way animals are tracked by hunters in the forest, but more ruthlessly.
The aim was to wipe out a "nation," all the way to the last person who carried that contaminated "drop of blood," even if it came from most distant
forefathers. Once someone was defined as a "Jew" he was not a man but an
"insect" in the eyes of the authorities.

All this took place in the very heart of western civilization, in Christian
Europe, while the top hierarchs of the Catholic Church were silent.

What were the feelings of those who found themselves in this situation, people who were condemned and exterminated one after another?
Did many Poles attempt to use their imagination to reproduce the psychological state of those who were perishing, and those few who survived
(thanks to Polish help, I'll grant it), but who lived with a constant sense of
danger throughout the war years? People who were treated like insects—
people endowed with consciousness, sensitivity, intelligence, imagination,
dignity. . . .

A moment of reflection about the fate of our fellow citizens would
make it possible to understand that in comparison to Jews—despite all our
suffering—we were a very privileged nation. We were persecuted but still
considered human. We could make choices: heroism in the fight against the
occupier, attempts to secure physical survival, or even villainy and betrayal.
To a large extent, our fate and our exposure to danger depended on our
choices.

Barbara Engelking clearly conveys this asymmetry in the situation of
Poles and Jews: "Poles who carried out their war against Germans did not
need Jews in this war. When Jews wanted to avoid sure death at the hands
of the Germans, however, they could not manage without Poles. They were
sentenced to the Poles' brotherly love, compassion, decency, hatred, indifference, or greed." And further down: "For Jews—generally speaking—the
war did not bring the experience of a positive sense of community. Their
war (. . .) was a cursed time. Jews did not die for the Fatherland. (. . .) For
what then? In fact, they did not even die—they were killed."

The asymmetry of our experiences also manifested itself in the asymmetry of the situation of the Poles who rescued Jews—and the Jews who were
rescued. Poles knew that if they risked their lives, it was because they had

made a heroic choice. When they felt fear, they could simultaneously have a sense of moral satisfaction because they were offering help to another human being. A hiding Jew necessarily remained in the position of a "dependent debtor." His was not a death for honorable moral choices; it was the death of an animal which had been tracked down, and which, by the very fact of "biologically" being himself, also put others in danger. In other words—the very possibility of rescuing Jews, regardless of whether anyone took advantage of it—was one of the signs of our privileged position.

Two Childhoods

If anyone finds the thesis proposed here iconoclastic or difficult to grasp, he should read Michał Głowiński's recently published book *Czarne sezony* (*The Black Seasons*).[3] It was only after many years that the author, a professor at the Literary Studies Institute of the Polish Academy of Sciences, a man of rare wisdom, humility, detachment, and objectivity, mustered the will to write a book in which he shows his wartime experiences—the experiences of a Jewish child. He recreates this history in fragments, as it was preserved in his memory. He does it objectively, parsimoniously, using unpretentious, beautiful language.

We learn about the experiences of a single Jewish child, and this child— let us remember—is privileged in relation to the whole nation because Głowiński's family was able to make it to the "Aryan" side and survive. He himself was ultimately rescued by nuns from Our Lady of Turkowice monastery; they provided refuge to and rescued over thirty Jewish children.

I recommend this book, above all, to those who were children during the occupation and the war. It was thanks to this book that I was able to experience that ASYMMETRY of Polish and Jewish fate, with much greater clarity than during the war. Four years older than the author, I was among those Polish children who were not touched by the worst cataclysms. My entire immediate family survived; no one was arrested or deported, and I was under my mother's care the entire time.

On the other hand, however, I was a natural participant in the Polish fate. I survived bombings, street fighting, the death of friends and relatives. I lived through expulsion from our apartment and, after which we were thrust into horrible conditions; I was worried about my father, who disappeared after the 1939 offensive, and who then had to hide (he joined the resistance).

I knew hunger; I was so undernourished that I suffered a deadly illness. The house where we lived burned down together with all our belongings. In the end—like all Vilnius intellectuals who did not want to remain in the USSR—I had to leave my native city. I knew the taste of life-threatening situations, the fear of being arrested and having my father arrested; I knew adversity, humiliation, and hunger.

And yet, as I was reading *The Black Seasons*, I once again experienced my immense privilege in comparison to Jewish children. During the entire war I held my head high. Like other children, I was carefree as I played, I did not have to shudder at the thought of being tracked down and annihilated because of my background; I did not have to deny my identity. I could dream about fighting the enemy and realize these dreams in ways fit for a child. And I could—also in my childish ways—help Jews.

To Understand that Horror

Polish-Jewish conflicts can be grasped in a variety of ways. But the drastic difference between our experiences, which unfolded SIDE BY SIDE, in the same place—a difference of existential importance—makes it necessary to approach this problem from the perspective of axiology.

Even though I recognize that the awareness of the drama of war, together with its tragic and dreadful dimension of the Holocaust, was too much to bear, I also believe that after the war it was the moral responsibility of the Poles to offer kindness and help to surviving Jews, in order to compensate for the fact that the wartime situations of the two groups were so different, for that fact that, consumed by our own suffering and exposure to danger, we were unable to help those who died. For the fact is that our countrymen sometimes committed heinous deeds.

That moral imperative also flows from our belonging to a single human family, and the denial of human attributes to one nation is a way of dishonoring humanity as such.

Had we developed an inner understanding of the essence of the Holocaust right after the war, Polish-Jewish relations, I think, would have evolved differently. First, we would have been able to soberly asses the role played by Jews during the era of Stalinist terror. We would have noticed that many Poles also participated in the apparatus of violence, and that there were many noble and wise Jews among us who had nothing to do with communism, and thus emphatically nothing to do with the apparatus of terror.

And thus in the first years after the war, we would not have irrationally and unfairly transferred our attitudes toward the terror apparatus onto our attitudes toward Jews.

Second, perhaps the so-called folk anti-Semitism would not have made such a forceful appearance. It made itself known in the Pogrom in Kielce (even if it was provoked, a provocation is possible only when there already are "potential attitudes" among the provoked); it was partially present in 1956, and finally in 1968. It is true that in March of 1968 we were dealing with "institutional" anti-Semitism of the Polish Communist Party (PZPR), but, unfortunately, it resonated with a significant part of our society.

Let us suppose, however, that a tangle of external causes bound Poles and Jews into a knot of mutual misunderstandings and conflicts, and that Poles' various behaviors toward Jews can be ascribed to the disorienting and destructive influence of communism. But today we live in a free country. And since we are settling various kinds of accounts, this could also be the time for deep and honest reflection about this issue. Meanwhile, it is precisely today that we see "gas the Jews" graffiti, that certain priests incorporate anti-Semitic themes into their sermons (the example of Reverend Henryk Jankowski[4] is well known), the National Armed Forces are honored, anti-Semitic texts appear in the streets and in private conversations, and openly anti-Semitic political parties are being formed. It is today, finally, that the conflict around Auschwitz has broken out.

Even if we assume that only a minority of the population are involved in these behaviors, they are nonetheless taking place at a time when Poland is free. It is symptomatic that many Poles—who are certainly no anti-Semites themselves—look upon all this with indifference. These incidents are seen as "folklore": nonthreatening and unimportant, not deserving attention. Most members of the Catholic Church hierarchy, even if their own attitudes are not anti-Semitic, are reacting to these phenomena with obstructive guardedness. In a word, the atmosphere in Poland feels as if the Holocaust never took place on our soil.

In my opinion, this is testimony to the fact that its inhuman terror has still not been processed by the vast majority of Poles. It does not even occur to them that for those who survived—as well as for Jews and people with Jewish backgrounds who were not directly affected by the Holocaust but whose psyche is marked by this terror—every sign of anti-Semitism brings back the time of the Holocaust.

Let me bring up Głowiński's book once again. The author recalls a post-war Polish school and a priest who, during religion classes, repeated that all Jews, with no exception and for all generations, are responsible for crucifying Christ. Influenced by these teachings, two classmates beat up young Michał. His reaction is very characteristic:

> It was one of those situations when I felt that my world was collapsing, that something was happening to deprive the world of sense, and to direct it in its entirety against me. It was a great shock (. . .) in a deeper sense, because that sudden attack allowed me to see, or so I thought, that I would always be alien-ated, that neither in Pruszków nor anywhere else would I ever find a place for myself. I felt the shock as an extension of the occupation, which I still carried inside myself.[5]

We can regard Głowiński's experiences from this period as a very typical example of the ways in which people affected by the Holocaust react to all, even incidental, manifestations of anti-Semitism. And that is why I believe that if Poles truly understood and inwardly experienced the terror of the Jewish fate, they would become painfully sensitized to all symptoms of anti-Semitism—and they would react sharply, immediately, and decisively. The lack of such reactions testifies to what I already said: even though our expe-riences unfolded side by side, on the same land, most Poles never under-stood the terror of the Holocaust.

A Cross that Appropriates

This can be seen most clearly and most drastically in the conflict about the cross at Żwirowisko. But that conflict concerns the pivotal territory of the Holocaust—the main site of the Shoah. Moreover, it concerns a place that is symbolic in a certain sense—it was precisely here that extermination was carried out in a "cold" and "pure" manner, with the use of modern technology so that millions of people could be annihilated at the lowest possible cost, without leaving any traces. The most inhuman essence of the Holocaust was expressed in this territory.

The presence of Polish victims at Auschwitz—and their number was incomparably smaller—can be emphasized discreetly. In a way that does not hurt the feelings of a people who were dealt such an inhuman blow during the war. This is the only thing that we, as a society, can do for Jews today—in the name of the memory of the Holocaust.

This is why, even though I try to somehow explain certain Polish behaviors, in this case I cannot find any explanation.

And I am not thinking about the emotionally and mentally primitive fanatics dedicated to "the defense of the cross." People with such predispositions can be found in any society. But today the conflict has taken on a broader and more general character. This is because for quite a while now the government has consistently kept "washing its hands"—and thereby refusing to come to the defense of the Holocaust victims. For quite a long time, the Church has not taken the floor. Recently, the top Church official, Cardinal Józef Glemp, declared that the huge cross must remain at Żwirowisko.

Moreover, Jews who demand that the cross be moved to a different place are designated as "extremists." In "enlightened" circles it is rather common to claim that equally rightful claims of the two sides are at odds here, and a "peaceable" compromise should be sought, in the spirit of reconciliation and mutual respect for religious symbols. And in the end, people pose a question that is "naïve" in its blindness and egocentricity: why are Jews bothered by a cross—a symbol of love and peace?

This question is the quintessential expression of group egoism that disregards all points of view other than its own.

The cross is a symbol of love and peace only for Christian religions. For nonbelievers and members of other religious communities it is simply a sacred sign of one specific religion—nothing more. For Jews, its dominant presence in Auschwitz can rightfully also arouse negative associations.

And it is not important to "inquire" whether these associations are right or fully justified from the Christian (Polish Catholic) point of view. Because respect for mourning the Holocaust victims is tantamount to unconditional acceptance of that interpretation of Auschwitz symbols which Jews themselves embrace. It is a great monument to their people's martyrdom, and basic sensitivity should convince us to respect their feelings, convictions, and beliefs. After all these years, do we really not understand what Jews—our fellow citizens—went through?

There is one more very important factor. After the watershed of 1989,[6] the behaviors of certain Polish Catholics have caused the cross to cease being simply a religious symbol. It has become a sign of "appropriation" of a territory by a specific group, a signal that all who are different are second-class citizens in this territory—or basically unwanted intruders. And this is precisely the signal given by the enormous cross at Żwirowisko, a cross so large it can be seen from afar, and dominates over the town of Oświęcim. It insults Holocaust victims and people who want to honor them.

The fact that the conflict focuses on the size of the cross is tangible proof of the fact that precisely a signal of "appropriation" is at stake here. In its religious dimension, the cross is always one and the same symbol, regardless of size. Thus if the fight is about the cross being enormous—and about placing many other enormous crosses there—then it is doubtless not about honoring the Catholic victims of murder, but about emphasizing that Auschwitz, which is located in Poland, is primarily a "Polish cemetery," that other victims are unimportant, and the feelings and beliefs of those who want to honor them are of no concern to us. The presence of the cross is to testify that for Poles the Holocaust is a marginal issue of secondary importance. The Holocaust did not concern us—it concerned "them."

How can one speak about the claims of "both sides" and a measured compromise in this context? One could claim instead that the indifference of Poles—and the indifference of the Polish government and the Catholic Church—to the rightful claims that Jews have in this conflict becomes identical to inhuman indifference to the Holocaust. This is what I see as our disgrace—and it cannot be erased.

I wrote this article with great difficulty. It concerns a problem which moves me deeply, and which is the source of shame and pain. The tragedy of the Holocaust cannot be expressed in words. Silence is more appropriate. But the situation has nonetheless forced me to speak. I wanted to bear witness to the fact that this way of viewing the Oświęcim conflict is also possible on the Polish side.

I am sure that there are many more people who think as I do. Krzysztof Śliwiński's stance and the statement made by Father Musiał testify to this. Others are silent. Perhaps because they are afraid that an awkward expression can be seen as profanation of the cross? Or perhaps because it is immensely difficult to find words to express an obvious truth, a truth that evokes events so tragic that they defy understanding.

Editors' Notes

1. For an analysis of this conflict and its implications, see, for example, Genevieve Zubrzycki, *The Crosses at Auschwitz: Nationalism and Religion in Post-Communist Poland* (University of Chicago Press, 2006).

2. The National Armed Forces (NSZ) are discussed in "Poles and Jews during the Holocaust" in the Introduction to this volume.

3. Głowiński's book *Czarne sezony* is available in Marci Shore's translation: Michał Głowiński, *The Black Seasons* (Northwestern University Press, 2005).

4. We discuss an example of Rev. Jankowski's anti-Semitic statements in the Introduction.

5. Głowiński, *The Black Seasons*, 150.

6. We provide a brief overview of the 1980s and the fall of communism in Poland in the Introduction.

20

The Holocaust

MARIA JANION

Editors' Introduction

Maria Janion (b. 1926) is a historian of literature and ideas. Born in the town of Mońki in northeastern Poland, she spent the Second World War in Vilnius, where she was an underground courier of the Polish Scouting Association. She studied Polish literature in Łódź and began publishing in the progovernment weekly *Kuźnica* (*The Forge*) in 1947. She joined the Communist Party (PZPR) in 1949 and taught literature first at the University of Warsaw and later in Gdańsk; over the decades, she has also worked with the Polish Academy of Sciences. In Gdańsk, she was popular among students willing to question the communist government, and she was therefore removed from her teaching post in 1968. She returned to teaching at the newly formed Gdańsk University in 1973 and became involved in democratic opposition initiatives in the 1970s, which led to her expulsion from the Communist Party in 1979. Over time, Janion moved from her early involvement with Marxism to left-leaning liberal views, always with an emphasis on individual liberty. Since 1990 she has been living and teaching in Warsaw.

In her research, Janion is most interested in the Polish Romantic tradition and is one of the foremost authorities on the subject. Her most important books include *Romantyzm i historia* (*Romanticism and History*, 1978, coauthored with Maria Żmigrodzka) and *Do Europy tak, ale razem z naszymi umarłymi* (*Let Us Join Europe but Let Us Bring Our Departed*, 2000). The essay reproduced here was originally published as an appendix in Janion's book *Bohater, spisek, śmierć. Wykłady żydowskie* (*Hero, Plot, Death: Jewish Lectures*), (Wydawnictwo WAB, 2009).

Even if we are not always aware of this, the Holocaust determines the entire contemporary system of culture and all the questions and dilemmas of modernity. In Poland, in many disciplines there is still too little thinking that draws conclusions from the Holocaust, which—by a terrible decree of history—took place primarily "on Polish soil."

> The Holocaust was a unique phenomenon. From time immemorial in the history of the world, imperial wars were waged and struggles against different types of political systems were undertaken. At no other point in modern history, however, was there such a forceful explosion of hatred and destruction. What is meant here is not an abstraction or a metaphor, but destruction in the literal sense of the word. The goal of the Nazis was to exterminate an entire nation by means of starvation, executions, gassing, and burning. (. . .) An entire culture was to disappear from the face of the Earth.

This is why there is strong resistance against all attempts to "relativize or trivialize the Holocaust, or give it a semblance of 'normality' by drawing analogies to the actions of other dictators."[a]

The uniqueness of the Holocaust forces us to work on revising many convictions. We are still too burdened by nineteenth-century heroic-martyrological schemas, stereotypes of "honorable" and "disgraceful" death, "heroic" and "unheroic" attitudes, and so on. It seems that perennial humanist questions, and humanist reflection on lying in particular, call on us to bring up the Holocaust—the facts and their interpretations. This is the only way to fulfill Zygmunt Bauman's injunction to introduce conclusions drawn from the Holocaust into the mainstream of our study of modernity.[b]

"Honorable" and "Disgraceful" Death

> No path led from death in Auschwitz to *Death in Venice*.
>
> —Jean Améry

A wonderful story ("O wojnie wielkich Niemiec z Żydami Warszawy" (On Great Germany's War against Warsaw's Jews) was penned by Stefan Ernest,

---

[a] N. Orland, "Żydzi w obliczu nazizmu" (Jews in the Face of Nazism), in *Nowy Leksykon Judaistyczny* (*The New Jewish Lexicon*), trans. S. Lisiecka, Z. Rybicka, and E. Ptaszyńska-Sadowska (Warsaw, 2007). German original: J. H. Schoeps, ed., *Neue Lexicon des Judentums* (München: Bertelsmann Lexicon Verlag, 1992).
[b] Zygmunt Bauman, *Modernity and the Holocaust* (Cornell University Press, 1989; reprint 2001).

about whom we still do not know much, when he was hiding in Warsaw's Jewish district in May 1943. This report, written right after the defeat of the Ghetto Uprising, which the author observed from hiding, drastically poses a problem that weaves its way through hundreds of memoirs, novels, and studies: the juxtaposition between the passive attitude of most of the exterminated Jews ("like sheep going to the slaughter") and the active resistance of the Uprising participants, who saved, as many stressed, the honor of a nation which was being massacred with impunity. Comments collected by the historian Paweł Szapiro from the other side—the Polish underground press[c]—also emphasize the contrast between the masses who passively went to their death and the Uprising heroes. "Under the ruins lie those who did not want to give themselves over to the executioners without resistance." They died "choosing a fate more beautiful than what became the lot of their compatriots who were deported to murder depots in Treblinka or Bełżec. They died like fighting men, like men inspired by that Warsaw spirit, which always called on the capital's citizens to walk the path of honor and struggle."[d] Elsewhere, praises were sung for those who "preferred a soldier's death to a slave's death," people who truly responded to the call to "die with honor." A pathetic article in *Prawda Młodych* (an organ of the Front for National Revival [FON]), published in April–May 1943, offered a characteristic interpretation—streaked with anti-Semitic prejudice—of Jewish armed resistance in the Ghetto when it juxtaposed the fighters against the disdainfully styled Jewish masses:

> For a year now, with indignation and pity, Polish society has been watching a terrible crime that is being perpetrated without any attempt at resistance on the part of the murdered. Tens of thousands of Jews went passively to gas chambers and execution line-ups, despicably bowing and scraping before the enemy. And here, suddenly, the very same Jewish people take up arms. The very same nation fights heroically.

In this, one can hear tones of anti-Semitic propaganda which often resorted to comparisons between Jews and insects: they are fighting "to die like people, not like vermin." What follows is a stereotyped description of the low, cowardly, and treacherous character of Jews: "For the first time in eighteen

[c] In a conversation I had with Paweł Szapiro, he mentioned the possibility that Ernest was inspired by Polish underground journalism from this period.
[d] "Wojna żydowsko-niemiecka, polska prasa konspiracyjna 1943–1944 o powstaniu w getcie Warszawy" (The Jewish-German War. Polish Underground Press about the Warsaw Ghetto Uprising, 1943–1944), selection and editing by P. Szapiro (London, 1992).

centuries they have awakened from degradation." During these eighteen centuries Jews were parasites on the bodies of European nations. "They fought against everyone, but only by treachery, never openly, and never bearing arms. (. . .) They seemed not to participate in anything. Jewish cowardice has become proverbial. They lost their human dignity." These are harsh and terrible words. Praise for taking up arms borders on contempt for the defenseless. Jews have a chance to redeem themselves, however, when, having shaken off their parasitic lifestyle, they sacrifice themselves on the altar, making their ordeal into "a sacrificial pyre that hastens rebirth," removing the curse that hangs over them. Because in the face of death they can convert to the true faith and redeem themselves with the baptism of blood. These lofty messianic fantasies drew inspiration from models of romantic, military heroism and a crusading spirit.

In underground journalism there appeared a claim that during the 1943 Uprising Jews took up arms for the first time in eighteen centuries (counting from the second-century Bar Kokhba rebellion against the Romans; there were also frequent mentions of the earlier revolt of the Maccabees).[e] *Głos Demokracji* (*The Voice of Democracy,* published by the Polish Democratic Party), challenged this conviction by showing that "the Jewish proletariat in Russia and Poland, pulled as it was into the orbit of struggling against the tsar, could boast of numerous representatives in fighting organizations; they either died fighting, or, after assassinations, gave up their lives for the cause of freedom." The aforementioned *Prawda Młodych* was not, however, interested in this type of fighting heroism.

Irrespective of their political nuances, statements collected by Paweł Szapiro from the underground press, which aspired to express the opinion of the entire Polish society—all of "us-Poles"—contain a certain characteristic type of judgment: a typical juxtaposition of general Polish and Jewish attitudes. The Polish attitude is characterized by devotion to fighting and honor, and by powerful heroism; the Jewish attitude is characterized by petty passivity that comes close to degradation, and by proverbial cowardice and effeminate softness and acquiescence. In the Home Army's *Biuletyn*

---

[e] In her depiction of the Zionist interpretation of life in the Ghetto, which is often cited in Israel, Idith Zertal stresses that Zionists placed the 1943 military undertaking and the Maccabee and Masada rebellions in the same symbolic register. They showed the gesture of the participants of the Ghetto Uprising as an act of expiation for the passivity of the masses of the Jewish diaspora. See Idith Zertal, *Israel's Holocaust and the Politics of Nationhood* (Cambridge University Press, 2005; English translation of the original Hebrew edition from 2002).

Informacyjny (*Information Bulletin*) one often finds words of praise for Jews, who in the Uprising unexpectedly displayed their "manly will to resistance," "manly, soldierly decisions," and "manly, determined protest." A slogan that expresses this attitude says: "A choice between honorable death and life at any cost was made." In "nationally" oriented press in particular, there are words that draw an especially harsh and arbitrary contrast between the two attitudes: "Jews only think about preserving their lives, while we Poles are focused on a single idea and know that an individual's life is nothing when compared to the sacred cause for which we fight." The underground press treats Jews locked up in the Ghetto as citizens of the Polish state, but one can also encounter the view that they become citizens only when they take up arms. Only then do they gain qualities typical for citizens of the Polish Republic. Armed struggle is to give meaning to Jewish death in general. "Earlier passive death of the Jewish masses did not create new values—it was useless; death on the battlefield can bring new values into the life of the Jewish people, giving the Jewish ordeal in Poland the glory of armed struggle for the right to life."[f] The Polish myth of heroism once again confirms its overwhelming influence, and divides deaths into "worthless" and "valuable."

Demanding armed heroism from Jews imprisoned in the Ghetto testified to a complete lack of understanding of the mental and emotional situation of this particular civilian population. At the same time, people did not know anything about—or perhaps did not appreciate—the impressive educational, social, charitable, scholarly, cultural and political activities carried out in the Warsaw Ghetto.[g] There was also no appreciation for the "Jewish war" for survival, conducted from hiding. As usual, Henryk Grynberg, author of the excellent *Żydowska wojna* (*The Jewish War*),[1] expressed this truth most emphatically and most harshly when he recalled places "where we fought in the spring of 1943, my mother and I, during the Jewish war for life, in

---

[f] This is a passage from the Home Army's *Biuletyn Informacyjny* (*Information Bulletin*); it was reprinted by other underground papers.

[g] Agnieszka Arnold, director of the 1993 film about the Ringelblum Archive, an extraordinary collection from the Ghetto, says: "In Ghetto memoirs and reports in the Ringelblum Archive, one can see great cultural and intellectual resistance very shortly before the Holocaust (...). It was an eruption of talent and human abilities. And in this, I saw an exceptional kind of heroism and humanity—which was realized through social resistance. I was surprised that, except for Ruta Sakowska, no one writes about this and it remains hidden. This is why I made a film about the Ringelblum Archive." *Nienazwane i niesłyszane. Z Agnieszką Arnold rozmawia Sebastian Matuszewski* (*Unnamed and Unheard. Sebastian Matuszewski Speaks with Agnieszka Arnold*), Kos, 2007.

ceaseless retreat." When he cites General Bor-Komorowski's report from August 1943 about robbery attacks on manors and peasant farms carried out by armed groups that hid in the woods—Jewish groups among them—Grynberg comments:"It sometimes happened that Jews came, arms in hand, and took food and clothing (often post-Jewish), like partisans who were under the General's command, but partisans had the right to do it because they were fighting for Poland, while Jews did not have that right because they were only fighting for their lives."[h] This great sentence expresses Polish understanding of fighting and heroism well. All of Grynberg's works are permeated by a striving to describe Jews' courageous struggle to survive—precisely in opposition to the disgusting phrase that they went "like sheep to the slaughter." There is also another dimension of Jewish heroism: the heroism of death, brought out very often by none other than Marek Edelman, a leader of the 1943 Ghetto Uprising:"People who did not fight were heroes, too. Someone who joined his mother so she would not go to her death alone was as much a hero as someone who died fighting."[i]

Julian Tuwim had most sweeping intentions when in his famous manifesto "We, Polish Jews," written in New York in April 1944, he predicted: "On the armbands which you wore in the ghetto the star of David was painted. I believe in a Poland in which that star, the one from the armbands, will be one of the highest decorations awarded to the most valiant Polish soldiers and officers. They will wear it on their breast with pride next to the ancient Virtuti Militari."[2] It is not even worth mentioning that Tuwim's dreams had no chance of coming true. However, they testify to the fact that the poet unambiguously envisioned honoring the fate of persecuted Jews in the categories of heroism. This converges with the feelings of the author of a moving diary from the Warsaw Ghetto: "life and a Jew's desire to continue it under the Nazi yoke constitutes undeniable heroism. (. . .) Every one of us is basically a hero, common, quiet, undecorated by any Cross of Merit."[j]

Eva Hoffman aptly describes the difference between Holocaust victims and soldiers afflicted by a war neurosis and a sense of humiliation

[h] H. Grynberg, *Monolog polsko-żydowski* (*The Polish-Jewish Monologue*), (Wołowiec, 2003).
[i] Cited by W. Bereś, and K. Burnetko in *Marek Edelman. Życie. Po prostu* (*Marek Edelman. A Life. Just That*), (Warszawa, 2008).
[j] P. Weiser, ed., "Patrzyłam na usta . . . Dziennik z warszawskiego getta" (I Looked at Lips . . . A Diary from the Warsaw Ghetto), (Krakow, Lublin, 2008).

during the First World War (which was, temporally, the closest experience of catastrophe).

> But the victims of the Holocaust had been forced into a greater passivity, subjected to deeper violations. They were not, after all, engaged in a war, and most of them were not in a position to fight in any way. *They were assaulted not for reasons of state, or as enemy combatants, but simply because of who they were.* There is no framing of *that* in any meaningful structure, and there was mostly no meaningful action through which they could respond. (my emphasis—M. J.)[k]

To survive outside concentration camps they could only hide in the most humiliating of conditions.

It is characteristic that by juxtaposing rebels against the masses, people in the state of Israel created a "total conceptual and existential split" between the participants of the 1943 Uprising and the rest of the Jewish population, which did not take up arms.[l] This, as Idith Zertal emphasizes, resulted from the fact that the "Zionist 'theory of [beautiful] death' was projected from afar on to the unprecedented circumstances of both existence and annihilation in the ghettos and the death camps, *of which people in Palestine could not have had the slightest understanding*" (my emphasis—M. J.).[m] In Poland, the imposition of soldierly attitudes and heroic ideals onto civilian Jewish masses imprisoned in ghettos was in line with the Romantic belief in the necessity of dying in a heroic fight. Heroic death as an honorable and aesthetic death was juxtaposed against disgraceful death, base and cowardly death, as it was referred to in the aforementioned article from *Prawda Młodych*.[n]

The lesson of the Holocaust makes it necessary to think through the meaning of civilian death. The distinction between "valuable" and "worthless" death must be redefined. Michał Głowiński rightly argues against

---

[k] Eva Hoffman, *After Such Knowledge: Memory, History, and the Legacy of the Holocaust* (PublicAffairs, 2004), 43–44.

[l] "It was as if to say that the rebels had not emerged from within this people, had not been raised on its traditions; as if it were not in protest against the outrage to and murder of this very people that they had risen up and died." At that time, Zionist ideologists, who for the most part came from Poland, could have been inspired by the Polish romantic images. [Editors' note: Zertal, *Israel's Holocaust and the Politics of Nationhood*, 30.]

[m] Zertal, *Israel's Holocaust and the Politics of Nationhood*, 26.

[n] The stereotype of Jew-the-coward, unable to use weapons or outright afraid of them, also influenced decisions about delivering arms to underground activists in the Ghetto. Asked about "issuing weapons for self-defense to Jews in the country," General Grot-Rowecki, top commanding officer of the Home Army, replied: "I issued some guns to try it as an experiment, but I am not sure whether they'll use them at all." In January 1943, a counterintelligence officer from the Home Army General Command reported: "One cannot count on Jews to put up the kind of resistance

"foolish [and] thoughtless" judgments about death during the Holocaust and emphasizes that one must clearly say, "everyone who died as a result of those criminal decrees died with dignity."[o]

Roman Polański understands this perfectly well. In *The Pianist* there is a scene where Szpilman observes the fighting Warsaw Ghetto through a window in his hideout home. For a moment, he is accompanied by a principled Polish woman, who expresses her admiration for Jewish fighters, reminds him that Jews were always thought to be cowards, and assures him that Poles will soon come to join the fight. Szpilman hears that the fighting Jews died with dignity, and he remains silent. The viewer, who has been with him from the very first days of the war, knows something the woman does not know—and does not want to know. By endowing fighting Jews with dignity, the Polish woman looking at the Ghetto denies dignity to Szpilman's father, mother, and siblings, who die in Treblinka.

Lying

One of the more interesting debates in recent years has focused on Małgorzata Melchior's 2004 book *Zagłada a tożsamość. Polscy Żydzi ocaleni "na aryjskich papierach." Analiza doświadczenia biograficznego* (*Holocaust and Identity. Polish Jews Saved with the Help of "Aryan Papers." An Analysis of Biographical Experiences*). Assuming an anthropological perspective, the author diligently examines various stories and personal documents of Polish Jews who hid on the "Aryan" side. At that time, "being someone else" meant, above all, as she writes, "not being a Jew." But a change of documents and personal information did not

---

that would warrant giving them weapons. German losses will not be equivalent to the value of the weapons, and Jewish resistance will not even come to merit mentions about "the honor of Polish Jews." Żbikowski, ed., *Polacy i Żydzi pod okupacją niemiecką 1939–1945. Studia i materiały* (*Poles and Jews under the German Occupation 1939–1945. Sources and Analyses*), (Institute of National Remembrance [IPN], 2006). In a study included in this volume [Janion's book *Hero, Plot, Death*] and entitled "ZWZ-AK i delegatura rządu RP wobec eksterminacji Żydów polskich" (Home Army's Union of Armed Struggle and the Representative Office of the Government of the Polish Republic on the Extermination of Polish Jews), Dariusz Libionka provides a detailed description of the "tactical, worldview-related, and psychological factors" which played a role in arming the Jewish Military Organization (ŻOB). Among these he lists "the stereotype that denied Jews any military abilities and military men's conviction that Jews were indifferent toward military service." The *Jewish Lexicon* says that "Jews' resistance against Nazism is documented by their participation in the military defeat of Hitler's Germany. More than 1.5 million Jewish men and women fought in the anti-fascist Allied armies" (*The New Jewish Lexicon*).
[o] Michał Głowiński, *The Black Seasons*, trans. Marci Shore (Northwestern University Press, 2005).

take care of everything. Deeper metamorphoses became necessary: changing one's way of acting and speaking, and learning the social code—often an anti-Semitic one—to which one had to be able to respond in an appropriate way.

Melchior has collected a great number of self-descriptions proving that those who were hiding fully realized that acting became a way of life, and they knew how the "Aryan audience" could threaten them. They talk about "costumes," "getting into their role," "playing a role," "putting on a mask," "playing a comedy," or "tragicomedy," and "pretending." Their eyes and ears remained constantly vigilant. If these "actors" played ineptly they could pay with their lives. No wonder that for this reason, too, many of those hiding on the "Aryan" side emphasized that they hated their tragicomedy, that it was difficult for them to stay in character when a life-threatening unmasking could take place at any moment.

In *Czarne sezony* (*The Black Seasons*), when writing about his mother who went through the hell of hiding with "Aryan papers," Michał Głowiński says that the unforgettable and "most severe psychological wound" inflicted on his mother was connected with a "House beneath the Eagles" in Otwock.[p] It was here that, working as a maid serving her mistress, she could not reveal that she recognized her son, supposedly an orphan, when the house was visited by children from an orphanage run by the nuns. One can surmise that this wound was most painful because—in a very seriously dangerous situation—it necessitated such an all-encompassing lie.

As Melchior shows, the new identity could be treated as a tool of survival but it could also become a starting point of a deeper transformation. Nechama Tec admits: "I became a double person, one private and one public. When I was away from my family I became so engrossed by my public self that I did not have to act the part; I actually felt like the person that I was supposed to be." Thanks to the internalized duality, as the author-actress writes, "life became easier, and I felt less threatened when Jews were mentioned. I could listen to anti-Semitic stories indifferently, and even laugh heartily with someone else about some Jewish misfortune. I knew that they were abusing my people, but *part of me was like them*." Tec was not proud of these changes.[q] On the whole, Tec's autobiographical story

[p] Głowiński, *The Black Seasons*, 89

[q] Nechama Tec, *Dry Tears, The Story of a Lost Childhood* (Oxford University Press, 1984).

is a moving testimony of hiding the secret of one's origins and feeling as if one is betraying one's parents.

Duality could make life easier. The most striking thing for us is that some of those who were rescued from the Holocaust felt pangs of conscience or a sense of guilt because they had pretended and lied. It is not that someone else accused them of fraud; they accused themselves. Melchior collected shocking pieces of evidence that testify to this attitude.

She also brings up possible ways of morally justifying the "Aryan" lie. For example, Maria Ossowska writes that "there are circumstances when we are allowed to abandon truthfulness." Anna Pawełczyńska writes that this could take place in borderline situations, when the individual is faced by a direct threat to his life and the annihilation of his nation. But—and Melchior mentions this as well—some of those who resorted to lies in order to survive would agree with Leszek Kołakowski's conviction that "even when lying is justified in the name of some other, greater moral good, it is still not itself morally good."[3]

Although at the beginning of his essay "O kłamstwie" (On Lying) Kołakowski mentions complications in human affairs where an absolute imperative against lying under any circumstances "is not only unlikely to be fulfilled; in some circumstances it can conflict with other imperatives, such as kindness to our fellow-men, or with the public interest." And, significantly, in order to illustrate this utterly nonfictional type of situation, he gives an example taken precisely from the Holocaust: "If a Jew is hiding in your house, and the SS knocks on your door looking for him, do you, does anyone with a shred of conscience, hand him over to certain death in the name of the noble imperative which enjoins us never to lie?" Even though Kołakowski is not entirely consistent, the Holocaust draws certain boundaries here. Yet his conclusions—including the aforementioned claim that lying is not morally good even when it is meant to serve a greater good—signify that he did not fully think these boundaries through.[r]

Bringing Kołakowski's claim into the context of judging Holocaust survivors provoked important reactions. On the one hand, Joanna Tokarska-Bakir

[r] L. Kołakowski, *Mini-Wykłady o Maxi-Sprawach* (Brief Lectures about Significant Issues), Krakow, 1997. The cited sentence about complications of human and Jewish affairs was probably influenced by Kołakowski's experiences from his youth: in 1943, he lived in Warsaw in a building which was "practically an underground hideout, where Jews who escaped from the Ghetto were hidden" (See *Czas ciekawy, czas niespokojny. Część I. Z Leszkiem Kołakowskim rozmawia Zbigniew Mentzel* (*Interesting Time, Restless Time. Part I. Zbigniew Mentzel Speaks with Leszek Kołakowski*), (Znak, 2007).

questioned his opinion and Melchior's decision to cite him in the context
of lies told by hiding Jews and concluded: "There is only one case in which
I could agree with the philosopher: if right after proclaiming this kind of lie
as 'morally bad,' he would say the same about truth in this type of situation."[s]
On the other hand—and in connection with Melchior's book—Bronisław
Świderski has made the most far-reaching indictment of Holocaust lies. He
believes, for example, that the price of survival could consist in permanent
demoralization of the saved life. "Yes, they survived, but it was precisely
because they groveled, pretended, and fibbed." Those who survived inherited lying and continued to resort to it under communism ("we saw the
state's lies as something natural," etc.). Świderski uncompromisingly claims
that "Kołakowski is more correct here" and praises his "moral rigor."[t]

Asystent śmierci (*Death's Assistant*) implies that for Świderski lies were
entangled in the whole drama of the author-narrator's family: the mother,
who, having lost a family of sixty in Treblinka did not admit to being
Jewish until her death in 1992, and the father—who was a hardline communist. But the mother in *Death's Assistant* lies in the same way as the
Jewish woman who appears in Melchior's book. She was silent about her
background in front of her Polish friend, who rescued her and immediately
admitted to being an anti-Semite. The anti-Semitism of the surroundings
necessitates lying and intensifies the lies of the hiding Jews (they sometimes
hide throughout their entire post-Holocaust life)—and Świderski is well
aware of this situation.[u]

Reading the stories collected by Melchior leads one to suppose that we
are often dealing with images of "honorable" and "disgraceful" life, and
with a creation of a moral hierarchy of different types of death. Surviving
is not by itself treated as a heroic and moral deed. Głowiński opposes this

---

[Editors' note: Selections from Kołakowski's *Mini-Wykłady o Maxi-Sprawach* appear in
Kołakowski, *Freedom, Fame, Lying and Betrayal: Essays on Everyday Life*, trans. Agnieszka
Kołakowska (Westview Press, 1999). Cited here from the Kindle edition, locations 262–263,
and 265–267, respectively].

[s] J. Tokarska-Bakir, "Bez próby losowej" (Without Random Sampling), *Tygodnik Powszechny*,
October 24, 2004).

[t] B. Świderski, *Asystent śmierci. Powieść o karykaturach Mahometa, o miłości i nienawiści w Europie*
(*Death's Assistant. A Novel about Mohammed's Caricatures and Love and Hate in Europe*), (Wydawnictwo
W.A.B., 2007).

[u] He writes, after all: "The fact that Jews had to lie in order to survive says a lot about the moral
fabric of Polish society. After arriving in Denmark in 1970, I was surprised to hear that to survive
Danish Jews had to tell the truth. People simply rescued those who admitted to being Jewish."

schema for understanding what is noble and heroic, a schema so popular in Poland: "[C]onspiratorial activity (. . .) included not only things military and political but also assistance in saving the lives of those who succeeded in getting out from behind the walls."ᵛ The Holocaust introduced knowledge about a change in the canon of heroism, but it has not yet managed to become widespread.ʷ Grynberg expresses the conviction that in this absolutely extreme situation, Jewish moral resistance was an act of the highest order. "Under the conditions of the Holocaust—i.e., the breaking of fundamental moral norms—this resistance was more difficult than armed resistance."ˣ The evaluation of the ethos of the Ghetto and that of the "Jewish war for survival" forces us to abandon ossified stereotypes.

Lies of the hiding Jews do not submit to schemas that emanate from the humanistic glow of goodness, truth, and beauty; they refuse placement in canons that separate "pure" and "noble" life from "sullied" and "base" survival. Conventional limits of tragedy were overstepped. Lying about one's identity meant life, and here one cannot posit that there are values more important than life, because during the Holocaust life was the highest value. Tokarska-Bakir cites the wartime words of Nacht-Samborski, as quoted by a woman who worked with the Council to Aid Jews (Żegota): "Wanda, Poland will win without you, stop distributing these underground pamphlets and rescue Jews instead, a single rescued Jew means more than everything else."ʸ

One does not have to see this as disrespect for the independence-oriented underground. Paradoxically, the importance of the life of just a single rescued Jew is revealed here. To see it, however, one has to abandon ethical arrogance.ᶻ

ᵛ Głowiński, *The Black Seasons*, 56
ʷIn the second part of Agnieszka Arnold's film *Sąsiedzi* (*Neighbors*), Antonina Wyrzykowska rescues Jews, and at one point her daughter says: "My mother is, after all, a greater hero than the partisans since she did not even have a gun." While discussing this part of the film, Arnold comments: "This simple woman said something very obvious and at the same time very incongruous with the ethos of Polish heroism. (. . .) Heroism can still pertain only to partisans—simple human love for one's neighbor is not yet heroism. And I want equal treatment for both these types of heroism." *Nienazwane i nieusłyszane* (*Unnamed and Unheard*).
ˣ Monolog polsko-żydowski (*Polish-Jewish Monologue*).
ʸ Tokarska-Bakir, "Bez próby losowej" (Without Random Sampling)
ᶻ "Ethical arrogance" is Slavoj Žižek's expression, used in the context of a moralistic evaluation of "Muslims," the most humiliated prisoners in Nazi concentration camps; see *The Puppet and the Dwarf: The Perverse Core of Christianity* (MIT Press, 2003), 159.

Editors' Notes

1. Available in English as *The Jewish War and The Victory* (Northwestern University Press, 2001).
2. Julian Tuwim, "We, Polish Jews," reproduced in this volume, citation from page 65.
3. "On Lying," trans. Agnieszka Kołakowska, in Leszek Kołakowski, *Freedom, Fame, Lying and Betrayal: Essays on Everyday Life* (Westview Press. 1999). Kindle edition (Kindle locations 329–330).

PART
IX

After 2000: Against
the Conformity of Silence

21

The Burning Barn and I

WALDEMAR KUCZYŃSKI

Editors' Introduction

Waldemar Kuczyński (b. 1939) is an economist and journalist. Born in the city of Kalisz, he studied economics at the University of Warsaw, where he later worked in the Department of Economics. He joined the Communist Party (PZPR) in 1959, but in 1966 he was expelled from both the party and his university for his revisionist views and involvement with the Political Discussion Club led by the historian and antigovernment activist Karol Modzelewski. Kuczyński participated in the March 1968 protests at the University of Warsaw and spent six months in prison. He remained active in the democratic opposition movement in the 1970s, and in August 1980 became an expert adviser to the workers' strike committee led by Lech Wałęsa at the Gdańsk Shipyard. He was imprisoned during martial law in 1981, and left Poland a year later to live in Paris, where he taught at the École des Hautes Études en Sciences Sociales and wrote for leading Polish émigré periodicals like *Kultura* and *Aneks*. He returned to Poland in 1989 and became active in politics, serving, among other things, as adviser to Prime Ministers Tadeusz Mazowiecki and Jerzy Buzek. His most important book is the analysis of Edward Gierek's policies *Po wielkim skoku* (*After the Great Leap*, 1979).

The essay reproduced here was originally published in the weekly *Wprost*, in Poznań, on March 25, 2001. It was Kuczyński's contribution to the fierce public debate that broke out in Poland after the publication of Jan Gross's book *Neighbors* (2000), in which Gross analyzed how and why the Polish inhabitants of the northeastern Polish town of Jedwabne murdered their

Jewish neighbors during the Second World War.[1] The Jedwabne Pogrom took place on July 10, 1941, shortly after the Nazi invasion of the Soviet Union on June 22. In the power vacuum created when the Soviet occupying forces fled and the German administration was not yet established, Poles carried out several pogroms in the towns and villages in the Podlasie region, often resorting to the canard of "Judeo-Bolshevism," which stipulated Jewish collaboration with the Soviet Union to undermine Polish sovereignty. Historians estimate that there were hundreds of victims in the pogroms in Radziłów on July 7, Wąsosz on July 5, and other towns, but the largest massacre took place in the town of Jedwabne. For several days in early July, Poles from Jedwabne and surrounding villages taunted and lynched Jews, and on July 10, they forced a few hundred of their Jewish neighbors into a barn and set the barn on fire.

When Gross's book was published in Poland, it met intense resistance and many sought to either minimize or outright deny the Poles' culpability. In May 2001, however, Polish bishops prayed for forgiveness for the Jedwabne Pogrom, and in July, President Aleksander Kwaśniewski publicly acknowledged the Poles' responsibility for this crime. Over time, debates around Jedwabne have given rise to a large body of scholarship and to rigorous studies of the attitudes and behaviors of Poles toward Jews during the Shoah.[2]

There is a barn outside of town. And Poles from the town and its vicinity are driving Jews to this barn. Whether they are driving 1,600 or 100 Jews is completely irrelevant—neither as an extenuating nor an aggravating circumstance. Extenuating circumstances do not apply to the evaluation of the act they are about to commit or to judgments we make about this act in our conscience—I emphasize this because that is the type of evaluation and judgment I have in mind. The possibility that the number of Jews forced into the barn was smaller than what people discuss was important for those who found themselves beyond the persecutors' reach; today it is important for historians. The behavior of Jews under the Soviet occupation is also of no consequence for how we judge this genocide in the realm of our conscience. That behavior is significant only for Jewish consciences and for Jewish examinations of conscience.

They are driving Jews of all ages to the barn, men and women, infants in their parents' arms. Let us free our imagination from its shackles, from the certainty that blocks it—the certainty that we, Poles, would have been incapable of something like this. We have to free ourselves from this blockage when we approach this barn that has been burning for sixty years, or else we will fail to understand anything. Let us see the people who are being herded in, and if we cannot see them as our neighbors, then let us at least put ourselves in their shoes. Let us put our children and our grandchildren in their shoes. Let us see how our countrymen are closing this barn and setting it on fire, how smoke and fire billow inside. And inside, let us see—I will repeat—if not our neighbors, then at least ourselves and our loved ones. And let us hear those screams "that could be heard two kilometers away"— as witnesses say—and let us imagine that we are the ones screaming, that people we love most are screaming, devoured by the terrible heat, with no way out. And only when we feel tears welling up in our eyes– seeing these scenes with the eyes of a freed imagination—will we be able to say that we gave our conscience a chance to speak, that we felt the terror of the crime of our countrymen, we felt it through grief for those devoured by the fire. Not grief for display, but authentic grief, underneath our eyelids.

This crime incriminates us. Let us have no illusions that we will free ourselves from it by pushing it away and multiplying excuses and justifications. In the barn, they did not murder a specific Jew for a specific reason; they did not commit a common crime that incriminates only the criminal or a group of criminals. In this barn, it was not the margins, but a fragment of the Polish people that burned a fragment of the Jewish people. So long as we consider ourselves a people, that is, a community of past, present, and future generations, this deed, committed by those from a generation now mostly gone, will continue to incriminate us. We are not responsible for it as individuals, but we are responsible for it as members of a nation. This is not collective responsibility, which must not be evoked, but national responsibility, which cannot, and must not, be evaded. At work here is the same moral law that makes it possible to see our forefathers' great deeds as our own, to take pride in them and also rightfully claim that there was a sliver of the Polish people that rescued and saved a sliver of the Jewish people. In the vicinity of that barn there was even a hideout where, until the end of the war, Antonina Wyrzykowska hid seven Jews who escaped from "our" hands. This hideout is a place of national pride, while the nearby barn is a place of dishonor. National dishonor!

And so we cannot cast off and remove from our conscience that burning barn from sixty years ago, that screaming "that could be heard two kilometers away." The barn still burns and the screaming still resounds. The barn will continue to burn and the screaming will continue to resound so long as we continue to push away the burden of this—our—genocide. To be able to remove it, and to have it removed from us, we have to accept it. We have to use the eyes of our imagination to walk that path from a half century ago, all the way into the center of the fire; and if we shed tears over those who perished there, we will gain a chance to remove the anti-Semitic poison from the body of our nation, a poison which continues to debase so many of us to this day. I had tears in my eyes when I wrote this and saw how people were getting burned alive. This is all I can do to put out the embers of that burning barn, and soothe the cries of the dying.

Editors' Notes

1. Jan Gross, *Neighbors: The Destruction of the Jewish Community in Jedwabne, Poland*, (Princeton University Press, 2001; initially published in Polish by Fundacja Pogranicze in 2000).
2. In the final section of the Introduction to this volume, we briefly discuss the debates initiated by Gross's book about the Jedwabne massacre.

22

Helplessness

JERZY JEDLICKI

Editors' Introduction

Jerzy Jedlicki (b. 1930) is a historian and essayist. Born in Warsaw, he studied history at the University of Warsaw and worked at the Institute of History of the Polish Academy of Sciences from 1954 to 2009. In 1953, he joined the Communist Party (PZPR), which he left in March 1968 to protest the government's brutal repression of student protests. Throughout the 1970s and 1980s he was active in the anticommunist democratic opposition movement, and he was imprisoned when General Jaruzelski's government introduced martial law in 1981. In 1989, Jedlicki became the head of the History of Intelligentsia Section at the Polish Academy of Sciences. He later served as President of the Council of the "Open Republic" Association Against Anti-Semitism and Xenophobia.

In his research, Jedlicki has been interested in the history of ideas and intellectuals, and his most important books include *Klejnot i bariery społeczne. Przeobrażenia szlachectwa polskiego w schyłkowym okresie feudalizmu* (*Jewel and Social Barriers: The Transformation of Polish Gentry During the Decline of Feudalism*, 1968), *Jakiej cywilizacji Polacy potrzebują. Studia z dziejów idei i wyobraźni XIX wieku* (1988), available in English as *A Suburb of Europe: Nineteenth-Century Polish Approaches to Western Civilization* (1999), and *Świat zwyrodniały. Lęki i wyroki krytyków nowoczesności* (2000), available in English as *A Degenerate World* (2016). The essay reproduced here was originally a talk given at a seminar of the Emanuel Ringelblum Jewish Historical Institute in Warsaw and published in Polish in *Gazeta Wyborcza* on June 27, 2009.

The last twenty years have brought a rich outpouring of historical and anthropological studies devoted to the situation, culture, faith, and changing fortunes of Jews in Poland throughout the centuries—and a concomitant focus on Polish and Catholic attitudes toward Jews and their fate.

This wealth of documents, printed volumes of source materials, testimonies and memoires, local studies, survey articles, monographs, and ambitious syntheses is too great to lend itself to any comprehensive overview. And Polish-Jewish topics have started to attract not only renowned scholars, but also an ever-growing multitude of their students from nearly every corner of the country—and researchers from many foreign universities.

The central place within this framework is occupied by investigations that focus on the recent past—the interwar years and the Holocaust, along with its consequences. It is as if there is a desire to make up for the long years of negligence, distortions, censorship, and researchers' avoidance of the most painful and conflictual topics.

The new works, ones that meet critical methodological standards, tend not to avoid drastic topics anymore—topics that used to be inadmissible in public discourse, and often even in the awareness of historians. Only in the last twenty years have we seen the publication of source materials and studies about prewar, wartime, and postwar anti-Semitic press and journalism; about the humiliation of Jewish students at Polish universities; about pogroms and mob rule in 1918–1919, 1940–1941, and 1945–1946; about blackmailers and the denunciations handed over to the Gestapo; about killings of Jews who managed to survive; about the 1968 libels, purges, and expulsions; and about other matters which—until recently—were either euphemized or passed over in silence. The new publications also include source documents and analyses bearing on how the various subdivisions of the Polish Underground State and the Home Army related to the Holocaust, and how the stance of the Church and the clergy evolved over time.

Knowledge and Phantasms

This epistemological watershed has no precedent in earlier historiography, where Jewish topics were largely isolated and cultivated primarily by researchers for whom they had deep personal relevance. By contrast, within the current upsurge of studies it has become conventional—a habit that was only weakly started in the Polish People's Republic—that one does not have to have Jewish ancestors or experiences to feel called to the duty of recreating the buried traces of the life and extermination of a community that was obliterated from the memory of generations.

Yet the greater our ability to learn—should we wish to—about the events of the past century, and the more thorough our studies, the more helpless we feel in the face of our knowledge.

Restraining our sense of terror, we have learned to talk about events that shock us as human beings, Europeans, Poles, or inhabitants of a particular region, town, or village. We know how to recall circumstances and search for motivations capable of unleashing yet another wave of murderous hatred or calculated policies in one nation or another. But we remain helpless before phantasms which—ebbing and flowing—have survived two thousand years as an irremovable component of Christian civilization.

We are aware of their religious genesis, investigated by many scholars.

A liturgical prayer for the conversion of devious Jews—which was at the heart of a recent controversy within the Church—preserved an ancient trace of the disappointment felt by a messianic sect, which transformed itself into a powerful Church, while celebrating apostolic, missionary, and political successes in the lands of polytheist cultures, but which was contemptuously rejected by the followers of one God—a community from which it originated, and which, more than anything else, it immediately wanted to convince and convert.

This painful disappointment can explain the fierceness of early Christian tracts against Jews, or the theological hostility, which is, by the way, mutual; it does not, however, have the power to explain the later inheritability of superstitions, magical fears, and bloody phantasms, whose durability was so vividly shown in Joanna Tokarska-Bakir's great recent book *Legendy o krwi* (*Legends about Blood*).[1] Anthropological and historical studies make one thing clear: the various European Christians' stubborn hostility toward Jews was not, as is often supposed, one of the countless biases of "us" against "them" that permeate the past and present of our cultural realm.

Anti-Judaism—ancient or modern, it makes no difference—is a unique phenomenon because it concentrates certain irreducible components with an intensity not found in even the bloodiest tribal, national, or religious antagonisms.

These are demonic components, impervious to all attempts to explain them in rationalizing categories, such as the conflict of economic interests or the effect of the foreignness of customs or language.

Elżbieta Janicka is right to say that "anti-Semitism is a mental structure that organizes the world," and contains potential acquiescence to "the final solution."[a] Yet we still have the sense that this structure contains a core which we cannot explain—its indifference to the effects of time, civilizational change, and experience.

Let us note that in nineteenth- and early twentieth-century Europe, none of the rival affiliation strategies enabled Jews to erase the stigma of despised and excluding otherness: neither isolation nor emancipation; neither orthodoxy nor baptism; neither Zionism nor most authentic patriotism toward the country where they settled; neither conservatism nor revolutionary zeal; neither growing rich nor disdain for temporal goods; neither the cultivation of the Jewish cultural idiom nor a denial of it—no choice overcame divisions and isolation; none offered full entry into the civic community.

This was also the case in Poland, where the problem kept growing, especially starting in the second half of the nineteenth century. Works by Alina Cała, Helena Datner, Agnieszka Jagodzińska, Anna Landau-Czajka, and Monika Natkowska have shown convincingly that even those who most ardently sought to integrate with the Polish intelligentsia were, for the most part, unable to overcome the invisible barrier, and, at least before 1939, they remained a nation "in between"—alien to both sides.

A Cultural Norm and Circumstances

In light of the newest research, the distinction between ancient religious anti-Judaism and modern racist anti-Semitism loses the meaning typically attributed to it because it signifies a change not in the excluding attitude itself, but only in its justification. Anti-Semitic racism erected a new impassable and allegedly biological barrier—one could see this especially vividly in Germany—since cultural barriers and legal obstacles were already overcome by Jews who were diligently undergoing Germanization. This was not as necessary in Eastern European countries because here barriers of language, customs, and separate settlements, not to mention religion, were crossed by only a negligible minority of the Jewish population. This does not change the fact that here, too, the popularity of racism was a response to

[a] "Mord rytualny z aryjskiego paragrafu" (Ritual Murder under Aryan Statutes), *Kultura i Społeczeństwo* (*Culture and Society*) 2 (2008).

emancipatory and assimilatory tendencies, in the face of which traditional principles of discrimination were losing their prohibitive effectiveness.

But were Jews denied equal rights and equal respect because they were Christ's murderers, had dealings with the devil, poisoned wells, kidnapped and bled innocent children, or profaned the Host? Or because they grew side curls, jabbered in jargon, made peasants into drunkards, traded and made loans with interest, and isolated themselves? Or the opposite—pushed their way everywhere, hated Christians and especially Poles, were racially foreign, depraved by the teachings of the Talmud and the Shulchan Aruch (the Code of Jewish Law), sat on piles of gold, stunk of onions, corrupted Polish, Russian, or Hungarian culture, Jewified progress, undermined the social order, spied, and secretly plotted to rule the world? What difference does it make?

These were all secondary, interchangeable rationalizations, and the twentieth century was to bring them on in even greater abundance. They get blurred together, and, in fact, the criteria for differentiating between traditional, modern, religious, and racist justifications have not been clearly defined; they are still not defined today because, under the right circumstances, they all led equally easily to collective acts of aggression, pogroms, expulsion, and extermination.

We should certainly not disregard historical circumstances because—starting with the Middle Ages—Jews tended to be killed when killing was allowed or even encouraged, when there was no punishment, and when it was even possible to get a reward if one made an effort. Slaughters and pogroms took place primarily when state power was weakened or when it was being transferred, when the social order was destabilized and lost its legitimacy. The backdrop of incidents like those in Jedwabne or Kielce[2] consists precisely in the fact that killing was permitted, or at least seemed to be permitted, though it was sometimes possible to make a miscalculation.

This is why I agree with Elżbieta Janicka, when in the (aforementioned) insightful argument against Jan T. Gross's *Fear*, she minimizes the significance of circumstances like depravation by the Nazis, the postwar "moral vacuum," the desire to eliminate competition, or the simple temptation to robbery. Of course, any of these may have motivated specific individuals, but only because the permissibility of performing "ritual murder" on Jews was a powerfully entrenched cultural norm over the course of many centuries, and in the shadow of Hitler's Holocaust (i.e., during the Holocaust and in its aftermath) one could indulge oneself.

In his book *Bondage to the Dead: Poland and the Memory of the Holocaust*, the American historian Michael Steinlauf explained postwar acts of aggression against Jewish survivors in Poland by evoking a suppressed sense of guilt on the part of the "passive witnesses of the Holocaust."[3] In light of the knowledge we have today, this subtle psychoanalytical explanation seems to be wrong, or it could be ascribed only to a small number of people who have a hard time dealing with ethical ambivalence. I would be more inclined to agree with the supposition that most of the population—excluding only some intellectual milieus, and individual people with high ethical sensitivity who are dispersed and present everywhere—experienced no trauma at all on account of the Holocaust that was taking place right before their eyes. People had enough of their own suffering and sacrifices and these were not their own.

In her book *Urwany lot* (*Unfinished Flight*), Hanna Świda-Ziemba cites testimonies that show that after the war, even in intellectual families, people talked about Jews as if nothing had happened, "as if the world turned back to prewar times, and the Holocaust never took place." One could cite countless casual observations and sociological polls to support this view.

The Holocaust, I believe, was neither experienced nor worked through in the collective Polish consciousness. It was not included in our national history—until recently its documents, accounts, and commemorations have remained separate, unassimilated by the patriotic rites of memory. Only lately have there been belated attempts at such integration, and they reveal the solitude of the dying—a solitude acknowledged by poetry before historiography, by historiography before textbooks, and by textbooks before human hearts.

The Curtain

When it comes to the current picture of prejudices and emotions that accompany them, sociologists and their polls seek to convince us that things are getting better since at most half—or less—of the population seems to foster stereotypes that are hostile to Jews. We are supposed to celebrate this statistic, which, if it proves anything at all, perhaps only proves, once again, the ineffectiveness of rational education in this realm, even among the educated. And scholarly knowledge about humans and society is likewise proving awkward. When we face the phenomenon of anti-Semitism as an intractable European— and largely also a Polish—cultural norm, which is sometimes recessive and sometimes dangerously active, we remain—I repeat—intellectually helpless, even though we have our vast store of knowledge.

Meanwhile, the immediate significance of anti-Jewish biases seems to be weakening, since those who perpetuate them have lost the perceptible object of their obsessions, and are increasingly inclined to turn against gays or foreigners who have a different skin color; which is an important problem in itself, but one that requires a separate analysis. The past is what provides for unextinguished conflagrations of Polish-Polish conflicts.

This in no way indicates that we are zealously interested in history. On the contrary, the public cuts itself off from knowledge amassed by scholars by means of a rather tight curtain of indifference, which the media penetrate only infrequently. The tomes of documents and studies I mentioned at the beginning, including ten volumes of the excellent yearly *Zagłada Żydów* (*Holocaust Studies and Materials*), edited by Dariusz Libionka; the book *Prowincja noc* (*Province Night*), edited by Barbara Engelking, Jacek Leociak, and Dariusz Libionka; and even the Institute of National Remembrance (IPN) volume *Polacy i Żydzi pod okupacją niemiecką* (*Poles and Jews under the German Occupation*), edited by Andrzej Żbikowski, along with related monographs, drew neither broad interest nor the attention of our fervent defenders of national dignity. This kind of reading is perhaps too difficult for them to digest.

Jan T. Gross's two books, however, did manage to pierce through the curtain and reach a wider audience: *Neighbors*, which actually uncovered a dismal episode in 1941, not previously described by historians, and *Fear*, which stood out against the extensive available studies of the 1946 Kielce Pogrom because of its compelling prose and a certain dose of moralizing. We remember the storm of emotions these books provoked.

Both subjective observations and sociological measures seem to suggest that the only perceptible result of these disputes was to create greater polarization of opinion on a subject that reveals so much about the worldview of those who were surveyed—both sides of the argument gained more adherents and people became more entrenched in their convictions, while the undecided middle weakened.

Indeed, Poland now seems to be more and more clearly and deeply divided into two camps: nationalist-clerical and liberal-leftist, or whatever one calls them. Their relative proportions depend on the question asked. And (if we disregard insults) communication between them has become practically impossible.

Without Anesthesia

It is important to realize, however, that many people with traditional patriotic views perceive the evocative books by Gross and Anna Bikont (*My
z Jedwabnego*),[4] along with other similar reliable historical narrations, as a
threat to their sacred sphere, their sense of collective identity, and thus also,
indirectly, to their sense of their own worth. Such an attack causes pain
and activates defensive reactions, especially when information or judgments
come from outside the country.

Sometimes the answer consists in the refusal to acknowledge facts that do
not cohere with patriotic mythology, and thus also to accept the drastic stories that bring these facts together—stories, which get perceived as intentional depreciation of national values, dictated by suspect motives. I wrote
about this in "Wiedza jako źródło cierpień" (Knowledge as a Source of
Suffering, *Tygodnik Powszechny*, 2004).

We should not be too quick to relegate such reactions to the realm of
anti-Semitic prejudice, however, even if we see unpleasant subtexts in them,
because this only gives ammunition to the charlatans who exploit them.
After all, defenders of an idealized vision of history are well aware of how
much the Holocaust has changed European sensibility and the binding
norms of decency, and they automatically try to make their—not entirely
forgotten—homegrown knowledge and collective images fit in with these
realities. This must be a painful process and not always a consistent one, and
it is hard to say whether brutal teaching is more effective here than more
delicate and gradual approaches.

It depends on the goal we set for ourselves. If the goal is to overcome
hardened hostility that has been feeding on anti-Semitic biases, psychologists suggest using artful indirect strategies, meant to soften the blow caused
by the confrontation between documented knowledge and the heroic
canon of inheritable Polish *nobilitatis*.

If, however, the goal is ruthless historical truth and the need for Polish
Catholics to come to terms with the stains on their own national and
religious history, the task cannot be carried out under anesthesia. After
such a long period of accumulating legends, the restoration of the right
proportions, and criticism of socially inherited convictions, must cause
pain and resistance, and we have to resign ourselves to the fact that such
education—at least for the time being—will intensify suspicions of under-
handed, most likely racial and self-serving, motives among historians and

anthropologists, whether they are Polish or foreign. And it follows that initially this education will intensify rather than soften distrustful, hostile, and ossified attitudes.

We are helpless in the face of this constellation. It is too late to return to the land of cowardly silence and euphemisms, where the courage of the Righteous and the noble solidarity of the empathetic allegedly eclipsed and redeemed everything else, including their own—deeply justified—fear of their neighbors' denunciations and their neighborhood's opinion. Historians will write and say what they know, knowing the price one pays for the truth of facts and claims that contradict articles of faith.

"To utter certain things"—Joanna Tokarska-Bakir writes—"one has to overcome one's own and others' reflex of pulling back from pain. And there are a great number of reasons to overcome this reflex. We can only argue about what is better: the hypocrisy of a past that does not hint at what people are capable of, or the sad knowledge of what people can actually do at times—and the need to somehow go on living with that knowledge."[b]

Despite all this, however, there is no lack of heartening news. In dozens of Polish cities and towns there are loners who are stubbornly working on discovering a lost world and reading its palimpsests; and they are gradually attracting the youth.

Perhaps work at the foundations, work that is often literally excavatory, along with lessons and workshops that seek to immunize children and youth against the toxins of prejudice and phobias—perhaps such initiatives can give us hope for good outcomes: gradual changes in mentality and "cultural norms," and readiness for honest confrontation with the past. But this will happen very slowly. It might take generations.

Editors' Notes

1. Joanna Tokarska-Bakir, *Legendy o krwi. Antropologia przesądu* (*Legends about Blood: The Anthropology of Prejudice*), (Wydawnictwo W.A.B., 2008).
2. The Kielce Pogrom is discussed in the introduction to Stanisław Ossowski's essay "With Kielce in the Background" in this volume on pages 114–115.

[b] Joanna Tokarska-Bakir, "Strach w Polsce" (Fear in Poland), in *Wokół Strachu. Dyskusja o książce Jana T. Grossa* (*Around Fear: A Discussion about Jan T. Gross' Book*), ed. Mariusz Gądek (Wydawnictwo Znak, 2008).

3. Michael C. Steinlauf, *Bondage to the Dead: Poland and the Memory of the Holocaust* (Syracuse University Press, 1997).

4. Anna Bikont's 2005 book *My z Jedwabnego* (*We from Jedwabne*) was published in English as *The Crime and the Silence: Confronting the Massacre of Jews in Wartime Jedwabne* (Farrar, Straus and Giroux, 2015).

Index